LEGALIZED FAM]
OF BORDERED G~~LOBALIZATION~~

Providing a panoramic and interdisciplinary perspective, this book explores the interrelations between globalization, borders, families and the law. It considers the role of international, multi-national and religious laws in shaping the lives of the millions of families that are affected by the opportunities and challenges created by globalization, and the ongoing resilience of national borders and cultural boundaries. Examining familial life-span stages – establishing spousal relations, raising children, and being cared for in old age – Hacker demonstrates the fruitfulness in studying families beyond the borders of national family law, and highlights the relevance of immigration and citizenship law, public and private international law and other branches of law. This book provides a rich empirical description of families in our era. It is relevant not only to legal scholars and practitioners but also to scholars and students within the sociology of the family, globalization studies, border studies, immigration studies, and gender studies.

DAPHNA HACKER is an associate professor at the Tel Aviv University Law Faculty and Women and Gender Studies Program. She is an interdisciplinary researcher and holds LL.B and LL.M degrees as well as a Ph.D in sociology. Her socio-legal work focuses on the intersection of law, families and gender. She teaches family law, families and globalization, feminist jurisprudence, and qualitative methods.

GLOBAL LAW SERIES

The series provides unique perspectives on the way globalization is radically altering the study, discipline and practice of law. Featuring innovative books in this growing field, the series explores those bodies of law which are becoming global in their application, and the newly emerging interdependency and interaction of different legal systems. It covers all major branches of the law and includes work on legal theory, history, and the methodology of legal practice and jurisprudence under conditions of globalization. Offering a major platform on global law, these books provide essential reading for students and scholars of comparative, international and transnational law.

LEGALIZED FAMILIES IN THE ERA OF BORDERED GLOBALIZATION

DAPHNA HACKER

CAMBRIDGE
UNIVERSITY PRESS

CAMBRIDGE
UNIVERSITY PRESS

University Printing House, Cambridge CB2 8BS, United Kingdom

One Liberty Plaza, 20th Floor, New York, NY 10006, USA

477 Williamstown Road, Port Melbourne, VIC 3207, Australia

4843/24, 2nd Floor, Ansari Road, Daryaganj, Delhi – 110002, India

79 Anson Road, #06-04/06, Singapore 079906

Cambridge University Press is part of the University of Cambridge.

It furthers the University's mission by disseminating knowledge in the pursuit of education, learning, and research at the highest international levels of excellence.

www.cambridge.org
Information on this title: www.cambridge.org/9781107144996
DOI: 10.1017/9781316535004

First published 2017

Printed in the United Kingdom by Clays, St Ives plc

A catalogue record for this publication is available from the British Library.

Library of Congress Cataloging-in-Publication Data
Names: Hacker, Daphna, author.
Title: Legalized families in the era of bordered globalization / Daphna Hacker.
Description: New York : Cambridge University Press, 2017. |
Series: Global law series | Includes bibliographical references and index.
Identifiers: LCCN 2017002747| ISBN 9781107144996 (hard back : alk. paper) |
ISBN 9781316508213 (paper back : alk. paper)
Subjects: LCSH: Domestic relations – Social aspects. |
Law and globalization – Social aspects.
Classification: LCC K670 .H33 2017 | DDC 346.01/5–dc23
LC record available at https://lccn.loc.gov/2017002747

ISBN 978-1-107-14499-6 Hardback
ISBN 978-1-316-50821-3 Paperback

For all those who endeavor to be part of a nurturing family

CONTENTS

ACKNOWLEDGMENTS

The journey that yielded this book started four years ago at Hong Kong University, where I gave a course on Globalization of the Family on behalf of Duke University Law School. I wish to thank Supreme Court Justice Daphne Barak-Erez, who was my dean at the time, for encouraging me to look beyond my nation's borders and to explore the interrelations between families, law, and globalization.

This has been the most enjoyable of all my intellectual journeys so far, thanks to many people – those who, like me, think that families are the most interesting study subjects and whose research forms the basis of this book; those who shared with me their familial *globordered* stories and reminded me that, behind the theories and generalizations, there are unique individuals and families; and those who gave me indispensable assistance that enabled the completion of this book.

I thank the Colton Foundation and the Cegla Center for Interdisciplinary Research of the Law at Tel Aviv University for their generous support. I thank David Nelken, the series coeditor, for being my guiding angel. I am forever grateful to Amanda Dale for accompanying me with the best editing experience I have ever had and becoming a true partner in shaping the text. My deepest appreciation to my colleagues who read different chapters of this book, according to their fields of expertise, and provided invaluable feedback: Rhona Schuz, Noam Peleg, Einat Albin, Tamar Morag, Zvi Triger, Sharon Bassan, Sharon Shakargy, Ayelet Blecher-Prigat, Ruth Zafran, Uri Ram, Sylvie Fogiel-Bijaoui, Adriana Kemp, Kinneret Lahad, Yael Hashiloni-Dolev, Adi Moreno, Lena Salaymeh, Yehouda Shenhav, Yishai Blank, Michael Birnhack, Tally Kritzman-Amir, Arianne Renan Barzilay, Irit Porat, Michael Kagan, Lidia Rabinovich, and Israel Doron. I am also thankful to my research assistants, and especially to Daniel Findler and Eynat Meytahl who invested hundreds of hours in bibliographic searches and footnote editing. I thank Morag Goodwin, the series coeditor, and Finola O'Sullivan at Cambridge University Press, for all their assistance and support.

I thank you, the readers, for taking the time to take part in the outcome of my journey. I hope you will enjoy reading the book as much as I have enjoyed writing it, and that you find in it inspiration for future study and for reflecting on your own familial experiences. I know that, for me, this book has been another opportunity to appreciate my familial good fortune and to be thankful for the love and nurturing I receive from my parents Ilan and Tamar Hacker, my spouse Alon Dror, and my children Yasmin and Aviv. I know now, more than I ever knew before, that they are the pillars of my existence.

Introduction

This book is perhaps best introduced through the story of Bara and Nickel. In the 2011 HBO documentary "When Strangers Click," director Robert Kenner acquaints us with Bara Jonson, a Swede, who looks to be in his fifties. We meet Bara after he has lost his business in the United States and moved to Tärnö, a remote island in the southeast of Sweden, where he now lives with his elderly mother. Becoming bored in this extremely peaceful and secluded place, Bara finds himself visiting the website Second Life, creating an avatar, and setting up a virtual bar. The documentary shows Bara standing in his kitchen, playing the guitar and singing his original songs while plugged into the computer, so his avatar performs live in the virtual bar in front of other avatars.

His performing avatar becomes popular and is soon visited by a gorgeous female avatar who tells Bara that, although his singing is great, his avatar needs a makeover. One thing leads to another, and the two avatars fall in love and get married in the virtual world – in a wedding for which Bara and Nickel, the woman behind the female avatar, pay $500 in real money.

One day, the owner of an independent record company from New York, who also got to know Bara through Second Life, invites him to the United States to record his songs. Bara accepts the invitation and takes the opportunity to initiate a nonvirtual meeting with Nickel, who lives in a small city in Missouri. After recovering from the shock of seeing how they look in real life, and maybe because of it, Bara and Nickel get drunk, have intercourse, and a very real baby is born as a result, whom they name Christopher. However, since Bara and Nickel are not married according to the law, and as Christopher will be eligible to petition for a visa for his father only when he turns 21,[1] Bara cannot obtain a residency permit in

---

[1] For US family-based visa regulations, see "Family of U.S. Citizens," US Citizenship and Immigration Services, www.uscis.gov/family/family-us-citizens. All websites in this book were last visited on August 19, 2016. See also discussion on familial citizenship in Chapter 5.

the United States and reluctantly returns to Sweden. As Nickel says: "The countries don't make it easy for you to actually live with someone for a while, to see if you want to get married." Bara claims, "We are still family even though we are just in separate places." Indeed, the film ends with us watching Nickel watching her computer, in which the couple's avatars are sitting in a virtual living room, watching a virtual screen onto which pictures of Nickel and baby Christopher, taken in reality, are projected.[2]

Watching the film, one starts to wonder: Are Bara, Nickel, and Christopher a transnational family, or is Nickel a single mother like so many others? Can people have a significant familial life in virtual dimensions, or should the term *family* be reserved only for physical familial relations? Are we heading for a future in which people will establish and maintain families without ever meeting each other, through communication and fertility technologies? Do sperm and ova exportation and international surrogacy prove that this future is already here?

Indeed, the story of Bara and Nickel is an interesting example of the impact of globalization on familial biographies and on our understanding of what a family is. In this case, cross-border movement of communication and people allowed two people separated by a significant geographical distance to establish what at least they perceived as a family. In other, much more common, cases, globalization brings together people through immigration, studies abroad, and tourism, and some of these interactions lead to the creation of cross-border families. Globalization also separates families, especially as labor migration becomes an opportunity and a necessity for both men and women, who are also spouses, parents, children, or siblings. Moreover, the movement of ideas, through a variety of means such as the media and international law, changes what people know and think about familial possibilities, and eventually how they choose to live their own vision of a family.

Hence, *family* as an adjective – that is, referring to "sets of practices which deal in some way with ideas of parenthood, kinship and marriage and the expectations and obligations which are associated with these practices"[3] – cannot be understood in our era detached from globalization. *Familiality* (my term for how such practices are lived and experienced, which I use throughout this book) is opened up by globalization

---

[2] For details on the documentary, see the HBO website: www.hbo.com/documentaries/when-strangers-click. For an interview with the avatars of Bara and the director, see *HBO "When Strangers Click" with Documentary Maker Robert Kenner and Bara Jonson on Tonight Live*, available at: www.youtube.com/watch?v=mMxbnwlZhjI.

[3] David H. J. Morgan, *Family Connections* (Cambridge: Polity Press, 1996), at 11.

and exposed to new options, liberties, and flexibilities, as well as challenged by it and faced with new complexities and confusions.

Though families are shaped by globalization in many profound ways and are, at the same time, contributing to the ever-changing meaning of globalization, surprisingly, very little attention has been given to families in the rich literature on globalization. As I write these lines, I have several books on my desk that have *globalization* in their titles and that strive to offer a wide perspective on the phenomenon. I find it almost inconceivable that not even one out of the eleven works that contain a subject index has *family* as a category, particularly as they include a reader[4] and a handbook,[5] which hold about 500 pages each, and a book entitled *Globalization and Everyday Life.*[6] Moreover, although there are growing numbers of studies that look into specific case studies in which families are affected by globalization, especially within immigration studies,[7] the links between the social institution of the family and globalization are also theoretically underdeveloped within family studies. One goal of the present book is to contribute to the exploration of this *"terra incognita,"* as it has been called by the prominent sociologists Ulrich Beck and Elisabeth Beck-Gernsheim;[8] in so doing, it adds to the first signs of the much-needed theoretical attention to the current interrelations between globalization and families.[9]

Although Bara and Nickel's story is about the new, globalized, cross-border movement – which enables us all to even blur the boundary between fiction and reality in novel, exciting, and puzzling ways[10] – it is also about the ongoing existence of borders. Not only the geo-political and

---

[4] Frank J. Lechner & John Boli (Eds.), *The Globalization Reader*, 4th edn. (Oxford: Wiley-Blackwell, 2012).

[5] Jonathan Michie (Ed.), *The Handbook of Globalization*, 2nd edn. (Cheltenham, UK: Edward Elgar, 2011).

[6] Ray Larry, *Globalization and Everyday Life* (London: Routledge, 2007).

[7] For example, Deborah Bryceson & Ulla Vuorela (Eds.), *The Transnational Family: New Frontiers and Global Networks* (Oxford: Berg, 2002); Jennifer Cole & Deborah Durham (Eds.), *Generations and Globalization* (Bloomington: Indiana University Press, 2007); May Friedman & Silvia Schultermandl (Eds.), *Growing Up Transnational: Identity and Kinship in a Global Era* (University of Toronto Press, 2011).

[8] Ulrich Beck & Elisabeth Beck-Gernsheim, *Distant Love* (Cambridge: Polity Press, 2014), at 7.

[9] Bahira Sherif Trask, *Globalization and Families Accelerated Systemic Social Change* (New York: Springer, 2010); Harry Goulbourne, Tracy Reynolds, John Solomon, & Elisabetta Zontint, *Transnational Families, Ethnicities, Identities and Social Capital* (London: Routledge, 2010); Beck & Beck-Gernsheim, *Distant Love*.

[10] Tom Boellstorff, *Coming of Age in Second Life: An Anthropologist Explores the Virtually Human* (Princeton, NJ: Princeton University Press, 2008).

legal borders, of the kind that prevent a Swedish man from living with an American woman and their baby for a 'relationship test period,' but also the national economic borders that force and allow Bara to move back to his homeland, a generous welfare state, and a gender border that makes the choice of preferring the mother–child dyad over the father–child dyad an unspoken one, entirely taken for granted. Hence, the answers to questions regarding who can cross borders, who wants to cross borders, and who must cross borders, are part of the global movement itself. In that sense, we cannot understand globalization without understanding the current national, social, economic, legal, and other kinds of borders that interrelate with it. Indeed, as this book will argue, we cannot understand families today without contextualizing them within *bordered globalization* – the conceptual framework I develop in Chapter 1 of this book, which includes a typology of the antagonistic, cooperative, and complex inter-relations between globalization and borders.

One reason for the ongoing centrality of borders in the familial context is that there is no global moral and normative consensus on what a family is and how family members should be treated by one another, by the country of their nationality, and by other countries. While Bara and Nickel are both from a western secular background, one can only imagine the challenges that could have been added to the already complex story if, for example, Bara had found out that behind the female avatar he married virtually lived a gay man who could not even take the risk of creating a homosexual avatar, let alone experiencing nonvirtual intimate relations with another man, in fear of social and legal retaliation in his country. Or what if Nickel had discovered that behind the avatar she loved hid a man who was already married to three wives, which was perfectly acceptable according to his religion and the law of his country of residency? Although these scenarios sound almost ludicrous, they are entirely possible in an era in which globalization and borders are in constant interplay, bringing together different national, religious, cultural, and legal perceptions of the family, and thus creating familial opportunities and challenges for people all over the world.

As hinted earlier, the law acts as a family-shaping border in itself, as it reinforces cultural borders between the allowed and the forbidden in familial terms, as well as reflects the ongoing global, national, and parochial controversies about what a family is and what the rights and obligations of family members are vis-à-vis each other and the state. Indeed, as will be explained in detail in Chapter 2, the law – national, international, and subnational – on the books and in action – will be applied in this book as the central analytical perspective from which to explore the interrelations between globalization and borders in the familial context.

Before briefly justifying the choice of the legal prism here, allow me to offer another way of contextualizing the relevance and importance of analyzing the interrelations between globalization, borders, and families, while mentioning the themes on which the chapters in this book focus. I wish to point to what I detect as a *new familial dictionary*, which has evolved in recent years and which demonstrates the many ways families shape, and are shaped by, bordered globalization. This dictionary includes entirely new terms as well as new additional definitions attached to existing terms used until recently only in the local or national context. Tracing these terms and definitions, and assembling them together here, illuminate the argument at the heart of this book – that contemporary family structures, practices, and displays[11] are affected, with increasing intensity and in many significant ways, by bordered globalization.

One group of terms in this emerging new dictionary is related to spousal relations and how these are established and maintained. *Split household, living apart together,* and *long-distance relationship* are three terms describing a situation in which a couple, married or not, have an intimate, more or less exclusive, relationship, while each lives in a different place.[12] Although these terms can describe spouses who live in separate dwellings within the same country, due to globalization these terms are also relevant to more and more people who, like Bara and Nickel, sustain such spousal relations while living in different countries. *Split household* also refers now to situations in which the spouses used to live together but are currently separated due to immigration.[13] *Mobile intimacy*[14] captures such couples' ability to stay intimate, through technological means, while living apart.

The terms *cross-border marriage, multinational marriage, mixed-marriage, cross-cultural marriage, interfaith marriage,* and *interracial*

---

[11] Janet Finch, "Displaying Families," *Sociology*, 41(1) (2007), 65–81.

[12] Irene Levin, "Living Apart Together: A New Family Form," *Current Sociology*, 52(2) (2004), 223–40.

[13] Cindy C. Fun & San Mingjie, "Migration and Split Households: A Comparison of Sole, Couple, and Family Migrants in Beijing, China," *Environment and Planning*, 43 (2011), 2164–85.

[14] Gerard C. Raiti, "Mobile Intimacy: Theories on the Economics of Emotion with Examples from Asia," *Journal of Media and Culture*, 10(1) (2007), available at: http://journal.media-culture.org.au/0703/02-raiti.php.

marriage all refer to the growing number of cases in which people marry outside their group of origin.[15] This phenomenon can be explained first and foremost by the physical and virtual exposure to different nationalities, religions, and races that is the outcome of globalization, as well as by growing tolerance for exogamy rising from the globally spreading Western perception of the family as aimed at fulfilling individual, rather than collective, needs and wishes. This cross-border spousal mixing is part of what Beck and Beck-Gernsheim call the "normalization of diversity,"[16] and, as will be elaborated in Chapters 2 and 3, can also be seen as part of what they describe as the global normal chaos of love, in which people from different places and cultures must negotiate the meaning of their familial relations with no agreed-upon familial social scripts.[17]

Intimate citizenship is another term I would add to the evolving dictionary's spousal section. As developed by Plummer,[18] the notion of intimate citizenship is a broad conceptual framework drawing attention to the interplay between individual intimate choices, such as marriage and procreation, and public debates and constraints, such as those surrounding same-sex marriage and surrogacy. Although this term can relate to many conflicts and dilemmas arising from bordered globalization, I will narrow it here so it echoes the formal term *spouse visa,* and will attribute it a very pragmatic, yet controversial, meaning regarding whether a country should grant citizenship to an outsider because that person is the spouse of one of that country's citizens. As we shall see in Chapter 5, which centers on what I term *familial citizenship,* the answer to this and other questions related to family-based naturalization reveal many examples of national authorities endeavoring to impose ever-more effective borders between insiders and outsiders. For example, *sham marriage, fraudulent marriage, fictive marriage,* and *marriage of convenience* are all terms used by the authorities to try to differentiate between marriages based on love and those used merely

---

[15] Daphna Hacker, "From the Moabite Ruth to Norly the Filipino: Intermarriage and Conversion in the Jewish Nation State" in Hanna Herzog & Ann Braude (Eds.), *Gendering Religion and Politics: Untangling Modernities* (New York: Palgrave Macmillan, 2009), pp. 101–24.

[16] Ulrich Beck & Elisabeth Beck-Gernsheim, "Families in a Runaway World" in Jacqueline Scott, Judith Treas, & Martin Richards (Eds.), *The Blackwell Companion to the Sociology of Families* (Malden, MA: Blackwell Publishing, 2004), pp. 499–514, at 505.

[17] Beck & Beck-Gernsheim, *Distant Love.*

[18] Ken Plummer, *Intimate Citizenship, Private Decision and Public Dialogue* (Seattle: University of Washington Press, 2003).

as an immigration license, as if it were possible to separate authentic spousal feelings from material and other interests.[19]

Two additional terms, which can be found in the group of spousal-related terms, are *mail-order brides*[20] and *leftover women*.[21] These terms remind us that mixed marriages are not gender-neutral since, in most cases, it is the woman who leaves her country of origin to live with the man in his country.[22] Among other reasons for this gendered tendency is that, in some countries where women have gained some degrees of freedom and independence, men are seeking women from less developed countries, whom they perceive as more traditionally-minded women. Hence, the industry surrounding mail-order brides is much more significant than that of *mail-order grooms*, and there are also *leftover women* – those in the more developed country who are left single, among other reasons, because of this male preference for foreign brides. In some countries, such as Singapore, Korea, and Taiwan, this phenomenon is very significant. In Singapore, about 35 percent of marriages are of local men with women from less developed Asian countries, leaving many local women unmarried. In the case of Taiwan, in 2004 some 22 percent of marriages were between Taiwanese men and foreign women. By 2008 this had declined to around 10 percent due to government-strengthened immigration policy aimed at discouraging the importation of brides.[23] Notwithstanding, in the poorer countries from which the brides emigrate, such as Vietnam, there are *leftover men*, who either import brides from even poorer countries or remain single.[24]

---

[19] See also Viviana A. Zelizer, *The Purchase of Intimacy* (Princeton, NJ: Princeton University Press, 2005).

[20] Yu Kojima, "In the Business of Cultural Reproduction: Theoretical Implications of the Mail-Order Bride Phenomenon," *Women's Studies International Forum*, 24(2) (2001), 199–210.

[21] Xin Meng, "In the 'New China' Educated, Unmarried 'Leftover Women' are Still Stigmatized," Xpat Nation (April 18, 2016), available at: http://xpatnation.com/in-the-new-china-educated-unmarried-leftover-women-are-still-stigmatized/.

[22] Catherine Dauvergne, "Globalization Fragmentation: New Pressures on Women Caught in the Immigration Law-Citizenship Law Dichotomy" in Seyla Benhabib & Judith Resnik (Eds.), *Migration and Mobilities: Citizenship, Borders and Gender* (New York University Press, 2009), pp. 333–54.

[23] Daiji Kawaguchi & Lee Soohyung, "Cross Border Marriages and Female Immigration," Harvard Business School, Working Paper No. 12–082 (2012), available at: www.hbs.edu/faculty/Publication%20Files/12-082.pdf.

[24] Danièle Bélanger & Tran Giang Linh, "The Impact of Transnational Migration on Gender and Marriage in Sending Communities of Vietnam," *Current Sociology*, 59(1) (2011), 59–77.

Finally, in the spousal-related group of terms, I would suggest importing *portability*, used mainly in social security law,[25] to family law and family-related legal documents. *Portable spousal agreement* and *portable divorce agreement* can be useful terms that point to the need to draft such legal documents in a way that will secure their meaning and enforceability in different countries. As will be demonstrated in Chapter 3, which centers on the theme of coordinating expectations, the relevance of prenuptial agreements is relatively obvious for cases in which the spouses are from different countries, have different expectations of the marriage, and are connected to competing legal systems. However, the questions surrounding prenups' desirability and portability, as well as the portability of other familial legal agreements and documents, such as last testaments, become relevant to all couples in an era in which one cannot be sure that both parties will live in the same country all their lives. *Divorce tourism* is another relevant term that relates to forum shopping on the part of ex-spouses in an attempt to secure the jurisdiction most favorable to them.[26] For example, according to *The Times*, London is a global capital for divorce tourism, with marriage break-ups involving foreign nationals accounting for a sixth of all divorce cases put before the courts.[27] Apparently, ex-wives, and their lawyers, are aware of the English courts' reputation as being more generous than others toward the domestic partner when it comes to splitting the matrimonial property.[28]

Another group of terms in the new familial dictionary relates to the different cross-border ways of bringing a child into the world. The terms *fertility tourism, procreative tourism, infertility exile, reproduction emigration,* and *cross-border reproduction care* all refer to the same phenomenon in which people in one country travel to another to buy gametes (mostly ova) or pregnancy-related services (surrogacy or delivery).[29] People can also stay put, and import gametes (ova and sperm) from another country.[30] For the first time in human history, a child can be born from sperm

---

[25] For example, see "General Rules of Portability," Australian Government website, available at: http://guides.dss.gov.au/guide-social-security-law/7/1/2/10.

[26] Beck & Beck-Gernsheim, *Distant Love,* at 180.

[27] Frances Gibb, "'Divorce Tourists' Take Over the Court," *The Times* (April 10, 2012), available at: www.thetimes.co.uk/tto/law/article3379227.ece.

[28] Cecilia Rodriguez, "Divorce Tourism: London Is Still the Top Destination," *Forbes* (August 23, 2013), available at: www.forbes.com/sites/ceciliarodriguez/2013/08/22/divorce-tourism-london-is-still-the-top-destination/.

[29] Richard F. Storrow, "The Pluralism Problem in Cross-Border Reproductive Care," *Human Reproduction,* 25(12) (2010), 2939–43.

[30] Marcia C. Inhorn, "Rethinking Reproductive 'Tourism' as Reproductive 'Exile'," *Fertility & Sterility,* 94 (3) (2009), 904–6; Eric Blyth, "Fertility Patients' Experiences of Cross-Border

produced in one country and an ovum retrieved in another country, which are then transplanted as an embryo into a woman from a third country, who gives birth in a fourth country, to a baby designated to be handed over to intended parents from a fifth. However, as the different terms demonstrate, this new option is not normative-neutral.

Chapter 4 frames abortion as another cross-border reproduction service, and discusses it together with inter- and multinational surrogacy. I will argue that the ability to purchase reproduction services abroad, and the disagreement about the moral acceptability of abortion and surrogacy, lead to what I call *familial globordered hypocrisy* – a situation in which one country enacts restrictive family-related legislation while assuming this will not lead to active external or internal opposition since that country's citizens can satisfy their familial needs in another country where there is different and more enabling legislation. In this case, globalization and borders are in symbiotic relations, as a nation-state can preserve its *nomos* thanks to the global supply of reproduction services, while the global reproduction industry profits from national restrictive policies.

The final group of terms in the new familial dictionary relates to parent–child relations. *Left-behind child* is a term referring to cases in which one or both of the parents emigrate, leaving the child to be raised by the remaining parent or grandparents or other family members. There are millions of left-behind children around the world, living in countries with a markedly high incidence of emigration such as the Philippines, Sri Lanka, Moldova, and Mexico. Millions more, especially in China, are left behind because of their parents' need to emigrate afar within their own country, a phenomenon also reinforced by global capitalism and its impact on agriculture and urbanization.[31] *Transnational motherhood* is the mirror term of *left-behind child* as well as another example of the parentally gendered border that leads to greater emphasis being placed on the mother–child dyad,[32] though the gender-neutral term *transnational families* is increasingly in use, describing families that are split

Reproductive Care," *Fertility & Sterility*, 94(1) (2010), e11–e15, available at: www.fertstert.org/article/S0015-0282(10)00106-8/fulltext.

[31] See "Migration, Displacement and Children Left Behind," The International Center for Migration, Health and Development (August 12, 2013), available at: http://icmhd.wordpress.com/2013/08/12/migration-displacement-and-children-left-behind-clbs/.

[32] Sarah K. van Walsum, "Transnational Mothering, National Immigration Policy, and European Law: The Experience of the Netherlands" in Seyla Benhabib & Judith Resnik (Eds.), *Migration and Mobilities, Citizenship, Borders and Gender* (New York University Press, 2009), pp. 228–51.

between two countries or more.[33] Additional related terms are *teleparenting* and *mobile-phone mum*, which captures the technology-assisted attempts of transnational parents to keep in touch with their left-behind children on a regular basis.[34] Chapter 6 will look at remittances, sent by parents working abroad to their left-behind children, and place this phenomenon, together with child labor and international adoption, in the broader context of the question of who should be obliged to secure children's economic needs in our era.

Parachute kid is another term in the lexical parent–child group, developed to capture the phenomenon of children sent to live in a new country, alone or with a distant family member or a paid caregiver, while the parents stay in the country of origin. If the child is accompanied by one of the parents and siblings while the breadwinner parent stays behind in the country of origin, he or she is termed a *satellite kid,* and the absent breadwinner is referred-to as an *astronaut parent,* left detached to provide for the rest of the family.[35] In both cases, the children's change of location is usually aimed at securing good schooling and higher education for them. For example, during the 1990s it was estimated that about 40,000 unaccompanied Taiwanese minors aged 8–18 were studying in the United States.[36] Although in most cases the family's assumption is that the child will return to the homeland, in others the expectation is that the child will remain in the host country and, possibly, will be joined at some point by his or her parents and other adults.[37] Two further terms, used to derogate parents who try to secure citizenship of another country by a short-term move, are *anchor baby* and *birth tourism.*[38] These terms relate to cases in which expectant parents deliberately time the baby's delivery and choose its location to coincide with a country that grants citizenship on the basis of geographic place of birth, such as the United States.

---

[33] For example, Laura Meria (Ed.), *Transnational Families, Migration and the Circulation of Care: Understanding Mobility and Absence in Family Life* (New York: Routledge, 2014).

[34] Burghardt et al., in Beck & Beck-Gernsheim, Distant Love, at 112; Ernesto Castañeda and Lesley Buck, "Remittances, Transnational Parenting, and the Children Left Behind: Economic and Psychological Implications," *The Latin Americanist*, 55(4) (2011), 85–110, at 91.

[35] Yuying Tsong & Yuli Liu, "Parachute Kids and Astronaut Families" in Nita Tewari & Alvin N. Alvarez (Eds.), *Asian American Psychology: Current Perspectives* (Mahwah, NJ: Erlbaum, 2008), pp. 365–79.

[36] Ibid.

[37] Ibid.

[38] See Wikipedia entry, *Birth Tourism*, available at https://en.wikipedia.org/wiki/Birth_tourism (as of August 14, 2016).

Indeed, in the United States, the authorities are trying to combat the phenomenon,[39] and the question of abolishing birthright citizenship was part of the recent presidential campaign.[40] Recently, a new term has emerged in the global sphere of children crossing borders. *Unaccompanied minors* relates mainly to the tens of thousands of teenagers from Africa and the Middle East who, since 2010, have reached European countries without their parents. They seek asylum or try to stay unnoticed by the authorities. The motivations of these minors and their families, which fuel the decision to take this highly risky route, include the need to escape war or poverty, and are still in need of a much deeper study, both in the countries of origin and the destination countries.[41]

A very different term in this parent–child lexical group, and the last one I will refer to in relation to the emerging and dynamic new familial dictionary, is *left-behind parent*. This term refers to cases in which a child is kidnapped from one parent, by the other, and taken to another country.[42] This reminder of the dark side of family life will be discussed in Chapter 7, together with other forms of familial violence and abuse affected by bordered globalization.

Interestingly, in my research for this book I did not come across any new shared familial terminology related to the growing proportion of the elderly population separating from their family due to 'return migration', in which older people who emigrated when they were younger choose to retire to their birth country or, due to immigration to a warmer or more affordable country. Nor did I find any new terms that reflect the familial impact of elderly people's reunion with their children, where the latter immigrated in the past and now bring their parents across so they can care for them in old age. Likewise, I did not detect any new familial terms related to the rising phenomenon of elderly people cared for by workers

[39] For example, Leo Timm, "Chinese 'Birth Tourists' Getting Attention from US Authorities," *Epoch Times* (Sep. 11, 2013), available at: www.theepochtimes.com/n3/283563-chinese-birth-tourists-getting-attention-from-us-authorities-2/.

[40] Tal Kopan, "Birthright Citizenship: Can Donald Trump Change the Constitution?," CNN (August 18, 2015), available at: http://edition.cnn.com/2015/08/18/politics/birthright-citizenship-trump-constitution/.

[41] European Commission, *Policies, Practices and Data on Unaccompanied Minors: In the EU Member States and Norway* (2015), available at: http://ec.europa.eu/dgs/home-affairs/what-we-do/networks/european_migration_network/reports/docs/emn-studies/emn_study_policies_practices_and_data_on_unaccompanied_minors_in_the_eu_member_states_and_norway_synthesis_report_final_eu_2015.pdf.

[42] "International Child Abduction: A Guidebook for Left-Behind Parents," Government of Canada website, available at: https://travel.gc.ca/travelling/publications/international-child-abductions.

who have emigrated from another country, that will be discussed in the eighth and final chapter of the book. This might be so since many people in the developed world would like to continue to treat these caregivers as invisible migrant workers. However, the little research that exists on this phenomenon shows that, in some cases, these foreign paid caregivers eventually become *child substitutes* or *surrogate grandchildren* and establish significant semifamilial relations with the cared-for person, who might become a *grandparent replacement* to the caregiver.[43] The intense daily and intimate care of the elderly in the destination country, on the one hand, and the distance of the caregiver from his or her family in the country of origin, on the other hand, create new identities and roles that cross the socially constructed border between family and strangers, and the legally constructed border between employment contracts and intimate ties. Like *split household, mail-order bride, transnational motherhood*, and *parachute child, child substitute* in the context of the elderly is an example of the new challenges to familial care, intimacy, authority, obligations, and rights in the era of bordered globalization, to be explored in this book.

Like the story of Bara and Nickel, the new familial dictionary detailed here demonstrates the many ways in which bordered globalization is part of contemporary families' biographies. Moreover, terms such as *spouse visa, portable spousal agreement, divorce tourism*, and *anchor baby*, also point to the role of law in shaping the interrelations between globalization, borders, and families. Indeed, this book strives to provide answers to the following questions:

• What are the opportunities that bordered globalization offers families?
• What are the difficulties and challenges faced by families due to bordered globalization?

---

[43] The term *surrogate daughter* is used by Liat Ayalon in the context of older Israelis cared for by Filipina migrant workers. See Liat Ayalon, "Family and Family-Like Interactions in Households with Round-the-Clock Paid Foreign Carers in Israel," *Ageing & Society*, 29(5) (2009), 671–86, at 681. Another term used in the literature to describe the relations that develop between elder care recipients and their paid care providers, though not necessarily in the context of globalization and migrant care workers, is *fictive kin*. See Tracy X. Karner, "Professional Caring: Homecare Workers as Fictive Kin," *Journal of Aging Studies*, 12(1) (1998), 69–82. Interestingly, *fictive kin*, a term developed by anthropologists to describe family-like relations that are not based on blood or marriage but on religious rituals or close friendship, is also the term used by Helen Rose Ebaugh and Mary Curry to describe the web of relations that immigrants constitute in the destination country. See Helen Rose Ebaugh & Mary Curry, "Fictive Kin as Social Capital in New Immigrant Communities," *Sociological Perspectives*, 43(2) (2000), 189–209.

- What role does the law play in shaping these opportunities, difficulties, and challenges?

Hopefully, this investigation will also provide substantial food for thought about what role the law should play in the lives of families in the bordered globalization era. Here I am inspired by Robin West's claim that legal scholarship should not be satisfied only by answering the question 'what is the law?'. Rather, it must also insist on trying to understand why the law is what it is, and what the law should be, so that it contributes to a humane and just society and world.[44] However, this book does not point to concrete desired legislative reforms. Rather, it highlights the importance of legal contextualization as well as the lack of satisfying empirical knowledge on families in the era of bordered globalization, needed for informed policy making.

Although the choice to use the law as the prism through which to study families in the era of bordered globalization is explored in detail in Chapter 2, I will end this Introduction by referring to the main differences between this book and other books on family law.

First, unlike most books on family law, the chapters of this book are not organized around the classic division of marriage, divorce, property, and child custody and support. Rather, as mentioned earlier, after developing the concept of bordered globalization in Chapter 1 and connecting it, generally, to families and law in Chapter 2, its impact on spousal and parental relations will be discussed in subsequent chapters that center on the themes of 'coordinating familial expectations', 'transnational reproduction services', 'familial citizenship', 'feeding children', 'familial violence', and 'old age'. This thematic organization echoes the familial life-span stages – establishing spousal relations, conceiving a child, caring for one's children (or sadly neglecting them), and being cared for in old age. It also allows us to look afresh at issues that, at first glance, might appear unconnected – for example, prenuptial agreements and relocation conflicts as part of the challenge inherent in coordinating expectations between spouses before marriage or after its breakdown; spouse visas and labor migrant-family rights as part of the interrelations between citizenship and family; or remittances and child labor as part of the question about who should be responsible for supporting children – and to see the conceptual connections they share within the bordered globalization framework.

---

[44] Robin West, "A Reply to Pierre," *Georgetown Law Journal*, 97 (2009), 865–75.

Second, unlike most family law scholarship that centers on one particular national legal system, this book looks at family law in different
countries. It will explore mainly three legal systems – namely, those of the
United Kingdom (UK), as an example of a Western country that was still
a part of the European Union (EU) when this book was written and that
is challenged by incoming immigration and a recent decision to enhance
its national borders (following the Brexit referendum); the United States
(US), as an example of a Western superpower, which faces massive legal
and illegal emigration; and Israel, as an example of a relatively multicultural traditional society, with a dual system of religious and secular family
law. In addition, many more countries and legal systems will be discussed
in this book, both from the Global North and the Global South, to provide a panoramic and contextual analysis of the impact of bordered globalization on families and the role the law plays in shaping it.

Third, in contrast to most other works on family law, law in this book
does not just refer to family law in the traditional sense, but to *families
laws* – that is, all laws that impact families affected by bordered globalization. These include, of course, family law, but also other branches of law
such as immigration law, labor law, criminal law, and public and private
international law. In saying that, I join those who argue that, even from a
narrow doctrinal perspective, one can no longer understand the law as it
pertains to families only by looking at national family law.[45] The era of bordered globalization forces family lawyers and judges to become acquainted
with these other branches of law, as well as with relevant laws of other
countries and the religious laws of minority groups, otherwise they are left
trapped by "methodological nationalism,"[46] unable to properly attend to
the family members with whom they come into professional contact.

Fourth, and perhaps most importantly, unlike most other books on
family law, including those few that escape the methodological nationalism trap,[47] in this book the law is not only an interesting research subject

---

[45] Barbara Stark, *International Family Law: An Introduction* (Aldershot, UK: Ashgate,
2005); Ann Laquar Estin & Barbara Stark, *Global Issues in Family Law* (Eagan, MN:
Thomson/West, 2007); Marianne D. Blair, Merle H. Weiner, Barbara Stark, & Solangel
Maldonado, *Family Law in the World Community: Cases, Materials, and Problems in
Comparative and International Family Law*, 2nd edn. (Durham, NC: Carolina Academic
Press, 2009); David Hodson, *The International Family Law Practice*, 2nd edn. (Bristol:
Family Law, 2012); Zvi Triger, "Introducing the Political Family: A New Road Map for
Critical Family Law," *Theoretical Inquiries in Law*, 13(1) (2012), 361–84.

[46] Ulrich Beck, "Unpacking Cosmopolitanism for the Social Sciences: A Research Agenda,"
The British Journal of Sociology, 57(1) (2006), 1–23.

[47] See supra note 45.

matter in itself but also an analytical perspective and a methodological prism through which the social, cultural, and moral dimensions of familial lives in our era are explored. As a scholar trained in both law and sociology, I cannot understand the law but as a social field, and a relatively weak one, because it is shaped by political and economic forces.[48] Yet, the law is meaningful enough to limit our imagination and to contribute to the creation of relatively consensual social scripts – and more rarely to open up our minds to challenge these scripts.[49] Moreover, as our collectively agreed-upon private conflict solver, the law highlights the falseness of the alleged separation between the private and the public spheres, as well as the problematic treatment of family members as belonging to one harmonious unit, while ignoring power relations and conflicting interests within families – two insights well developed by feminist jurisprudence.[50] Finally, as the law is perhaps the last meta-narrative to survive postmodernism and identity politics on the national level,[51] and the dominant language in the international sphere,[52] it is a fascinating public discursive arena in which global forces, nations, communities, families, and individuals meet and different perceptions related to families interact, clash, converse, and are reshaped. Hence what better a lens than the law through which to study the interrelations among globalization, borders, and families?

The socio-legal perspective of the book leads to its *methodological bricolage*. This is not a family law doctrinal book, limited to the analysis of legal rules and cases. Rather, it offers a synthesis of innovative theoretical conceptualization, empirical and legal literature integrative reviews, focused and overview comparative analyses, qualitative research, cultural artifacts analysis, and historical socio-legal genealogy. All this is tailored to provide what I consider the most important, thought-provoking, and challenging narratives of the phenomenon of legalized families in the era of bordered globalization.

---

[48] Pierre Bourdieu, "The Force of Law: Towards a Sociology of the Juridical Field," *Hastings Law Journal*, 38 (1987), 814–53.

[49] Patricia Ewick, "Consciousness and Ideology," in Austin Sarat (Ed.), *The Blackwell Companion to Law and Society* (Malden, MA: Blackwell Publishing, 2004), pp. 80–94.

[50] For example, see Frances E. Olsen, "The Myth of State Intervention in the Family," *University of Michigan Journal of Law Reform*, 18 (1985), 835–64; Suzan Okin Moller, *Justice, Gender, and the Family* (New York: Basic Books, 1989).

[51] Shulamit Almog, *Law and Literature* (Jerusalem: Nevo, 2000) (Hebrew). All translations from Hebrew are either official or those of the author.

[52] Orna Ben-Naftali & Yuval Shany, *International Law between War and Peace* (Tel Aviv: Ramot, 2006) (Hebrew).

Allow me to end this Introduction with two warnings. First, this book aims to provide a panoramic overview of the interrelations between globalization, borders, families, and laws. Each chapter could have been developed further to include many more topics, arguments, examples, and references, and there is no presumption to exhaust any of the issues raised, let alone refer to all the relevant literature. I hope this task will be ably performed by others convinced by the basic arguments in the book and enriched by the synthesis and analysis it provides. Second, reality changes so fast in the era of bordered globalization that sociological data, legal descriptions, and socio-legal analyses can become obsolete even days after they are presented. The Brexit debate and resolution, the candidacy and triumph of Donald Trump, and the massive and frequent terrorist attacks in Europe are but three examples of the more dramatic and unpredicted events that took place while this book was written, and which might have significant implications for legalized families affected by bordered globalization. Hence, the data in this book should be consumed with caution, in context, and in light of updated information, and in no event should be confused with legal advice.

1

Our Era

In this chapter, I will lay down the general theoretical framework that will accompany us throughout the book. I call this framework *bordered globalization,* and at its heart stands my claim that we live in an era in which globalization and borders are two extremely important forces that interrelate in ways that affect every aspect of our lives, including the familial dimension. By taking this view, I depart both from those arguing that our world is a global village in which people, capital, and ideas move with little interruption across geo-political borders and social boundaries," as well as from those arguing that "borders and boundaries are so significant that globalization should be perceived as a phenomenon affecting only the mobile elite or only specific areas of activity, such as commerce or communication technology." Furthermore, in the last part of this chapter, I will move away from the common conceptualization of globalization and borders as two oppositional forces, to join those who suggest a more multifarious perception of the interrelations between the two. I will offer a typology that adds cooperative and complex relations to the antagonistic one, to highlight the richness of the dynamics between globalization and borders, and to emphasize my argument that the one cannot be understood without the other. This typology is crucial to understanding the opportunities offered to families, as well as the challenges they face in our era, and to understanding the role the law plays in shaping them both, as will be explored in the following chapters.

Before presenting my *bordered globalization* theoretical framework and typology, I will first discuss the much-deliberated concept of *globalization*, to make clear the meaning I ascribe to this overarching term. Next, I will discuss *borders*, for those less familiar with the fascinating themes developed in recent years within border studies, to capture the many ways borders are constructed by political, social, and cultural forces and are, in turn, constructing all aspects of our lives. Three well-known examples epitomizing globalization – McDonald's, London, and the Internet – will be presented, to subsequently highlight their inseparability from borders, hence leading us to the concept of *bordered globalization*, with which this chapter will conclude.

Globalization

Our era has already had many labels attributed to it, including *late modernity*, *second modernity*, *postmodernity*, and *liquid modernity*. Similarly, the current world society is described by scholars as the *post-industrial society*, *post-traditional society*, *information society*, *network society*, *risk society*, *transnational society*, and *cosmopolitan society*. Notwithstanding, the term that has most powerfully captured the imagination of scholars from a variety of disciplines as best describing the most significant periodic change since the 1980s, is *globalization*.

Indeed, globalization is perceived by many to be at the heart of the very processes that lead to the search for other terms, such as those already mentioned, that will capture the essence of the era following modernity.[1] Although there are ongoing disagreements about what globalization is, how new it is, what it does and to whom, and whether it is good or bad,[2] there is a near consensus that we live in a globalized era and society. As the prominent sociologist Anthony Giddens argues, in just a few years during the last decade of the twentieth century, the term *globalization* "had come from nowhere to be almost everywhere" – a rapid linguistic spread, which is an example of globalization itself.[3]

Let me state up front that I concur with those who think globalization is real, new, and dramatic in its harmonizing and differentiating impact in relation to all aspects of life, with complex, dynamic, and contradicting moral dimensions. Furthermore, its interrelations with the social institution of the family are understudied; hence, in respect to this and other mezzo- and microlevels of our current social existence, globalization is still far from being fully understood.

---

[1] For example, see Zygmunt Bauman, *Globalization: The Human Consequences* (Cambridge: Polity Press, 1998); Anthony Giddens, *Runaway World: How Globalization Is Reshaping our Lives* (New York: Routledge, 2000); Ulrich Beck, "Unpacking Cosmopolitanism for the Social Sciences: A Research Agenda," *The British Journal of Sociology*, 57(1) (2006), 1–23.

[2] Guillén F. Mauro, "Is Globalization Civilizing, Destructive or Feeble? A Critique of Five Key Debates in the Social Science Literature," *Annual Review of Sociology*, 27 (2001), 235–60.

[3] Giddens, *Runaway World*, at 25.

In the last half-century, an extensive body of literature has evolved around the topic of globalization.[4] As Thomas Hylland Erikson, the former president of the European Association of Social Anthropologists, demonstrates, the sheer volume of this literature is almost overwhelming.[5] I will point here to what I perceive to be the most convincing descriptions of the major components of globalization, being fully aware that there are competing definitions and emphases.[6] I will later argue that even the most convincing descriptions are partial and misleading since, in my opinion, our era is not the era of globalization but rather that of *bordered* globalization.

To my understanding, globalization is first and foremost about intense movement across national borders. This movement has three major components: movement of capital (virtual and physical money, commodities, products, and other kinds of economic goods); movement of people (due to voluntary and forced emigration, tourism, business trips, studies abroad, and other personal and political circumstances); and movement of messages (private, commercial, political, cultural, and other kinds of communications). There are also – as melting icebergs, HIV, and toxic waste all demonstrate – additional and significant, at least partially manufactured, global movement components that shape our current world, but which I will not discuss here.[7]

The intensity of the movement across national borders is what differentiates globalization from previous historical epochs. At least since Homo Sapiens emigrated from Africa to other parts of the world about 70,000 years ago – pushing away other Homo species to become the only

---

[4] The magnitude of scholarly writings devoted to globalization is truly breathtaking. According to Bahira Sherif Trask, *Globalization and Families: Accelerated Systemic Social Change* (New York: Springer 2010), at Ch. 1, fn. 6, there are over 61,000 books and articles dealing with various aspects of globalization. For important examples, see Arjun Appadurai (Ed.), *Globalization* (Durham, NC: Duke University Press, 2003); Thomas Hylland Erikson, *Globalization: The Key Concepts* (Oxford: Berg, 2007); Frank J. Lechner & John Boli (Eds.), *The Globalization Reader*; Jonathan Michie (Ed.), *The Handbook of Globalization*; George Modelski, Devezas Tessaleno, & William R. Thompson (Eds.), *Globalization as Evolutionary Process* (London: Routledge, 2008); Saskia Sassen, *A Sociology of Globalization* (New York: W. W. Norton, 2007); Jan Aart Scholte, *Globalization: A Critical Introduction*, 2nd ed. (New York: Palgrave Macmillan, 2005).

[5] Erikson, *Globalization*.

[6] Nayef Al-Rudhan, "Definitions of Globalization: A Comprehensive Overview and a Proposed Definition," Geneva Center for Security Policy (2006), available at: www.scribd.com/doc/56147025/Definitions-of-Globalization-A-Comprehensive-Overview-and-a-Proposed-Definition.

[7] See Giddens, *Runaway World*, at 25; Ulrich Beck, *Risk Society: Towards a New Modernity* (London: Sage, 1992); Erikson, *Globalization*, Ch. 7.

rulers of the earth – people, goods, and ideas have moved across huge geographic distances to shape and be shaped by other people, goods, and ideas.[8] However, never in human history has the movement of all three components of globalization been so massive, so intense, and so much a part of everybody's lives as in our era. There are countless examples of this dramatic movement, but here I will present three of my favorites that epitomize the phenomenon, one for each component.

A well-known example of the movement of capital, which also highlights the interrelations between this component of globalization and the other two, is McDonald's, the fast-food chain.[9] According to the company's website, it opened its first restaurant in the United States in 1955. Today, there are more than 36,000 McDonald's restaurants in more than 100 countries, serving tens of millions of customers every day and employing 1.9 million people, including managers from the United States who have relocated to run McDonald's branches in other parts of the world.[10] The company's website, however, does not mention how many cows are bred to be slaughtered, how many trees are destroyed, and how many tons of waste are produced daily in the process of running the business, or how these costs are spread globally.

McDonald's is an example of what Jan Aart Scholte calls *hypercapitalism*, which is the economic outcome of globalization. According to Scholte, the creation of thousands of transnational companies and commercial alliances, the appearance of innumerable global products, and the huge expansion of borderless monetary flow lead to the expansion of commodification and to a greater organizational efficiency of accumulation – and hence to global hypercapitalism.[11] As the terms *McDonaldization* and *McWorld* – used in the literature on globalization – demonstrate, this hyperglobal economic activity has political and cultural meanings, as it is seen by many scholars and laypeople alike as a new kind of imperialism, in which Western economies and cultures, and especially the United States, are conquering the world with monetary and symbolic violence rather than with physical force.[12]

---

[8]   Yuval Noah Harari, *Sapiens: A Brief History of Mankind* (London: Harvill Secker, 2012).
[9]   Uri Ram, "McDonaldization" in George Ritzer (Ed.), *The Wiley-Blackwell Encyclopedia of Globalization* (Malden, MA: Blackwell Publishing, 2012), pp. 342–7.
[10] Data extracted from McDonald's Official Global Corporate Website. Available at: www .aboutmcdonalds.com/mcd/our_company.html.
[11] Scholte, *Globalization*.
[12] Benjamin Barber, *Jihad versus McWorld* (New York: Times Books, 1995).

Indeed, during what is called the era of globalization, economic inequalities between developed and developing countries continue to widen, if China and India are left out of the equation. These two rising national economic powers complicate the oft-used West–East descriptive and analytical division, suggesting the North–South division as a more accurate reflection of the current global power imbalance.[13] Moreover, unrestrained global capitalism is the major reason for the growing economic inequality within nations as local elites manage to benefit from global opportunities and faraway markets while the poor are left far behind. Not only are the poor less able to mobilize themselves, and not only do they have no fortune with which to invest in the global economy, but national governments are also less able to secure their citizens' minimal welfare in the face of global competition and transnational companies that set the economic rules.[14]

These economic gaps between and within countries have led to a reality in which, according to the World Bank, 8 percent of the world population (the latter currently estimated at about seven and a half billion),[15] enjoy 50 percent of the world's income, whereas 20 percent of the world's inhabitants earn less than $1 per day and a further 30 percent are only marginally better off. That said, globalization has also improved the absolute position of the world's poor, as the percentage of people earning less than $1.25 a day decreased from 44 percent in 1988 to 23 percent in 2008.[16] Still, the attraction of other, wealthier countries is stronger than ever for poor people as, unlike a few decades ago, nowadays one's geo-political location within the global system has become a stronger predictor of income than economic class within one's nation state.[17] For example, the poorest French person earns more than do 72 percent of the world's population, and the richest 5 percent of rural India are poorer than the poorest 5 percent of the people of France.[18]

---

[13] The term "Global North" is also misleading as it includes Australia and New Zealand.

[14] Ulrike Schuerkens, "Theoretical and Empirical Introduction: Globalization and Transformation of Social Inequality" in Ulrike Schuerkens (Ed.), *Globalization and Transformation of Social Inequality* (New York: Routledge, 2010), pp. 3–28.

[15] For a useful "population clock," see "U.S. and World Population Clock," the United States Census Bureau, available at: www.census.gov/popclock/.

[16] Branko Milanovic, "Global Income Inequality in Numbers: In History and Now," *Global Policy*, 4(2) (2013), 198–208; "GNP per Capita," The World Bank Group, available at www .worldbank.org/depweb/english/modules/economic/gnp/print.html; Branko Milanovic, "The Real Winners and Losers of Globalization," *Let's Talk Development* Blog (December 14, 2012), available at http://blogs.worldbank.org/developmenttalk/voices/nasikiliza/ developmenttalk/health/developmenttalk/the-real-winners-and-losers-of-globalization.

[17] Branko Milanovic, "Evolution of Global Inequality: From Class to Location, From Proletarians to Migrants," *Global Policy*, 3(2) (2012), 125–34.

[18] Branko Milanovic, "Globalization and Inequity" in David Held & Ayse Kaya (Eds.), *Global Inequality* (Cambridge: Polity Press, 2007), pp. 26–49, at 41.

Indeed, this relative global economic inequality is the major reason for the second component of globalization – accelerating cross-border movement of people.[19] According to the United Nations (UN), in 2013 there were 232 million international immigrants. Between 1990 and 2013, the volume of international migration rose by 50 percent, with 69 percent of the 77 million immigrants in this period received by developed countries, and 78 percent of these 53 million born in the southern hemisphere. Notwithstanding, since 2000 the average annual growth rate in international migrant stock in the developing countries has outpaced that of migration to the developed ones: 1.8 percent versus 1.5 percent per year, respectively. Still, immigrants account for about a tenth of the population in the developed regions, compared to less than 2 percent in the developing ones.[20]

Moreover, since 2014, armed conflicts in Syria and other countries, such as Afghanistan and Iraq, have contributed to mass emigration, mainly to Europe. For example, 1.26 million asylum applications were submitted to EU countries in 2015, compared to half that number in 2014, and to less than 200,000 a decade earlier.[21] Indeed, it is important to try to distinguish between voluntary and forced emigration. According to a recent UN report,[22] a global total of 59.5 million forcibly displaced people documented in 2014 represents the highest number ever recorded. In 2014 alone, 13.9 million people became newly displaced – four times the number of the previous year. Many of them were children. Globally, one in every 122 humans is now either a refugee, internally displaced, or seeking asylum. These are people who were forced to leave their homes due to persecution, conflict, generalized violence, or human rights violations. Whereas 38.2 million were displaced inside their own countries, the rest were forced to leave their homeland and to become *refugees, asylum seekers, job-seekers, undocumented migrants,* or *infiltrators* – with each label carrying different political, legal, and social sanctions and

[19] Stephen Castels & Mark J. Miller, *The Age of Migration: International Population Movements in the Modern World,* 2nd ed. (Hampshire, UK: Macmillan Press, 1998).

[20] See United Nations, *International Migration Report* (2013), available at www.un.org/en/development/desa/population/publications/pdf/migration/migrationreport2013/Chapter1.pdf.

[21] "Asylum Statistics," Eurostat Statistic Explained, available at http://ec.europa.eu/eurostat/statistics-explained/index.php/Asylum_statistics.

[22] "Worldwide Displacement Hits All-time High as War and Persecution Increase," UNHCR: The UN Refugee Agency (June 18, 2015), available at www.unhcr.org/news/latest/2015/6/558193896/worldwide-displacement-hits-all-time-high-war-persecution-increase.html.

privileges.[23] Notwithstanding, the attempt to draw a clear line between voluntary and forced emigration is often futile, as the many kinds of circumstances and factors that affect it create a vast spectrum of opportunities and restrictions leading to people's relocation on the inside or the outside of their birth country's border.

One of the examples epitomizing the movement-of-people component of globalization is London, Europe's largest city and the sixth richest in the world. Over 300 languages are spoken by London school children;[24] only 45 percent of Londoners identify themselves as white British;[25] and fewer than half identify themselves as Christian.[26] It is important to note that London, like other global cities,[27] is an emigration destination for people from all classes in their country of origin. However, its economic structure centers around the high- and low-paying ends of the scale, from the privileged hypermobile manager of a large global corporation, to the undocumented migrant woman who cleans his house. Hence, London itself, like many of its other global counterparts, contributes to the polarization of inequality.[28]

Moreover, many do not come to London for long-term emigration yet experience the city for a significant period of time. Foreign students are one example. In 2013, some 102,965 non-UK students were studying in London's universities and colleges; this figure represents 26 percent of the international students in the UK who, in turn, account for 18 percent of all students in the UK. Within this group there are more Chinese and Indian students than European Union (EU) students.[29] Interest among the Chinese

[23] Roger Zetter, "Labelling Refugees: Forming and Transforming a Bureaucratic Identity," *Journal of Refugee Studies*, 4(1) (1991), 39–62.

[24] Javier Espinoza, "More than 300 Different Languages Spoken in British Schools, Report Says," *The Telegraph* (July 24, 2015), available at www.telegraph.co.uk/education/educationnews/11761250/More-than-300-different-languages-spoken-in-British-schools-report-says.html.

[25] Office of National Statistics, *2011 Census: Key Statistics for England and Wales* (2011), available at www.ons.gov.uk/peoplepopulationandcommunity/populationandmigration/populationestimates/bulletins/2011censuskeystatisticsforenglandandwales/2012-12-11#key-points.

[26] Office of National Statistics, *Religion in England and Wales* (2011), Figure 4, available at www.ons.gov.uk/peoplepopulationandcommunity/culturalidentity/religion/articles/religioninenglandandwales2011/2012-12-11.

[27] On the concept of the global city, see Saskia Sassen, *A Sociology of Globalization* (New York: W. W. Norton), Ch. 4; Saskia Sassen, *The Global City: New York, London, Tokyo* (Princeton, NJ: Princeton University Press, 1991).

[28] Sassen, *The Global City*.

[29] "International student statistics: UK higher education," UK Council for International Student Affairs, available at www.ukcisa.org.uk/Info-for-universities-colleges–schools/Policy-research–statistics/Research–statistics/International-students-in-UK-HE/#International-%28non-UK%29-students-in-UK-HE-in-2012–13.

in studying abroad is notable in other places as well. For example, more than a quarter of the 819,664 international students who studied in the United States in 2013 were from China.[30] One can only speculate on the implications for China of such exposure to democracy as an everyday experience among this growing and accumulating mass of educated citizens.

Going back to London as the epitome of the global movement of humans, it is also, notably, one of the most popular tourist destinations in the world. In 2015, a record high of 18.6 million overseas tourists visited London (more than twice the number of Londoners), spending a total of £11.9 billion during their visit to the city.[31] Hence, although London belongs to England and is home to its most significant functional and symbolic national institutions, it cannot be understood without its international tourist context. Indeed, unlike previous times, in our era tourism is a major engine for human movement across national borders. Around the globe, there are around 880 million international passenger arrivals each year, and the travel and tourism industry is one of the largest in the world, accounting for 9.4 percent of world GDP and 8.2 percent of all employment. However, most of the tourism-related activity takes place within the developed countries.[32]

One of the most fascinating characteristics of globalization is that being part of it does not necessarily have to involve leaving one's home. As prominent sociologist Zygmunt Bauman said in his book on the human consequences of globalization: "All of us are, willy-nilly, by design or default, on the move. We are on the move even if physically we stay put: immobility is not a realistic option in a world of permanent change."[33] Globalization comes to us even if we do not come to it, by its influence on national economies and politics and by our personal acquaintance with, and sometimes dependency on, people who leave the *local* to become part of the *global*. Yet it is the third component of globalization, the movement of messages, which creates a global awareness – even among those who stay at home and (apparently) continue to live just as their parents did.

[30] Associated Press, "Chinese students boost U.S. universities to all-time high foreign enrollment," *PBS NewsHour* (November 11, 2013), available at www.pbs.org/newshour/rundown/chinese-students-boost-us-universities-to-all-time-high-foreign-enrollment.
[31] Office of National Statistics, *Travel Trends* (2015), available at www.ons.gov.uk/peoplepopulationandcommunity/leisureandtourism/articles/traveltrends/2015#travel-trends-2015-main-findings.
[32] John Urry & and Jonas Larsen, *The Tourist Gaze 3.0* (Los Angeles: Sage, 2011).
[33] Bauman, *Globalization: The Human Consequences*, at 2.

The example I have chosen to illustrate the global movement of messages is that of the Internet. Indeed, in my opinion, nothing supports the arguments that the world has become a borderless global village[34] and is flattening[35] more than the expansion of the Internet and its uses. Even if one does not accept these metaphors (and, as will be elaborated in this chapter, indeed I do not) it is hard to overstress the significance of the Internet in creating global interconnectedness that simply did not, and could not, exist in previous eras.

According to Internet World Stats, in June 2016 there were more than 3.5 billion Internet users around the globe, with penetration rates ranging from 89 percent in North America, 73.9 percent in Europe, 59.8 percent in South America, and 52.5 percent in the Middle East, to 28 percent in Africa. Though the latter presents the lowest take-up, it holds the record in change over time during the third millennium, witnessing 7,288 percent growth in penetration in 2000–2016.[36] Hence almost half of the world's inhabitants are connected to each other through a virtual, yet very real, technological web. For them, especially if the regime under which they live does not try to block their online access, the vivid description provided by the media sociologist Christian Fuchs rings very true:

> On the Internet, we search for information, plan trips, read newspapers, articles, communicate with others by making use of e-mail, instant messaging, chat rooms, Internet phone, discussion boards, mailing lists, video conferencing; we listen to music and radio, watch videos, order or purchase by auction different goods, write our blogs, and contribute to the blogs of others; we meet others, discuss with others, learn to know other people, fall in love, become friends, or develop intimate relations; we maintain contact with others; we protest, access government sites, learn, play games, create knowledge together with others in wikis, share ideas, images, videos; we download software and other digital data, and so forth.[37]

Not only does the Internet have a global reach and an extensive range of possible uses, but it is also characterized by an extremely

[34] Ohmae Kenichi, *The Borderless World* (New York: Harper Business, 1990); Yaacov Baal Shem & Duv Shinar, "The Telepresence Era: Global Village or 'Media Slums'?" *IEEE Technology and Society Magazine,* 17(1) (1998), 28–35.

[35] Thomas L. Friedman, *The World Is Flat: A Brief History of the Twenty-First Century* (New York: Picador, 2007).

[36] Data provided by Internet World Stats, available at www.internetworldstats.com/stats.htm.

[37] Christian Fuchs, *Internet and Society: Social theory in the information age* (New York: Routledge, 2008), at 1.

intense level of activity. According to Pingdom, a company dedicated to enhancing website efficiency in 2012 some 144 billion e-mails were sent each day; 634 million websites existed; 1 billion Facebook users pressed *Like* 2.4 billion times a day; 1.2 trillion searches were conducted through Google; 4 billion hours were spent every month on watching videos on YouTube; and more than 58 photos were uploaded every second to Instagram,[38] amounting to 2.1 billion photos a month during 2015.[39] The yet-to-be-studied global hysteria triggered by the *Pokémon Go* craze of the summer of 2016, with its overnight gains in terms of millions of players and billions in Nintendo share values, is another example of the scope and intensity of the Internet.[40] For a short while, *Pokémon Go* even managed to beat *porn* – one of the most popular search terms on Google.[41]

The Internet is therefore both a very useful everyday tool and also a catalyst for the global hypercapitalism mentioned earlier. Moreover, its significance as the epitome of the third component of globalization goes much further than its being a platform for economic messages. Together with other related cross-border technologies, such as satellites and mobile phones, the Internet is part of what Arjun Appadurai, a prominent anthropologist of global culture, calls *mediascapes* which constitute narratives of self and others.[42] The exposure to information about faraway places and societies, to images produced outside one's culture, to political messages from groups from all over the world, and to the personal stories of strangers, opens our imagination to "globally defined fields of possibility."[43] Indeed, the effects of the quick, massive, cross-border transformation of messages are far more dramatic than pragmatic interconnectivity. Such transformation allows us to compare ourselves to others from all over the world, creating global consciousness and global subjectivity. Whether it leads us to global

[38] Pingdom, *Internet 2012 in Numbers* (2013), available at http://royal.pingdom.com/2013/01/16/internet-2012-in-numbers/.

[39] Pingdom, *Year in Review: The Web Performance* (2015), available atwww.pingdom.com/2015.

[40] Claire Lampen, "These Numbers Show Just How Staggering the 'Pokémon Go' Phenomenon Really Is," *Mic* (July 11, 2016), https://mic.com/articles/148390/these-numbers-show-just-how-staggering-the-pok-mon-go-phenomenon-really-is#.TWpmJwpaS.

[41] Jacob Wolinsky, "Nintendo Shares Soar as Pokemon Go Overtakes Porn On Google Trends," *ValueWalk* (July 10, 2016), www.valuewalk.com/2016/07/nintendo-shares-pokeman-go/.

[42] Arjun Appadurai, *Modernity at Large: Cultural Dimensions of Globalization* (Minneapolis: University of Minnesota Press, 1996), Ch.2.

[43] Ibid., at 31.

solidarity, manifested in projects such as global eco-activism and volunteering in faraway disaster areas, or to counterreactions such as joining a local or a global violent group promoting a separtist ideology, or even if we just stay passive in the face of these new and global *mediascapes*, we are changed, and the way we understand ourselves can no longer be separated from our exposure to the global. Indeed, in my opinion, it is this component of globalization – the movement of messages across national borders – more than the other two, that most affects the masses around the world, making everyone part of the global, regardless of geographic placement, economic position, or ideological perception of globalization as good or bad.

Scholte distinguishes between four common notions of globalization which he rejects as redundant – internationalization, liberalization, universalization, and westernization – and globalization as he understands it. He defines the concept as "the spread of transplanetary – and in recent times also more particularly supra-territorial – connection between people." It is through the process of globalization – that is, the process via which the globe as a whole becomes a distinctive and significant space beyond territorial space – that "people become more able – physically, legally, linguistically, culturally and psychologically – to engage with each other wherever on planet Earth they might be."[44] Although I agree with Scholte, and suggested that the three aforementioned components are at the heart of this process, I can only accept his definition of supraterritoriality – referring to cases in which "place is not territorially fixed, territorial distance is covered in no time, and territorial boundaries present no particular impediment"[45] – as an abstract notion and not as a realistic description. Indeed, the concept of *bordered globalization* that I offer insists that, at least currently, borders – territorial and other – are always of "particular impediment" - so much so, that describing our era as the era of globalization, as characterized so far in this chapter, and our society as a global society,[46] is, at the very least, incomplete and might even be distorting.

Borders

Of the many global phenomena that characterize our era, of particular note is the growing interest in borders. On the geo-political level we live

44 Scholte, *Globalization*, at 59.
45 Ibid., at 62.
46 Giddens, *Runaway World*, at 37.

in an era with more borders than ever before in human history.[47] In addition to the approximately 200 countries and the 300 land borders that separate them from one another, there are also some 600–800 cultural groupings in the world, many of which are striving for a national independent existence within internationally recognized geo-political borders.[48] Furthermore, after the 9/11 terrorist attacks and in the face of massive uninvited emigration, borders – at least those of the developed countries – have become more intensely scrutinized and militarized, and an industry of border security has emerged, based on the logic of suspicion and surveillance.[49] Hence, it is the globalization process itself, of which global emigration and terrorism are part, that enhances states' interest in preserving their borders and that makes borders so much more present and violently upheld in the third millennium than in the second.

A striking fact is that only 3.2 percent of the world's population, as of 2013, live outside their country of birth,[50] whereas, at the beginning of the twentieth century, a tenth of the world's population were immigrants.[51] Taken together with the harsh effects of global inequality, described earlier, this figure suggests that many who would like to internationally relocate to better their lives are blocked by physical and legal borders that separate them from their wished-for destination. A horrific example is the estimation that more than 2,510 people lost their lives in the first five months of 2016, in their illegal attempt to cross the Mediterranean Sea, from Africa and the Middle East to Europe.[52] Moreover, even among those who belong to the minority that managed to cross national borders for a long-term stay in another country, only a small fraction are privileged enough to be able to treat borders more or less as a bureaucratic nuisance. The majority "will face the most serious impacts of borders."[53]

---

[47] Thomas M. Wilson & Hastings Donnan, "Borders and Border Studies" in Thomas M. Wilson & Hastings Donnan (Eds.), *A Companion to Border Studies* (Malden, MA: Wiley-Blackwell, 2012), pp. 1–25, at 1.

[48] Anssi Paasi, "A Border Theory: An Unattainable Dream or a Realistic Aim for Border Scholars?" in Dorit Wastl-Walter (Ed.), *The Ashgate Research Companion to Border Studies* (Surrey: Ashgate, 2011), pp. 11–31, at 13.

[49] Brenda Chalfin, "Border Security as Late-Capitalist 'Fix'" in Wilson & Donnan (Eds.), *A Companion to Border Studies*, pp. 283–300.

[50] United Nations Department of Economics and Social Affairs: Population Division, *International Migration Report 2013* (2013), Ch.1, available at: www.un.org/en/development/desa/population/publications/pdf/migration/migrationreport2013/Chapter1.pdf.

[51] Daniel Cohen, *Globalization and Its Enemies* (Cambridge, MA: MIT Press, 2007), at 27.

[52] UN News Centre, "As Mediterranean Death Toll Soars, Ban Urges Collective Response to Large Refugee and Migrant Movements" (May 31, 2016), available at: www.un.org/apps/news/story.asp?NewsID=54092#.V5muI_l97IU.

[53] Paasi, "A Border Theory," at 21.

Similarly to the growing political interest in borders, in academia, the paradoxical influence of globalization has also encouraged scholars from a variety of disciplines to join geographers in their treatment of borders as an important subject of study, and to produce counternarratives to the narrative often found in globalization literature of a borderless and deterritorialized world.[54] Indeed, the last two decades witnessed "a flourishing renaissance" of border studies, with numerous conferences, research institutes, and publications exclusively dedicated to the topic.[55] The field has become so rich and developed that its canonization is already materializing, with two companions published recently.[56]

The incorporation of political scientists, sociologists, anthropologists, legal scholars, and researchers from other disciplines into the field of border studies broadened the understanding of borders, beyond their physical existence on the surface of the land, to include more abstract and nonspatial conceptions.[57] The border (material and conceptual, formal and informal, as a process, an institution, and a state of mind) became a subject of study, a methodological prism, and a metaphor for researchers endeavoring to understand groups – how they are created and how they include and exclude.

Although some of the discussions within border studies relate to borders and boundaries as synonymous concepts, I would like to emphasize here that I refer to borders, first and foremost, as geo-political spatial barriers. However, I expand the definition of borders to include also what Michèle Lamont and Viràg Molnár call "social boundaries" – that is, "objectified forms of social differences manifested in unequal access to and unequal distribution of resources (material and nonmaterial) and social opportunities."[58] In that sense, as will be demonstrated in this book, the law can be – and in many cases is – a border, as are other kinds of institutionalized mechanisms that turn symbolic boundaries – that is, conceptual categorizing distinctions[59] such as us–them, man–woman, or white–black – into an excluding and discriminatory reality.

---

[54] David Newman, "The Lines that Continue to Separate Us: Borders in our 'Borderless' World," *Progress in Human Geography,* 30(2) (2006), 143–61.

[55] Doris Wastl-Walter, "Introduction" in Wastl-Walter (Ed.), *The Ashgate Research Companion to Border Studies,* pp. 1–10, at 1.

[56] Ibid.; Wilson & Donnan (Eds.), *A Companion to Border Studies.*

[57] Newman, "The Lines that Continue to Separate Us," 143–61.

[58] Michèle Lamont & Viràg Molnár, "The Study of Boundaries in the Social Sciences," *Annual Review of Sociology,* 28 (2002), 167–95, at 168.

[59] Ibid.

Similarly to the theoretical, descriptive, and normative controversies over globalization, border-studies scholars are divided on many questions, including the proper definition of borders, whether borders are closing or opening, and whether they are a social necessity or a social construct that can, and should, be eliminated. Again, I will not delve into these discussions but rather point to several themes within the border-studies field that I find convincing and useful for investigating the interrelations between globalization, borders, families, and the law, which are at the heart of this book.

The first theme, already mentioned earlier, is that national borders still matter very much to people's everyday lives and to their sense of identity. Indeed, within the more general debate over the role of nation-states in the face of globalization, between those who argue for the decline of the nation-state and those who argue for its ongoing significance,[60] most border-studies scholars are for the latter.[61] As the data presented earlier demonstrate, although every year millions cross national borders (by their own free will, by force, or by constrained choice), the vast majority of people are born, live, and die in the same nation-state. Hence, whether enjoying the ability to travel, to study, or to do business abroad, or not being so fortunate, most people have what is called in legal language a *domicile* – in other words, one permanent residency controlled by a specific national jurisdiction. Likewise, although terms such as *deterritorialization,*[62] *denationalization, multiscalar system,*[63] and *global governance*[64] point to the growing interest in subnational and transnational forces and their transformation of nation states, the political framework that governs almost all the world's inhabitants, and the central political categories organizing our understanding of the public sphere – *sovereignty* and *citizenship*, remain fundamentally organized according to the national sphere and its rationale.[65]

[60] David R. Cameron, Gustav Ranis, & Anaalisa Zinn (Eds.), *Globalization and Self-Determination: Is the Nation-State under Siege?* (London: Routledge, 2006).

[61] Thomas M. Wilson & Hastings Donnan (Eds.), *Border Identities Nation and State at International Frontiers* (Cambridge University Press, 1998); Paul Ganster & David E. Lorey (Eds.), *Borders and Border Politics in a Globalizing World* (Lanham, MD: SR Books, 2005).

[62] M. Kearney, "The Local and the Global: The Anthropology of Globalization and Transnationalism," *Annual Review of Anthropology*, 24 (1995), 547–65.

[63] Saskia Sassen, "Globalization or Denationalization?" *Review of International Political Economy*, 10(1) (2003), 1–22.

[64] John Gerard Ruggie, "Global Governance and 'New Governance Theory': Lessons from Business and Human Rights," *Global Governance*, 20 (2014), 5–17.

[65] Étienne Balibar, *We, the People of Europe? Reflections on Transnational Citizenship* (Princeton, NJ: Princeton University Press, 2004); Erikson, *Globalization*.

Hence, at least currently, the central living experience of most people is that of belonging to a nation, to an *us* that is different from the *other* who lives across the national border. From early childhood, people are socialized to "learn what are the legitimate and hegemonic national meanings attached to these borders and what are the pools of emotions, fears and memories that we have to draw on in this connection."[66] Even among those who emigrate, many practice *long-distance nationalism*, through strategies such as remittances, ongoing communication, maintaining the homeland language and culture, importing a spouse from the homeland to marry their children, or political activism aimed at influencing the action taking place in their homeland.[67]

The second important theme within border studies centers on the understanding that although national borders are currently the most significant ones, they are not the only ones that matter. For example, presently, one of the most significant mass-emigration movements is that of the Chinese within China. At first glance, this could point to the absence of inner borders and to free movement that brings together the rich and the poor, the agricultural and the urban, the ruling elite and ordinary citizens. However, the fact that, currently, about 70 million Chinese children are left behind by one or both parents due to the difficulty of securing education and health services for them outside of their birth province[68] demonstrates that the lived experiences surrounding intranational borders can be as dramatic as international ones. Indeed, border studies as a field goes beyond borders that separate states, to include other territorial borders such as those between provinces, cities, and neighborhoods. Thus, Henk van Houtum, a prominent border studies scholar, suggests a broader definition of spatial borders: "A border today is dominantly understood as a belief in the presence and continuity of a spatially binding power, which is objectified in everyday sociopolitical practices."[69]

Moreover, some scholars are even willing to abandon the spatial dimension of borders and to relate to nonspatial borders as "delimiters of social, economic and cultural categories no less than the geographical."[70]

[66] Paasi, "A Border Theory," at 23.
[67] Erikson, *Globalization*, Ch.5.
[68] "Migrant workers and their children," China Labor Bulletin, available at: www.clb.org.hk/en/view-resource-centre-content/110306.
[69] Henk van Houtum, "Remapping Borders" in Wilson & Donnan (Eds.), *A Companion to Border Studies*, pp. 405–18, at 406.
[70] David Newman, "Contemporary Research Agendas in Border Studies: An Overview" in Wastl-Walter (Ed.), *The Ashgate Research Companion to Border Studies*, pp. 33–47, at 34.

As manifested in my definition of *borders* mentioned earlier, this is the reason the distinction between border studies and the study of social boundaries – usually focused on the constructed stratifying lines between social groups – might be blurred.[71] Indeed, many people emigrate in an attempt to settle in another nation, only to learn that the cultural, racial, ethnic, and economic borders within the host society might be harder to cross than geo-political ones.[72] For example, in the face of massive labor migration and significant numbers of asylum seekers arriving in Israel since the 1990s, the Israeli authorities currently restrict the conversion of noncitizens to Judaism, in an attempt to prevent their naturalization, as Jewish immigrants receive immediate Israeli citizenship. Hence, the regulation of what is usually perceived as the most intimate aspect of life – one's religious faith – is used to strengthen the border between insiders and outsiders.[73] This example is one of many in which spatial borders interrelate with symbolic boundaries based, for example, on religious categorization, and can amount to social boundaries, which are part of borders as defined here. The Israeli example also demonstrates the capacity of nonspatial borders, such as conversion and citizenship regulations, to be just as rigid and restrictive as spatial ones. Moreover, just like spatial national borders enhanced by globalization, 'indigenous' nonspatial borders are in many cases strengthened as a counter-globalization reaction.[74]

Gender is another important example, very relevant to this book, of a symbolic boundary that has attracted growing attention among border-studies scholars. This attention is inspired by feminist and queer theories on the centrality and significance of the socially constructed, hierarchical, and metaphorical line between the sexes, and connects these theories to spatial and other kinds of social borders. As Henric Altink and Chris Weedon describe in the introduction to *Gendering Border Studies,* edited together with Jane Aaron, in the last decade and a half, border studies scholars have started to investigate the following themes: how

[71] Andreas Wimmer, "Boundaries (Racial/Ethnic)" in George Ritzer (Ed.), *Blackwell Encyclopedia of Sociology Online* (2007), available at: www.sociologyencyclopedia. com/public/tocnode?query=Boundaries+(Racial%2FEthnic)&widen=1&result_ number=1&from=search&id=g9781405124331_yr2015_chunk_g97814051243318_ ss1-42&type=std&fuzzy=0&slop=1.

[72] Newman, "Contemporary Research Agendas in Border Studies."

[73] Daphna Hacker, "From the Moabite Ruth to Norly the Filipino: Intermarriage and Conversion in the Jewish Nation State" in Hanna Herzog & Ann Braude (Eds.), *Gendering Religion and Politics: Untangling Modernities* (New York: Palgrave Macmillan, 2009), pp. 101–124; "Conversion for Non-Citizens," ITIM Website, available at: www.itim.org.il/en/conversion-for-non-citizens.

[74] Erikson, *Globalization.*

gender ideologies, within sending and receiving countries, shape the patterns, causes, experiences, and effects of crossing national borders; how crossing national borders challenges such gender ideologies to free and empower women and to allow them to cooperate with women from different ethnic and religious groups; how the gendered prices of crossing the borders between countries operate, including, for example, in the case of sex trafficking and detached motherhood; and how territorial borders contribute to the construction of gendered national, ethnic, and religious ideologies, which in particular use women as the "symbolic border guards" who have a duty to embody the line between the us and the *other*, and hence, for example, are expected to practice endogamy, procreate, and socialize the children into the group and are at risk of being raped in wartime.[75]

Notwithstanding, Altink and Weedon criticize the existing scholarly focus on women in the field of gender and borders – neglecting men and other gendered sexual options – and the relative emphasis on receiving countries compared to sending ones. Moreover, they claim that scholars are ignoring the intersectionality between gender and other markers of difference, such as class and race, and being too optimistic about the consequences of border-crossing for women[76] This book follows the route they pave, and pays gender special attention within the study of legalized families in our era, including in the context of boys and gay men, sending countries, intersectionality, and the harmful consequences of crossing borders.

The third significant theme within border studies is that borders are relational, contextual, and dynamic. Indeed, much of the current study regarding borders is not about the demarcation of borderlines, but about *bordering* – the continuous construction and reconstruction of borders, which is the outcome of time- and place-specific configurations of social relations and networks.[77] Furthermore, since, in most cases, borders do not act as physical barriers that are literally impossible to cross, *borderlands* are created in proximity to many spatial borders, in which people from different categories mix and, in some cases, create a third and hybrid category.[78] Indeed, some perceive borders as *connective tissue,* creating

---

[75] Henrice Altink & Chris Weedon, "Introduction" in Jane Aaron, Henrice Altink, & Chris Weedon (Eds.), *Gendering Border Studies* (Cardiff: University of Wales Press, 2010), pp. 1–15.

[76] Ibid.

[77] Van Houtum, "Remapping Borders," 406.

[78] Newman, "Contemporary Research Agendas in Border Studies."

and enabling new networking opportunities.[79] The term *borderland* has also been used in the literature as a concept denoting a constant psychic state of transition "created by the emotional residue of unnatural boundary."[80] The subjective and nationally, economically, and culturally dependent meaning of borders also supports the claim of leading border-studies scholar Sarah Green that what she calls "*borderness*" can be experienced in multiple ways, in the sense that what might be regarded by some as a border will not even be noticed by others or will be perceived by them as something else.[81]

Notwithstanding, Green reminds us of the common resilience of borders, usually established to last a long time: "The fact that borders are the outcome of ongoing activity [...] does not necessarily mean there is either much activity going on at any given time, or that the activity varies a great deal, or that the outcome of that activity will be a discernible change from what had existed the day, or even the year, before."[82] Furthermore, she argues: "there is a strong association between borders and stopping things from happening, and also stalling things, as well as generating endless waiting. Border dynamics can be the opposite of dynamic, as it were."[83]

Indeed, a related theme is that power relations are a major variable in the process of bordering, if not the most significant one. As the political geographer David Newman argues, borders are created by those who have the power to separate between their collective and those who are perceived as a threat to that collective. This power blocks the *other*'s entry into the collective, but in some regimes and ethnic and religious groups also blocks exit from the purportedly protective collective.[84] Moreover, in many cases, the opening of borders happens when the most powerful in the collective realize that such an opening will serve their interests. This *openness* is relative and hierarchical, transforming borders into what the philosopher Étienne Balibar calls "detention zones" and "filtering systems" aimed at allowing

---

79 Anthony Cooper, Chris Perkins, & Chris Rumford, "The Vernacularization of Borders" in Reece Jones & Corey Johnson (Eds.), *Placing the Border in Everyday Life* (Surrey: Ashgate, 2014).

80 See Gloria Anzaldúa's quote in Stefanie Kron, "The Border as Method: Towards an Analysis of Political Subjectivities in Transmigrant Spaces" in Wastl-Walter (Ed.), *The Ashgate Research Companion to Border Studies*, pp. 103–20, at 106.

81 Sarah Green, "A Sense of Border" in Thomas M. Wilson & Donnan Hastings (Eds.), *A Companion to Border Studies* (Malden, MA: Wiley-Blackwell, 2012), pp. 573–92.

82 Ibid., at 576.

83 Ibid.

84 Newman, "Contemporary Research Agendas in Border Studies."

freedom of movement among the powerful while suspending basic human rights among the disempowered and marginalized.[85]

Yet for all their power, borders will always be contested. First, because they are always arbitrary in the sense that they are never entirely congruent with the alleged and imagined absolute categories they strive to divide.[86] Second, because, once established, they have a rigidity that typically fails to adapt to the social dynamics that change the categories they were designed to separate.[87] And third, because they so very often create hierarchies and thus are constantly challenged by those who find themselves on the relatively underprivileged side of the line. The concept of *borderland*, mentioned earlier, is used by several scholars to emphasize the ability of the *border-crossers* – thanks to their history, presence, practices, and strategies – to negotiate and transgress physical and social boundaries and hence to create a space that challenges attempts to uphold strict national, economic, and cultural borders.[88]

Moreover, although a specific border might be originated by the powerful group, it can, paradoxically, become a means of empowering the individuals kept behind the line, who start to conceive themselves as a group and act collectively for their advancement. Furthermore, in an increasing number of cases, people who find themselves discriminated against or harmed by the dominant collective develop strategies to bypass the border created by this collective. For example, cause lawyers representing national and ethnic minorities challenge the nation state, both by using international law in their litigation in national courts and also by bringing their grievances against the state in front of international political and legal bodies, for actual remedy as well as for diplomatic shaming.[89]

The last theme I will mention is that of the impact of borders on everyday life within the private sphere, an issue emphasized by several scholars in the border-studies field. Seemingly, national borders are related only to the public sphere and are the concern of states, politicians, armies, diplomats, and international public law. However, many border scholars are

[85] Balibar, *We, the People of Europe?*, at 111.

[86] On the concept of imagined communities, see Anderson Benedict, *Imagined Communities: Reflections on the Origin and Spread of Nationalism*, rev. edn. (London: Verso, 1991).

[87] Newman, "Contemporary Research Agendas in Border Studies."

[88] Stefanie Kron, "The Border as Method: Towards an Analysis of Political Subjectivities in Transmigrant Spaces" in Wastl-Walter (Ed.), *The Ashgate Research Companion to Border Studies*, pp. 103–20.

[89] Hassan Jabareen, "The Rise of Transnational Lawyering for Human Rights," *Maʾasei Mishpat*, 1 (2008), 137–51 (Hebrew).

not interested in studying the political emergence of intrastate cartography and international political relations and conflicts over borders but, rather, in examining how national and other kinds of political and social borders are manifested in people's ordinary lives and are constructed by their routine praxis. Through intense fieldwork and qualitative methods, border-studies researchers extract personal border stories, narratives, and representations, and learn about the impact of borders on daily life experiences and practices.[90] Moreover, they may look at materials such as the life stories told by mail-order brides[91] or data on the practices that help relatives to continue to connect with one another despite being divided by a border separating neighboring states in conflict,[92] to study how the private sphere constructs, challenges, and reshapes borders. Indeed, border scholars contribute, though not always consciously, to the feminist project of revealing the fallacy of the notion of two distinct public and private spheres and to the demonstration of the feminist understanding that the personal is political.

Some fear that the broadening of border theory beyond geo-political or spatial borders could transform the *border* into a useless analytical concept, because it tries to capture so much that it means nothing.[93] Indeed, at its extreme, the *border* might collapse into other well-known general theoretical notions such as Claude Lévi-Strauss's famous *binary oppositions*[94] or Pierre Bourdieu's *distinctions*.[95] Although no one is suggesting getting rid of *globalization* – even though, as a concept, it is no less all-encompassing than *border* – I would still like to further stress the meaning of *border* as used in this book. First, as distinct from other analytical concepts of lines between categories, in this book *border* signifies, and is limited to, social hierarchal categorization, reinforced by physical or symbolic violence. Second, as mentioned earlier, borders, in this book,

---

90 Newman, "Contemporary Research Agendas in Border Studies."
91 For example, see Donna R. Lee, "Mail Fantasy: Global Sexual Exploitation in the Mail-Order Bride Industry and Proposed Legal Solutions," *Asian American Law Journal*, 5 (1998), 139–79.
92 For example, see Sarah J. Mahler, "Transnational Relationships: The Struggle to Communicate across Borders," *Identities*, 7(4) (2001), 583–619.
93 Amanda Conroy, Book Review, "Jane Aaron, Henrice Altink and Chris Weedon (Eds.), Gendering Border Studies, Cardiff: University of Wales Press," *European Journal of Women's Studies*, 19 (2012), 399–402.
94 Claude Lévi-Strauss, "The Structural Study of Myth," *The Journal of American Folklore*, 68(270) (1955), 428–44.
95 Pierre Bourdieu, *Distinction: A Social Critique of the Judgment of Taste*, Richard Nice (Trans.) (Cambridge, MA: Harvard University Press, 1984).

are first and foremost national borders, and, indeed, almost all the issues discussed in the book are the outcome of the existence of national borders and of their crossing. Notwithstanding, families will be studied here, with special attention paid to other kinds of social borders – in particular the law – that reinforce gendered, economic, ethnic, and religious symbolic boundaries, and to their interrelations with the national ones and with globalization. With these definitional boundaries in mind, we are ready to move onto the discussion of *bordered globalization* as the conceptual framework I suggest for understanding the interrelations between borders and globalization in our era.

Bordered Globalization

Around 2000 we entered a whole new era: Globalization 3.0. Globalization 3.0 is shrinking the world from a size small to a size tiny and flattening the playing field at the same time. And while the dynamic force in Globalization 1.0 was countries globalizing and the dynamic force in Globalization 2.0 was companies globalizing, the dynamic force in Globalization 3.0 – the force that gives it its unique character – is the newfound power for *individuals* to collaborate and compete globally.[96]

Globalization has had its impacts on some cross-border flows, such as cyberspace and the flow of capital, but it is clear to all scholars of borders that we live in a hierarchical world of rigid ordering and that borders – be they territorial or aspatial – are very much part of our daily lives.[97]

By offering *bordered globalization* as the conceptual framework for this book, I wish to challenge both those who belittle the significance of borders and also those who belittle the significance of globalization, as well as to argue that the one cannot be understood without the other. Globalization and borders are both so important in our era and so interlinked that analyzing the one separately from the other is limited and incomplete, and might generate a biased, distorted picture. Even by returning to the three epitomes of globalization presented in the first part of this chapter (McDonald's, London, and the Internet), we can see that they cannot be fully understood if detached from the ongoing presence of borders.

As the collection of articles on McDonald's restaurants in Asia demonstrates,[98] it is impossible to understand the phenomenon of global

[96] Friedman, *The World Is Flat*, at 10.
[97] Newman, "Contemporary Research Agendas in Border Studies," at 156.
[98] James L Watson, *Golden Arches East: McDonald's in East Asia*, 2nd edn. (CA: Stanford University Press, 2006).

McDonaldization[99] without also understanding the national context in which it operates. In Beijing, for example, young people enter McDonald's though many of them dislike the food, because it is perceived as a liberating cross-border act. In South Korea, though the food is suited to local cultural tastes, some perceive eating a Big Mac as an act of treason. In Hong Kong, McDonald's introduced a previously unknown service culture that has impacted local restaurants and other commercial facilities, characterized by clean toilets and orderly queues, for example. Still, Hong Kongese clients do not necessarily dispose of their tray or leave the table when eating is over, and are not easily impressed by smiling members of staff.

Furthermore, in recent years McDonald's started to sell state-tailored food, such as *Quiche de Queijo* in Brazil, Red Bean Pie in Hong Kong and *Caldo Verde* soup in Portugal, and takes pride in its sensitivity to the national cultural context.[100] More importantly, the prices of the different products sold in McDonald's restaurants and the employment conditions enjoyed or suffered by the employees selling them differ from country to country and are shaped by local economic conditions, and the latter are also affected by national labor law, enforcement, and unionization.[101] For example, in Australia, McDonald's employees earn twice as much as their United States counterparts, largely due to the former's minimum wage law enforcement. This gap has not gone unnoticed by US employees who fight to raise their salary, with some signs of partial success.[102] To conclude, McDonald's not only changes national culture and economy, but it is also changed by them. It is often used as a border-related political symbol, varying in its meaning depending on the country in which it operates, and it performs flexibility and risks local protests in the face of competing national concepts of employment fairness.

As for the second epitome of globalization discussed earlier – London – nongovernmental organizations (NGOs) such as London NoBorders, which calls for "No Borders, No Nations, No Deportations!"[103] offer a

---

99 Ram, "McDonaldization."
100 "The Great McDonald's International Menu," Fast Food Menu Prices, available at: www.fastfoodmenuprices.com/great-mcdonalds-international-menu/.
101 Mary Joyce Carlson, "Combating Wage Theft in the Global Fast Food Industry," paper presented at the ABA International Labour & Employment Law Committee, Tel Aviv (2014).
102 Jordan Weissmann, "The Magical World Where McDonald's Pays $15 an Hour? It's Australia," *The Atlantic* (August 5, 2013), available at: www.theatlantic.com/business/archive/2013/08/the-magical-world-where-mcdonalds-pays-15-an-hour-its-australia/278313/; Phil Wahba, "McDonald's Says its Wage Hikes Are Improving Service," *Fortune* (May 9, 2016), available at: www.fortune.com/2016/03/09/mcdonalds-wages/.
103 London NoBorders website: http://london.noborders.org.uk/whoweare.

reminder of London sharing with the UK as a whole the border immigration apparatus, which does not allow in all those who wish to enter
and deports those who entered uninvited or allegedly stayed too long.
Moreover, global cities such as London are experiencing spatial changes,
including the collapse of older inner borders and the creation of new
ones, which are part of the complex outcomes of the globalizing process.
These border-related changes include high-income residential and commercial gentrification and a sharp increase in spatially concentrated poverty.[104] Finally, although 60 percent of Londoners voted recently against
the UK leaving the EU, demonstrating a more global perception than the
rest of Britain, they, and London as a global city, will have to face the
consequences of the reestablishing of the border between the UK and
the rest of the European continent.[105] Especially if its global banking sector is taken as a preliminary test case, there are already indications that
Brexit will "fundamentally transform" London.[106]

   Even the Internet, allegedly the most borderless epitome of globalization, cannot be understood if detached from national borders. As mentioned earlier, the Internet penetration rate is very different in developed
and developing countries. National borders also affect other characteristics of Internet use, such as the rate of women's participation in the
Internet[107] and the content it is permitted to convey.[108] The most famous
example is perhaps that of the Chinese government's attempts to block
virtual searches related to topics such as democracy, Tibet, or sex, and to
monitor and filter what it perceives to be dangerous political online text
messages. These censoring efforts are not only carried out by the 2,800
official surveillance centers but are also assisted by non-Chinese Internet
companies, including the global giants Yahoo!, Microsoft, and Google.[109]
Finally, the fact that about half of all websites available globally are not
in English, and the dominant popularity of local websites as opposed to

[104] Sassen, *The Global City*, at 251.
[105] "EU Referendum: Most London Boroughs Vote to Remain," BBC NEWS (June 24, 2016),
     www.bbc.com/news/uk-politics-eu-referendum-36612916.
[106] John Manning, "What Does Brexit Mean for UK and European Banking?" *International
     Banker* (June 29, 2016), available at: http://internationalbanker.com/banking/brexit-mean-
     uk-european-banking/.
[107] Eszter Hargittai & Yuli Patick Hsieh, "Digital Inequality" in William H. Dutton (Ed.), *The
     Oxford Handbook of Internet Studies* (Oxford University Press, 2013), pp. 129–50.
[108] Christian Sandvig, "The Internet as Infrastructure" in William H. Dutton (Ed.), *The
     Oxford Handbook of Internet Studies* (Oxford University Press, 2013), pp. 86–106.
[109] Larry Ray, *Globalization and Everyday Life* (London: Routledge, 2007), at 118–9.

transnational ones[110] point to the ongoing national contextualization of this allegedly borderless communication technology.

Although most theorists and researchers of globalization and border scholars are aware of the fact that globalization and borders interact, the interrelations between the two remain, surprisingly, severely under-theorized. One of the most-developed attempts to address the intersection between globalization and subglobal phenomena, and certainly the most referred to, is captured in the portmanteau *glocalization*. This term was first used to describe those strategies employed by global commercial entities to tailor and advertise their goods to appeal to differentiated local markets.[111] It was later developed to refer to the erosion of the nation state, both from above, by global, supranational and international powers, and also from beneath, by local, subnational, and even individual forces.[112] Finally, it is currently perceived as the term that best captures the simultaneity and interpenetration of the global and the local.[113]

I would like to join these conceptualizing efforts by offering a typology of the possible interrelations between globalization and borders that can serve as a theoretical framework for the study of families and law in our era, as well as the study of many other current social phenomena. This typology differs from the first use of *glocalization* as it is relevant to all social spheres – not just to the commercial realm –and it understands the relations between the global and the subglobal as bilateral rather than unilateral. It differs from the second use of *glocalization* because it does not assume the erosion of the nation state. On the contrary, it is based on the presumption (that may be rebutted in the future) of the current importance of national borders. It correlates with Roland Robertson's third understanding of *glocalization* as signifying simultaneity and inter-penetration,[114] and it strives to further develop schematic drafting of the interrelations between the global and the subglobal. However, my typology insists on globalization and on borders as two separate, meaningful, and explanatory terminologies and analytical concepts, which should be compounded into *globorderization* (globe-borderiztion) only in cases of hybridity and synthesis, as I further explain here.

[110] Erikson, *Globalization*.
[111] Roland Robertson, "Globalisation or Glocalisation?" *Journal of International Communication*, 18 (2) (2012), 191–208.
[112] Erik Swyngedouw, "Globalisation of 'Glocalisation'? Networks, Territories, and Rescaling," *Cambridge Review of International Affairs*, 17 (1) (2004), 25–48.
[113] Robertson, "Globalisation or Glocalisation?" 191–208.
[114] Ibid.

The first group in my typology of relations between globalization and borders is that of antagonistic relations. Within the existing literature, these kinds of relations are the most frequently discussed. Seemingly, the relation between globalization and borders is only that of oppositions that are in constant tension and mutual enmity. On the face of it, it looks as if globalization is about movement, freedom, and universalism, whereas borders are about status quo, restrictions, and group politics. Some might even go further and attach normative qualities such as progress and enlightenment to globalization, whereas traditionalism and fundamentalism is ascribed to borders.[115] For example, when discussing domestic violence asylum in Chapter 7, I will demonstrate the potential impact of the global human rights discourse and cross-border movement on women's liberation from abusive intimate relations within patriarchal countries. However, although in many cases globalization and borders are empirically and normatively antagonistic, I would argue that in many other cases they are not and that we must develop a much more complex and attuned typology of the relations between these two dynamic and contingent social phenomena.

The second group within the typology centers on cooperation between globalization and borders. In many cases, the two are interdependent, use each other, and might even create mutually constitutive and symbiotic relations. Balibar, for example, argues that global capitalism needs national borders to segregate the poor in distinct territorial zones and to triage and regulate their entrance to the wealthiest territories. The free movement of capital, on the one hand, and the growing discriminatory restrictions on human movement, on the other, are conceptualized by Balibar as *global apartheid*, which replaces old colonial and post-colonial apartheids.[116] The geographer Erik Swyngedouw likewise argues that the global economic order is dependent on the national–territorial organization and the regulation of markets, money, ownership, security, and service delivery.[117]

Furthermore, strong nations can become even stronger by taking advantage of economic, political, and military global options, gaining "new power" as they lose "traditional sovereignty."[118] Even poor countries can economically benefit from globalization, for example by attracting transnational companies that look for relatively cheap labor. In Chapter 4,

---

[115] Erikson, *Globalization*, at 58–62.
[116] Balibar, *We, the People of Europe?*, at 113.
[117] Swyngedouw, "Globalisation of 'Glocalisation'?" 25–48.
[118] Scholte, *Globalization*, at 192.

I will provide an example of the mutual benefits that nation states and global economic entities extract from each other through cross-border reproduction services. This internationally nonregulated industry enables nation states to preserve their ideological borders thanks to the global entities that profit from these countries' citizens' use and abuse of global reproduction services. Likewise, in Chapter 5, I will show how developed nation states enjoy global options for cheap labor while using their borders to prevent labor migrants from fulfilling their familial rights, and how the international treaty aimed at addressing this abusive situation is signed only by countries sending laborers to other nations, hence demonstrating international law's cooperation with strong nations' antifamilial borders.

In addition to the antagonistic and cooperative groups of relations between globalization and borders, my typology includes a third group of more complex kinds of relations that demonstrates the artificiality often embedded in the attempt to distinguish between the two ideal types of the previous groups. Among other aspects, attention should be paid to the possibility of dialectic relations, which may lead to synthesis between the two phenomena. Globalization and borders do not interact as two finalized processes but rather are shaped as reactions and counterreactions to each other. Here I am referring not only to the counterreactions to globalization, manifested in the reinforcement of nationalist, racist, and patriarchal borders observed by many, but also to the counteractions of globalization to the counteractions of borders, and the hybrid manifestations that might result.

Jihad is the term coined by the political scientist Benjamin Barber to describe local, often violent and zealous, reactions to the global forces he labels *McWorld*.[119] Such reactions are aimed at redrawing sectorial boundaries and social borders and securing religious, tribal, and parochial identities. Although Barber predicted in 1995 that the *McWorld* will eventually out-win *Jihad*, events such as the terrorist attacks of 9/11 – and the bloody civil war in Syria that engendered no substantial international intervention even though it already produced more than 250,000 deaths, 4.5 million refugees, and an additional 6.5 million internally displaced victims[120] – suggest that the battle between global powers and group bordering is far from being decided. Moreover, Al-Qaeda, involved in both, is

---

[119] Barber, *Jihad versus McWorld*.
[120] "Syria: The Story of the Conflict," BBC News (March 11, 2016), available at: www.bbc
.com/news/world-middle-east-26116868.

an example of how *Jihad* can reshape globalization and also become part of it. Indeed, the dialectic nature of the relations between globalization and borders can lead to such a hybrid synthesis as a sectorial sub-national terrorist global movement.

A thousand times different, and providing more gladdening examples of *globorderization* – the portmanteau I offer to mark a possible synthesis between globalization and borders – are world music and fusion cuisine.[121] Likewise, global families, including international, interfaith and multiracial families, which are central to this book, are an example of such a synthesis, as they embody a hybridity of global options, movement, and ideas, and intimate, legally bordered, and exclusive small social units, with varying degrees of bordering identities passed on to the children through socialization.[122] Because they are also always located within bordering territories and societies, I suggest calling them *globordered families*.

This theoretical typology can include additional possible relations between borders and globalization, such as: deliberate disregard relations, which belong to the antagonism group, in which the one tries to act as if the other did not exist (as is the case in the religious marriage law of certain groups, discussed in Chapter 3); inventive relations, which can belong to either the cooperative or the antagonistic groups, in which global forces imagine and invent borders, and bordering groups reconstruct themselves in the face of what they imagine as global powers (the issue of violence against children, discussed in Chapter 7, might provide examples of such inventive relations);[123] dilemmatic relations, which belong to the third group of complexities, in which the situation created by bordered globalization yields unsatisfying outcomes both for global and national forces, that must be chosen-from (as is the case in international adoption and child labor, discussed in Chapter 6); and abusive

---

[121] Erikson, *Globalization*, at 113.

[122] Daphna Hacker & Roni Liberson, "Cross Boarders Families in Israel: Between Individualism, Globalization and the Ethnos," *College of Management Law Review*, 15(2) (2010), 509–29 (Hebrew).

[123] As will be discussed in Chapter 7, global carriers of the human-rights discourse imagine there to be a rigid distinction or border between *abusive* actions against children, such as female genital mutilation and male circumcision, and *accepted* actions concerning children, such as child beauty pageants, hence contributing to the invention of a hierarchal border between alleged child-protecting societies and alleged child-abusing societies. In the opposite expression of these inventive relations, a country might change its policy related to violence against children in fear of international pressure based on global norms that, in fact, have not yet materialized. By doing so, it will help to create those very global norms.

relations, which can belong to each of the three groups, depending on the context (antagonistic, cooperative, or complex), and can refer to one- or multiple-sided abuse, depending on the specific power-relations configuration. Indeed, the typology I offer here is only a tentative one, in the sense that it is open to refinements, adjustments, and decompositions by additional theorization and empirical observations.

As mentioned here, the debates over globalization include moral presuppositions, which in many cases ascribe it positive value. It is important to briefly note, as this chapter is coming to its end, my understanding of the moral dimensions of globalization, borders, and the interrelations between them. There are no presuppositions underlying this book about any intrinsic moral aspects of globalization or borders. However, my moral view is that humans should be able to shape their personal biographies free of spatial and other kinds of social borders based on national, gender, race, religious, nonmeritocratic class, and other symbolic boundaries. At the same time, I realize that, for many, being part of national, cultural, ethnic, and religious bordering groups is the realization of this freedom. Hence, this book does not strive to offer any simple how-to moral guidelines for humane regulation in our era, because there is no such script. Rather, and at least as a minimal ethical standard, this book will offer contextual answers to these questions: Who benefits from bordered globalization and enjoys relative freedom in shaping their familial biographies? Who is excluded, harmed, and dehumanized by bordered globalization in ways that infringe this freedom? What role do national, international, and subnational laws play in the matrix yielding these outcomes?

2

Legalized Families

Of all the human spheres, it would seem that family and law are among the most radically opposed. The former is supposed to be all about intimacy, privacy, unconditional love, and long-lasting mutual care, whereas the latter is the domain of public rules, conflicting rights, and adversarial relations. Whereas we wish families to be centered on positive emotions, and we value each familial relation as unique, we hope the law is rational, uniform, general, and impartial. However, as this and the following chapters will demonstrate, the familial and the legal social institutions do not represent two unrelated separate spheres, but rather are entangled in various and complex ways. In fact, we cannot understand what family is without also understanding how the law constitutes familiality. Likewise, we cannot responsibly evaluate and shape the law that affects families, without understanding how people understand and perform their family lives while identifying with the law, using it as a resource, or resisting it.[1]

Because there are many approaches to defining and understanding *family*, and *law*, this chapter sets the foundations for the meaning ascribed to each of these terms in this book. Furthermore, it presents my understanding of the mutual interconnections between families and the law in the era of *bordered globalization* – the theoretical framework presented in the previous chapter. The first part of this chapter is devoted to *family*. It sketches the sociological and legal attempts to define what a family is, and the current competing descriptive and normative positions attached to the institution of the family. The second part centers on *law*. It details the three major functions of the law in democratic societies – all extremely relevant to the creation, maintenance, and breakdown of families. It also briefly discusses the *law and society* approach to the study of the law, in which this book is embedded and through which the interconnections

---

[1] For a theoretical typology of the law's presence in people's everyday lives, based on a comprehensive study in the United States, see Patricia Ewick & Susan S. Silbey, *The Common Place of Law* (The University of Chicago Press, 1998).

between the law and families are explored. Finally, the chapter ends with a discussion of the complex legal universe that affects families in the era of bordered globalization and that includes international, national, and sub-national laws and legal institutions. This complex legal amalgam affects families not only through laws that are part of classical family law, such as marriage and divorce laws, but also through other legal branches, such as immigration law, labor law, and human rights law.

Family

What Is a Family?

Oxford Dictionaries offers the following definitions for the word *family*: "A group consisting of two parents and their children living together as a unit," and "A group of people related by blood or marriage."[2] Each of these two structural definitions is partial and anachronistic. In an era in which there are countries, such as France, Mexico, and Norway, where the major-ity of children are born to unmarried parents, and others, such as the US and England, not far behind,[3] to leave out of the definition of *family* single parents (as the first definition does), or cohabitation (as the second defini-tion does) is to ignore two of the most important structural forms of fami-lies in the twenty-first century. Indeed, these two family forms, together with others such as polygamous families, same-sex families, polyamorous families, and multigenerational families create a real challenge for those striving to find one comprehensive structural definition of *family*.

Sociologists and legal scholars alike have been struggling with the ques-tion of defining *family*, not only due to the many structural forms it can, and does, take, but also because many consider the structural emphasis lacking, and therefore add to – or replace – it with a functional one. The anthropolo-gist George Murdock, in what became a dominant definitional paradigm in the second half of the twentieth century, offered economic cooperation, sexual reproduction, and common residence as the three universal func-tions of families. Childless couples, a widow and her grown-up children, national and international living-apart-together couples, and parenthood

[2] *Family*, Oxford Dictionaries, available at: www.oxforddictionaries.com/definition/english/family.

[3] OECD Social Policy Division, Directorate of Employment, Labour and Social Affairs, *Share of Births Outside of Marriage* (2016), available at: www.oecd.org/els/family/SF_2_4_Share_births_outside_marriage.pdf.

[4] Bahira Sherif Trask, *Globalization and Families: Accelerated Systemic Social Change* (New York: Springer, 2010), at 24.

through reproduction technologies, all demonstrate the limitations of this paradigm and its growing irrelevance in the twenty-first century.

Indeed, the institution of the family has witnessed rapid changes since the mid-twentieth century, which has led anthropologists and sociologists to depart from the universalistic structural and functional perceptions of the family, and to develop theories on the dynamic and contextual social construction of kinship.[5] The rapid changes include dramatic demographic shifts, such as the decrease in marriage and childbirth rates; the increase in divorce rates and life expectancy; technological developments, which diminish the time and energy needed to perform housework and provide new ways to bring children into the world; and ideological changes, including individualism, feminism, and the LGBT rights movement. All these developments, which affect families all over the world to varying degrees, not only alter and pluralize family structures but also shake up our conventional understanding of *the family*, as well as everyday familial practices and power relations between family members, and between them and the state and community.[6]

One theoretical path developed to cope with the growing pluralization of the structure and the concept of family, while still trying to distinguish between families and other social groups, is to focus on the unique quality of familial relations. The interest in familial emotional relations can already be found in the work of the anthropologist Bronislaw Malinovsky[7] who argued that to study the family's role without paying attention to the "personal affections," such as those existing between husband and wife, parents and children, is absurd. More recent attempts to define *family* do not assume structure or function, but center, instead, on the actual relations established between adults, and between adults and children. According to some legal theorists, including, for example, Martha Minow, Mary Shanley, and Ruth Zafran,[8] it is less important

---

[5] For example, Janet Carsten, *After Kinship* (Cambridge University Press, 2004); Marilyn Strathern, *Kinship, Law and the Unexpected: Relatives Are Always a Surprise* (New York: Cambridge University Press, 2005).

[6] For concrete examples of the legal changes that followed these developments in several different countries, see John Eekelaar & Rob George (Eds.), *Routledge Handbook of Family Law and Policy* (Abingdon: Routledge Handbooks, 2014).

[7] Bronislaw Malinowski, "The Group and the Individual in Functional Analysis," *American Journal of Sociology*, 44(6) (1939), 938–64, at 962.

[8] Martha Minow & Mary Lyndon Shanley, "Relational Rights and Responsibilities: Revisioning the Family in Liberal Political Theory and Law," *Hypatia*, 11(1) (1996), 4–29; Ruth Zafran, "The Relational Discourse as a Theoretical Basis for Resolving Family Disputes: Some Thought about Care and Justice" in Orna Ben-Naftali & Hannah Naveh (Eds.), *Trials of Love* (Tel Aviv: Ramot, 2005), pp. 605–55 (Hebrew).

whether a couple is married or not, or if a child is biological, genetic, adopted, or conceived through surrogacy. What should count, in defining a family, is the quality of relations between the adults and between the adult and the child. If these relations are long-term relations of care, dependency, intimacy, and support then they should be recognized and protected as familial relations, regardless of structure. Indeed, some sociologists go as far as defining a family as broadly as "a group of people who love each other and care for each other."[9] However, this relational emphasis is problematic as a definitional criterion because it calls for subjective and culturally varied understandings of such vague notions as care. Moreover, these relational definitions raise questions around the differences between a family and a football team or roommates, and the place of abusive relations, such as those created under spousal or parental violence, within the definition of *family*.

The difficulties with establishing an inclusive, yet meaningful, definition of *family* are evident in case law. The Burden sisters' case is a famous example of the possible unfortunate outcomes of familial structuralist definitions, which reached the European Court of Human Rights (ECtHR) in 2008. The two elderly, single Burden sisters had lived together all their lives, and for more than thirty years they did so in a house they owned in equal shares in southwest England. Although they signed mutual wills in which each bequeathed the other her share of the house, they anticipated that when one of them passed away the surviving sister would have to sell the house in order to pay the 40 percent inheritance tax, mandatory in the UK, and would find herself, in old age, expelled from her home. At the ECtHR, the sisters argued that they were being discriminated-against by their country's law, compared to married and cohabiting couples, who enjoy an inheritance tax exemption given to the surviving partner. The Grand Chamber rejected their claim. It adopted a narrow structural definition of cohabitation that privileges marriage and civil partnership over siblingship – as "marriage confers a special status on those who enter into it," and because civil partnership is a declared contract – and that rejects "the length or the supportive nature of the relationship" as a criterion for legal protection of familial relations.[10]

[9] Sylvie Fogiel-Bijaoui, "Families in Israel: Between Familism and Post-Modernism" in Dafna Izraeli, Ariella Friedman, Henriette Dahan-Kalev, Sylvie Fogiel-Bijaoui, Manar Hassan, Hannah Herzog, & Hannah Naveh (Eds.), *Sex, Gender and Politics* (Tel Aviv: Hakibbutz Hameuchad, 1999), pp. 107–66, at fn. 2 (Hebrew).
[10] Case 13378/05, *Burden v. United Kingdom* [2008] ECtHR.

Although the Burden sisters' case calls for a relational definition of family,[11] other legal cases demonstrate the problems that can arise from replacing structural definitions with relational ones – for example, the struggle of Diane Blood over her right to be inseminated by her dead husband's sperm, which was retrieved while he was in a coma in 1995.[12] Although the British Human Fertilization and Embryology Authority, and the High Court, refused to allow Diane the use of the sperm as it was retrieved without the husband's consent, leading UK legal and political figures argued that she should be allowed to give birth to a child carrying her late husband's genes, as a continuation of her relationship with him. In 1997, the Court of Appeal allowed Diane to travel to Belgium for artificial insemination with her husband's sperm, as part of her right for medical treatment in any of the European Community (EC) member states, but prohibited any future cases of retrieval of sperm without the man's consent. Although a number of countries, such as Australia and several US states, share the UK demand for consent, other countries, such as Germany, Sweden, Italy, France, Malaysia, and Taiwan, are more restrictive, and totally ban posthumous reproduction. Only one country, Israel, is less restrictive, allowing posthumous sperm retrieval and use, not only by the deceased's spouse but also by his parents, without his pre-mortem consent, and with the assistance of a woman their son did not know.[13] These different legal attitudes manifest the different balance, struck by each country, between the spouse's or the parents' right to a relationship with a future offspring of their beloved deceased family member, the deceased's bodily integrity and familial wishes, and the future child's best interests, compared, for example, to the option that child will be conceived through anonymous sperm donation, with no option to get to know, or have a relationship with, the child's genetic father's family. Hence, the technological option of posthumous fatherhood reveals the subjectivity embedded in the relational definitions of *family,* and the difficulty of prioritizing some kinds of familial relations over others.[14]

---

[11] Ruth Deech, "Family Relations and the Law: Family Members," Gresham College, Lecture (February 2, 2010), transcript available at: www.gresham.ac.uk/lectures-and-events/sisters-sisters-there-were-never-such-devoted-sisters.

[12] Carsten, *After Kinship*, at 1–2.

[13] Yael Hashiloni-Dolev, "Posthumous Reproduction (PHR) in Israel: Policy Rationales Versus Lay People's Concerns, a Preliminary Study," *Culture, Medicine, and Psychiatry*, 39(4) (2015), 634–50.

[14] For more on the relevance of relational theory to family law, and on its normative limitations, see Robert Leckey, *Contextual Subjects: Family, State, and Relational Theory* (University of Toronto Press, 2008).

The challenges inherent in finding one accurate definition of *family* have led some sociologists to forsake the endeavor altogether and to argue that "no single definition of family may be possible."[15] Likewise, many legal systems lack a definition of *family*, and there is no common-law definition of *family* to be found either.[16] Several legal theorists go as far as arguing for the abolishment of any kind of familial legal definitions, such as marriage, because they are, by definition, discriminatory toward the familial and familial-like relations they exclude. In accordance with the relational approach, these scholars call for the legal protection of relations of dependency and care, detached from rigid familial legal categories.[17] Similarly, several scholars within the social sciences have moved away from the sociology of the family to the study of *intimacy, relatedness*, and *personal life*, in an empirical and normative rebellion against the (Western) heteronormative tendency of placing exclusive significance on *the family*.[18]

Although I think the broadening of the research agenda to embrace significant human relations that do not collapse down to the family is extremely important and inspiring, I agree with those who argue that studying families (in their plural manifestations) and *family* as a sociological category – rather than *the (heteronormative) family* – is still crucial. For better or for worse, *family* is still very central to most people's lives and to public policy makers, and, as such, must be studied as a distinct and central category.[19] Likewise, although I find the possibility of avoiding familial legal definitions appealing in its egalitarian promise, I think it is problematic, primarily because I believe the ambiguity embedded in the relational thesis might leave vulnerable family members – children, women, and the poor in particular – without the necessary legal protection. I agree with those who argue that long-term spousal relations and parent-child relations create special vulnerabilities – and responsibilities – which must be

---

[15] Sherif Trask, *Globalization and Families*, at 24.

[16] Alison Diduck & Felicity Kaganas, *Family Law, Gender, and the State: Text, Cases and Materials* (Oxford: Hart Publishing, 2006), at 18.

[17] For example, Martha Albertson Fineman, "Why Marriage?," *Virginia Journal of Social Policy & Law*, 9 (2001), 239–71; Nancy Polikoff, *Beyond (Straight and Gay) Marriage, Valuing All Families under the Law* (Boston: Beacon Press, 2008).

[18] For example, see Eleanor Wilkinson & David Bell, "Ties that Blind: On Not Seeing (or Looking) beyond 'The Family,'" *Families, Relationships and Societies*, 1(3) (2012), 423–9.

[19] For example, see Rosalind Edwards & Val Gillies, "Farewell to Family? Notes on an Argument for Retaining the Concept," *Families, Relationships and Societies*, 1(1) (2012), 63–9.

acknowledged by law.[20] Any such acknowledgment is bound to demand some kind of legal differentiation between *family* and *stranger*, and so will suffer from the difficulties in determining family and familial relations discussed earlier.

Although, in my opinion, defining familial relations is legally justified, and indeed inevitable, the impossibility of finding a universalist definition supports Pierre Bourdieu's inspiring claim that:

> The family is indeed a fiction, a social artifact, an illusion in the most ordinary sense of the word, but a "well-founded illusion", because, being produced and reproduced with the guaranty of the state, it receives from the state at every moment the means to exist and persist.[21]

Indeed, as detailed in the next part of this chapter, the law plays a major role in the creation of the "well-founded illusion" that is the family, even if it does not include a definition of *family*.[22] Although this book focuses on families as social units of spousal and parental relations, by no means do I offer this as an exclusive descriptive or normative definition of *family*. Rather than trying to find the ultimate definition, in my view, it is much more interesting and important to study how social and legal understandings of family are shaped and reshaped, not only by the state, as Bourdieu suggested, but also by individuals, subnational communities, and transnational forces. Along similar lines, I do not limit the discussion in this book to *transnational families* – that is, families with "one or more family members located in different countries"[23] – or to the broader definition of *world families* – namely, those in which family members are "living in, or coming from, different countries or continents."[24] Although, indeed, most of the issues discussed in the following chapters are related to such *international* and *cross-border families*, I am

---

[20] For example, Mary Lyndon Shanley, *Just Marriage* (New York: Oxford University Press, 2004); Carol Sanger, "A Case for Civil Marriage," *Cardozo Law Review*, 27 (2006), 1311–23; Marsha Garrison & Elizabeth S. Scott, "Legal Regulation of Twenty-First Century Families" in Marsha Garrison & Elizabeth S. Scott (Eds.), *Marriage at the Crossroads* (New York: Cambridge University Press, 2012), pp. 303–25.

[21] Pierre Bourdieu, "On the Family as a Realized Category," *Theory, Culture & Society*, 13(3) (1996), 19–26, at 25.

[22] See also Frances E. Olsen, "The Myth of State Intervention in the Family," *University of Michigan Journal of Law Reform*, 18 (1985), 835–64.

[23] Valentina Mazzucato, "Transnational Families, Research and Scholarship" in Immanuel Ness (Ed.), *The Encyclopedia of Global Human Migration* (2013), at 1, available at: http://onlinelibrary.wiley.com/doi/10.1002/9781444351071.wbeghm541/abstract.

[24] Ulrich Beck & Elizabeth Beck-Gernsheim, *Distant Love* (Cambridge: Polity Press, 2014), at 2.

also interested in the effect of bordered globalization on families that do not fit these definitions, such as those that remain in the same country but find themselves affected in some way by the cross-border movement of other people, or by international law or the laws of other nations. Chapter 4, for example, reveals how bordered globalization and the lack of international regulation around reproduction services shape the familiality of people who only need to leave their country of origin for a short time to use such services or do not even leave at all as they are the providers of the fertility service. My assumption is that all families are potentially affected by bordered globalization, and my mission in this book is to explore and discuss the role of the law in shaping these effects, as well as how the law is changed by them.

In this regard, I would offer a further refinement of Bourdieu's thesis on the family. He claimed that the family is a *habitus*, a social category so deeply institutionalized and agreed-on as to be perceived as natural and taken for granted, as well as to make individuals integrate into this instituted unit, as if this was the only possible way of living, by feeling and practicing "obliged affections and affective obligation."[25] Although I agree that this was, and is, true, for a variety of societies, and for long historical periods, I would argue that in our era of bordered globalization, we are more aware than ever of competing social and legal notions of family, and face growing difficulties in creating a common and institutionalized perception of: what a family is; what the legal obligations that family members owe to each other are; and what privileges, if any, should be granted, by law, to families by collective entities, such as the nation state and the international community. The major competing conceptions of *family* and their normative implications will be discussed next, and that will complete the discussion of the *family* needed before turning to the role of the law in shaping familiality in the era of bordered globalization, discussed in the second part of this chapter.

Axes of Competing Conceptions of Family

My approach to mapping the controversies surrounding the different notions of family is to think in terms of four axes, or spectra, along which conceptions of family and family-related policy are located (see Figure 2.1 for a graphic representation of this conceptual map).

[25] Bourdieu, "On the Family as a Realized Category," at 25.

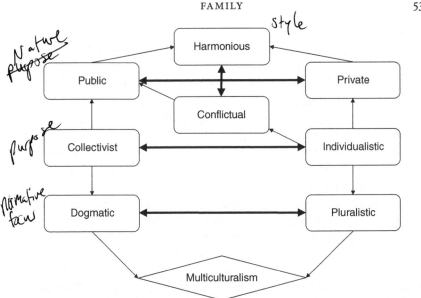

Style [handwritten]

Nature purpose [handwritten]

purpose [handwritten]

normative focus [handwritten]

Figure 2.1 Conflicting Conceptions of Family
Legend: bold arrows = antagonistic axes; pale arrows = analytical compatibility

As will be explained in detail, I argue that the different competing conceptions of family can be grouped into four axes with contrasting extremes, as marked by opposing bold arrows in Figure 2.1: (1) collectivist–individualist; (2) dogmatic–pluralistic; (3) public–private; and (4) harmonious–conflictual. Moreover, there are analytical connections between the ends of these axes (marked by the pale arrows in Figure 2.1). The collectivist, dogmatic, and public perceptions of family usually go hand-in-hand, whereas the individualistic perception usually correlates with the pluralistic view and with the notion that families ought to be kept separate from the public sphere. However, the extremes cannot be organized into two separate groups, because some of those who perceive family as a private sanctuary of individuals share the notion that family is harmonious – as most of those who view families as a public matter do – whereas others within the individualistic camp argue that family is a site of conflict, and emphasize the crucial interdependency between the private and the public sphere's in constructing families. Figure 2.1 also positions multiculturalism as an important normative view related to families, which does not belong to any of the axes and which can be reached from both of the two competing dogmatic and pluralist notions of family. Let us now briefly examine each of the four axes in turn.

The collectivist–individualist axis: One of the most widely contested issues regarding the meaning of family is between those who perceive it as a social unit in the service of the larger collective, be it the religious or ethnic group or the nation, and those who understand family as a unit in the service of the individual. This tension is captured in the collectivist-individualist axis, placed at the center of Figure 2.1.

Many prominent social theorists, including Adam Smith, Herbert Spencer, and Emil Durkheim, understood families as organic units aimed at socializing their members to be productive members of the larger collective. Under this perspective, through sexual reproduction, economic and emotional support, role-modeling, and education, families are generating the next generation, which will be culturally molded according to the values and perceptions of the current one. The notion that the family is first and foremost the building block of society is echoed in the Universal Declaration of Human Rights' recognition that "the family is the natural and fundamental group unit of society and is entitled to protection by society and the State."[26]

At the opposite end of this collectivist–individualist axis we find those who claim that families exist because they serve the individuals who are part of them, including their biological, psychological, and economic needs. According to this view, held by prominent philosophers and social researchers such as Jean-Jacques Rousseau and Malinovsky, the individual preexists the family, and not the other way around.[27]

The dogmatic–pluralistic axis: The collectivist perception of family is usually joined by a normative perception aimed at securing and nurturing the family as a social institution. This posture holds that since every social group, big or small, depends on the family for its biological and cultural survival, society not only has an obligation to protect the family, but should also enjoy the power to control families. This view is reflected in the analytical connection between the collectivist and dogmatic extremes, shown by the pale arrow connecting the two in Figure 2.1. According to the dogmatic end of the dogmatic–pluralist axis, because families are the major socializing force, they must reflect the social values of the larger collective, including those values related to sexuality, gender roles, and the proper education children ought to receive. Accordingly, any deviation from what the specific collective perceives as legitimate family forms

---

[26] Article 16(3) of the Universal Declaration of Human Rights 1948, available at: www .un.org/en/documents/udhr/.

[27] For a review of the scholars at both ends of this axis, see Mattat Adar-Bunis, *Families in Sociological and Anthropological Perspective* (Raanana: The Open University of Israel, 2007), pp. 18–25 (Hebrew).

or practices is a threat to the collective's values and should be duly prevented or punished. This is the reason certain orthodox groups, such as Amish Christians, Wahhabi Muslims, or Haredi Jews, are preoccupied with only channeling their members toward certain family forms, such as heterosexual marriages, and punish – by excommunication or by law – those who try to establish an alternative family.

By contrast, the individualist perception of family often correlates with a pluralistic normative standing vis-à-vis family forms and practices, as shown by the pale arrow connecting the two in Figure 2.1. According to this pluralistic worldview, since the social function of families, and their moral justification, is to fulfill individuals' needs, they should be shaped according to these needs. Human needs are varied and dynamic; therefore family forms and practices can, and should, also be so. Society has no right, under this view, to channel individuals toward only one legitimate familial way of life, and should allow each individual to shape his or her own familial biography and everyday life, as long as they do not harm the individual rights of others.[28]

As we shall see in the following chapters, when discussing issues such as polygamy, female genital mutilation, and religious family courts, the tension within this dogmatic–pluralistic axis becomes extremely complex, in light of the realization that many individuals identify – through socialization – with, or choose to belong to, dogmatic collectives. Hence, as captured by the rhombus placed below the dogmatic–pluralistic axis in Figure 2.1, and its analytical connections to both ends of this axis, one can endorse a multicultural normative stance on families, from both the collectivist–dogmatic and also the individualist–pluralistic perspectives. Indeed, in several of the discussions in the chapters to come, multiculturalism will occupy a significant space and will be contrasted with liberal feminism and other normative perceptions. In my opinion, the most important difference between the collectivist–dogmatic and the individualist–pluralistic endorsement of multiculturalism is that the latter will insist on the right to exit the collective, including the right to exit the family as determined by the collective.[29]

The harmonious–conflictual axis: The right to exit the family is especially acute in the eyes of those who argue that family is not a harmonious unit of solidarity and mutual care, but rather a site of conflict. The harmonious end of the harmonious–conflictual axis presented in the

---

[28] See also Pinhas Shifman, "On the New Family: Introductory Notes," *Tel Aviv Law Review*, 28(3) (2005), 643–70 (Hebrew).

[29] Annamari Vitikainen, *Limits of Liberal Multiculturalism* (Helsinki: Theoretical Philosophy, 2013), Ch. 5.

upper-middle part of Figure 2.1 is, first and foremost, the outcome of the functionalist understanding of families, held by most of those who belong to the collectivist camp. According to this view, each individual within the organic unit of the family has a role designated to him or to her, in perfect correlation with their intrinsic relative strengths, to the benefit of the familial unit and of society as a whole. One of the most prominent exponents of this theory is the American sociologist Talcott Parsons,[30] who argued that the nuclear family is a universal familial form, in which the man maximizes his masculine instrumental strengths by taking on the role of the breadwinner and by representing the family in the larger collective, while the woman, with her feminine expressive abilities, takes responsibility for the emotional and integrative dimensions of family life. The normative conclusion that stems from this analysis is that since this gender-based role division is the most utilitarian, as far as the family unit and society are concerned, it is, by definition, legitimate and just.

A very different perception to this harmonious position can already be found in the nineteenth century writings of Fredrick Engels. He argued that the nuclear family, of a married heterosexual couple and their biological children, is the social mechanism through which men make sure their wealth is transferred to their offspring.[31] More recently, it is feminist theorists, such as Susan Okin Moller, who have worked to unveil the myth of family harmony, by revealing the high price women pay for their domestic role, including economic dependency, discrimination in the labor force, and domestic violence.[32] Likewise, the socio-legal scholar Leon Sheleff pointed to the conflictual nature of families by analyzing the inherent generational hostility between parents and children, and to families as a site of violation of children's basic human rights.[33]

The public–private axis: Logically, the collectivist–dogmatic–harmonious extremes correlate with the public end of the public–private axis, as signaled by the pale arrows connecting them in Figure 2.1, because these three views understand family as a major public concern and as a realm that should be governed by public norms and forces to secure harmonious socializing units. Likewise, it is not surprising to see the pale arrows that connect the individualist–pluralist extremes to the private one. The famous saying "a man's home is his castle" epitomizes the

---

[30] Talcott Parsons, *Social Structure and Personality* (New York: Free Press, 1964).

[31] Friedrich Engels, *The Origin of the Family, Private Property and the State* (Harmondsworth: Penguin, 1985).

[32] Suzan Moller Okin, *Justice, Gender, and the Family* (New York: Basic Books, 1989).

[33] Leon Sheleff, *Generations Apart: Adult Hostility to Youth* (New York: McGraw-Hill, 1981).

liberal perspective that the family should be treated as a private sanctuary, secured from any public interference. Interestingly, this view shares the harmonious understanding of the family, characterizing the collectivist-dogmatic–public extremes of the axes, as it conceptualizes the family as a safe haven, equally protecting all its members.

In contrast, feminists, who also belong to the individualist camp, insist on revealing the fallacy of the public–private dichotomy and argue that this false dichotomy is, in fact, a central strategy used by the patriarchal society to allow men to do to their wives as they please.[34] Unlike classical liberals, feminist individualist perceptions of the family lead to the public end of the public–private axis, albeit not as a desired policy, as understood by the collectivists, but as a critical observation: "the personal is political," including within the family. According to feminist theories, domestic labor division and power dynamics cannot be understood detached from gender power relations in general, and from the politics of the public sphere, including the paid-labor market and the law.[35] Hence, feminist theorists create complex analytical linkages between the individualist, conflictual, and public extremes, as marked by the pale arrows connecting them in Figure 2.1.

As can be seen, then, using the axis metaphor to map the four major controversies over the family helps us see how the radical descriptive and normative ends of the spectra intersect. Furthermore, I suggest this metaphor to emphasize the importance of what happens between the extremes of the spectra. In my view, most of the social action takes place in-between the radical ends, as families and family policies can be differentiated according to their varying and dynamic placements along the collective–individual, dogmatic–pluralistic, harmonious–conflictual, and public–private spectra.

Examples of this in-between at play, as manifested in everyday life, can be easily drawn from my own, quite ordinary, familial life, shaped in the shadow of Israeli familial legal policies. Regarding the collectivist–individualist axis, to satisfy my conservative mother-in-law and the law of my country, which only acknowledges religious marriage, and against my individualist feminist worldview, I have married in the only collectively agreed-upon and legally sanctioned way in Israel – in a patriarchal religious ceremony. At the same time,

---

[34] Olsen, "The Myth of State Intervention in the Family."
[35] For example, see, ibid.; Okin, *Justice, Gender, and the Family*; Joan Williams, *Unbending Gender* (Oxford University Press, 2000).

I have established, with my husband, egalitarian relations, based on the understanding that our spousal relations are justified only if, and as long as, they satisfy us both, individually. Curiously, even if I had not married but had chosen to cohabit with my spouse, the laws of Israel would have treated me and my spouse as a married couple for almost all practical matters.[36] Hence, both my personal marital experience and the spousal law of Israel are not located on the collectivist or the individualist ends of the spectra, but rather placed along them, with Israeli spousal law located closer to the former, and my spousal relations located closer to the latter.

Regarding the dogmatic–pluralist axis, although I believe I hold relatively pluralist views in relation to family forms and practices, I am still, somewhat dogmatically, confounded when people, seriously, relate to their pet as their child. Yet one Israeli family court judge has already ruled on custody and visitation rights relating to a dog and a cat belonging to a separated couple, applying the same legal categories as those applied to children upon their parents' divorce.[37] However, another judge has since ruled that the decision, regarding which partner the couple's dog will live with, should be determined according to property law, and not custody law.[38] These examples show the importance of the spectra between the radical pluralist and dogmatic ends of the axis, and demonstrate the possibility that the same legal system might include inconsistent and conflicting judicial familial worldviews, placed at different points along the spectra.

Regarding the harmonious–conflictual axis, my relations with my two children are a mixture of harmony and conflict, with deep love, devotion, and joy accompanied by more clashes and quarrels than I wish to admit. Sometimes, at the height of an argument over issues such as tidying their rooms, they remind me that children have rights, and threaten – I hope jokingly – to report me to the authorities. Although these are relatively minor conflicts, they are governed by Israeli law, which prohibits corporal punishment by parents.[39] Although this law strives to promote harmonious familial relations, it would not have been necessary if, indeed, parent–child relations were consistently, and naturally, harmonious.

---

[36] Shahar Lifsitz, *Cohabitation Law in Israel: In Light of a Civil Law Theory of the Family* (Haifa University Press, 2005) (Hebrew).

[37] FC (TA) 32405/01 *P v. A* (2004) (Israel).

[38] FC (Krayot) 24585-11-09 *D v. K* (2011) (Israel).

[39] CrimA 4596/98 *A v. The State of Israel* (2000) (Israel).

Finally, regarding the public–private axis, while fully aware of the public and political dimensions of my family life, including, for example, the state benefits I enjoy as part of a legitimate family, and the labor market-related price I have paid as a mother in a country with no real incentives for paternity leave, I also cherish the privacy of my family home and the fact that I can write this book in my pajamas, with only my close family members to see me (one of the reasons I prefer working at home rather than in my office on campus). Hence, just as in the case of the other axes, both descriptively and normatively, family life and the laws that govern families can comprise public–private mixtures rather than being a radical endorsement of one of the extremes of the axis.

Indeed, although many citizens of the world hold a very coherent perception of family, such as a collectivist–dogmatic–harmonious–public one, and try to hold to it all their lives – among other reasons for fear of social and legal retaliation if they don't – many others are enjoying the increasing ability to shape their familial biographies as they wish, along the spectra I have mapped. The degrees of freedom and flexibility are shaped by bordered globalization: the more an individual is exposed to global information about familial options or to people from different familial cultures, and is a part of a nation with pluralist family law or can travel to shop around for the legal system that tolerates the familial option he or she desires, the greater freedom and flexibility he or she enjoys. Notwithstanding, as will be discussed in Chapter 3, this freedom and the growing instances of conjunctions – due to bordered globalization – between people and normative systems located at different points along the spectra are often accompanied by familial confusion, conflict, and, at times, even breakdown. Beck and Beck-Gernsheim went as far as arguing that, in our era, *world families* might experience "religious wars" in their everyday lives, as conflicting perceptions of family, held by Western and non-Western family members, collide with one another.[40]

To set the stage for understanding the role of the law in broadening or narrowing familial freedom, and in mitigating the growing potential for familial confusion and conflict in our era, the next section will elaborate on the functions of the law and on its meaning as conceptualized in this book, and on the complex legal arena affecting families in the era of bordered globalization.

---

[40] Beck and Beck-Gernsheim, *Distant Love*, at 3.

The Law

The Three Main Functions of the Law

The law in modern societies has three main functions: to resolve disputes, to guide behavior, and to redistribute resources.[41] All three are relevant to families, as we shall now see.

A well-known function of the law is to resolve conflicts. Although people are allowed to resolve their conflicts in many ways, such as through private negotiation or with the assistance of a mediator, the legal system, in democratic countries, is the only social institution that is allowed to resolve conflicts among citizens by using coercion and violence to enforce its resolutions. As a society, we allow the law to do to us things we would not allow any other social system or fellow citizen to do – to lock us up, to fine us, to take our money and to give it to someone else, and – in some legal systems that allow the death penalty – even to murder us. We are willing to grant the law the power to harm our basic rights and freedoms because we understand how important it is that only the law will have the power to resolve conflicts (and guide behavior and redistribute resources) through the use of force. Hence, while in the past a duel was considered an honorable way of resolving a conflict, today the winning party would be tried for murder.

A commonly-used argument is that the law is not suitable for resolving family conflicts. Its adversarial positioning of one party against the other, its disinterest in feelings, and the winner-takes-all rationale of its outcomes might well serve disputes between strangers but are ill-suited to resolving disputes among family members. Familial disputes, it is claimed, need a resolution mechanism that will acknowledge the network of relations in which the parties are embedded, including the emotional ones, and must strive to find creative solutions that will fit the specific family and facilitate post-crisis channels of communication, especially when children are involved.[42] Therapeutic evaluations, mediation, and collaborative divorce, are among the alternatives developed in an attempt to save familial relations from adversarial legal procedures and outcomes.

Notwithstanding, the monopoly of the law over violence in resolving disputes brings all alternative forms of conflict-resolution under its

[41] For a similar, though not identical, typology, see Hadar Aviram, "Does the Law Achieve Its Goals? Answers from the Empirical Research World" in Daphna Hacker & Neta Ziv (Eds.), *Does the Law Matter?* (Tel Aviv University, 2010), pp. 27–62 (Hebrew).

[42] Jay Folberg & Ann Milne (Eds.) *Divorce Mediation Theory and Practice* (New York: Guilford Press, 1988).

shadow.[43] Although two parties may choose an alternative forum for seeking resolution, other than the courts, each is likely to do so while calculating his or her chances of achieving the outcome they want, knowing that they can abandon this alternative and ultimately turn to a judge if they believe this will improve their odds of success. The choice of the alternative forum and these kinds of calculations depend on the legitimacy – or lack thereof – that the state's legal system designates to the alternative forum and to the outcomes it produces. For example, a religious couple, living in a Western country, might prefer to turn to their religious community leader, rather than to a judge, in their attempt to agree on their divorce conditions. However, if that mentor were to suggest that the woman should relinquish all her property rights, since she is the guilty party in the marriage breakdown, she would probably bring that consultation to an end and turn to the court, with its no-fault property division legal rules, adopted in all Western countries.[44] Still, as will be explored in Chapter 3, if the couple had signed an arbitration contract, in which both spouses had granted the religious leader authority to decide their divorce conditions, the civil court might have no choice but to force the woman to honor the arbitrator's decision, if the law of that particular Western country allowed such arbitration contract and outcomes. Hence, it is the state's divorce, property, and arbitration laws that shape the possibility and content of out-of-court alternative familial dispute resolutions.

Although many are used to thinking of the law, first and foremost, as a system aimed at resolving conflicts, an equally important role of the law is to prevent conflicts from occurring in the first place. This is achieved by the law's second function: guiding behavior. The law guides our everyday interactions with each other, through criminal law, with its determination of moral right and wrong, and through the civil branches, such as tort law, contract law, and family law, which provide the normative frameworks for such cognitive schemas as *reasonable person*, contractual *offer* and *acceptance*, and *the best interests of the child.*

Legal systems that recognize marital rape, for example, regulate the most intimate aspect of spousal relations. They do so not only in the sense that a husband who rapes his wife can be jailed, but also because they signal that marriage should include only consensual sex and that a man does not own his wife's body. Likewise, a law that assumes

---

[43] Robert H. Mnookin & Lewis Kornhauser, "Bargaining in the Shadow of the Law: The Case of Divorce," *Yale Law Journal*, 88 (1979), 950–96.

[44] Mary Ann Glendon, *The Transformation of Family Law* (University of Chicago Press, 1989), Ch. 5.

community property among married spouses signals what the proper marital economic relations should be like, hence adding to the marital rape statute, in constructing what good marriage is and how so-called normal spouses are expected to act toward each other. As the legal scholar Ayelet Blecher-Prigat argues, the law provides families with "background rules," which contribute to, and even shape, the content of familial relationships and their social and personal meanings. These background rules not only signal what normal and good familial relations should look like but also help in coordinating expectations among family members.[45] This is why, when people who come from different legal systems try to establish a family, they might experience a lack of shared undertakings and clashes of familial expectations, as will be examined in Chapter 3.

Moreover, the law narrows our imagination.[46] When a legal system allows only heterosexual and monogamous marriages, most people will not imagine the options of same-sex or polyamorous marriage. Likewise, and as detailed in Chapter 4, when legal systems recently started allowing surrogacy, the option of using another woman's uterus to become parents – not seen since Biblical times – became imaginable. On similar lines, total disinheritance of children from one's will is unimaginable in most of the European continent, as the law of inheritance in this part of the world includes forced shares for children. By contrast, in countries such as England, the United States, and Israel, total disinheritance of children is an option, as the law promotes absolute freedom of testation, including that of parents.[47]

As social beings, in most cases, most of the time, people identify with the society they live in and wish to belong to it. Thus, they usually and willingly follow the behavioral guidelines that the laws of their society set, and do not do so in fear of legal retaliation. In many cases, the obedience to the law is not even conscious, as its guidelines are internalized as

---

[45] Ayelet Blecher-Prigat, "The Family and the Law?" in Daphna Hacker & Neta Ziv (Eds.), *Does the Law Matter?* (Tel Aviv University, 2010), pp. 275–304 (Hebrew).

[46] David M. Trubek, "Back to the Future: The Short, Happy Life of the Law and Society Movement," *Florida State University Law Review,* 18 (1990), 1–55; Douglas Lawrence, Austin Sarat, & Martha Merrill Umphery, "Theoretical Perspectives on Lives in the Law: An Introduction" in Austin Sarat, Lawrence Douglas, & Martha Merrill Umphery (Eds.), *Lives in the Law* (Ann Arbor: University of Michigan Press, 2006), pp. 1–20.

[47] Daphna Hacker, "The Rights of the Dead through the Prism of Israeli Succession Disputes," *International Journal of Law in Context,* 11(1) (2015), 40–58, at 54; Daphna Hacker, "Disappointed 'Heirs' as a Socio-Legal Phenomenon," *Oñati Socio-Legal Series,* 4(2) (2014), 243–63.

reflecting the state of nature, or as the only way things can be.[48] Of course, this book is all about the problems arising when people come from different socio-legal systems or move from one to the other, or when they forum shop in another country or are exposed to contradicting behavioral guidelines found in the laws of their religious community, their country, or the international community. The growing intensity of such cases in the era of bordered globalization shakes Bourdieu's argument, mentioned earlier, that the family is an agreed upon *habitus*, and exposes the growing difficulty of the law in producing agreed upon familial guidelines.

The third function of the law, perhaps less visible than the other two, but nonetheless extremely important, is to redistribute public resources. Tax law is the means by which the nation state collects revenues from its citizens; and welfare law, health law, and education law are examples of branches of law that redistribute these revenues back to the public, according to the governing regime's agenda. The redistribution of resources is not only monetary (such as in the form of a social security pension) but also includes services (for example, public schools) and permission to use public resources (such as water). Furthermore, the law distributes non-monetary resources, such as occupational monopoly (as is given to lawyers) and citizenship.

At first glance, it might appear as if this third role has nothing to do with families, but the truth is that it is extremely relevant to the creation of families and their practices. People might choose to marry or have more children than they had originally planned, if married couples and parents of larger families enjoy more generous governmental housing benefits than cohabitants or parents with only one or two children. Likewise, the availability and cost of public childcare services or care for the elderly affect the labor division within families, the power relations between family members, and their daily interactions with each other and with local or migrant paid caregivers, as discussed in Chapter 8. Finally, as explored in Chapters 5, 7, and 8, the law's definition of citizenship eligibility shapes families' ability to be created and maintained, family members' living arrangements – together or apart – and family members' freedom to escape domestic violence. Indeed, as mentioned in the previous chapter, citizenship is perhaps the most valuable resource held by developed nation states in the era of bordered globalization. Hence, to understand familiality in this era demands close attention to citizenship laws.

---

[48] Hadar Aviram, "Does the Law Achieve Its Goals?"; Menachem Mautner, "Three Approaches to Law and Culture," *Cornell Law Review,* 96(4) (2011), 839–68.

To conclude, by resolving conflicts, guiding behavior, and redistributing monetary and nonmonitory public resources, the law shapes familial forms, praxis, and perceptions, in times of familial peace and in times of familial wars. In that sense, all families are legalized, and no family escapes legal intervention.[49] However, the law not only shapes families but is also shaped by them. This is so since the law is not a static, monolithic, and isolated entity but rather, as will be explained next, a social field that is in constant interaction with the society of which it is a part.

Law and Society

This book is embedded in the *law and society* intellectual movement, also known as socio-legal studies.[50] So it is important to set out, even if only briefly, this movement's basic understanding of the law and its points of departure from the formalist perception of the law held by many legal scholars, judges, lawyers, and laypeople.

According to legal formalism, the legal system in democratic nations can, and should, be autonomous. It should function independently of other social systems, including the political, the economic, and the religious ones. Judges can, and should, exercise the law objectively, while relying on valid legal resources (mainly statutes and precedents) and applying interpretation principles, through which such sources yield legal rules (such as linguistic meaning, internal consistency, and legislative purpose), and reasoning principles, by which legal rules and facts are made to yield legal conclusions (mainly analogy and deduction).[51] Hence, if a judge acts rationally, she or he will come to the only one possible legal conclusion in a specific dispute, as would all other rational judges if they had been assigned to decide the same specific case. Although different formalist theoreticians argue over the scope of the interpretational resources a judge is allowed to use, they all agree that these resources must be internal to the legal system and should not be imported from other social realms. Formalist legal research, then, centers on doctrinal substantive and procedural legal rules and does not look to other fields of knowledge as they are external, and thus irrelevant, to the law.

In what seems, at first glance, to be in complete opposition to the formalist concept of the law, the law and society movement – inspired by

---

[49] Olsen, "The Myth of State Intervention in the Family."

[50] Philip A. Thomas, "Socio-Legal Studies: The Case of Disappearing Fleas and Bustards" in Philip A. Thomas (Ed.), *Socio-Legal Studies* (Aldershot: Dartmouth, 1997), pp. 1–22.

[51] Brian Leiter, "Positivism, Formalism, Realism," *Columbia Law Review*, 99 (1999), 1138–64.

legal realism in the United States and by the sociology of law in Europe[52] – assumes that the law cannot be understood detached from the society in which it functions. According to this perspective, judges are not machines, and laws are never simply clear-cut black-letter legal texts. Hence, the law is the product of a continual task of interpretation by social agents, whose interpretative labor is influenced, in turn, by their personal and social circumstances.

The law and society movement further departs from the formalist perception of the law, as it realizes that *the law* happens in a much broader social field than the judiciary.[53] Lawyers, law professors, and law enforcement officers, among other professionals, as well as laypeople, take part in the creation of the law as they apply it, interpret it, accept it, or challenge it. Moreover, law and society research points to the shortcoming of the formalist emphasis on state law, by revealing the existence of other, parallel, formal, and informal legal systems, such as within religious communities, or certain trades, or the mafia.

Hence, law is constantly created and recreated by professionals, laypeople, and communities, which shape it according to their interests, world views, and relative power within the legal field. Even if these agents believe they are using and interpreting the law objectively, they do not and cannot do so, as their perception of the law – which, as mentioned, is open at all times to a variety of interpretations – is always embedded in their individual histories and social positioning.[54] For example, deciding on the best interests of the child in a parental custody dispute is never a matter of pure math, because this vague concept invites subjective judgments of good parenting, both generally and also in relation to the specific family handled by the judicial system. These subjective judgments are not an evil that must be replaced by objective custody measures (as the formalists would argue), because there are no such objective measures. Rather, the decision should be understood as a matter of judicial discretion, influenced by formal law, interactions in the courtroom, empirical knowledge, and personal and professional experiences, views, and common sense.

---

[52] Carroll Seron & Susan S. Silbey, "Profession, Science, and Culture: An Emergent Canon of Law and Society Research" in Austin Sarat (Ed.), *The Blackwell Companion to Law and Society* (Victoria, AU: Blackwell Publishing, 2004), pp. 30–59.

[53] Pierre Bourdieu, "The Force of Law: Towards a Sociology of the Juridical Field," *Hastings Law Journal*, 38 (1987), 814–53; Daphna Hacker, "A Legal Field in Action: The Case of Divorce Arrangements in Israel," *International Journal of Law in Context*, 4(1) (2008), 1–33.

[54] Alan Hunt, *Explorations in Law and Society* (New York: Routledge, 1993).

As to the empirical knowledge component, the growing emphasis within the law and society movement on quantitative data demonstrates that not all law and society scholarship is in stark contrast to the formalist vision of a rational and coherent legal system. In fact, much of this scholarship, currently within the empirical legal studies stream of the movement in particular, is aimed at assisting policy makers and judges to shape the most efficient policies and to reach the most scientific judgments. By providing allegedly accurate descriptions of the social reality and the legal system – that is, by gathering and analyzing statistical data – socio-legal scholars strive to assist the legal system, for example, in choosing the optimum deterring sentencing, channeling resources to the most urgent socio-legal problems, and achieving consistency in judicial outcomes[55]

Other streams of the movement are critical of these ambitions. Austin Sarat and Susan Silbey, in their famous warning against the "pull of the policy audience," argue that the wish to appeal to legislators and judges leads socio-legal researchers: to choose only those research questions that interest the elite; to use only, and uncritically, quantitative methods, because policy makers and judges are usually interested only in statistics, and mistake them for objective truth; and to forsake reflexive awareness of the political dimensions of their research. These choices, they argue, render socio-legal research shallow and lacking in the rich understanding of the law that can be yielded through critical, reflexive, interpretive, and pluralist studies.[56]

Interestingly, many of those who belong to the critical camp also strive to better society through the law, especially by pointing to the social ills created by the law but also by offering legal remedies to the social ills created by other social forces.[57] However, unlike the positivist camp, this scholarship, to which I subscribe, is engaged with the inherent political meaning of any research project and of the law, and is much more aware of the many possible gaps between the promises made by the law; of a linear correlation between the law on the book and social outcomes; and of the actual complex, hard-to-detect, unpredictable, and unintended relations between the law and the society in which it functions.

[55] Theodor Eisenberg, "Empirical Methods and the Law," *Journal of the American Statistical Association*, 95 (2000), 665–9.

[56] Austin Sarat and Susan S. Silbey, "The Pull of the Audience," *Law & Policy*, 10(2–3) (1998), 97–166.

[57] Javier Treviño, "The Sociology of Law in Global Perspective," *The American Sociologist*, 32(5) (2001), 5–9; Daphna Hacker, "Law and Society Jurisprudence," *Cornell Law Review*, 96 (2011) 727–48.

Family law scholars, practitioners, and policy makers, are increasingly interested in law and society theories and findings. They embrace the perception that doctrinal family law cannot be fully understood and developed without the study of "the elaborate and elusive ways that people behave in families" and how "the law interacts with families."[58] However, much of the socio-legal study of families still suffers from what Beck calls "methodological nationalism"[59] – that is, it centers on the legal system of a specific nation state and on the interrelations of family law and families within that state's national borders.[60] As this book strives to demonstrate, in the era of bordered globalization, this narrow national prism fails to reveal the full spectrum of familial socio-legal dynamics. I will end this chapter by sketching the legal universe that affects families in our era and that includes international and subnational legal systems as well as the national ones.

Families Laws in the Era of Bordered Globalization

The theoretical framework of *bordered globalization* presented in the previous chapter acknowledges the current ongoing centrality of national law but, at the same time, assumes the relevance of other legal systems and enquires into their connections with globalization as well as with national and other kinds of borders. The intense border-crossing of humans, capital, and ideas, as well as the ongoing persistence of borders, detailed in Chapter 1, takes place in a legal universe composed of an amalgam of international, national, and subnational laws and tribunals.[61] As illustrated in Figure 2.2, all these kinds of legal systems affect families.

National Law: The most obvious link between families and law, and for most families the most central of all, is the one that exists between family members and the national law of their home country, also captured by the legal term *domicile* mentioned in the Introduction and further discussed in Chapter 3. The principle of national sovereignty is that each nation state has exclusive jurisdiction over the people within its national borders. This internationally accepted principle is based on the right and freedom of

---

[58] Margaret F. Brining, Carl E. Schneider, & Lee E. Teitelbaum (Eds.), *Family Law in Action: A Reader* (Cincinnati, OH: Anderson Publishing, 1999), at xxi.

[59] Ulrich Beck, "Unpacking Cosmopolitanism for the Social Sciences: A Research Agenda," *The British Journal of Sociology*, 57(1) (2006), 1–23.

[60] Beck & Beck-Gernsheim, *Distant Love*, at 175.

[61] Paul Schiff Berman, *Global Legal Pluralism: A Jurisprudence of Law Beyond Borders* (New York: Cambridge University Press, 2012), at 6–8.

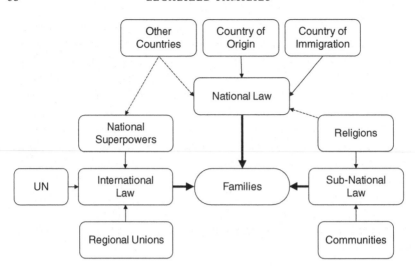

Figure 2.2 The Legal Universe Surrounding Families
Legend: bold arrows = exerts an effect; regular arrows = sources; dotted
lines = congruence

citizens of each nation to shape the laws that govern them.[62] Hence, the
laws of the country in which the family members live are the most relevant to their familial behavioral guidance, conflict resolution, and resource
distribution – the three functions of the law explained earlier in this chapter.

However, the principle of sovereignty is challenged by the global movement of people, capital, and ideas; and, indeed, in many cases, families in
the era of bordered globalization are affected by more than one national
legal system. As presented in the central section of Figure 2.2, the same
family can be affected by the national law of its country of origin or the
country to which its members emigrated, and by laws of other countries
in which the family bought property, hired a surrogate mother, or undertook other kinds of cross-border familial activities. As already mentioned,
it is important to note that these national laws are not only classical family
laws relating to marriage, divorce, or child custody and support but also
laws from other legal branches, including labor law, welfare law, immigration law, and criminal law. For example, as discussed in Chapter 5, family
members' ability to live together, or their living-apart forced reality, are

governed by the labor, immigration, family, and citizenship laws of destination countries with job opportunities.

The governance of the same family by different national legal systems can lead to conflict of laws, for example when a couple marries while studying abroad, in a ceremony recognized in the host country but not recognized by their home country, to which they return after graduation. Likewise, conflict of laws can occur when a parent dies, leaving a will that disinherits one of his children, while part of his property is in country A, which honors total freedom of testation, and another part is in country B, which has a legal system with reserved shares for all of the children of the deceased. Chapter 3 in particular, but also other chapters, will relate to different instances of conflict of laws arising in the familial context, and the legal mechanisms developed within national law and private international law to address them, such as the concept of *comity* – the recognition by one national legal system of the validity and effect of another national legal system (its laws, court decisions, and executive actions).

International Law: The left-hand side of Figure 2.2 captures the different sources that affect families in the legal international sphere. One of the most important manifestations of globalization is the development of this sphere, a process political scientist Jeremy Elkins calls "legal globalization."[63] The three main sources that build this sphere are: the UN, and in particular the international human rights law it develops;[64] regional unions (for example the EU) and their law and tribunals;[65] and national superpowers, such as the United States, which use transnational law to impact other nations.[66] Although most of the literature on international law and its sources centers on its relevance to public matters, such as commerce, armed conflicts, global pollution, and cyberspace,[67] this book demonstrates its relevance to families.[68]

---

[63] Jeremy Elkins, "Beyond 'Beyond the State': Rethinking Law and Globalization" in Austin Sarat, Lawrence Douglas, & Martha Merrill Umphrey (Eds.), *Law without Nations* (CA: Stanford University Press, 2011), pp. 22–65, at 24.

[64] Thomas Hylland Erikson, *Globalization: The Key Concepts* (Oxford: Berg, 2007), at 64.

[65] David Hodson, *The International Family Law Practice*, 2nd edn. (Bristol: Family Law, 2012).

[66] Daphna Hacker, "Strategic Compliance in the Shadow of Transnational Anti-Trafficking Law," *Harvard Human Rights Journal*, 28(1) (2015), 11–64.

[67] For example, Volkmar Gesneer & Ali Cem Budak (Eds.), *Emerging Legal Certainty: Empirical Studies on the Globalization of Law* (Aldershot: Darmouth, 1998); Paul Schiff Berman, *The Globalization of International Law* (Aldershot: Ashgate, 2005); Günther Handell, Joachim Zekoll, & Peer Zumbansen, *Beyond Territoriality: Transnational Legal Authority in an Age of Globalization* (Leiden: Martinus Nijhoff Publishers, 2012).

[68] See also Barbara Stark, "When Globalization Hits Home: International Family Law Comes of Age," *Vanderbilt Journal of Transnational Law*, 39(5) (2006), 1551–604.

For example, as demonstrated in Chapter 7, spousal and parental violence is governed not only by the national law of the family's domicile, but also by the "shared grammar" produced by international human rights law,[69] including the General Recommendation No. 19 on behalf of the UN Convention on the Elimination of All Forms of Discrimination against Women (CEDAW), and the UN Convention on the Rights of the Child (CRC), which set normative prohibitions on violence against women and children, including within their families. This anti-domestic violence international human rights legal framework is further strengthened by regional conventions, including, for example, the Council of Europe Convention on Preventing and Combating Violence against Women and Domestic Violence, and the African Charter on the Rights and Welfare of the Child. Furthermore, asylum status granted by several countries to victims of domestic abuse adds a transnational legal dimension to familial relations, because it provides an option for family members to escape their domestic abuser by moving to another country. Likewise, as demonstrated in Chapter 7, antitrafficking norms, produced both by the UN and by the United States, affect the discourse on domestic abuse, in particular in relation to mail-order brides and international child adoption. Finally, as discussed in Chapters 5, 6, and 8, the failures in producing international legal agreement over the familial rights of labor immigrants – let alone the outright refusal to do so – are examples not only of international legal lacunae but also of the ongoing resistance power of national legal systems in cases in which legal globalization does not serve their interests.

Subnational law: The right-hand side of Figure 2.2 highlights the possible impact of subnational legal systems on families in the era of bordered globalization. As discussed in the previous part of this chapter, the control over the family is perceived by many as crucial for the survival of the collective. The sense of urgency over controlling the family is most acute within native and immigration communities that live as cultural minorities within the nation state. Hence, families can find themselves affected not only by national and international laws but also by the religious and tribal laws of their subnational community. As mentioned here, and as elaborated-on in Chapter 3, the task of establishing agreed-upon familial social scripts that can help guide familial expectations, everyday practices, and breakdowns, therefore, becomes extremely difficult because conflict of laws arises not only between different national legal systems but also between national and subnational legal systems. This can be seen,

---

[69] Erikson, *Globalization*, at 64.

for example, in cases in which the religion of a couple allows polygamy or prohibits divorce, while the national law that governs the couple prohibits the former and permits the latter.

Returning to the typology of the relations between borders and globalization presented in the previous chapter, it is important to note that there is no complete overlap between international law and globalization, or between national and subnational laws and borders, and that antagonism is not the only kind of relationship that exists between the three bodies of law (international, national, and subnational). For example, as will be discussed in Chapter 3, minority groups use the language of international law, of the right for self-determination, to claim legal autonomy over family matters. Likewise, nation states resist these claims, among other reasons, in the name of the internationally acknowledged right to gender equality, which they argue is harmed by patriarchal religious family laws. Likewise, as explored in Chapter 6, international and transnational legislation, for example against child labor, is at times accused by national actors as enhancing the borders between the alleged enlightened North and the primitive South, with its insensitivity to familial needs, in a world of deep inequalities and global exploitation. Moreover, the existence of nation states that adopt religious family law[70] – as expressed in the dotted line on the right-hand side of Figure 2.2 – and global processes of legal isomorphism and legal transplantations,[71] in which a national legal system adopts legal models from other nation states and from international law, including models affecting families[72] – captured by the dotted line and arrows on the left half of Figure 2.2 – highlights the possible dynamic blurring of the borders between international, national, and subnational legal systems.

Indeed, the chapters to follow will explore the interactions between international, national, and subnational laws, which affect families as part of the complex interrelations between globalization and borders. This exploration will be conducted in light of the conclusion that can be drawn from the discussion in this chapter, that we should no longer study and

[70] See also Hadas Tagari, "Personal Family Law Systems: A Comparative and International Human Rights Analysis," *International Journal of Law in Context*, 8(2) (2012), 231–52.

[71] For example, Yves Dezalay & Bryant G. Garth (Eds.), *Global Prescriptions: The Production, Exportation, and Importation of a New Legal Orthodoxy* (Ann Arbor: University of Michigan Press, 2002).

[72] An example of an isomorphic legal process related to families is the abolishment of the "tender years" presumption in child custody law in all Western countries, during a very short period toward the end of the twentieth century. See Carol Smart & Selma Sevenhuijsen (Eds.), *Child Custody and the Politics of Gender* (London: Routledge, 1989).

practice *family law* but rather *families laws*, as there is no –nor should there be – one single kind of socially and legally recognized family but rather many kinds of families, whose expectations, practices, and crises are currently governed by an amalgam of international private and public laws, religious and tribal laws, and different branches of national law created in different countries.

For the scholars among us who are interested in families, this conclusion calls for interdisciplinary and international academic cooperation for the study of families in this exciting era. For the practitioners among us, what might seem at first glance to be an overwhelming realization (as no one lawyer can master all these kinds of laws) can and should lead to professional cooperation, such as in the form of ad-hoc teams of lawyers from different countries, and with expertise in different branches of law, working together to provide families with the best legal advice and representation they need in the era of bordered globalization.

Now, after setting the theoretical framework of *bordered globalization* in the previous chapter, and connecting it, generally, to *families laws*, in this chapter, we are ready to explore in depth specific issues related to the complex and fascinating interrelations between globalization, borders, families, and the law.

3

Coordinating Familial Expectations

Conflicting Familial Social Scripts

More than two decades ago, Ulrich Beck and Elisabeth Beck-Gernsheim argued that we live in a liminal era, in which the family is an open space – a space of no longer, but not yet. As old familial social categories have collapsed, in the face of individualism, secularism, and gender emancipation, and new agreed-upon categories have yet to emerge, Beck and Beck-Gernsheim recognized a new and chaotic phase in the history of the social institution of family:

> [I]t is no longer possible to pronounce in some binding way what family, marriage, parenthood, sexuality or love mean, what they should or could be; rather, these vary in substance, exceptions, norms and morality from individual to individual and from relationship to relationship. The answers to the questions above must be worked out, negotiated, arranged, and justified in all the details of how, what, why or why not, even if this might unleash the conflicts and devils that lie slumbering among the details and were assumed to be tamed.[1]

In their more recent work, these two prominent German sociologists acknowledged the Eurocentrism embedded in this universalist thesis.[2] Individualism, secularism, and gender equality are Western notions.[3]

---

[1] Ulrich Beck & Elisabeth Beck-Gernsheim, *The Normal Chaos of Love* (Cambridge: Polity Press, 1995), at 5.

[2] Ulrich Beck & Elisabeth Beck-Gernsheim, *Distant Love* (Cambridge: Polity Press, 2014), at 3.

[3] I would argue that even Beck and Beck-Gernsheim's repeated emphasis on *love* as the core and the *raison d'être* of families (evident in the titles of their two books devoted to the topic, see supra notes 1 & 2) should be contested as Eurocentric ideology. Although empirical evidence suggests that "there is a trend away from 'traditional' notions of family that emphasize the role of social obligation in the reproduction of kinship systems and toward globalizing models of family that are increasingly based on 'love' that is chosen, deeply felt, 'authentic', and profoundly personal" (see Padilla as mentioned in Lynn Jamieson, "Intimacy as a Concept: Explaining Social Change in the Context of Globalisation or Another Form of Ethnocentricism?," *Sociological Research Online*, 16(4) (2011), available at: https://core .ac.uk/display/6496696), different conceptions of spousal and parental love, and of their

Although these contribute to the declining rate of marriage and childbirth and to the relatively high rate of divorce and of women's paid employment in Western countries,[4] they are much slower to impact families in other parts of the world.[5] Moreover, in the Global South, the institution of family is severely destabilized by very different factors, including postcolonialism, war, poverty, and disease. For example, in poor post-apartheid South Africa, devastated by HIV, only 35 percent of children live with both their parents.[6] Unfortunately, the sociology of the family, with its Eurocentric bias, has done little to understand current familiality in this and other African countries in which many children live only with their mother, or are sent away to be fostered by a distant relative or in a non-familial household.[7] However, and as will be explored in Chapter 6, it is safe to generalize that the Global South is, by and large, closer to the collectivist edge of the collectivist–individualist familial axis, discussed in Chapter 2, than the Global North.

The values of individualism, secularism, and gender equality, and their embodiment in *families laws*, could create a backlash if individuals or communities holding collectivist–dogmatic familial perceptions and coming from legal systems that support such perceptions were to view them as a threat to their familial values, and as they try to preserve their community's borders.[8] This familial socio-legal clash is more likely to occur in our era of intense cross-border movement of people and ideas. Indeed, acknowledging our era as the era of bordered globalization, we become aware that no one lives in a familial normative vacuum in which

relevance to familial biographies, might constitute yet another hotbed of familial misunderstandings and clashes in our era.

[4] Beck & Beck-Gernsheim, *The Normal Chaos of Love*; Stanford N. Katz, John Eekelaar, & Mavis Maclean (Eds.), *Cross Currents: Family Law and Policy in the United States and England* (Oxford University Press, 2000).

[5] For international statistics on birth, marriage, and divorce rates, see United Nations, *Demographic Yearbook 2013* (2014), Tables 9, 23, and 25, available at: http://unstats.un.org/unsd/demographic/products/dyb/dybsets/2013.pdf; For data on women's employment worldwide, see International Labour Office, *Global Employment Trends for Women 2012* (2012), available at: www.ilo.org/wcmsp5/groups/public/@dgreports/@dcomm/@publ/documents/publication/wcms_171571.pdf.

[6] Debbie Budlender & Francie Lund, "South Africa: A Legacy of Family Disruption," *Development and Change*, 42(4) (2011), 925–46.

[7] Radhamany Sooryamoorthy, "Introduction to the Special Issue," *Journal of Comparative Family Studies*, 46(1) (2015), 1–8, at 1.

[8] Khosro Refaie Shirpak, Eleanor Maticka-Tyndale, & Maryam Chinichian, "Iranian Immigrants' Perceptions of Sexuality in Canada: A Symbolic Interactionist Approach," *The Canadian Journal of Human Sexuality*, 16(3–4) (2007), 113–28.

negotiations over familial biographies take place free of social or legal scripts, but rather that we are all exposed to conflicting socio-legal scripts about family, including in relation to marriage, divorce, motherhood, and fatherhood, and enjoy different degrees of freedom to maneuver our familial biographies in their shadow.

The existence of conflicting socio-legal familial scripts and the growing intensity of cross-border movement of people and ideas lead to the growing significance of two kinds of challenges in coordinating familial expectations: that of coordinating expectations among family members and that of coordinating exceptions between family members and the state. This chapter deals with both kinds of challenges and explores the role of the law in shaping and addressing them.

One example of such challenges relates to the minimum age and spousal consent in marriage. Gendered arranged and forced marriage[9] at an early age is extremely common in South Asia and sub-Saharan Africa, with half of girls in the former and one third in the latter being married before their eighteenth birthday.[10] With globalization, we witness early-age arranged and forced marriage also practiced in the Global North among some families that emigrated from these and other regions. This practice is used as a means to preserve ethno-familial and religious identity, as well as to prevent female premarital sex, and to ensure the patriarchal enforcement of women's roles as wives and mothers in what is perceived by their families as a predominant culture that is promiscuous, unduly liberal, and overly feminist.[11]

---

[9] Andrea Büchler distinguishes between: "forced marriage," which "occurs when the marriage takes place against the will of at least one of the spouses, when their refusal is ignored or when they do not dare to resist because the psychological, social and emotional pressure exerted by the family is too great, or even because physical coercion was applied or threatened"; and "arranged marriage," which "may often have been initiated or intermediated by relatives, [but] the future spouses have consented to it." See Andrea Büchler, *Islamic Law in Europe? Legal Pluralism and Its Limits in European Family Laws* (Surrey: Ashgate, 2011), at 42. In my culturally embedded view, any marriage before the age of 18, initiated by adult family members, is forced, because a minor, dependent on her parents, cannot give voluntary informed consent to be married. However, even some Western countries allow minor marriage. In Australia, for example, the minimum age of marriage is 18, but a person between 16 and 18 may be allowed to marry by a judge or magistrate in "exceptional and unusual" circumstances – See Marriage Act 1961, s. 12(2)(b).

[10] "Child Marriages: 39,000 Every Day," UNICEF Website (March 7, 2013), www.unicef.org/media/media_68114.html.

[11] Naima Bendriss, "Report on the Practice of Forced Marriage in Canada: Interviews with Frontline Workers" (2008), available at: www.justice.gc.ca/eng/rp-pr/cj-jp/fv-vf/fm-mf/fm_eng.pdf.

The practice of forced marriage has been recognized by the UN as domestic abuse and a gross violation of human rights,[12] and the British government, for example, has declared it must be fought by civil, criminal, and immigration law.[13] Critics of such a legal stand argue that educational, rather than legal, measures should be adopted, because the latter will cause the phenomenon to go underground (making it harder to assist its victims), will target minority groups for police harassment, and will be used by immigration authorities to prevent family reunification of immigrants.[14]

The phenomenon of forced marriage is not only an example of the possible difficulties in coordinating familial expectations between immigrating families and hosting governments in the face of conflicting Western and non-Western familial notions. The challenges associated with coordinating familial expectations over forced marriage are also an example of internal family "religious wars," as Beck and Beck-Gernsheim call them,[15] which affect the everyday lives of families in which the young generation adopts Western values and rebels against their immigrant parents' generation, or in which each spouse comes from a different culture. Indeed, in its first four years of operation, the UK special unit dedicated to enforcing antiforced marriage legislation, established in 2009, was approached by more than 7,000 individuals and organizations seeking advice or support.[16] In most cases the victim of the planned or performed forced marriage is a female under 21.[17] At least in some of these cases, it is the girl or woman herself who tries to find a way to oppose the marriage her parents have coerced her into, exposing the internal familial war over the meaning of marriage, sex, gender roles, and parental authority.

I would go even further and argue that in the era of bordered globalization all families are exposed, in varying degrees, to the potential

---

[12] See UN Resolution A/HRC/24/L.34/Rev.1 of September 23, 2013 ("Strengthening efforts to prevent and eliminate child, early and forced marriage: Challenges, achievements, best practices and implementation gaps"), available at: http://girlsnotbrides.theideabureau .netdna-cdn.com/wp-content/uploads/2013/10/HRC-resolution-on-child-early-and-forced-marriage-ENG.pdf.

[13] See the Anti-social Behaviour, Crime and Policing Bill of 2014; Louise McCallum, "Chapter 18: Forced Marriage" in David Hodson (Ed.), *The International Family Law Practice*, 2nd edn. (Bristol: Family Law, 2012), pp. 517–28.

[14] Bendriss, "Report on the Practice of Forced Marriage in Canada."

[15] Beck & Beck-Gernsheim, *Distant Love*, at 3.

[16] Forced Marriage Unit, *Statistics January to December 2013* (2014), available at: www.gov .uk/government/uploads/system/uploads/attachment_data/file/291855/FMU_2013_sta-tistics.pdf.

[17] Ibid.

challenges of internal coordination (among family members) and external coordination (between family members and the state), created by the lack of one globally agreed-upon familial ideology. In our era, there are familial ideological differences even between individuals born in the same country, and between states that allegedly belong to the same Western or non-Western bloc. Moreover, widespread cross-border communication results in the exposure of almost everybody to a wide variety of familial perceptions, practices, and policies, held and implemented by other people and promoted by other states and communities, near and far. Finally, the complex interplay created by bordered globalization between immigration, gender, race, citizenship, and economic status also shapes one's familial perceptions and aspirations, and one's relative power to insist on them. The result is a bricolage of familial opportunities and barriers that can change over the course of one's life and that must be negotiated among family members and with legislators and judges who might hold different views over familiality.

The story of Dafna, Itamar, Kai, and Tal, as presented in a documentary film entitled "Family Matters",[18] provides an excellent example of my argument that the interplay between globalization and borders creates internal and external coordination challenges among family members and between them and the state, even if they – at least allegedly – share the same Western familial ideology and live in the same developed country. I will now summarize their story here.

Dafna, an Israeli, is single and wants to become a mother. Itamar, also an Israeli, has lived in Israel with his male partner Kai, a German, for several years. Through an NGO that assists single women and gay men to bring children into the world, Dafna meets Itamar and Kai, and the three of them decide to have a child together, though it is unclear if they all see eye-to-eye regarding their future familial ties and if these ties were well defined in the legal contract signed by Dafna and Itamar. Dafna is inseminated with Itamar's sperm and gets pregnant. At first, it seems as if the threesome is on its way to becoming a happy and harmonious alternative family. Alas, as the pregnancy progresses, conflicting expectations are exposed. Dafna is heterosexual and Kai feels threatened by her intentions toward Itamar. In an act of reassurance to affirm their spousal relations, Kai and Itamar fly to Germany (where gay couples are allowed to get married) and tie the knot. When they return to Israel from their honeymoon, tensions increase as Dafna refuses to allow Kai to be present at the baby's

---

[18] *Family Matters*, dir. David Noy, Israel, Cinemax Productions, 2004.

birth. Things get worse after the birth of Tal. The first major clash arises when Dafna and Itamar circumcise Tal, despite Kai's repulsion at what he perceives as a barbaric act. The conflict deepens when Dafna refuses to allow the baby to sleep overnight at Itamar and Kai's apartment, arguing that long detachments from her will harm Tal. At this point, Itamar threatens Dafna with a lawsuit, and they turn to a legal mediator to try to solve their disagreement regarding the visitation schedule, out of court.

It is very clear from the film that Dafna, Itamar, and Kai are struggling to create, do and display their family, with no clear social scripts to guide them or assist them in negotiating their familial expectations. Is Kai Tal's father, and, if not, then what is he to him? Do Dafna and Itamar have a spousal, albeit platonic, relationship? Do all four belong to the same family? And what should their everyday family life look like? The lack of globally agreed upon familial scripts leaves the members of this family, and of many other families, with no clear, consensual role definition or behavioral guidelines. It leads to everyday experiences of gaps between national or communal familial scripts, and personal dynamics that do not fit them or are torn between them. At the same time that this lack of clear and binding familial scripts leaves much room for each family to shape its own practices,[19] it also makes doing and displaying family in the era of bordered globalization a complicated task.

Sociologist Janet Finch relies on David Morag's influential thesis that contemporary families are defined more by "doing" family – that is, "performing sets of activities which take on a particular meaning, associated with family" – than by "being" a family – that is, belonging to a specific social structure recognized as "a family."[20] Finch underlines the importance of what she calls "displaying family," and argues that it is crucial that people are able to convey the meaning of their actions so they may be understood by relevant others as constituting "family."[21] As the story of Dafna, Itamar, and Kai demonstrates, the importance of, and the challenges associated with, displaying family grow in correlation to the intensity of the family's exposure to bordered globalization, which makes it harder to coordinate familiality. Family members who come from different countries and religions, and hold different familial perceptions, find it hard to coordinate their familial expectations, for example, in relation to circumcision

---

[19] David H. J. Morgan, *Family Connections: An Introduction to Family Studies* (Cambridge: Polity Press, 1996); David H. J. Morgan, *Rethinking Family Practices* (Basingstoke: Palgrave, 2011).

[20] Janet Finch, "Displaying Families," *Sociology*, 41(1) (2007), 65–81, at 66.

[21] Ibid.

(internal challenges). At the same time, their ability to forum shop from more than one jurisdiction – introducing, for example, the foreign notion that two men can marry into the country in which they live – creates a coordination challenge between family members and the state (external challenges).

Indeed, the story of Dafna, Itamar, Kai, and Tal also demonstrates that although families affected by bordered globalization "find themselves forced to invent their own procedures and practices through a process of *reflexive negotiation*,"[22] they do so in the shadow of the law:[23] Are Itamar and Kai married under Israeli law? And where should they divorce, if things become unbearable between them? Must Itamar pay Dafna for Tal's financial support as his genetic father? Must Kai, as the genetic father's partner? Should the court have issued a prevention order against Tal's circumcision, if Kai had asked for it? Should the court oblige Dafna to let Tal spend nights at Itamar and Kai's home? And with whom should Tal live if Itamar and Kai decide to relocate to Germany?

As detailed in Chapter 2, the law provides a baseline of familial definitions, rights, and obligations, guiding family members in their familial expectations and negotiations and guiding judges in settling familial disputes. But can the law perform these socializing and stabilizing functions when it is part of bordered globalization itself? Can the law assist members of families affected by bordered globalization in coordinating their expectations among themselves, and between them and the state in which they live, or does it only add to the internal and external familial confusion and conflicts? This chapter will address these questions.

I could have chosen a variety of issues to demonstrate and discuss the impact of bordered globalization on current challenges to legally coordinate internal and external familial expectations. I have chosen to focus here on one of the most dramatic and difficult challenges, looking at the relevance of religious family law and courts to Western countries, by focusing on Islamic and Jewish law. The parallel existence of state secular family law and subnational parochial religious family law, with very different gendered perceptions and rules, causes internal and external tensions, as demonstrated by the example of forced marriage mentioned earlier. This formal and informal legal pluralism also

---

[22] Beck & Beck-Gernsheim, *Distant Love*, at 171.
[23] Robert H. Mnookin & Lewis Kornhauser, "Bargaining in the Shadow of the Law: The Case of Divorce," *Yale Law Journal*, 88(5) (1979), 950–96. Although Mnookin and Kornhauser analyze the shadow of the law in divorce, this shadow is also very relevant to familial negotiations in other contexts, as explained in Chapter 2.

highlights the difficulties of law in signaling coherent, consistent, and shared familial normative guidelines. Indeed, the difference in gender perceptions within secular and religious family law is one of the major barriers to the creation of a consensual global family legal order and hence a paradigmatic example of the challenges in coordinating familial expectations in our era.

In the face of the difficulties of coordinating external and internal familial expectations *ex post*, which I will explore next, the last part of the chapter examines prenuptial agreements as a means of attempting to coordinate these expectations *ex ante*. This legal mechanism is relevant not only to circumstances that include a religious family-law element, but also to much wider circumstances embracing Western–individualist–pluralistic family members, such as the gay couple and heterosexual woman who decide to bring a child into the world, presented earlier. This last part of this chapter exposes the limitations of the prenup option due to the contradicting legal perceptions of prenups' enforceability. More importantly, I will argue that many familial aspects should not be allowed to be privately regulated by prenups, even if a global agreement over their enforceability could be reached. In my view, the difficulties of genuinely and rationally agreeing on the terms of a family in the making, and the dangers for children and their primary caregivers in trying to do so, especially in the era of bordered globalization, should limit the liberty of spouses to contract their relations *ex ante*. Taken together, the next two parts of the chapter demonstrate the importance of coordinating familial expectations in the face of the lack of globally agreed on social and legal familial scripts, and the pragmatic difficulties and normative challenges in trying to achieve exactly that – coordinating familial expectations in a legally binding, just, and effective way – in the era of bordered globalization.

Coordinating Religious and Secular Family Laws

As Mary Ann Glendon's seminal study reveals, religion has played a major role within Western family law since the end of the first millennium, almost until the end of the second. During the tenth to twelfth centuries, the Church gained regulative control over marriage and divorce, which had been perceived until then as unregulated private acts. Church courts applying canon law were established, insisting on marriage as a life-long binding public act, entered into freely by a man and a woman, which could nevertheless come to an end through annulment based on limited grounds such as impotence or insanity.[24] Even after the Church lost its jurisdiction over marriage and divorce in Europe, during the six-teenth to eighteenth centuries, ecclesiastic norms continued to play a significant role, as secular legislators adopted the ready-made canon law rather than developing original family law.[25] In particular, the notion that the husband is the head of the family, the importance of fault in ending a marriage, and the ban on same-sex relations guided civil legislators and courts well into the twentieth century,[26] with the latter still echoing in many Western jurisdictions' ban on same-sex marriage.[27]

However, during the last century of the second millennium, and espe-cially since the 1970s, a secular revolution swept Western family law, introducing new concepts such as autonomy, gender equality, and chil-dren's rights – hence, formally divorcing family law from religious and traditional concepts of the family. Although family law, and related crimi-nal law and reproduction law, in different Western countries are far from being homogeneous, general shared trends based on secular notions of individualism and equality can be observed. These include: raising the legal marital age; recognizing married women's equal rights to property ownership and an equal share in the marital property; abolishing restric-tions around interracial marriages; attaching some legal implications to nonmarital unions; abolishing laws relating to bastardy and recognizing children's rights vis-à-vis their parents regardless of the parents' mari-tal status; introducing the concepts of no-fault and clean-break divorce; relaxing antiabortion and anticontraception laws; abolishing maternal child custody preferences and sole paternal support obligations; and criminalizing spousal and parental violence.[28]

---

[24] Mary Ann Glendon, *The Transformation of Family Law* (University of Chicago Press, 1989), at 23–30.

[25] Ibid., at 31.

[26] Ibid.; Mala Htun & Laurel S. Weldon, "State Power, Religion, and Women's Rights: A Comparative Analysis of Family Law," *Indiana Journal of Global Legal Studies*, 18(1) (2011), 145–65, at 149. For an interesting analysis of the development of family law in the US, see Janet Halley, "What Is Family Law?: A Genealogy Part I," *Yale Journal of Law & the Humanities*, 23(1) (2011), 1–109; Janet Halley, "What Is Family Law?: A Genealogy Part II," *Yale Journal of Law & the Humanities*, 23(2) (2011), 189–293.

[27] Mark Strasser, "Family, Same-Sex Unions and the Law" in John Eekelaar & Rob George (Eds.), *Routledge Handbook of Family Law and Policy* (Abingdon: Routledge Handbooks, 2014), pp. 45–60.

[28] Glendon, *The Transformation of Family Law*; Michael Grossberg, "How to Give the Present a Past? Family Law in the United States 1950–2000" in Stanford N. Katz, John Eekelaar, & Mavis Maclean (Eds.), *Cross Currents, Family Law and Policy in the US and England* (Oxford University Press, 2000), pp. 3–29; John Dewer & Stephen Parker, "English Family Law since World War II: From Status to Chaos" in Stanford N. Katz, John Eekelaar, & Mavis

Moreover, the carriers of family law – its institutions and practitioners – have transformed, with women allowed entry to the legal field as lawyers and judges,[29] and many jurisdictions introducing specialized family courts offering therapeutic and mediation services.[30] This latter structural shift can be understood as part of the move away from the emphasis on marriage and divorce as rigid statuses that should be regulated in a unified and public manner, toward regulative micromanagement of specific and private familial relations in crisis.[31] Although one should not assume that gendered norms and discrimination are gone from judicial nominations, the legal profession, specific rulings, and mediation processes in Europe and North America, these are perceived by the current ethos of legal systems in Western countries as unfortunate wrongs that should be corrected in an overall attempt to depart from patriarchy.

In other parts of the world, however, family law is still deliberately dominated by patriarchal traditional norms and religious laws. Interestingly, and somewhat paradoxically, in many countries this is the legacy of colonial ruling, either because the colonizer granted legal autonomy to different religious groups over family matters to ease resistance,[32] or because decolonization included national elites reinventing indigenous familial

---

Maclean (Eds.), *Cross Currents, Family Law and Policy in the US and England* (Oxford University Press, 2000), pp. 123–40; Shahar Lifshitz, "The Liberal Transformation of Spousal Law: Past, Present, and Future," *Theoretical Inquiries in Law*, 13(1) (2012), 15–75.

[29] Susan Ehrlich Martin and Nancy C. Jurik, *Doing Justice, Doing Gender: Women in Legal and Criminal Justice Occupations*, 2nd edn. (Thousand Oaks, CA: Sage Publications, 2007), Ch. 5; Sharyn Roach Anleu, "Women in the Legal Profession: Theory and Research," *Law Institutional Journal*, 66 (1992), 193–208.

[30] Jessica Pearson, "A Forum for Every Fuss: The Growth of Court Services and ADR Treatment for Family Law Cases in the United States" in Stanford N. Katz, John Eekelaar, & Mavis Maclean (Eds.), *Cross Currents, Family Law and Policy in the US and England* (Oxford University Press, 2000), pp. 513–31; Mavis Maclean and John Eekelaar, "Institutional Mechanisms: Courts, Lawyers and Others" in John Eekelaar, & Rob George (Eds.), *Routledge Handbook of Family Law and Policy* (Abingdon: Routledge Handbooks, 2014), pp. 372–80.

[31] I refer here to Michel Foucault's 'micro-power' thesis, but accept Alan Hunt and Gary Wickham's argument that Foucault was wrong in assuming that in modernity the law withdrew into the background while other disciplines employing micropowers took over governmentality. I share their view that the law has transformed and takes part in the micro-regulation of our most intimate and personal lives. See Alan Hunt & Gary Wickham, *Foucault and Law: Towards a Sociology of Law as Governance* (London: Pluto Press, 1994).

[32] Hadas Tagari, "Personal Family Law Systems: A Comparative and International Human Rights Analysis," *International Journal of Law in Context*, 8(2) (2012), 231–52, at 231.

traditions and using religious family law as a counter-Western nation-building block.[33] In most Middle Eastern and North African countries, for example, family matters are governed by the family law of the religion of the individuals involved, as it was in the days of the Ottoman, British, and French colonizers.

However, while in colonial times the carriers of family religious law were religious tribunals run by each religious group, after national independence different models have emerged combining state law with religious law. For example, in many Arab countries, Islamic family law was codified to become the state's family law, carried by civil courts, but in a few other countries, such as Lebanon and Israel, each religious group maintained sole or parallel jurisdiction over its family matters through state-recognized religious tribunals. These countries also differ in the changes introduced to the religion-based family law over the years, with some, such as Morocco, introducing significant gender-equalizing reforms – including those limiting the option of polygamy, raising the age of marriage, and recognizing women's equal right to inherit, whereas others refrain from making any such changes.[34]

Indeed, in their family law survey of seventy-one countries, published in 2011, political scientists Mala Htun and Laurel Weldon found a direct correlation between the secularization of family law and women's legal equality. Some thirty-three of the countries surveyed had eliminated formal gender inequality from their family law. All these countries are European or North and South American, with the exception of Botswana. At the other end of the spectrum we find Algeria, Bangladesh, Egypt, Iran, Jordan, Malaysia, Pakistan, and Saudi Arabia, all implementing strict versions of Islamic family law. In many of these jurisdictions, in general: girls and boys can be married at a very early age; wives are required to obey their husbands; a man can marry up to four wives, whereas polyandry is prohibited; a husband can divorce his no-fault wife via verbal repudiation (*ṭalāq*), whereas a wife must prove her case in a judicial process that will determine the husband's fault, or she must relinquish some or all of her economic rights in exchange for a divorce (*khulʿ*); the default assumption in many Muslim-majority states is that the father is the sole guardian of the children and the only parent obliged to support them, and he will often be granted physical

[33] Htun & Weldon, "State Power, Religion, and Women's Rights," at 150.
[34] Tagari, "Personal Family Law Systems"; Htun & Weldon, "State Power, Religion, and Women's Rights."

custody regardless of the children's best interests;[35] a child born out of wedlock has no legal claims on his or her father; there is no communal property regime stemming from marriage; and, unless stipulated otherwise in a will, women may inherit only half of what a male would in the same familial *parentela* (the same order of proximity to the deceased).[36] Moreover, in some of the countries that subordinate family law to religious law, only men can be judges, or represent the parties, or be nominated as mediators[37] – and hence be the carriers of the law, as I call these positions. Finally, in several legal systems, the procedures in tribunals deciding family matters based on religious law are governed by religious evidence law, which accords less weight to women's testimony than to men's on particular topics.[38]

What Htun and Weldon's survey fails to capture is the harm caused to women and children by allegedly gender-neutral family law adopted in the Global North. Given that, even in Western countries, in most heterosexual families the mother is the primary caregiver and the father is the primary breadwinner,[39] the recent legal revolutions that allowed no-fault divorce and eroded maternal custody preferences, male alimony obligations, and paternal sole child support obligations

---

[35] The four different Islamic schools of law have different physical custody rules, granting different weight to the sex, age, and will of the children. However, in three of the schools the mother is the preferred custodian of boys only up to the age of seven or puberty, and all agree that if the mother remarries, the children should be transferred to their father's custody. See Robin Fretwell Wilson, "The Perils of Privatized Marriage" in Joel A. Nichols (Ed.), *Marriage and Divorce in a Multicultural Context: Multi-Tiered Marriage and the Boundaries of Civil Law and Religion* (New York: Cambridge University Press, 2012), pp. 253–83, at 263; Aayesha Rafiq, "Child Custody in Classical Islamic Law and Laws of Contemporary Muslim World (An Analysis)," *International Journal of Humanities and Social Science*, 4(5) (2014), 267–77.

[36] Htun & Weldon, "State Power, Religion, and Women's Rights," at 159. For a detailed description of Islamic law and its distinctively different schools, see Wael B. Hallaq, *An Introduction to Islamic Law* (New York: Cambridge University Press, 2014).

[37] Tagari, "Personal Family Law Systems," at 240.

[38] Ibid., at 241. I strongly recommend two films that offer a glimpse of the patriarchal practices of religion-based state courts dealing with family matters: the documentary "Divorce Iranian Style" (1998), directed by Kim Longinotto and Ziba Mir-Hosseini (showing real court hearings in a family court in Tehran); and "Gett: The Trial of Viviane Amsalem" (2014), directed by Ronit Elkabetz and Shlomi Elkabetz (showing a fictional case heard by an Israeli rabbinical court).

[39] Joan C. Williams, *Reshaping the Work–Family Debate: Why Men and Class Matter* (Cambridge, MA: Harvard University Press, 2010); Janet C. Gornick & Marcia K. Meyers (Eds.), *Gender Equality: Transforming Family Divisions of Labor* (New York: Verso Press, 2009).

have led to relative poverty for women and children as a result of divorce.[40] Leonore Weitzman's famous study on the unintended economic consequences of what she called the "divorce revolution" in the United States revealed the gendered price that was paid for these Western divorce legal reforms in the mid-1980s. Weitzman found a decrease of 73 percent in women's standard of living following divorce, and an increase of 43 percent in men's.[41] Although the study's methodology was severely criticized, even the critics agree that a gender gap of 20 to 50 percent in standards of living is created in the United States[42] and other Western countries[43] postdivorce. In that sense, it can be argued that religious law – with institutions such as the dower (*Mahr*[44] and *Ketubah*[45]), aimed at securing some financial support for women after divorce, or with presumptions such as the Jewish and Islamic laws' preference for mothers as physical custodians at least while the children are young, or with gendered financial obligations, such as the legal Islamic and Jewish exclusively paternal duty to support the children – better reflects the gendered marital labor division and its care and economic dependency outcomes, than current secular family laws that ignore it. Still, although Western family law does not guarantee substantive gender equality, it at least strives to secure formal gender equality, whereas, within Islamic and Jewish

[40] Lifshitz, "The Liberal Transformation of Spousal Law," at 35–7.

[41] Lenore J. Weitzman, *The Divorce Revolution: The Unexpected Social and Economic Consequences for Women and Children in America* (New York: The Free Press, 1985).

[42] Richard R. Peterson, "A Re-Evaluation of the Economic Consequences of Divorce," *American Sociological Review*, 61(3) (1996), 528–36; Eleanor E. Maccoby & Robert H. Mnookin, *Dividing the Child: Social and Legal Dilemmas of Custody* (Cambridge, MA: Harvard University Press, 1992); Karen C. Holden & Pamela J. Smoke, "The Economic Costs of Marital Dissolution: Why Do Women Bear a Disproportionate Cost?," *Annual Review of Sociology*, 17 (1991), 51–78.

[43] See, for example, Hans-Jürgen Andreß, Barbara Borgloh, Miriam Bröckel, Marco Giesselmann, & Dina Hummelsheim, "The Economic Consequences of Partnership Dissolution: A Comparative Analysis of Panel Studies from Belgium, Germany, Great Britain, Italy and Sweden," *European Sociological Review*, 22(5) (2006), 533–60.

[44] The *Mahr* will be discussed in the second part of this chapter.

[45] The *Ketubah* is a mandatory document within Jewish marriage law. It stipulates the husband's duties toward his wife, and in particular a sum to be paid to her upon divorce or the death of her husband. There is a minimum sum dictated by the rabbis, but the parties can agree on a higher sum. See Michael J. Broyde, "New York's Regulation of Jewish Marriage: Covenant, Contract, or Statute?" in Joel A. Nichols (Ed.), *Marriage and Divorce in a Multicultural Context, Multi-Tiered Marriage and the Boundaries of Civil Law and Religion* (Cambridge University Press, 2011), pp. 138–63, at 140–4.

law, the modern, liberal concept of gender equality, in either of its meanings,[46] is a foreign one.[47]

One of the expressions of this difference is the adoption of the CEDAW convention by Western countries, by and large with no reservations related to family law and courts, whereas countries that adopt religious family law do express such reservations. Saudi Arabia, for example, ratified the convention while stating a general reservation, that: "In case of contradiction between any term of the Convention and the norms of Islamic law, the Kingdom is not under obligation to observe the contradictory terms of the Convention." Israel was more specific, stating that: "The State of Israel hereby expresses its reservation with regard to article 7(b) of the Convention concerning the appointment of women to serve as judges of religious courts where this is prohibited by the laws of any of the religious communities in Israel." In addition, and like most Muslim-majority countries, it expressed its reservation with regard to Article 16, which obliges states to take all appropriate measures to eliminate discrimination against women in all matters relating to marriage and family relations, "to the extent that the laws on personal status which are binding on the various religious communities in Israel do not conform with the provisions of that article."[48]

The parallel existence of two groups of very different family law systems – Western secular and formally gender equal, and Eastern-religious gender specific – provides a fascinating opportunity to examine the socio-legal coordination challenges created by bordered globalization. There are three main such challenges arising from the increasing presence of religious family law on Western soil.[49] The first challenge arises when

---

[46] The CEDAW Committee had distinguished between formal and substantive equality, stating that "The Committee has consistently concluded that the elimination of discrimination against women requires States parties to provide for substantive as well as formal equality. Formal equality may be achieved by adopting gender-neutral laws and policies, which on their face treat women and men equally. Substantive equality can be achieved only when the States parties examine the application and effects of laws and policies and ensure that they provide for equality in fact, accounting for women's disadvantage or exclusion." See Article 8 of the General Recommendation on Article 16 of the Convention on the Elimination of All Forms of Discrimination Against Women, CEDAW/C/GC/29 (2013), available at: www2.ohchr.org/english/bodies/cedaw/docs/comments/CEDAW-C-52-WP-1_en.pdf.

[47] Büchler, *Islamic Law in Europe?* at 99–101.

[48] Convention on the Elimination of All Forms of Discrimination Against Women 1979, Declarations, Reservations and Objections, available at: www.un.org/womenwatch/daw/cedaw/reservations-country.htm.

[49] A fourth challenge, which will not be addressed here, is whether to give any legal consideration to the familial norms of a minority culture that are allowed within the religious

individuals ask that legal acts based on state religious family law, which took place in one country, be recognized by another country that operates secular family law. This scenario may arise, for example when a Muslim husband, legally residing in France, asks to be reunited with his three wives who live in Saudi Arabia,[50] or to have the private unilateral divorce he was granted in his country of origin – which allows it even if the wife is not present – recognized in the Western country to which he emigrated.[51] The second challenge arises when individuals ask the legal system of the Western country in which they live to recognize a subnational religious family law relevant to an act that took place on its soil, such as when a Jewish woman asks the civil court to recognize her financial rights stemming from thirty years of unregistered religious marriage[52] or to assist her in forcing her husband to grant her a religious divorce.[53] The third challenge arises when a minority religious group promotes or demands some kind of autonomous subnational family law, such as through arbitration

family law in the country of origin, but are unacceptable from the perspective of the dominant culture within the host country. For example, should a civil court recognize a husband's claim for annulment of marriage after he discovers his wife is not a virgin? See Büchler, *Islamic Law in Europe?*, at 60. Or should a "cultural defense" be allowed in familial violence criminal cases? See Melissa Spatz, "A 'Lesser' Crime: A Comparative Study of Legal Defenses for Men Who Kill Their Wives," *Columbia Journal of Law and Social Problems*, 24(4) (1991), 597–639.

50 In the EU, family reunification can include only one spouse. See "Bringing Your Family Together," the EU Immigration Portal, at: http://ec.europa.eu/immigration/tab1.do?subSec=30; antipolygamy policy also shapes US immigration law – see Claire A. Smearman, "Second Wives' Club: Mapping the Impact of Polygamy in U.S. Immigration Law," *Berkeley Journal of International Law*, 27(2) (2009), 382–447.

51 For a discussion of two contradicting decisions on this matter, one granted by the New Jersey Appellate court, which respected a *Talaq* performed in Pakistan, and the other, by the Maryland Appellete court, which refused to grant comity to a *Talaq* performed in the Pakistani Embassy in Washington, see Linda C. McClain, "Marriage Pluralism in the United States: On Civil and Religious Jurisdiction and the Demands of Equal Citizenship" in Joel A. Nichols (Ed.), *Marriage and Divorce in a Multicultural Context: Multi-Tiered Marriage and the Boundaries of Civil Law and Religion* (New York: Cambridge University Press, 2012), pp. 309–40, at 324–6.

52 Within Western jurisdictions, courts may recognize some financial outcomes of unregistered religious marriages through cohabitation law or contract law. To my understanding, such judicial interpretation corresponds with the CEDAW Committee General Recommendation on Article 16 of the Convention on the Elimination of All Forms of Discrimination Against Women, CEDAW/C/GC/29 (2013).

53 For example, in *Avitzur v. Avitzur*, 459 NYS 2d 572 (NY App 1983) the court issued an order compelling the husband to appear at the *Beth Din* to take part in a religious divorce procedure initiated by the wife. The court based its decision on the terms in the couple's *Ketubah*, which granted authority to the rabbinical court, and treated it as a civil contractual obligation.

between divorcing couples, performed by a religious body.[54] Each of these challenges adds to the confusion, dilemmas, and conflicts in relation to the meaning of *family* and to doing and displaying family, within and among family members, and between family members and the state.

The first challenge is, in fact, the current version of the old problem of conflict of laws of two countries, which can be traced back to the fourteenth century when the first signs of systemic private international law – the legal branch aimed at resolving such conflicts – emerged.[55] The basic principles of national legal sovereignty are that the law of the state applies in, and only in, its territory; that all persons, permanently or temporarily present within the state's territory, are subject to its law; and that the power of the law of the nation exercised according to the previous two principles is recognized by other national legal systems as effective everywhere (the principle of *comity*).[56] Although private international family law recognizes these principles, it also recognizes the possibility that when a foreign element is involved – such as a marriage that took place in another country – foreign law might be relevant, and so the authorities of country A would be expected to recognize and implement the family law of country B.[57]

The basic principle guiding national jurisdictions in family matters is that these matters should be governed by the *personal law* of the individuals involved. Although some jurisdictions relate to the personal law as the law of the country of nationality, others refer to the law of domicile, that is the home country of the individuals involved, or to the law of the country that is the family members' habitual residence.[58] Although, in the past, the personal law principle usually guarantied legal predictability and certainty, in

---

[54] See discussion in the second part of this chapter.

[55] Hessel E. Yntema, "The Historic Bases of Private International Law," *The American Journal of Comparative Law*, 2(3) (1953), 297–317, at 304.

[56] Ibid., at 306.

[57] Although in some family matters the foreign element does not denounce the jurisdiction of the court of country A, in others it does. A clear example is that although several countries allow foreign couples to marry on their soil, in most cases they lack jurisdiction over the divorce of these foreign couples, as the common rule on jurisdiction over divorce demands nationality or domicile of at least one of the spouses. See Celia Wasserstein Fassberg, *Private International Law* (Jerusalem: Nevo, 2013), vol. I, at 651, 661 (Hebrew). This situation leads, for example, to complexities arising when same-sex couples evade the prohibition on same-sex marriage in their home country by marrying in a country that allows it, and later learn that they have nowhere to divorce if they wish to. See Doron Halutz, "The Road to Civil Marriage in Israel Runs Through Same-Sex Divorce," *Haaretz* (August 29, 2015), available at: www.haaretz.com/israel-news/.premium-1.673283.

[58] John Obrien, *Conflict of Laws*, 2nd edn. (London: Cavendish, 1999), Ch. 2–3.

the era of bordered globalization such predictability and certainty are much harder to achieve. Intense cross-border movement of people leads to growing numbers of incidents in which there is no overlap between nationality and domicile, family members do not hold the same nationality or share the same habitual residence, and people have more than one nationality or their domicile is unclear. Moreover, as some family-related acts might be dominated by the law of the place of the deed (*locus regit actum*), including the act of marriage[59] and the act of buying family real estate,[60] there is a growing number of complex cases in which people perform familial acts in one country, and litigate their meaning in another under the latter's law.[61]

A relatively simple example of the difficulties in coordinating familial expectations, in the face of the challenge of settling conflict of laws in our era, relates to the division of marital property (all assets acquired during the marriage, including the family home) of a couple married in one country and litigating its divorce arrangement in another. In countries such as Germany, France, and Spain, in which the law states that the outcomes of a marriage are governed by the couple's nationality,[62] a married Algerian woman who emigrated there with her husband would not be entitled to an equal share of the marital property on divorce, unless the couple gained citizenship in the host country. Instead, they would be subject to Algerian law, with its Islam-based legal principle of a separate marital property regime, which usually benefits the husband because more assets are registered under his name.[63] Even if the couple gained

---

[59] Ibid., at 423–4.

[60] Ibid., at 541. Although the general principle is that real estate is governed by the law of the property's location, some argue that in cases of marital property, the relevant law is the personal law of the spouses. See Wasserstein Fassberg, *Private International Law*, Ch. 16.

[61] For a rich account of the relevance of conflict of laws to family matters in our era, see Barbara Stark, *International Family Law: An Introduction* (Surrey: Ashgate, 2005); and Ann Laquar Estin & Barbara Stark, *Global Issues in Family Law* (Eagan, MN: Thomson/ West, 2007). Conflict of laws is also relevant when the issue of the legal validity of a familial legal act, such as marriage or divorce, is incidental to another, main, family-related legal question, such as the right to inherit or remarry. In such cases, the question arises about whether the incidental issue should be determined by the choice of law that would have governed it, were it the main question, or by the choice of law rules governing the actual main question. See Rhona Schuz, *A Modern Approach to the Incidental Question* (Netherlands: Springer, 1997).

[62] Büchler, *Islamic Law in Europe?*, at 28–31.

[63] Neil MacMaster, "The Colonial "Emancipation" of Algerian Women: the Marriage Law of 1959 and the Failure of Legislation on Women's Rights in the Post-Independence Era," *Vienna Journal of African Studies*, 12 (2007), 91–116; Ann Luerssen Crowther, "Empty Gestures: The (In)Significance of Recent Attempts to Liberalize Algerian Family Law," *William & Mary Journal of Women and the Law*, 6(3) (2000), 611–43.

citizenship in a new country, the woman would not get an equal share of the property if that country subjects the outcomes of marriage to the so-called matrimonial domicile – that is, the law of the country in which the couple lived at the time they married, as is the case under English law, for example.[64] If, however, the same couple immigrated to a country that subjects the outcome of the marriage to the couple's current domicile,[65] such as Switzerland, the wife would receive half of the marital property in a divorce thanks to the new home country's egalitarian matrimonial property law. I doubt if such potentially dramatic property outcomes are part of familial negotiations over the choice of country of destination, if such choice is available (and to the degree that such negotiations take place in patriarchal households), but this can be an interesting research question for future studies. Moreover, understanding, predicting, and coordinating the familial legal outcomes of emigration becomes an almost impossible familial task in some cases. For example, going back to the aforementioned Algerian couple, if the husband holds dual Algerian and Western citizenships and the wife only an Algerian one, the woman is a second wife in a polygamous marriage, and the relevant property is to remain in Algeria.

The most significant attempt to harmonize private international family law, on a global scale, is that of the Hague Conference on Private International Law (HCCH) – an intergovernmental organization with seventy-seven member states. Out of its forty conventions, drafted since 1955, fourteen address family law issues. However, although a few conventions, such as the Convention on the Civil Aspects of International Child Abduction, which will be discussed in Chapter 7, have gained broad support with their ratification by most member states and a significant number of nonmember states, the conventions seeking to unify the rules relevant to the recognition (though not to the outcomes) of marriage[66] and divorce[67] are far from achieving their goal, with the former ratified by only three member states, and the latter by twenty.[68] Moreover, these

---

[64] Büchler, *Islamic Law in Europe?*, at 37.

[65] Ibid., at 36–8.

[66] Hague Convention on Celebration and Recognition of the Validity of Marriages 1978, available at: www.hcch.net/en/instruments/conventions/full-text/?cid=88.

[67] Hague Convention on the Recognition of Divorces and Legal Separations 1970, available at: www.hcch.net/index_en.php?act=conventions.text&cid=80.

[68] For the text of all the conventions of the HCCH, and their ratification status, see "Conventions, Protocols and Principles," available at: www.hcch.net/index_en.php?act=conventions.listing.

conventions, as well as other attempts to harmonize private international family law, such as those of the European Union,[69] acknowledge states' right to refuse recognition of a legal act related to marriage or divorce that has taken place in another country, if that act is against its "public order."[70]

Indeed, this public order normative valve symbolizes, most significantly, the international recognition of the ongoing conflicts of perceptions between different countries with regard to marriage and divorce, and the internationally acknowledged right of every country to preserve its normative borders in relation to these issues. Some Western countries use this valve to refuse recognition of forced marriage,[71] polygamy,[72] and Islamic divorce[73] that have taken place in countries following religious family law, as well as same-sex marriages[74] performed in the few countries that allow them. Hence people who *do* family (in the case of marriage) or *undo* it (in the case of divorce), based on the law where the acts of marriage or divorce were performed, might find themselves *unfamilized* or *refamilized*, respectively, by the law of the country in which they live. Hence, conflicts of law not only challenge the ability of spouses to coordinate expectations between themselves, but can also create a gap between family members' understanding of their family status and their actual state recognition.

The gap between legal recognition and actual familial lives is also evident in the second challenge faced by Western countries due to increasing emigration from religious family law countries – that of religious legal acts taking place on their soil. Although many immigrants and

---

[69] Council Regulation (EC) No 2201/2003 of November 27, 2003 Concerning Jurisdiction and the Recognition and Enforcement of Judgments in Matrimonial Matters and the Matters of Parental Responsibility, repealing Regulation (EC) No 1347/2000.

[70] For example, Article 10 of the Hague Convention on the Recognition of Divorces and Legal Separations 1970.

[71] McCallum in Hodson, *The International Family Law Practice*, Ch. 18; Marianne D. Blair, Merle H. Weiner, Barbara Stark, & Solangel Maldonado, *Family Law in the World Community: Cases, Materials and Problems in Comparative and International Family Law*, 2nd edn. (Durham, NC: Carolina Academic Press, 2009), at 183.

[72] Stark, *International Family Law*, at 17.

[73] Büchler, *Islamic Law in Europe?*, at 50–3.

[74] Until recently, US courts were divided on the question of whether to recognize same-sex marriages performed in countries such as Belgium, Canada, and the Netherlands. See Blair, Weiner, Stark, & Maldonado, *Family Law in the World Community*, at 255. The recent US Supreme Court decision that there is a constitutional right to same-sex marriage will hopefully settle this dispute, as well as make it unnecessary for gay US citizens to travel to marry abroad. See *Obergefell v. Hodges*, 135 S Ct 2071 (2015).

their offspring choose to handle their family legal affairs only within the state secular legal system, many others – as well as veteran citizens with religious convictions or traditional attachment – practice family acts that have a legally binding meaning according to their religion's family law. Indeed, some argue that religious identity, established among other ways through conformity to religious family law, is enhanced within diaspora communities as part of their emigration coping strategies.[75] In that sense, globalization has the paradoxical outcome of establishing new and more rigid socio-legal religious borders within Western societies.

An example of the internal and external coordination challenges created by the practicing of family religious law in the Global North is that of unregistered marriages. An empirically based estimation is that at least one-third of Muslim couples living in England only perform a religious ceremony (nikāḥ) and do not become legally married under English law by registering their marriage.[76] This is so even though, according to English law, marriage registration can be performed through both a recognized civil entity and a religious facility, and mosques in England can register Islamic marriages with the state.[77] There is a mix of reasons behind this phenomenon, including a strong attachment to religion, a mistrust of the state's legal system, the existence of polygamous and underage marriages that cannot be registered, a lack of awareness that Islamic marriage is not recognized by the state without registration, and a male tendency to breach the promise to follow the religious marriage with an official registration to avoid financial obligations or to allow additional future marriages.[78] Indeed, the nonrecognition of these marriages by the state leaves the vulnerable spouse, usually the woman, without public or private benefits and protections.[79] Male and state powers lead to a situation in which Muslim women might think they have successfully coordinated with their spouse and with the state their expectation to be protected in the case of spousal separation, only

---

[75] Büchler, *Islamic Law in Europe?*, at 6–12.

[76] Ibid., at 77.

[77] "Getting Married in England and Wales: The Basis for a Valid Marriage," General Register Office, available at: www.gov.uk/government/uploads/system/uploads/attachment_data/file/347609/357c_V3.pdf.

[78] Büchler, *Islamic Law in Europe?*, at 77–8; Hodson, *The International Family Law Practice*, at 58.

[79] Ihsan Yilmaz, "The Challenge of Post-Modern Legality and Muslim Legal Pluralism in England," *Journal of Ethnic and Migration Studies*, 28(2) (2002), 343–54, at 349.

to learn that this is not the case because in the eyes of the law they are single, never-married women.

However, British Parliament has chosen to interfere in, and hence grant some kind of recognition to, religious marriages, even if they are not registered. In an amendment from 2002, it introduced the possibility of postponing a civil divorce until a religious divorce is conducted for cases in which, for instance, a husband is only willing to divorce via the civil route and does not agree to a religious divorce.[80] As the legal scholar Matthijs de Blois observes: "In this Act secular and religious law are in a sense linked together," mainly in an attempt to assist Jewish women who, under their religion's family law, are in a weaker position than their husbands in securing a divorce.[81] Hence, the presence of religious family law in Western countries, which they may object to due to its gender bias, is in fact changing their secular family law, as they attempt to address this bias.[82] However, it is important to note that although the Divorce (Religious Marriages) Act 2002 targets Jewish divorces, it invites other religious groups to subject themselves to it, but, to date, none has done so. So, currently, the Act cannot assist Muslim women who are refused a divorce by their husband.[83]

Indeed, the attempt to address the difficulties of women in obtaining a religious divorce is but one example of the dilemmas faced by secular Western law when endeavoring to stick to its concept of legal unity and monism while legal pluralism is practiced on the ground.[84] It is also an example of the limitation of secular law in its attempts to intervene and regulate religious family law. Within orthodox Muslim communities living in the West, for example, a civil divorce does not end a religious marriage, and a woman divorced in a civil procedure still needs a religious divorce so as not to be regarded as being married within her community and faith. Hence, she is

---

[80] Divorce (Religious Marriages) Act 2002, c.27.

[81] Matthijs de Blois, "Religious Law versus Secular Law: The Example of the *Get* Refusal in Dutch, English and Israeli Law," *Utrecht Law Review*, 6(2) (2010), 93–114, at 101. De Blois focuses on Jewish law that grants greater power to the husband to divorce his wife than vice versa, but, as discussed in this chapter, women's access to divorce is restricted also in Islam. See also Pascale Fournier, *Muslim Marriages in Western Courts: Lost in Transplantation* (Surrey: Ashgate, 2010), at 22–3.

[82] See also Rhona Schuz, "Divorce and Ethnic Minorities," in Michael Freeman (Ed.), *Divorce: Where Next?* (Aldershot: Dartmouth, 1996), pp. 131–57.

[83] Machteld Zee, "Five Options for the Relationship between the State and Sharia Councils: Untangling the Debate on Sharia Councils and Women's Rights in the United Kingdom," *Journal of Religion and Society*, 16 (2014), 1–18, at 12.

[84] Yilmaz, "The Challenge of Post-Modern Legality."

dependent on the will of her husband to divorce her, or her ability to find an Islamic tribunal that will agree to issue a religious divorce decree. Otherwise, any future marriage will be regarded as adulterous and her future children as bastards.[85] In Orthodox Judaism things are even more complex, as an interference by a civil court trying to pressure the husband to agree to a religious divorce decree (*Get*), by postponing the civil divorce, can lead the rabbinical court (*Beth-Din*) to conclude that a divorce cannot be arranged or should be annulled, because it was forced upon the husband against religious law.[86] Hence, in the era of bordered globalization, in which communities maintain "multi-tiered"[87] and "unofficial"[88] family law, state secular law finds it difficult to create uniformity and to enforce its understanding of marriage and divorce. Moreover, attempts to preserve such uniformity, carried out mainly in the name of women's equal rights, might paradoxically harm women, who find themselves subordinated to unrecognized subnational family religious law, carried out by unregulated religious forums.

The existence and proliferation of religious law forums in Western countries, such as the Islamic Councils in the United Kingdom, the United States, and Australia, which focus on family disputes,[89] are linked to the third, most recent and, in my opinion, most dramatic challenge faced by Western jurisdictions in the context of religious family law. While the first and second challenges can be seen as stemming from unorganized, individual, and sporadic acts, the third is characterized by organized attempts among religious communities to secure state legal recognition of their subnational family law. The two such attempts that have received the most political and scholastic attention relate to Muslim organizations in Canada and the United Kingdom. In both countries, these organizations argued that they should be allowed to offer arbitration services in family disputes, which would be conducted according to Sharia and enforceable through civil courts according to state arbitration laws. In both countries, this argument met fierce opposition, with opposite outcomes.

---

[85] Ibid., at 350.

[86] De Blois, "Religious Law versus Secular Law."

[87] Joel A. Nichols, "Multi-Tiered Marriage" in Joel A. Nichols (Ed.), *Marriage and Divorce in a Multicultural Context: Multi-Tiered Marriage and the Boundaries of Civil Law and Religion* (New York: Cambridge University Press, 2012), pp. 11–50.

[88] Ann Laquer Estin, "Unofficial Family Law" in Nichols (Ed.), *Marriage and Divorce in a Multicultural Context*, pp. 92–119.

[89] As Machtled Zee explains, it is the centrality of family law, including its regulation of gender roles, to the survival of the religious communities, which makes their tribunals focus on family law rather than any other branch of law. See Zee, "Five Options for the Relationship between the State and Sharia Councils," at 7.

In Canada in 2003, a small Muslim group declared its intention to establish a religious court in Ontario that would perform family arbitrations.[90] The decisions of this Islamic court would have been enforceable within the civil legal system as, according to the Ontario Arbitration Act of the time, parties to arbitration could have chosen any kind of law applicable to their disputes.[91] Indeed, Canadian Jewish communities used this Act in their rabbinical tribunals as a matter of routine.[92] Many within the Muslim community and also outside of it, both in Canada and beyond its borders, raised concerns about the possibility of state-recognized Sharia-based arbitration. These concerns focused on the fear that Muslim women could be forced to agree to such arbitration, which would harm their familial rights since Islamic law discriminates against women.[93] In 2005, the Canadian parliament responded to these concerns by amending the Family Statute Law to prohibit faith-based arbitration in family matters altogether,[94] including the long-recognized arbitrations within the Jewish community.[95] This has not ended the controversy over the matter, however. Faisal Kutty, for example, who served as the counsel to a coalition of Muslim organizations during the debate over faith-based arbitration in Ontario, argues that this amendment is in contradiction to international law, which includes states' positive duty to assist minorities

[90] This was the highlight of a seventeen-year effort by Syed Muntz Ali, a Muslim leader in Ontario. See Marie Ashe & Anissa Hélie, "Realities of Religio-Legalism: Religious Courts and Women's Rights in Canada, the United Kingdom, and the United States," *UC Davis Journal of International Law and Policy*, 20(2) (2013), 139–209, at 149–55.

[91] Ayelet Shachar, "Privatizing Diversity: A Cautionary Tale from Religious Arbitration in Family Law" in Lisa Fishbayn Joffe & Sylvia Neil (Eds.), *Gender, Religion & Family Law: Theorizing Conflicts between Women's Rights and Cultural Traditions* (Waltham, MA: Brandeis University Press, 2013), pp. 38–75, at 41–2; Faisal Kutty, "The Myth and Reality of Shari'a Courts in Canada: A Delayed Opportunity for the Indigenization of Islamic Legal Rulings," *University of St. Thomas Law Journal*, 7(3) (2010), 559–602, at 562.

[92] Natasha Bakht, "Family Arbitration Using Sharia Law: Examining Ontario's Arbitration Act and its Impact on Women," *Muslim World Journal of Human Rights*, 1(1) (2004), 1–24.

[93] Ashe & Hélie, "Realities of Religio-Legalism," at 155–6. Faisal Kutty argues that legitimate concerns were fueled by illegitimate Islamophobia. See Kutty, "The Myth and Reality of Shari'a Courts in Canada," at 562–71.

[94] This decision was in opposition to the recommendations made by a special government committee appointed to study the issue, to allow religious arbitration and mediation of family and inheritance matters, and to regulate them. See Marion Boyd, "Dispute Resolution in Family Law: Protecting Choice, Promoting Inclusion" (2004), available at: www.attorneygeneral.jus.gov.on.ca/english/about/pubs/boyd/executivesummary.pdf.

[95] Loraine E. Weinrib, "Ontario's Sharia Law Debate: Law and Politics under the Charter" in Richard Moon (Ed.), *Law and Religious Pluralism in Canada* (Vancouver: UBS Press, 2008), pp. 239–63, at 258.

in collectively preserving their culture and religion.[96] He also argues that, since this amendment, Sharia-based "back-alley family arbitrations" continue, unregulated and unsupervised, which might result in more exploitive settlements than would have been the case if faith-based arbitration had been recognized by the state law.[97] On the other side of the barricade, feminist legal scholar Beverly Baines has raised concerns that the Canadian Supreme Court might accept possible future petitions of religious bodies (which she terms "equality's nemesis") and allow them to arbitrate family matters in the name of freedom of religion.[98]

Two years after the Canadian parliament's prohibition of faith-based family arbitration, an initiative to promote the option of legally binding Islamic family resolutions in the UK was promoted by the Muslim Arbitration Tribunal (MAT). Islamic Councils in England, which constitute the most developed set of institutions for Islamic dispute mediation throughout all Western countries,[99] dealt with family conflicts prior to 2007. However, they did not do so according to the UK Arbitration Act,[100] although they could have, and thus their decisions were not legally binding or enforceable.[101] The initiative of MAT – and more so the support of religious-based arbitration announced by Rowan Williams, the Archbishop of Canterbury at that time, and by Worth Matravers, then Lord Chief Justice of England and Wales – created mass controversy.[102] Just as in the Canadian case, most opposition was based on concerns over women's rights. In addition, Muslim leaders and secular organizations pointed to findings according to which most Muslims

[96] Kutty, "The Myth and Reality of Shari'a Courts in Canada," at 566. Article 27 of the International Convention on Civil and Political Rights 1976, to which Kutty refers, states: "In those States in which ethnic, religious or linguistic minorities exist, persons belonging to such minorities shall not be denied the right, in community with the other members of their group, to enjoy their own culture, to profess and practice their own religion, or to use their own language." However, as Almas Khan has pointed out, and as previously discussed in relation to CEDAW, other international law duties can be in tension with recognizing sub-national religious family law. See Almas Khan, "The Interaction between Shariah and International Law in Arbitration," *Chicago Journal of International Law*, 6(2) (2006), 791–802.

[97] Kutty, "The Myth and Reality of Shari'a Courts in Canada," at 572.

[98] Beverley Baines, "Equality's Nemesis?," *Journal of Law and Equality*, 5(1) (2006), 57–80; Ashe & Hélie, "Realities of Religio-Legalism," at 160–1.

[99] Ashe & Hélie, "Realities of Religio-Legalism," at 161.

[100] Arbitration Act 1996.

[101] Rajnaara Akhtar, "British Muslims and the Revolution of the Practice of Islamic Law with Particular Reference to Dispute Resolution," *Journal of Islamic State Practices in International Law*, 6(1) (2010), 27–39.

[102] Zee, "Five Options for the Relationship between the State and Sharia Councils," at 1–2.

in the UK did not wish to be governed by Islamic law,[103] and argued that promoting Islamic law-based arbitration would result in further alienation and segregation of members of Muslim communities from the rest of society.[104] In 2011, a private bill was introduced in the House of Lords, aimed at amending the Arbitration Act by prohibiting any arbitration of family law matters, as well as sex-based discriminatory practices in general.[105] In 2013, a new version of this bill was introduced. Apparently due to political pressure, this version does not include the prohibition of family matters in arbitration, including religious arbitration, but rather only subordinates such arbitrations to the principle of sex equality.[106] Interestingly, although even this modified bill has not yet materialized in law, the vast majority of family dispute resolutions within Muslim bodies in the UK are still not conducted under the Arbitration Act, and so continue to be performed outside state law.[107] Most of these resolutions concern Muslim women's requests for religious divorce.[108] Although some suggest that this might be the outcome of social pressure and coercion,[109] one cannot ignore the fact that religious Muslim women are in much greater need of these family law subnational forums since, unlike men, they cannot perform unilateral religious divorce, as explained earlier, unless they stipulate their right to do so in their marriage contracts.[110] As in the Canadian case, the socio-legal reality in the UK demonstrates both the parallel existence of state secular and community religious family laws and also the dilemmas caused by the

[103] Samia Bano, "Islamic Family Arbitration, Justice and Human Rights in Britain," *Law, Social Justice & Global Development Journal*, 1 (2007), 1–26, at 3, also available at: www2 .warwick.ac.uk/fac/soc/law/elj/lgd/2007_1/bano/.

[104] Zee, "Five Options for the Relationship between the State and Sharia Councils," at 6.

[105] The Arbitration and Mediation Services (Equality) Bill of 2014–15, available at: http:// services.parliament.uk/bills/2014–15/arbitrationandmediationservicesequality.html.

[106] Ibid.; Ashe and Hélie, "Realities of Religio-Legalism," at 184.

[107] Zee, "Five Options for the Relationship between the State and Sharia Councils."

[108] For example, according to the Islamic Sharia Council in London, in 2011, 132 of the total of 571 applications it received were from men applying for *Talaq* and 439 were from women applying for *khul*. See "Statistics," available at: www.islamic-sharia.org/statistics/.

[109] Shaheen Sardar Ali, "Authority and Authenticity: Sharia Councils, Muslim Women's Rights, and the English Courts," *Child and Family Law Quarterly*, 25 (2013), 113–37; Ashe & Hélie, "Realities of Religio-Legalism," at 177–81.

[110] For fascinating empirical findings in this regard, see Julia Macfarlane, *Islamic Divorce in North America: A Shari'a Path in a Secular Society* (New York: Oxford University Press, 2012); Gillian Douglas, Norman Doe, Sophie Gilliat-Ray, Russell Sandberg, & Asma Khan, "Social Cohesion and Civil Law: Marriage, Divorce and Religious Courts," Report of a Research Study funded by the AHRC, Cardiff University (2011), available at: www .law.cf.ac.uk/clr/Social%20Cohesion%20and%20Civil%20Law%20Full%20Report.pdf.

realization that each of the possible reactions – allowing, ignoring, or prohibiting this plurality – may harm women.

As Machteld Zee's typology suggests, Western state jurisdictions' responses to religious tribunals can range from "full accommodation," in which the secular state delegates legislation and jurisdiction to religious tribunals, to "state intervention," in which it actively safeguards its legal monopoly,[111] with "partial independent accommodation" (enforcement of religious tribunals' decisions in secular courts), "partial dependent accommodation" (enforcement of religious tribunals' decisions in secular courts only when they do not conflict with state law), and "no accommodation, no intervention" (recognition of religious tribunals by the community, but not by the state) responses in-between.[112]

One of the most developed and widely cited theoretical attempts to outline a response that respects multiculturalism while safeguarding women's rights, including their right to religious identity and belonging, is that of Ayelet Shachar (who, like Zee, is both a political scientist and legal scholar). Shachar developed a *transformative accommodation* model to encourage, through dialogue, both the liberal state and the minority *nomos* groups to be more responsive to all their constituents. At the heart

---

[111] An example of this radical end of the spectrum can be found in the recent "Anti-Sharia" legislation adopted by several states in the United States. According to Marie Ashe and Anissa Hélie, by August 2013 anti-Sharia initiatives had been introduced into at least half the state legislatures and enacted into law in seven. See Ashe & Hélie, "Realities of Religio-Legalism," at 193. Following a decision of the 10th Circuit Court of Appeals, according to which Sharia-targeted legislation is probably unconstitutional – see *Awad v. Ziriax*, 670 F3d 1111 (10th Cir 2012) – the language of these initiatives has become "neutral," but all the more sweeping for that. In Kansas, for example, the law prohibits any ruling based "in whole or in part on any foreign law, legal code or system that would not grant the parties affected by the ruling or decision the same fundamental liberties, rights and privileges granted under Unites States and Kansas constitution, including but not limited to, equal protection, due process, free exercise of religion, freedom of speech or press, and any right of privacy or marriage." See Kan. Stat Ann. § 60–5103 (West, Westlaw through 2013 Sess.). By that, Kansas and other states that adopt similar laws not only prohibit religious arbitration performed on their soil, but also refuse to acknowledge the law of other countries, if based on religion, as well as any national or international law that they find differing on the aforementioned grounds. I agree with those who claim that this broad refusal is extremely problematic, among other reasons due to its contradiction of the basic principles of private international law. See Samir Islam, "The Negative Effects of Ill-Advised Legislation: The Curious Case of the Evolution of Anti-Sharia Law Legislation into Anti-Foreign Law Legislation and the Impact on the CISG," *Howard Law Journal*, 57 (2014), 979–1031; Ann Laquer Estin, "Foreign and Religious Family Law: Comity, Contract, and the Constitution," *Pepperdine Law Review*, 41(5) (2014), 1029–47.

[112] Zee, "Five Options for the Relationship between the State and Sharia Councils," at 9.

of this model are the precepts that any given legal matter can be divided into submatters that can be governed by different legal systems; that neither the minority group nor the state should wield exclusive control over a contested social arena that affects individuals both as group members and as citizens; and that all constituents must have clear options that allow them to choose between state jurisdiction and their group's jurisdiction. In the area of family law, Shachar explains, the first two principles could translate, for example, into a division of jurisdictional power where the minority group exercises authority over the submatter of demarcation (that is, status regulation) and the state has authority over the submatter of distribution (for instance, allocation of marital property upon divorce). The third element of choice of jurisdiction could be manifested in the selection of either a religious or civil marriage and, in the case of a severely discriminatory religious legal decision, the right to appeal to the civil court even after having opted for religious marriage.[113] In accordance with her general theory, Shachar is critical of Canada's decision to quash religious arbitration. She calls for a dialogue with religious communities that wish to perform family law arbitration. Through this dialogue, the state and the community would seek ways to allow religious arbitration, which would adopt a baseline of protection established by state law to prevent gender discrimination and the abuse of power imbalance. Only if the religious body were to adopt this baseline would its decisions be recognized as enforceable arbitrations by the state and its courts.[114] By that, state law would recognize religious law, and religious law would recognize state law. I would add, based on my empirical study of Rabbinical Courts in Israel[115] and Ido Shahar's ethnographic study of Islamic Courts in Jerusalem,[116] that such a dialogue is most likely to succeed if: (1) the state guarantees true choice of secular family law to allow forum shopping (what I term the institutional variable);[117] (2) the gender-equalizing accommodations required are not in stark contradiction to religious

---

[113] Ayelet Shachar, *Multicultural Jurisdictions: Cultural Differences and Women's Rights* (Cambridge University Press, 2001), Ch. 6.

[114] Shachar, "Privatizing Diversity," at 61–2.

[115] Daphna Hacker, "Religious Tribunals in Democratic States: Lesson from the Israeli Rabbinical Courts," *Journal of Law and Religion*, 27(1) (2012), 59–82.

[116] Ido Shahar, *Legal Pluralism in the Holy City: Competing Courts, Forum Shopping, and Institutional Dynamics in Jerusalem* (Surrey: Ashgate, 2015).

[117] This includes low court fees, free legal aid, and translators within court hearings, to allow women of the minority group genuine access to secular family law and courts, as well as sanctions when forced religious family law procedures are discovered.

commandments (the religious variable);[118] and (3) the religious arbitrators' cultural background shares similarities with the liberal majority's (the cultural variable).[119]

Of course, Shachar's *transformative accommodation* model, even if adopted by Western legislators and judges, would not necessarily result in a harmonious process of coordinating expectations between family members, religious communities, and secular states. Confusion and conflict are only to be expected over questions such as who represents the religious community, what gender equality is, and what true consent for arbitration means. Moreover, those communities that do not manage to gain state recognition through dialogue might continue to practice unregulated subnational family law. Indeed, I would argue that as long as religious communities in the Global North perceive religious family law as relevant to their family doing and displaying practices, the family-related legal conflicts and dilemmas, especially in relation to gender equality and to children's best interests (less discussed in the literature in relation to religious family law, but extremely relevant),[120] are here to stay. This is an unavoidable outcome of the dialectic nature of the relations between globalization and borders. As geo-political borders are extensively crossed, through massive emigration, so new ethno-religious borders are created within the same national territory. Furthermore, as the similarities between the actions taking place in Canada and England suggest, these internal borders are not only shaped by individual religious beliefs and collective identity politics, but also by cross-border inspiration – that is, whereby minority groups are inspired by the actions of other such groups in other countries, or by religious global movements.

The recent thesis of marriage as a relational contract, developed by legal scholar Sharon Shakargy, offers another approach relevant to the attempt to advance family-related legally binding coordinated expectations that are clear and stable, both internally and externally, in the face of the plurality of familial conceptions and practices stemming from the dialectics of bordered globalization. While some of the calls for religious

---

[118] For example, under Jewish law, equalizing men's and women's right to divorce stands in stark contrast to Prohibition Jewish Law (*dinei isurim*), while finding ways to equalize women's right to inherit is possible, as inheritance is covered under monetary laws (*dinei mamonot*). See Hacker, "Religious Tribunals in Democratic States."

[119] For example, if the arbitrators practice gender equality within their own families, it is more likely they will be willing to adopt state legal safeguards that protect women during family arbitration.

[120] Chapter 7 will look at religious and parochial practices that harm children. See also Robin Fretwell Wilson, "The Overlooked Costs of Religious Difference," *Washington and Lee Law Review*, 64(4) (2007), 1363–83.

legal subnational forums are embedded in the right of groups to cultural self-determination,[121] Shakargy argues that state law should recognize religious law through individuals' rights to autonomy and identity. Since marriage lost its power as a status and is perceived by legal systems and family members as a contract,[122] the parties to this contract should be allowed to choose the law that governs their relations. The parties' choice of law could be from any available legal system, including religious legal systems, regardless of the parties' nationality, habitual residence, or religion. Only if the parties did not agree on their choice of law would state law determine the relevant applicable law.[123] Although Shakargy limits her proposal to the law that governs the validity of marriage and the act of divorce, her thesis can be broadened to the outcomes of marriage and divorce, such as alimony and the division of matrimonial property, as well as to the outcomes of cohabitation of both heterosexual and same-sex couples.

Indeed, one could argue that the contractual route should be the leading mechanism by which to legally coordinate familial expectations in our confusing epoch. A prenuptial contract will not only enable the coordination of the internal expectations of both spouses, but will also coordinate the external expectations between the spouses and the countries in which they live or will live in the future, because all jurisdictions will recognize the contract and will enforce the spousal choice of law and other agreed on family-related terms. This coordinating mechanism is relevant to all families affected by bordered globalization, and not only to those affected by the parallel existence of religious and secular family laws. In the next and final part of this chapter, however, I argue that this contractual vision cannot be achieved in the current global legal universe, and nor should it be normatively promoted in the future.

Prenuptial Agreements

At first glance, prenuptial agreements[124] appear to be a very effective legal mechanism for coordinating familial expectations in an era in which

---

[121] Kutty, "The Myth and Reality of Shari'a Courts in Canada."

[122] Interestingly, as will be discussed in the next part of this chapter, the contractual understanding of marriage is not only a new secular one but is also embedded in Islamic and Jewish law. See Broyde, "New York's Regulation of Jewish Marriage"; Fournier, *Muslim Marriages in Western Courts.*

[123] Sharon Shakargy, "Marriage by the State or Married to the State: Choice of Law in Marriage and Divorce," *Journal of Private International Law,* 9(3) (2013), 499–533.

[124] Prenuptial agreements (prenups) are also known as premarital and antenuptial agreements. Although in this part of the chapter I center on prenups, and hence on couples

spouses do not necessarily share the same understanding of what a family is. In theory, this mechanism constructs a space in which two autonomous individuals discuss their plans for establishing a family together (which may or may not include children). Through the contractual dialogue, ideally accompanied by one or more legal experts, the couple learn about the legal meaning and ramifications of their familial plans and can choose the legal provisions that best capture these plans. This process is assumed to enable each of the spouses to formulate a conscious understanding of his/her familial expectations including such issues as the family constitution, the labor division between the spouses, and the spousal and parental rights and obligations during marriage and in the case of divorce or death – and to make sure that this understanding is mutual. When differences arise, they can be negotiated. Either a compromise is reached or the spouses reluctantly learn that marrying would not be such a good idea after all – a realization better arrived at before, rather than after, the wedding.

Based on the discussion earlier in this chapter, one could further argue that in the era of bordered globalization it is also important that the couple contemplate the law they wish to govern their marriage and its outcomes, as it can be governed by an unexpected jurisdiction and law if, for example, each spouse has a different nationality, if familial property has been accumulated in more than one country, or if they had the capacity to marry under the law where the marriage took place but not under the law of the country in which they litigate their separation. Hence, allegedly, it is important that the spouses use a prenup also as an opportunity to choose the law that will govern any possible future conflicts by including in it a choice of law provision. Likewise, it would seem important to reach an international understanding to promote the enforceability of prenups, and the right of spouses to choose the law that will govern their relations, and to widen the familial issues that can be agreed by the spouses by limiting the cogent part of family law.

Indeed, the supporters of prenups argue that the spouses know best what their needs and interests are and can make the most efficient decisions regarding their future family life. Moreover, they argue that prenups promote certainty in familial relations and prevent litigation when

who wish to marry and are permitted by law to do so, many of the arguments for and against the contractual route are relevant to cohabiting heterosexual and same-sex couples, as well as to other familial forms, such as polyamorous families. The discussion here is also relevant to the question of divorce agreements and whether all elements of divorce should be governed by a contract or whether some should remain cogent.

these relations fail.[125] One can add that prenups are a better option than divorce agreements to shape postdivorce family life, because the point at which mutual feelings are at their most positive is a much better basis on which to reach familial understandings than the phase of disappointment and resentment that is so often part of a breakup. One American writer went as far as arguing that prenups should be mandatory for all marrying couples and should include not only economic provisions that will be enforced in the case of divorce or death but also articles related to the creation and ongoing life of the family, including the relative importance of each spouse's career; the labor division of domestic chores; the family's domicile; whether the relations will be monogamous or not; features of child-rearing such as religion, surname, and care; and caring for elderly parents.[126]

Interestingly, until the 1970s, prenuptial agreements were conceived by Western legal systems, such as in the United States, as void and against public policy as they anticipate divorce, hence contradicting the understanding of marriage as a life-long commitment.[127] However, in the last four decades, most Western countries have recognized prenups as enforceable contracts. This legal change has been followed by growing numbers of couples signing prenups, as well as by changes in the typical profile of those signing such agreements. Whereas in the past most prenups were signed by the economic elite and by people entering their second or higher-order marriage (that is, after a divorce) and were initiated mostly by men, today they are prevalent in broader economic circles and are initiated also by women who, for example, have their own premarriage assets they wish to protect in the case of divorce.[128]

---

[125] Debbie Ong, "Prenuptial Agreements Affirming TQ v. TR in Singapore," *Singapore Academy of Law Journal*, 24 (2012), 402–32; Alison A. Marson, "Planning for Love: The Politics of Prenuptial Agreements," *Stanford Law Review*, 49 (1997), 887–916.

[126] Kaylah Campos Zelig, "Putting Responsibility Back into Marriage: Making a Case for Mandatory Prenuptials," *University of Colorado Law Review*, 64 (1993), 1223–45, at 1233–5.

[127] Robert E. Rains, "A Prenup for Prince William and Kate? England Inches Toward Twentieth Century Law of Antenuptial Agreements: How Shall It Enter the Twenty-First?" *Florida Journal of International Law*, 23 (2011), 447–80.

[128] Marson, "Planning for Love"; Sanette Tanaka, "The Growing Popularity of the Prenup," *The Wall Street Journal* (October 31, 2013), available at: www.wsj.com/articles/SB100014 24052702303615304579157671554066120. However, it is important to note that we know too little about the circumstances in which prenups are signed, the dynamics of the negotiations over them, and their outcomes, because there is hardly any empirical knowledge on prenups as a socio-legal phenomenon.

However, several social and legal barriers prevent prenups from becoming a dominant legal mechanism that can effectively function as a familial coordination tool in the era of bordered globalization. On the social level, most people suffer from an optimistic bias, believing that their marriage will never become a statistic of the national divorce rate. For example, in a small-scale survey (n=270) conducted in the United States at the beginning of the third millennium, although the respondents knew that the national rate of divorce is about 50 percent, they estimated their chance of divorcing, on average, at only 10 percent, with 50 percent of them stating there was 0 percent chance they would divorce.[129] Moreover, many people believe that asking for a prenup or signing one is a negative indicator of the chances of a successful marriage.[130] In the aforementioned survey, 64 percent of the respondents believed divorce would be more likely than otherwise if their fiancé/e asked them to sign a prenuptial agreement.[131]

The legal scholar Ted de Boer argues that there is no reason to think that couples in which the two parties are from different countries do not follow this same pattern of optimistic thinking: "As long as the spouses are still living in (pre)marital bliss, very few of them will contemplate the consequences of a breakup, and fewer still will think of something abstruse as a choice of the court that will handle their divorce, or the law they want to be applied."[132] Indeed, in a quantitative study I conducted with fourteen international interreligious couples living in Israel, none has signed a prenuptial agreement and all have very little knowledge of the legal framework relevant to their family in the hypothetical case of a separation.[133]

Even if spouses were more aware of the potential of prenups to help coordinate familial expectations, and more rationally willing to use them,[134] the current regulation of prenups worldwide is an additional

---

[129] Heather Mahar, "Why Are There so Few Prenuptial Agreements?," *Harvard Law School John M. Olin Center for Law, Economics and Business Discussion Paper Series* (2003), Paper 436, available at: www.law.harvard.edu/programs/olin_center/papers/pdf/436.pdf.

[130] Marson, "Planning for Love," at 893–4.

[131] Mahar, "Why Are There so Few Prenuptial Agreements?," at 16.

[132] Ted M. de Boer, "The Second Revision of the Brussels II Regulation: Jurisdiction and Applicable Law" in Katharina Boele-Woelki & Tone Sverdrup (Eds.), *European Challenges in Contemporary Family Law* (Antwerp: Intersentia, 2008), pp. 321–41, at 322.

[133] Daphna Hacker, "From the Moabite Ruth to Norly the Filipino: Intermarriage and Conversion in the Jewish Nation State" in Hanna Herzog & Ann Braude (Eds.), *Gendering Religion and Politics: Untangling Modernities* (New York: Palgrave Macmillan, 2009), pp. 101–24.

[134] On strategic rationality that might prevent the signing of a prenup, see Antonio Nicolò & Piero Tedeschi, "Missing Contracts: On the Rationality of Not Signing a Prenuptial Agreement," *University of Milano-Bicocca, Department of Statistics, Working Paper* (2006), available at: http://econwpa.repec.org/eps/game/papers/0406/0406001.pdf.

and substantial barrier to their uptake as a common and effective coordination tool. First, different jurisdictions treat the enforceability of prenups differently, with some, such as those of France, the Netherlands, and Belgium, granting them binding significance just like any commercial contract, and others such as those of England and Singapore granting the court broad judicial discretion to ignore the prenup's terms in the name of justice and fairness.[135] In addition, these different jurisdictions employ different procedural and substantial protection measures designed to ensure the free will of the two parties and to balance between the parties' autonomy and public policy.

The US example is a fascinating one. In 1983, a Uniform Premarital Agreement Act (UPAA) was completed. Although it focuses on economic issues, it allows the marrying couple to agree on "any other matter, including their personal rights and obligations, not in violation of public policy or a statute imposing a criminal penalty."[136] Over three decades since its drafting, only twenty-seven states have adopted it.[137] No less interesting is the fact that even the states that *have* adopted the UPAA have modified it differently, by introducing a variety of procedural safeguards such as a demand for notary authorization, legal counseling, and disclosure of financial information, as well as more substantial changes – including two states that allow same-sex couples to sign prenups.[138] This procedural and substantial variation in relation to, among other aspects, the ability of the parties to choose the law that will govern their prenup and the public policy concerns that justify ignoring such choice, have led to a situation in the United States whereby a prenup that was signed in one state might not be respected in another.[139] The difficulties in reaching a consensus in one federal republic are but an illustration of the immense challenges embedded in any attempt to reach such a consensus on a global scale.[140]

---

[135] Ong, "Prenuptial Agreements," at 403.

[136] Uniform Premarital Agreement Act 2001, 9C U.L.A. 35 (2001), s. 3(a)(1)-(8).

[137] See "Legislative Fact Sheet – Premarital Agreement Act," available at: www.uniformlaws .org/LegislativeFactSheet.aspx?title=Premarital%20Agreement%20Act.

[138] Amberlynn Curry, "The Uniform Premarital Agreement Act and Its Variations throughout the States," *Journal of American Academy of Matrimonial Lawyers,* 23 (2010), 284–355.

[139] Julia Halloran McLaughlin, "Premarital Agreements and Choice of Law: 'One, Two, Three, Baby, You and Me,'" *Missouri Law Review,* 72(3) (2007), 793–854.

[140] Indeed, the 1978 Hague Convention on the Law Applicable to Matrimonial Property, which allows spouses to choose the law that will govern their matrimonial property from a limited set of options, has so far been ratified by only three countries. See Article 3 to the Convention. For the list of ratifying countries, see "25: Convention of 14 March 1978 on the Law Applicable to Matrimonial Property Regimes," available at: www.hcch.net/en/ instruments/conventions/status-table/?cid=87.

Finally, even those jurisdictions that enforce prenups are in many cases reluctant to do so in relation to the ongoing life of the family while the couple remains married, and treat them as enforceable contracts only in the context of divorce.[141] Moreover, even in a divorce scenario, provisions related to child custody and support are not respected by courts if their enforcement does not correlate with the children's best interests.[142] Hence, although prenups that plan for divorce *ex ante* can limitedly affect each spouse's decisions while married – for example, staying at home to care for the children knowing substantial alimony is guaranteed in the case of divorce – they are a long way from allowing detailed coordination of daily family life predivorce.

Going back to the special challenges created by bordered globalization, as discussed in the previous part of this chapter, one must note the additional chaos created by spousal conflicts over the enforcement of religious prenups brought before courts in Western countries. Both Islamic and Jewish marriages include mandatory premarriage contractual elements, and I will now focus on the former.[143] According to Islamic law, marriage is a private contract between a man and a woman (the latter often represented by a male guardian). The marriage contract is described by Islamic family law scholars as a protective mechanism that affords a Muslim woman a chance to customize her marriage through provisions that guarantee her rights vis-à-vis her husband, such as her right to pursue higher education, to participate in the paid labor force, not to clean the house, and to initiate a divorce. Unfortunately, this contractual opportunity to secure women's rights during marriage is rarely used.[144] In practice, most Islamic prenups focus on the sum and conditions of the dower (*Mahr*) – the payment the wife is entitled to receive from the husband. Although the dower is a mandatory part of an Islamic marriage that can assist the wife in the case of divorce or the husband's death,[145] restricting the prenup

---

[141] Marson, "Planning for Love," at 900.

[142] Uniform Premarital Agreement Act 2001, § 10, 9C U.L.A. 27 9C U.L.A. 35; Curry, "The Uniform Premarital Agreement Act"; Jeffrey A. Parness, "Parentage Prenups and Midnups," *Georgia State University Law Review*, 31(2) (2014), 343–76.

[143] There is an ongoing debate within Jewish law over the covenantal and contractual elements of marriage, and the relations between the two. Notwithstanding, there is a rabbinical consensus that the *Ketubah* – the Jewish version of the *Mahr* and the *Dower* – is a precondition to every marriage. On the *Ketubah* and the question of its enforceability by American civil law, see Broyde, "New York's Regulation of Jewish Marriage."

[144] McClain, "Marriage Pluralism in the United States," at 323.

[145] In many cases, payment of the *Mahr* is divided into two parts – one that must be paid to the wife immediately upon marriage (*muajjal*) and a delayed part (*muwajjal*) that can become relevant upon divorce, the husband's death, or a set future date. Although

only to this narrow aspect leaves the woman's obligation to obey her husband (in return for his duty to support her) unconditioned by a broader and more detailed contract.

As the thorough analysis of legal scholar Pascale Fournier reveals, Western jurisdictions have responded to the question of the enforceability of the dower payment with a mixture of three different ideological approaches: the Liberal–Legal Pluralist approach, the Liberal–Formal Equality approach, and the Liberal–Substantive Equality approach.[146] According to the Liberal–Legal Pluralist approach, religious law is part of the legal pluralism governing people's family life that should be respected in the name of the right to identity of ethnic communities and individuals living in the Global North. Interestingly, under this approach, Fournier identified court decisions that enforced the dower, as well as court decisions that refused to do so. In Canada, for example, the court in British Columbia recognized the dower as a marriage agreement that can be enforced by civil courts according to the civil law governing prenups, whereas the court in Ontario decided it could not enforce the dower as it is a religious act that should not be interfered with by civil law and courts. Hence, both courts voiced a multicultural respect for the dower but came to contradicting results as to its enforceability. Meanwhile, the Liberal–Formal Equality approach perceives the law as a neutral, objective, and autonomous social sphere, detached from society and morality. Fournier found court decisions from Canada, the United States, Germany, and France that rely on this formalist perception of the law and regard the dower as a secular contract that should be treated as any other. The judges in these cases approached Islamic evidence on the dower as irrelevant, and ruled on the validity of the monetary obligation only according to the civil law governing prenups or the civil right of the two parties to choose the law that would govern their marriage. Whereas some of these decisions enforced the dower, because the judges believed it to follow the civil law requirements, other decisions refused to enforce it, arguing that in the specific circumstances the dower's (contract's) conditions were too vague or abstract, or there was lack of consent. Finally, the Liberal–Substantive Equality approach, which places gender fairness and gender power imbalance at its center, refuses to treat the dower either as a group expression

according to the *Halafi* and the *Malike* schools, a part of the *Mahr* must be paid immediately upon marriage, the *Shafi'I* and *Hanbali* schools allow the whole sum of the *Mahr* to be delayed, for example, until divorce. See Fournier, *Muslim Marriages in Western Courts*, at 12, 20–3.

[146] Fournier, *Muslim Marriages in Western Courts*, Ch. 3.

of Muslim subjectivity, as the first approach does, or as a private secular prenup, as the second approach does. Rather, this third approach views the dower as a public institution that should be subjected to state intervention in the name of substantive equality. This approach has led a court in Quebec to enforce a dower, although it was the wife who initiated the divorce (*khu1*) and although, according to the Islamic law relevant to the couple, a woman is entitled to the dower only if the husband is the one divorcing her. However, the Liberal–Substantive Equality approach can also lead to the conclusion that a dower should not be enforced. Indeed, Fournier traced decisions from several countries, including Canada, that refuse to enforce the dower – either in the name of the husband's right to equality and justice, which deems that he should not be made to pay more than he is obliged to under civil alimony and property law, or in the name of the wife's right to equality and justice that is jeopardized by Islamic law, which allows her the dower but does not recognize her right to half of the marital property. As Fournier concludes, not only can all three very different ideological approaches be found, simultaneously, in the same jurisdiction, but each approach also leads to inconsistent and contradicting judicial rulings in relation to prenups' enforceability.

I would like to end this part of the chapter by arguing that even if we could, theoretically, overcome these legal barriers by drafting an international convention that could be signed by all the world's countries to achieve the harmonization of the substantial and procedural conditions needed for enforceable prenups (capable of regulating broad areas of family life and including a choice of law provision), we should not, normatively, strive to do so. In my opinion, prenups are, by and large, a bad idea. My antiprenuptial stance is based on arguments related to spousal relations, parental relations, and the relations between the family and the state.

Starting with spousal relations, the so-called optimistic bias mentioned earlier is most severe among couples on the verge of their wedding – becoming, in effect, a honeymoon bias. The combined level of romantic love, trust, and feelings of emotional security is usually at its peak. It is unrealistic to expect the spouses to envision, in any meaningful manner, future tensions, conflicts, or betrayals at this point in their lives.[147]

Even for couples not blinded by love, a prenup might not be the result of autonomous rational choice. In the case of arranged marriages, the prenup will not necessarily reflect the wishes of the spouses. In nonarranged marriages, the problem might be the power imbalance

[147] Ong, "Prenuptial Agreements," at 408–9.

between the spouses, characterizing many marriages, especially in our era. One such imbalance that is well-known and widely studied is that relating to gender.[148] Women usually have less capital than their male spouses,[149] experience greater societal pressure than men to marry,[150] and can be more risk averse[151] – all of which can weaken their position in the negotiation over the prenup.[152] In the era of bordered globalization, one should add emigration-related power imbalance. As will be detailed in Chapter 5 on citizenship, an immigrating spouse might suffer from status dependency and might agree to an unfair prenup for fear of deportation. Because most immigrating spouses are women,[153] and because the immigrating spouse lacks, in many cases, economic power and the support of the family of origin, an especially vulnerable intersectional position emerges, whereby the woman has significantly less bargaining power than the man. In such cases, the notion of a prenup as an agreement between two autonomous individuals who negotiate freely their familial expectations and interests could not be further from the truth.

As for the parental relations to be governed by the prenup, I would argue that it is impossible to imagine the emotional and economic consequences of parenthood. Becoming and being a parent are so unlike any previous life experiences that one cannot understand their meaning or envision their impact before they are even a reality. Moreover, especially in the era of bordered globalization, any plans for a long-lasting spousal, let alone parental, relationship, will undoubtedly face unpredicted and shifting circumstances. Enforcing the preliminary and premature terms of the contract might be impossible and, even if possible, harmful, especially for children.[154] Children cannot be parties to their parents' prenup and were only potential children at the time of its drafting, rather than

---

[148] Ibid., at 407–8.

[149] Gail Frommer Brod, "Premarital Agreement and Gender Justice," *Yale Journal of Law and Feminism*, 6 (1994), 229–95, at 239–42.

[150] Daphna Hacker, "Single and Married Women in the Law of Israel – A Feminist Perspective," *Feminist Legal Studies*, 9(1) (2001), 29–56.

[151] For a critical literature review of studies showing that women are more risk-averse than men, pointing to the empirical challenges of testing the gendered dimensions of risk aversion, see Julie A. Nelson, "Are Women Really More Risk-Averse than Men?" Global Development and Environment Institute, Working Paper No. 12-05, Tufts University (2012).

[152] See the dissenting opinion of Lady Hale, in *Radmacher (formerly Granatino) v. Granatino* [2010] UKSC 42.

[153] See Introduction, fn. 22.

[154] See also Ong, "Prenuptial Agreements," at 406–7.

actual children with their unique and dynamic personalities, preferences, and interests. To bind the children to a contract they were not party to, which was signed by their parents when attempting to envision their imaginary future offspring, is actually to overlook the children. Indeed, as mentioned earlier, courts around the world tend to ignore prenups' custody and child-support provisions if they are deemed to contradict the actual children's best interests.

But child custody and support are not the only problematic parenting-related provisions in prenups. It is important to note here Blecher-Prigat's argument that the common distinction between horizontal spousal relations and vertical parental relations distorts our understanding of the interrelations between these two dimensions. Parenting a child together gives birth to a new meaning of horizontal spousal relations that simply does not exist when the couple is child-free. From the moment the child is conceived, vertical spousal relations are embedded within, and affected by, the joint parenthood project. Hence, even the prenup's conditions that are supposedly related only to the spousal relations, such as how the marital property will be distributed, should be judged in the context of the economic consequences of the parental division of labor.[155] Furthermore, Blecher-Prigat has another, even more radical, argument that I find very convincing and inspiring in the context of prenups. She argues that the marital property should be conceptualized as the family property. When two adults bring children into the world, they implicitly agree to support these children together. Hence, she asserts, children have a birth-right to their parents' property.[156] A prenup that agrees that the marital property will be divided equally between the spouses in the case of a divorce – for example, in the scenario of a family with three children and sole maternal custody – creates an unjust distribution: one family member, the father, receives half of the family property, while four family members – the mother and the three children – are left with the remaining half between them. The shift of conceptualization, suggested by Blecher-Prigat, could lead to the children having property ownership rights, or at least to a recognition of their right to stay in the family home with their custodian parent until they are grown and economically independent.[157]

---

[155] Ayelet Blecher-Prigat, "The Costs of Raising Children: Towards a Theory of Financial Obligations between Co-Parents," *Theoretical Inquiries in Law*, 13(1) (2012), 154–207.

[156] Ayelet Blecher-Prigat, "On Spousal Property Law and Children's Interests in Israel," a lecture given at the International Conference on Children's Right – Theory and Practice, The Minerva Center for Human Rights, The Hebrew University, Jerusalem (2005).

[157] See also Lifshitz, "The Liberal Transformation of Spousal Law," at 46.

As for the prenups coordinating the expectations between the couple and the state, the latter has a legitimate concern that the prenup may externalize the burdens of divorce, even if these can be internalized by the couple or by one of the spouses. This is one of the concerns at the heart of legal scholar Julia McLaughlin's argument that spouses should not be allowed to condition future marital property rights in jurisdictions with marital property law aimed at leaving the dependent spouse financially secure. According to McLaughlin, marital property rights should be understood as materializing only when the couple divorce, and so no individual should be allowed to waive them until they mature. This is so not only in the name of the economically dependent spouse's right to personal integrity (best performed ex-post the materialization of her rights, rather than ex-ante) but also in the name of the general public's interest that the dependent spouse – and, I would add, also her children – should not become an economic burden on the welfare system.[158] Spousal, parental, and family–state relations are interrelated, and jointly point to the limitation of prenups to capture them in a morally ex-ante way.

One particular issue that is highly connected to bordered globalization and that also demonstrates the problematic nature of prenups, and hence my argument that we should not strive to encourage them by internationally harmonizing the law surrounding them, is that of provisions on relocation. One could argue that in our era, it is crucial for couples to negotiate the possibility of relocation in a prenup, for three reasons: first, because there is no global legal consensus on the circumstances in which parental relocation is allowed;[159] second, as relocation becomes relevant to more families due to voluntary short- and long-term cross-border emigration; and third, because the ability or inability to relocate can dramatically affect

---

[158] Julia Halloran McLaughlin, "Should Marital Property Rights Be Inalienable? Preserving the Marriage Ante," *Nebraska Law Review*, 82(3) (2003), 460–98.

[159] Countries disagree on what factors should be considered by the court when ruling over a request for parental relocation, and who should bear the burden of proof – the parent asking to relocate or the parent objecting to it? See Theresa Glennon, "Divided Parents, Shared Children: Conflicting Approaches to Relocation Disputes in the USA" in Katharina Boele-Woelki (Ed.), *Debates in Family Law around the Globe at the Dawn of the 21st Century* (Antwerp: Intersentia, 2009), pp. 83–106; Christina G. Jeppesen de Boer, "Parental Relocation, Free Movement Rights and Joint Parenting" in Boele-Woelki (Ed.), *Debates in Family Law around the Globe at the Dawn of the 21st Century*, pp. 107–20. Relocation law around the globe is gender-biased so long as it restricts only the freedom of movement of the parent who wishes to relocate with the children – usually the mother – while allowing the parent who wishes to relocate without the children – usually the father, to do so, though the expected distance between him and the children might have a detrimental effect on their relationship.

each of the spouses and their (future) children. During marriage, it can affect each spouse's studies and career opportunities, their connections with extended family and friends, and their cultural environment. After divorce, it can additionally affect parent–child relations and the children's ties with extended family members, friends, and cultures. However, both a prenup that states that each spouse is free to relocate and one that sets an international radius limitation clause, also known as a relocation clause (that is, prohibiting each spouse from relocating outside the country of current residence without the consent of the other) are problematic.

Let us think of a hypothetical, yet plausible, scenario of an international couple: Jim was born and still lives in Washington DC, where he works as a lobbyist and where he met Julia, who came to Washington from Costa Rica to study. They fall in love and decide to marry. On the initiative of Jim's well-off parents, a prenup is signed, stating among other things that the domicile of the couple is to be the District of Columbia and that if, and as long as, the couple have minor children, each spouse will not leave the District without the consent of the other. The prenup duly signed, they marry and go on to have two children. Seven years later, Jim falls in love with another woman and initiates a divorce. Julia wishes to move back to Costa Rica and to take the children – now five and two years old – with her. Jim objects, arguing she cannot as she is obliged by the prenup to stay in DC until the children reach the age of 18. Should a court be allowed to intervene? Well of course it must, since (as detailed in Chapter 2) one of the law's roles in relation to families is to resolve family disputes, and as even under contractual doctrine a party can argue in court that a contract should not be enforced. Should the court prevent Julia from relocating with the children? It may, but in my opinion there are many possible reasons that it should not.

As we have already touched upon, enforcing a prenup is not a straightforward matter as there are several factors at play. First, Jim and Julia might have suffered from honeymoon bias syndrome and found it hard to imagine not wanting to live in the same country one day. Second, even if Julia had wanted to leave the option of returning to her homeland open, it could be argued that her emigration dependency and familial isolation, coupled with the relative weakness of her situation based on her gender and economic vulnerability, probably made her relinquish this option in the face of pressure from Jim and his parents. Third, while during the prenup negotiation Julia might have thought that staying in DC in the case of a divorce would not be such a bad scenario, she could not have imagined the intense daily demands of motherhood once the children were born. This intensity, coupled with the increased expenses that come with children and the higher income her husband enjoyed (as a native English speaker, a more experienced employee, and a man)[160] led Jim and Julia to decide that he would invest all his energy in his lobbying career in Congress, while she would suspend her own career aspirations and would instead stay at home full-time to take care of the young children. Now, as a divorced mother with no independent income, she wishes to move back to Costa Rica, where the cost of living is cheaper and where she can be assisted with childcare by her parents. Fourth, the children were not even born when their parents' radius limitation clause was signed, so their current needs and interests must be considered by the court regardless of their parents' prechildren agreement. It might be the case, for example, that one of the children has special health needs that can be better served by the Costa Rican public health services, which are known to offer high quality care. In the case of the five-year-old, he might have already voiced an opinion about the possibility of relocation, which should be heard and taken into account by the court.[161] Finally, if the court defers Julia's request, it should consider altering other provisions in the prenup, so as to make sure that neither she,[162] nor the DC tax payers, have to bear the costs of the deferral if Jim can do so through alimony, child support, and property division. Hence, even if an international consensus could theoretically be reached, to ensure that relocation provisions in prenups are enforced – regardless of past and present circumstances, and independently of other contractual provisions – such consensus would be morally wrong. Needless to say, if past and present circumstances are taken into

---

[160] On the maternal penalty in the US, see Tamar Kricheli-Katz, "Choice, Discrimination, and the Motherhood Penalty," *Law & Society Review*, 46(3) (2012), 557–87.

[161] Article 12 of the Convention on the Rights of the Child states: "1. States Parties shall assure to the child who is capable of forming his or her own views the right to express those views freely in all matters affecting the child, the views of the child being given due weight in accordance with the age and maturity of the child. 2. For this purpose, the child shall in particular be provided the opportunity to be heard in any judicial and administrative proceedings affecting the child, either directly, or through a representative or an appropriate body, in a manner consistent with the procedural rules of national law." There are debates over the minimal age relevant to children's right to participate in judicial procedures, and I agree with those who argue that even young children can voice an opinion, if approached properly. See "Fact Sheet: The Right to Participation," UNICEF, available at: www.unicef.org/crc/files/Right-to-Participation.pdf; Gerison Lansdown, "The Realisation of Children's Participation Rights: Critical Reflections" in Bary Percy-Smith & Nigel Thomas (Eds.), *A Handbook of Children and Young People's Participation: Perspectives from Theory and Practice* (London: Routledge, 2010), pp. 11–23, at 12.

[162] Blecher-Prigat, "The Costs of Raising Children."

account, and additional relevant contractual provisions altered, prenups lose their potential to function as a tool to guarantee comprehensive and long-lasting coordination between the two spouses, and between them and the state. This loss of functionality, in my opinion, is a price that should be paid.

While prenups can be used as a socio-legal platform for spousal anticipatory dialogue, and should be used to try to overcome state or parochial religious discriminatory or otherwise harmful family law,[163] their binding force, especially if the couple have children together, should be made weak – within an overall attempt by the law to protect caregiving parents, children, and the general public's interest in fair and just outcomes of marriage.

Conclusion

This chapter exposes the growing difficulty of coordinating familial expectations, as more and more families become *globorderized* – that is, shaped by a synthesis of globalization and borders. Families in which each spouse comes from a different country, families in which each spouse belongs to a different religion, families that were created through religious law and move to a civil family law country, and immigrating families that live in a civil family law country but practice subnational religious family law, all embody a mixture of crossing borders and maintaining and at times even strengthening them.

Although globalization invites or forces people to move across national borders, family law is still, primarily, national. With the exception of the EU's attempts to harmonize family law,[164] no harmonizing international law has so far materialized in most areas relevant to marriage, divorce, or parenting. Hence, people moving from one country to another carry with them their or their ancestors' country of origin's family law (as may their

---

[163] For example, a few feminist activists and rabbis have drafted prenups with special provisions aimed at deterring Jewish husbands from using their greater power in keeping their wife locked in an unwanted marriage (the *Agunah* problem). The effectiveness of these provisions is debated both in civil and religious courts – see Michelle Greenberg-Korbin, "Religious Tribunals and Secular Courts: Navigating Power and Powerlessness," *Pepperdine Law Review*, 41(5) (2014), 997–1012; Yehiel Kaplan, "Solving the Distress of Women Who Are Refused a *Get* through Punitive Alimony," *Hamishpat,* 10 (2005), 381–448 (Hebrew).

[164] For example, see the efforts of the Commission of Europe on Family Law to advance the harmonization of family law in member states. See the Commission's website at: http://ceflonline.net/.

offspring). Thus, a clash between two national family law systems may emerge, with the country of origin's family law turning, in some cases, to subnational law in the host country. As shown in this chapter, this *legal intercourse* can create socio-legal confusion, conflict, and chaos, especially in relation to gender equality.

As the Canadian case of abolishing family arbitration and the anti-Sharia laws in some states in the United States[165] demonstrate, globalization can lead to a backlash reaction that tightens legal national borders and reduces tolerance to other national laws and to subnational laws that might govern families. However, the experience from England (dramatically altered by the recent Brexit referendum) demonstrates that backlash is not the only possible reaction, and that national family law and subnational family law interact in the era of bordered globalization in different ways that change them both.

The lack of one global family law and the diversity of responses of nations, communities, and individuals to the multiple and dynamic families laws make the law a part of the global familial chaos, rather than a stable, predictable, and certain framework that can assist *globorderized* families to coordinate their mutual expectations and their expectations vis-à-vis the states relevant to their lives. As I have argued in the third part of this chapter, trying to overcome this chaos through privatizing the legal framework, via prenups, is both pragmatically and normatively problematic. Indeed, the debate over prenups is a good example of the fallacy of the idea that the family is, and is only, a private entity.[166] Society's interest in having functioning and economically independent families, as well as its responsibility toward vulnerable family members, rightfully prevent spouses from crafting *private marriage* and *private parenthood* through a contract.[167]

So are families doomed to confusion and conflict in the era of bordered globalization, or can the law assist them somewhat? I believe countries can make their law clearer and more known to the public, in and outside their borders. By doing so, they can educate potential newcomers on the impact of their law on families within their territory. For those who

---

[165] Discussed earlier. See earlier note 111.

[166] Lifshitz, "The Liberal Transformation of Spousal Law," at 45–49.

[167] For opposing opinions, supporting private regulation of families through contracts, see, for example, Marjorie Maguire Shultz, "Contractual Ordering of Marriage: A New Model for State Policy," *California Law Review*, 70(2) (1982), 204–334; Yehezkel Margalit, "Determining Legal Parentage by Agreement," PhD Dissertation, Bar-Ilan University (2011) (Hebrew).

have a choice of destination, this information might make a difference. Those with a choice can also coordinate their expectations through a pre-nup if they wish, and choose to live in a jurisdiction that will enforce it. However, the lack of coordinated international private law, even on basic issues such as the validity of marriage and the law applicable to divorce and its outcomes, the intensity and resilience of the forces making people cross national borders and the dynamic and vulnerable nature of family relations make such efforts pragmatically marginal and normatively undesirable. Indeed, we must conclude that the more people affected by globalization need the law to assist them in coordinating their conflicting expectations with their family members or with the state in which they live, the more unlikely it is that the law can meet the challenge.

4

Transnational Reproduction Services

Introduction

The first cross-border reproduction service[1] story is as old as the Old Testament itself. In the Book of Genesis we are told about Abraham, God-chosen first monotheist, who immigrated from what is present-day Turkey, and settled in Canaan (ancient Israel) with Sarah, his beloved and beautiful wife. After realizing she was barren, Sarah offered Hagar, her Egyptian female slave, to Abraham, so he could inseminate her. Sarah was planning to take the baby boy who would be born to Hagar to be her son and the patriarch's successor. But things did not go as planned. Feeling that pregnant Hagar was becoming arrogant and taking advantage of her new status as the carrier of the patriarch's future child, Sarah tortured Hagar so badly that she fled to the desert. Only after being promised by an angel that her son would live and prosper did she return to Abraham's camp to give birth to Ishmael. Later, to Sarah's delight, despite her age and years of infertility she miraculously fell pregnant and gave birth to Isaak. To secure her son's primogeniture, she pressured Abraham to outcast Hagar and Ishmael, and he reluctantly sent them away. Again, thanks to divine intervention, Hagar and Ishmael were saved and Ishmael was prosperous, as foretold. He went on to become, according to both Jewish and Islamic traditions, the father of the Arab–Islamic nation.[2]

---

[1] As detailed in the Introduction, the literature uses the terms *fertility tourism, procreative tourism, infertility exile, reproduction emigration,"* and *cross-border reproduction care* to refer to the phenomenon of people in one country traveling to another to buy gametes or pregnancy services. I suggest *transnational reproduction services* and *cross-border reproduction services* as terms that avoid both the holiday and suffering connotations embedded in *tourism* and *exile*, respectively, and that emphasize the commercial aspect of this phenomenon. These terms are also broader than the others as they capture, in addition to fertility and pregnancy services (surrogacy and delivery) administered abroad, the importation of reproduction-related materials, such as sperm and contraceptives, and abortion, which is often excluded from the discourse on reproduction in the global era.

[2] Tamar Katz Peled, "Surrogate Motherhood in Israel: Legal, Social, and Cultural Construction," PhD Dissertation, Haifa University (2014) (Hebrew).

The biblical custom of taking an enslaved woman from another nation to become a surrogate mother for an infertile privileged couple was legally recognized by several Ancient Eastern societies.[3] It echoes the power imbalance embedded in modern international surrogacy, discussed in the third part of this chapter. Nowadays, the cross-border reproduction movement includes not only the use of ovum and pregnancy services of "foreign" women but also sperm export and international travel for fertility treatments, delivery services,[4] and abortion – the latter discussed in the second part of this chapter. Indeed, while continuity over the generations is of significance, four recent developments have made the cross-border reproduction services of our era unprecedentedly common, diverse, and complex.

First, infertility is on the rise. According to one recent international estimate, approximately 16 percent of heterosexual couples around the world are currently affected by life-time infertility.[5] The World Health Organization (WHO) highlights multiple factors – infectious, environmental, genetic, and dietary in origin – as possible contributors to infertility, as well as the phenomenon of people postponing attempts to become parents until a later age.[6] Thanks to globalization, more and more people facing the challenge of infertility are seeking reproduction services, wherever they can find and afford them. In Europe alone, it is estimated that at least 24,000–30,000 assisted reproduction interventions (intrauterine insemination and *in vitro* fertilization) are performed annually on, at least, 11,000–14,000 women who cross their nations' borders to receive this service in another country within the EU.[7] These figures

---

[3] Ibid., 94–5.

[4] On the controversies over "maternity tourists" in the United Kingdom, see Jack Doyle, "One in 14 New Mothers are Maternity Tourists: £182m Bill for Births to Short Term Migrants and Visitors," *Mail Online* (July 18, 2014), available at: www.dailymail.co.uk/news/article-2697892/One-14-new-mothers-maternity-tourists-182m-bill-births-short-term-migrants-visitors.html.

[5] Karl Nygren, David Adamson, Fernando Zegers-Hochschild, & Jacques de Mouzon, "Cross-Border Fertility Care – International Committee Monitoring Assisted Reproductive Technologies Global Survey: 2006 Data and Estimates," *Fertility and Sterility*, 94(1) (2010), e4–e10, available at: www.fertstert.org/article/S0015-0282(09)04298-8/pdf.

[6] Maya N. Mascarenhas, Seth R. Flaxman, Ties Boerma, Sheryl Vanderpoel, & Gretchen A. Stevens, "National, Regional, and Global Trends in Infertility Prevalence since 1990: A Systematic Analysis of 277 Health Surveys," *Plos Medicine*, 9(12) (2012), e1001356, available at: www.plosmedicine.org/article/info%3Adoi%2F10.1371%2Fjournal.pmed.1001356#s3.

[7] Françoise Shenfield, Jacques De Mouzon, Guido Pennings, Anna Pia Ferraretti, Anders Nyboe Andersen, Guido De Wert, Goossens Veerle, & the ESHRE Taskforce on Cross Border Reproductive Care, "Cross-Border Reproductive Care in Six European Countries," *Human Reproduction*, 25(6) (2010), 1361–8.

do not include the many Europeans who travel for fertility treatments, including for surrogacy, outside the EU.

The second development, which highlights the distortion embedded in infertility statistics that center only on heterosexual couples, as the 16 percent statistics mentioned earlier, is the growing legitimacy of single and of gay, lesbian, and other nonheterosexual kinds of parenthood. This legitimacy has created a new audience for reproduction services, including services through the global market. Indeed, in the aforementioned European survey that yielded the estimation of cross-border reproduction cycles, 6 percent of those treated identified themselves as being single, and almost 10 percent as homo- or bisexual.

The third development encouraging cross-border reproduction movement is technological in nature. Current fertility technology allows procedures such as sperm and ova storage and export, and the transplantation of the fertilized ovum of one woman into another woman's uterus, and thus enables long-distance reproduction services not possible in the past. The United States, for example, is the number-one sperm-exporting nation. It sends sperm to 60 other countries and dominates 65 percent of this multi million dollar global market.[8] Interestingly, it is Denmark that has one of the largest sperm banks in the world and it is estimated, for example, that 10 percent of sperm used in the UK is Danish in origin.[9] The success of this small country at exporting sperm – via commercial clinics using such slogans as "Congratulations! It's a Viking!" – points to the racist component in this phenomenon manifested in intended parents' preferences for blond and blue-eyed babies.[10] Such slogans are also an example of the contribution of global media technology – especially the Internet, as discussed in the first chapter – which exposes millions around the globe to the possibility of becoming consumers of, and providers for, the global reproduction industry.

Both the US's and Denmark's success in the global sperm market cannot be understood detached from the existence of diverse national regulations – the fourth development that increases the global movement

---

[8] Jay Newton-Small, "Frozen Assets: America is the Largest Exporter of Sperm. But what Happens When All Those Kids Grow Up and Decide to Go Looking for Daddy?" *Time* (April 5, 2012). Available at: http://content.time.com/time/magazine/article/0,9171,2111234,00.html?pcd=pw-hl.

[9] Sandra Nielsen, "Viking Sperm-Sales are Plummeting Right Now" *NewStatesman* (May 1, 2013). Available at: www.newstatesman.com/business/2013/05/viking-sperm-sales-are-plummeting-right-now.

[10] Charlotte Kroløkke, "Click a Donor," *Journal of Consumer Culture*, 9(1) (2009), 7–30.

of gametes, of people who cannot conceive unassisted, and of new-borns. It is the fact that some countries allow anonymous sperm banks, whereas others demand full or partial disclosure of the genetic father; that some countries allow ovum donation or sale and some prohibit it; and that some allow surrogacy, whereas others ban it completely or restrict it to heterosexual couples as intended parents, that creates, motivates, and sustains a global market of reproduction services.[11] This regulatory diversity among nations in matters of reproduction, together with states' inability or unwillingness to control their citi-zens' reproduction-related activities outside their borders, together with the lack of international regulation and enforcement, constitutes the most significant impetus to current cross-border reproduction movement.[12]

In this chapter, I will discuss two examples of this movement. The first is cross-border abortion movement, focusing on the movement of women who seek abortion from the Republic of Ireland to England and Wales.[13] Though many do not perceive this kind of movement as part of the global reproduction services phenomenon, I do.[14] Abortion is part of the quest for individual control over reproduction, and an unintended or risky pregnancy is an accident of fertility, as is infertility. As declared in the Programme of Action of the UN International Conference on Population and Development, signed by 179 countries in 1994, "reproductive health is a state of complete physical, mental and social wellbeing and not merely the absence of disease or infirmity, in all matters relating to the reproduct-ive system and to its functions and processes." It includes the "capability to

[11] Richard F. Storrow, "The Proportionality Problem in Cross-Border Reproduction Care" in Glenn Cohen (Ed.), *The Globalization of Health Care: Legal and Ethical Issues* (Oxford University Press, 2013), pp. 125–47; Kimberly M. Mutcherson, "Open Fertility Borders: Defending Access to Cross-Border Fertility Care in the United States" in Cohen (Ed.), *The Globalization of Health Care: Legal and Ethical Issues*, pp. 148–63.

[12] Richard F. Storrow, "Assisted Reproduction on Treacherous Terrain: The Legal Hazard of Cross-Border Reproductive Travel," *Reproductive BioMedicine Online*, 23(5) (2011), 538–45, available at: www.rbmojournal.com/article/S1472-6483(11)00412-3/fulltext.

[13] I refer here only to the Republic of Ireland, though the case of Northern Ireland shares similar traits. See Fiona Bloomer & Kellie O'Dowd, "Restricted Access to Abortion in the Republic of Ireland and Northern Ireland: Exploring Abortion Tourism and Barriers to Legal Reform," *Culture, Health & Sexuality*, 16(4) (2014), 366–80; Marie-Louise Connolly, "Abortion: Appeal Against High Court Ruling begins in Belfast," BBC News (June 20, 2016), available at: www.bbc.com/news/uk-northern-ireland-36574902.

[14] See also Christabelle Sethna & Marion Doull, "Accidental Tourism: Canadian Women, Abortion Tourism, and Travel," *Women's Studies*, 41 (2012), 457–75.

reproduce and the freedom to decide if, when and how often to do so."[15] Hence, when using the term *reproduction services* I am including those services that prevent, or end, an unwanted pregnancy (contraception and abortion) as well as those that assist in cases of infertility (artificial insemination, *in vitro* fertilization, or surrogacy).

From this perspective, the thousands of Irish women who cross the border to the UK each year to seek an abortion because their country does not allow it, and the UK clinics that provide abortion services to Irish women, are part of the interplay between globalization and borders in the reproduction context. Moreover, the Irish case study is particularly fascinating because it exposes the potential influence of the public, media, medical, and legal discourses related to reproduction autonomy that are taking place outside the nation-state, even on the most restrictive, stubborn, and religiously-driven national legislature in matters of reproduction.

The second case study explored in this chapter is that of international and multinational surrogacy, in particular as it was, until recently, manifested by the relations between India, as the home country of the surrogate mothers, and Israel, as the home country of the intended parents, who often used ova from a third country. This case study highlights the complex power relations between providers (the countries and individuals providing reproduction services) and recipients (the countries and individuals receiving those services) and the national and international legal systems' role in shaping these relations.

The chapter will end with a discussion on the insights that can be drawn regarding the interrelations between globalization, borders, familiality, and the law, from placing cross-border abortion alongside cross-border surrogacy.

Cross-Border Abortion – The Case of the Republic of Ireland and the UK

The only time I saw a real person dying in front of a TV camera was on the third episode of the 2011 BBC series "Toughest Place to Be a ...".[16] In this cross-border series, each episode accompanied one British worker who traveled to a developing country to try to do the job he

---

[15] See United Nations *Report of the International Conference on Population and Development* (1994), available at: www.un.org/popin/icpd/conference/offeng/poa.html.

[16] "Toughest Place to Be a ...," available at: www.bbc.co.uk/programmes/b00z5868.

or she did at home. Although the series centered on occupations, it also contributed to our familial global awareness, allowing us a comparative glimpse in relation to social and legal experiences relevant to becoming and being a parent. In this specific episode, a midwife from Birmingham was sent to work in an obstetric hospital in Monrovia, the capital of Liberia in West Africa. Liberia is one of the world's poorest countries,[17] where one in 120 women dies in childbirth,[18] and abortion for social or economic reasons is illegal.[19] The most horrendous case from this episode started when a woman entered the hospital in a very bad condition. It took the staff some time to realize that she suffered from an infection caused by a poisonous leaf she had inserted into her vagina, a customary practice aimed at inducing an abortion. Even after identifying the cause of the worsening condition of the woman, very little could be done for her. There was a shortage of basic antibiotics that could have saved her life. She was dying in front of the camera, and we, like the hospital staff and the shocked British midwife, were helpless. Whereas locals had seen many cases like this before, it presented outsiders from abroad with an astonishing scenario.

This horrible case is a reminder of what women, throughout history and in our times, were and are willing to do to terminate an unwanted pregnancy in the face of a patriarchal society trying to rob them of their reproduction autonomy. This is true not only in extremely poor and undeveloped countries such as Liberia,[20] but also in Western countries such as Ireland, Poland, and Italy, which, like Liberia, perceive the fetus as a human being and abortion as murder. Although, in these more developed countries, death is rarer, each year their antiabortion laws cause tens of thousands of their female citizens to suffer shame, humiliation, suffering, health problems, and economic debts due to the termination of unplanned or risky pregnancies. Many more avoid abortion and instead experience forced parenthood, with its resultant emotional, health, and

---

[17] "The Poorest Countries in the World," *Global Finance*, available at: www.gfmag.com/global-data/economic-data/the-poorest-countries-in-the-world?page=8.

[18] World Health Organization, *Liberia: Maternal and Perinatal Health Profile* (2015), available at: www.who.int/maternal_child_adolescent/epidemiology/profiles/maternal/lbr.pdf.

[19] Section 16.3 of Liberia: Penal Code, July 1976.

[20] Mexico is another country with abhorrent anti-abortion law consequences for women and for girls as young as 13. See, for example, the recent case of a 13-year-old girl who was refused abortion because the judge in the criminal case against her attacker refused to convict him of rape. See Nina Lakhani, "Mexican Rape Victim, 13, Denied Access to Abortion," *The Guardian* (August 1, 2016), available at: www.theguardian.com/world/2016/aug/01/mexican-victim-13-refused-access-to-abortion.

economic burdens, laid not only on the mother but also on the father, on the new-born child, and on its older siblings.

I have chosen to focus on the story of the Republic of Ireland's abortion policy and its cross-border outcomes, as I find it a striking demonstration of the connection between, on the one hand, the phenomenon of limited national access to abortion and, on the other, bordered globalization. It adds to our understanding of the complex interrelations between national borders and the movement of people, ideas, and commodities associated with global reproduction, and highlights the role of domestic, neighboring countries' and international laws in shaping these interrelations, which impact women's lives, health, and autonomy.

As reflected in the fascinating historical accounts of Jeffrey Weinstein,[21] legal scholar Bryan Mercurio,[22] and Irish legal scholar and politician Ivana Bacik,[23] on which the following narrative is largely based, until 1939 Ireland shared with the UK the prohibition and criminalization of abortion, and no abortion travel existed between the two. The relevant law, enacted in 1861, deemed it a felony punishable by life imprisonment for any person to procure an elective abortion and a misdemeanor for any person to supply an instrument to provoke an abortion.

The phenomenon of pregnant Irish women traveling to England for abortion started in 1939 following an English court decision in the case of a young girl who was gang-raped by a group of soldiers. The court relaxed English law, allowing doctors to perform an abortion to preserve the life of a pregnant woman and in cases in which the effect of continuing the pregnancy would cause the woman substantial physical or mental damage. The availability of abortion in England thus reduced the number of prosecutions for abortion in Ireland, this rising again only during World War II when travel from Ireland to England was restricted.

The numbers of women traveling to the UK from Ireland increased further after 1967, when the British Parliament enacted a law that legalized abortion in a range of circumstances, including when "… the continuance of the pregnancy would involve risk, greater than if the pregnancy were terminated, of injury to the physical or mental health of the pregnant

---

[21] Jeffrey A. Weinstein, "An Irish Solution to an Irish Problem: Ireland's Struggle with Abortion Law," *Arizona Journal International and Comparative Law*, 10 (1993), 165–200.

[22] Bryan Mercurio, "Abortion in Ireland: An analysis of the Legal Transformation Resulting from Membership in the European Union," *Tulane Journal of International and Comparative Law*, 11(2003), 141–80.

[23] Ivana Bacik, "The Irish Constitution and Gender Politics: Development in the Law on Abortion," *Irish Political Studies,* 28(3) (2013), 380–98.

woman or any existing children of her family," or when there was "... a substantial risk that if the child were born it would suffer from such physical or mental abnormalities as to be seriously handicapped."[24] In practice, today, many women manage to secure an abortion even if these conditions are not met, as demonstrated, for example, by the recent public commotion in the UK over sex-selection-based abortion.[25]

In Ireland, on the other hand, fear from judicial activism, especially after the famous US *Roe v. Wade* case, and the Irish Supreme Court's approval of married couples' right to import contraception, led in 1979 to a re-enactment of the 1861 articles criminalizing abortion, and in 1983 to a referendum-based amendment of the Constitution that states that the right to life of the fetus is equal to that of the pregnant woman who carries it, interpreted by many as granting the value of fetal life an absolute protection in the name of public interest.[26] This constitutional amendment was followed by attempts by prolife groups to close the international abortion corridor, which for years allowed Irish women to bypass their country's policy. However, these attempts led to an unintended and countering result, which I would describe as a widening of the cracks in the antiabortion Irish jurisprudential wall, through which European law has started to trickle.

Indeed, since Ireland joined the EU in 1973, and especially since the drafting of the Maastricht Treaty in the early 1990s, the latter being designed to promote economic, monetary, and political union among the European Community, the country is vacillating between its wish (and economic need) to be a full and cooperative EU member, and its wish to preserve its restrictive pro-life ideology and law.[27] At first, it seemed that Ireland had been successful in handling the tension between the need to allow free movement between countries embraced by the EU and the

---

[24] Abortion Act, 1967, article 1, available at: www.legislation.gov.uk/ukpga/1967/87/section/1.

[25] See editorial opinion, "Abortion on Demand," *The Telegraph* (October 7, 2013), available at: www.telegraph.co.uk/comment/telegraph-view/10360989/Abortion-on-demand.html; John Bingham & Laura Donnelly, "Women Wanting Abortion Will Not Have to See Doctors," *The Telegraph* (January 15, 2014), available at: www.telegraph.co.uk/health/healthnews/10575108/Abortion-on-demand-gets-Government-green-light.html; "Q&A: Abortions for Fetal Abnormality," Royal College of Obstetricians and Gynaecologists, available at: www.rcog.org.uk/en/news/campaigns-and-opinions/human-fertilisation-and-embryology-bill/qa-abortions-for-fetal-abnormality/.

[26] Ruth Fletcher, "National Crisis, Supranational Opportunity: The Irish Constitution of Abortion as a European Service," *Reproductive Health Matters*, 8(6) (2000), 35–44.

[27] Mercurio, "Abortion in Ireland," 141–80.

Council of Europe (CoE) and the growing desire felt by some parts of its society to prevent Irish women from traveling to the UK to obtain an abortion. On the one hand, the Irish voted for the Maastricht Treaty, and on the other hand they made sure that it included a protocol that excluded Ireland's antiabortion constitutional article from the Treaty's orders.

But things were even more complex than they seemed. Shortly before the vote on the Treaty, in March 1992, the Irish Supreme Court had to intervene in the case of a 14-year-old girl who had traveled to England with her parents to procure the termination of a pregnancy caused by rape. As the parents contacted the Irish authorities to find out if the aborted fetus could be used for DNA testing to assist legal procedures against the rapist, they were ordered not to go ahead with the abortion. Upon returning to Ireland, they were then ordered by the High Court – which was not convinced that the circumstances, including the suicidal condition of the girl, justified the termination – not to travel to the UK for abortion again. This outrageous decision led to local protests, as well as to expressions of horror and shock among observers outside Ireland. Indeed, the Irish Supreme Court changed the High Court decision by ruling that the termination of a pregnancy was to be allowed on Irish soil, and hence travel to obtain an abortion abroad was also to be permitted, if the pregnancy presented a real and substantial risk to the life (as distinct from the health) of the pregnant woman (or girl), including the risk of suicide. However, three of the five judges suggested that, if no such risk existed, then the woman's right to travel to other countries for abortion might be restricted – hence limiting, in fact, Irish women's access to abortion.

Following this case, and other Irish courts' decisions that tried to limit access to information regarding the option of procuring an abortion abroad and that were challenged in the early 1990s in European tribunals, the Irish Prime Minister, Albert Reynolds, tried to convince the other parties to the Maastricht Treaty to allow Ireland to amend the aforementioned protocol that had allowed Ireland to exclude its antiabortion law from the Treaty's free movement rationale. This move by Prime Minister Reynolds was designed to ensure it would be clear that Ireland did indeed recognize the right to travel for abortion and the right to receive information about this option. The Prime Minister was afraid that the referendum on the Treaty would fail because of public opinion favoring these rights and objecting to attempts to close the abortion corridor to the UK. The other parties refused in fear of a re-opening of the Treaty by other states, but allowed a declaration, with no clear legal status, which mentioned that the protocol was not meant to limit the freedom to travel from Ireland to other member states and to obtain information related to services provided in those states.

Shortly after the Irish voted in favor of the Treaty, after being promised a referendum on the debatable questions related to abortion, the European Court of Human Rights of the Council of Europe (ECtHR) ruled that the Irish judicial ban on family-planning clinics providing information on abortion options in the UK was too broad and disproportionate. Furthermore, the Court of Justice of the European Union (CJEU) suggested that Ireland's restrictions on abortion-related information might be in conflict with its obligation to allow its citizens free access to "services" provided by another EU member state. To handle the internal pressure from prolife groups calling to constitutionally prevent abortion with no exceptions, and external pressure on behalf of European law and courts to relax Irish abortion-related restrictions, Prime Minister Reynolds brought to the Irish public yet another referendum (together with general elections after he lost power in Parliament), which included three questions that can be summarized thus: Should the right to travel for abortion be guaranteed? Should the right to receive information about this option be guaranteed? And should abortion be allowed in Ireland if the pregnancy risks the life of the woman, *not* including the risk of suicide? The Irish voted "Yes" on the first two questions, and "No" on the last, as prolife believers thought it too broad and prochoice supporters thought it too limiting. Hence, the Irish Constitution was amended and now specifically states that the 1983 amendment "shall not limit freedom of travel between the State and another State," and refers to the "freedom to obtain or make available ... information relating to services lawfully available in another state."[28]

Hence, the Irish Constitution embraces what I would call *globordered hypocrisy*, a situation in which a nation state uses global options for the movement of products (such as the importation of contraception), people (such as the exportation of pregnant women), and messages (such as locally-provided information about external abortion options) to preserve its restrictive and exclusive national ideology, while satisfying global forces, such as commercial pressures from global companies and normative pressures exerted by regional and international legal bodies. This *globordered hypocrisy* can also be seen as a national, political, and

---

[28] Constitution of Ireland, article 40.3.3, available at: www.irishstatutebook.ie/en/constitution/index.html#article40.

moral internal "safety valve," as termed by legal scholar Richard Storrow.[29] It allows the national legislator to satisfy oppositions by adopting and maintaining restrictive local perceptions (regarding reproduction, for instance) while channeling citizens' needs that cannot be answered due to these very perceptions (such as those related to reproduction autonomy) outside the country, toward other jurisdictions where they *can* be addressed. As mentioned in the Introduction, when this strategy is used in relation to the issues discussed in this book, I call it *familial globordered hypocrisy.*

The true number of Irish women procuring abortion in the UK is not known, as many do not disclose their personal details, for example in fear of condemnation from their family or community.[30] Based on figures regarding those who do state their country of origin, currently at least 4,000 women travel every year from the Republic of Ireland to the UK for an abortion. This number is somewhat lower than during the beginning of the third millennium, arguably because of growing illegal importation and home-use of the "morning-after pill" (which prevents pregnancy by delaying ovulation or preventing ovum implementation) and the "abortion pill" (which terminates an early pregnancy). The Irish women who still need to use the abortion corridor to the UK pay around £600–£2,000 to cover the costs of the journey and treatment.[31]

One could argue that this cross-border movement linked to human reproduction is an example of the benefits that nation states and individuals can gain from transnational legal pluralism in the bordered globalization era. Ireland can preserve its prolife Catholic ideology, while its female citizens can opt out by obtaining abortion in nearby England, and British doctors and clinics make a profit – apparently, a win-win-win situation. Unfortunately, traveling to another country to get an abortion can be a dangerous and traumatic ordeal.

The experiences, perceptions, and legal consciousness of Irish women who cross the border for abortion are yet to be explored. Surprisingly, and disappointingly, their voices are missing from the studies on the issue – the main heroines of this socio-legal story "have yet to speak in their own

---

[29] Richard F. Storrow, "Quest for Conception: Fertility Tourism, Globalization and Feminist Legal Theory," *Hastings Law Journal,* 57 (2005–2006), pp. 295–330, at 305.

[30] Ann Rossiter, *Ireland Hidden Diaspora: The "Abortion Trial" and the Making of a London-Irish Underground, 1980–2000* (London: IASC Publishing, 2009).

[31] Bloomer & O'Dowd, "Restricted Access to Abortion in the Republic of Ireland and Northern Ireland."

name."[32] Still, some idea of the hardship these women face and the price they are forced to pay can be grasped by the legal tales of A, B, and C in their cases versus Ireland, submitted to the ECtHR in 2004, and decided by the Grand Chamber of 17 judges, in 2010.[33]

The woman titled A told the court that she became pregnant unintentionally, believing her partner to be infertile. At the time, she was unmarried, unemployed, and poor. She already had four children, one with a disability, and all placed in foster care due to her alcoholism. She had experienced depression during all five of her pregnancies and was struggling to keep sober so as to regain custody of her children. She was afraid that having another child at that point in her life would jeopardize the wellbeing, and the hoped-for reunification, of her family. She had to borrow €650 for her trip to England, at a high interest rate. Afraid that her condition would be discovered by the social workers reviewing her request for custody, she traveled alone and in secrecy. She flew back home the day after the abortion so as not to miss the contact visit with her youngest child. On the train home from the airport, she started bleeding, and an ambulance was called to meet the train and take her to a hospital, where she underwent dilation and curettage.

Applicant B also became pregnant unintentionally. She believed she could not care for a child on her own, and was told by two doctors that there was a substantial risk of ectopic pregnancy. She did not have a credit card and had to borrow her friend's to book the flights to, and back from, England, where she concealed her identity so her family would not find out about the abortion. She had decided to go ahead with the termination despite knowing the pregnancy was not ectopic by the time she managed to get an appointment. On her return to Ireland she started passing blood clots, and two weeks later, being unsure of the legality of her abortion in England, sought treatment at a Dublin clinic affiliated with the clinic in London.

---

[32] Rossiter, *Ireland Hidden Diaspora*, at 23. An interesting recent attempt to give these women "much-needed face," is the online X-ile Project that uploads pictures of Irish women who had to travel to another country for abortion. See the X-ile Project website: www.x-ileproject.com/new-page/. The fact that these women are willing to reveal their faces in the most public way possible is, perhaps, an indication that the social atmosphere is slowly changing in Ireland and Northern Ireland after the socio-legal developments detailed later.

[33] *A, B and C v. Ireland*, App. no. 25579/05, ECtHR (2010), available at: http://hudoc.echr.coe.int/eng#{"appno":["25579/05"],"itemid":["001-102332"]}.

Unlike applicants A and B, who were Irish nationals, applicant C was a Lithuanian residing in Ireland. She became unintentionally pregnant after undergoing three years of chemotherapy for a rare form of cancer. Though she wanted to become a mother, she was afraid that her medical past would harm the fetus and that the pregnancy might trigger the cancer that was in remission. Although she approached several Irish doctors for advice, she could not get a clear answer regarding the pregnancy-related risks, due to what she alleged to be "the chilling effect of the Irish legal framework." Though she was at an early stage of pregnancy, she could not identify a clinic in England that was prepared to provide her with a medical abortion induced by drugs, because she was a nonresident and would need follow-up consultations. So it was eight weeks before she could secure an appointment at an English clinic for the much more complicated and dangerous surgical abortion. Indeed, upon returning to Ireland, she suffered from complications caused by an incomplete abortion, including prolonged bleeding and infection.

All three applicants based their claims mainly on Article 8 of the European Convention on Human Rights (ECHR) that guarantees the right to privacy, which was interpreted through various ECtHR decisions as a broad right encompassing, among other privacy interests, personal autonomy, physical and psychological integrity, and the decision to have or not to have a child.[34] Ireland, on its behalf, argued that Article 8 had never been interpreted by the Convention bodies as relevant to abortion and that, even if relevant, Ireland's abortion-related conduct was in keeping with this Article's limitation clause, which allows restriction of the right to privacy that is "in accordance with the law and is necessary in a democratic society in the interests of national security, public safety or the economic wellbeing of the country, for the prevention of disorder or crime, for the protection of health or morals, or for the protection of the rights and freedoms of others".[35]

In its decision, the Court cited the important resolution of the CoE on "Access to safe and legal abortion in Europe" from 2008. This resolution, voted-in by 102 to 69 (including, of course, the four opposing Irish representatives), declared that restrictions on "effective access to safe, affordable, acceptable and appropriate abortion services" had discriminatory effects

---

[34] Brynn Weinstein, "Reproductive Choice in the Hands of the State: The Rights to Abortion under the European Convention on Human Rights in Light of A, B & C v. Ireland," *American University International Law Review*, 27 (2012), 391–437.

[35] Article 8 of the European Convention on Human Rights, available at: www.echr.coe.int/ Documents/Convention_ENG.pdf.

against poor women who could not afford abortion "tourism," and did not lead to fewer abortions but only to more clandestine, dangerous, traumatic, and costly ones.[36] The Court further noted Ireland's failure to address concerns about its abortion law expressed by the CoE Commissioner for Human Rights, the UN CEDAW Committee, and the UN Human Rights Committee. Notwithstanding, the Court only accepted the application of C, arguing that as long as Ireland allows women to travel abroad to abort for health and wellbeing reasons, and provides information on this option together with medical preintervention and follow-up care, the prohibition of such abortions on Irish soil was within the "margin of appreciation" accorded to the Irish state, as it was based on "the profound moral views of the Irish people as to the nature of life … and the right to life of the unborn".[37] As to applicant C, the Court ruled that the fact that Ireland had no legislation in place to provide accessible and effective procedures by which she, and other women whose pregnancies might put their lives at risk, could have learned if they qualified for abortion in Ireland or not, was a violation of Article 8. The Court awarded applicant C €15,000.

Hence, the ECtHR legitimates Ireland's *familial globordered hypocrisy* while using the global movement option as a justification to allow a member state to act in a way that contradicts the broad agreement established within Europe regarding women's right to an abortion if their health and wellbeing require it. The Court portrays the journey from one country to another as hard but possible, and as a solution to the need of the CoE to accept that "State authorities are in principle in a better position than the international judge to give an opinion on the 'exact content of the requirements of morals' in their country, as well as on the necessity of a restriction intended to meet them."[38] Hence the ECtHR adds *compromising relations* to the typology of *bordered globalization* introduced in Chapter 1, which, in this case, demand very little from patriarchal nation states, at the expense of women. This compromising strategy is evidence of legal scholar Ronli Sifris's claim regarding the phallocentrism of international law in relation to abortion.[39] Another evidence is the lack of discourse on the obligation of the European community toward women in Europe, regardless of nationality. For example, as far as I know, suggestions such as

---

[36] Council of Europe Parliamentary Assembly, Resolution 1607 (2008), available at: http://assembly.coe.int/nw/xml/XRef/Xref-XML2HTML-en.asp?fileid=17638&lang=en.

[37] *A, B and C v. Ireland*, para. 241.

[38] Ibid., para. 223.

[39] Ronli Sifris, *Reproductive Freedom, Torture and International Human Rights: Challenging the Masculinisation of Torture* (London: Routledge, 2014).

CoE- or EU-funded abortion clinics in England, which would allow Irish women to receive the best care and much-needed postabortion bed rest for free, are not on the table.

The story has another tragic chapter to be told. It took two-and-a-half years, one dead woman, and intense internal and external campaigns that followed her unnecessary death, for Ireland to comply with the ECtHR's minimal demand for clear regulation of the option, or lack thereof, to terminate life-threatening pregnancies there. On October 21, 2012, Savita Halappanavar, a 31-year-old Hindu Indian citizen working in Ireland as a dentist, sought medical care at a hospital in Galway. She was suffering a miscarriage of her 17-week pregnancy, later assessed to be most likely due to a bacterial infection. She asked for a termination but was told that since the fetus's heart was beating, it was illegal to terminate the pregnancy. Two days later she collapsed while still in hospital, and on the twenty-fourth day the remains of the fetus were removed. But this was too late, and on the twenty-eighth day, Savita passed away. Her death received immense global coverage by both old and new media, and protests followed in Ireland, India, England, and other parts of Europe.[40] An official investigation team concluded a year later that there was "a failure in the provision of the most basic elements of patient care to Savita Halappanavar and also the failure to recognize and act upon signs of her clinical deterioration in a timely and appropriate manner."[41] Even before the team concluded its investigation, the Irish government responded to the national and international protests by passing the Protection of Life During Pregnancy Act, in July 2013, which allows abortion in Ireland if there is real and substantial risk of loss of the woman's life, including the risk of suicide, and that risk can only be averted by the termination of the pregnancy.

This last move does little more than put into law the aforementioned Irish Supreme Court's decision, from 1992, in the case of the raped and suicidal 14-year-old girl. Nevertheless, one *abortionially murdered*[42]

---

[40] See Wikipedia, *Death of Savita Halappanavar*, available at: http://en.wikipedia.org/wiki/Death_of_Savita_Halappanavar (as of August 3, 2016).

[41] Health Information and Quality Authority, *Investigation Into the Safety, Quality and Standards of Services Provided by the Health Service Executive to Patients, Including Pregnant Women, at Risk of Clinical Deterioration, Including Those Provided in University Hospital Galway, and as Reflected in the Care and Treatment Provided to Savita Halappanavar* (2013), at 22, available at: www.hiqa.ie/system/files/Patient-Safety-Investigation-UHG-Summary.pdf.

[42] Like few other feminists, I think the fetus should not be devoid of any value as it is a potential human being. See Fletcher, "National Crisis, Supranational Opportunity." Moreover, I consider abortion to be a physical and emotional risk to women and hence not a trivial

woman, as I would describe the case of Savita Halappanavar – who was not even Irish but paid the price of Irish law due to the global movement of people – together with external legal pressure and internal and external critical media coverage, forced Ireland's legislature, for the first time in its history, into recognizing women's right to life supremacy over that of the fetus, and to do so even without a referendum. Of course, although this is a significant step, it is still far from securing reproduction autonomy for women in Ireland. Indeed, recently, the UN Human Rights Committee (HRC) published a very critical opinion against Ireland, in a case of a woman who had to travel to England to terminate her pregnancy, after being refused abortion in her home country, although medical examinations revealed that the fetus suffered from a heart defect that would lead to its death in utero or shortly after birth. The HRC concluded that Ireland violated Articles 7, 17, and 26 of the International Covenant on Civil and Political Rights, as its treatment of the case "amounted to cruel, inhuman or degrading treatment," was "unreasonable and arbitrary," and "constituted discrimination." Unlike the ECtHR, the HRC refused to compromise and declared that Ireland is under an obligation to take steps to prevent similar violations occurring in the future, and that to this end it "should amend its law on voluntary termination of pregnancy, including if necessary its Constitution, to ensure compliance with the Covenant, including ensuring effective, timely and accessible procedures for pregnancy termination in Ireland, and take measures to ensure that health-care providers are in a position to supply full information on safe abortion services without fearing being subjected to criminal sanctions."[43] Although this is a very important international legal voice, it still leaves, every year, thousands of women who face a 'mundane' unwanted pregnancy, which is not life threatening or one with a dead fetus, with no answer but a cross-border journey abroad, with all the accompanied economic, physical, and emotional risks.

---

medical procedure. Notwithstanding, my position is that the phenomenon of unwanted pregnancies should be dealt with by means of education and contraception, and not with restrictions on abortion through the first two trimesters, as the pregnant woman's bodily autonomy outweighs, in my view, any other consideration. Moreover, at any stage of the pregnancy, if it risks the life or health of the woman carrying it, she should be allowed to terminate it as she is a whole person and the fetus is yet to become one. Hence, refusing to terminate a life-threatening pregnancy that then leads to the woman's death is, in my opinion, murder.

[43] United Nations, *International Covenant on Civil and Political Rights* (2016), available at: www.reproductiverights.org/sites/crr.civicactions.net/files/documents/CCPR-C-116-D-2324-2013-English-cln-auv.pdf.

Before discussing further the insights that can be drawn from the Irish–UK case study of cross-border abortion, let us move to another form of bordered globalization reproduction service and discuss India and Israel as examples of countries that are interdependently part of the dynamic multinational surrogacy industry.

Cross-Border Surrogacy – The Case of Israel and India

India, the giant subcontinent, and Israel, one of the smallest countries on earth, could both, until recently, be perceived as *fertility superpowers*, but in very different ways: whereas Israel is obsessed with producing children for (Jewish) Israelis,[44] India was preoccupied, until the second decade of the third millennium, with producing children for citizens of other countries. These two very different motivations have entangled the two countries together in the net of the growing global reproduction market. This entanglement is used in this part of the chapter to highlight how bordered globalization can lead to the legal objectification of humans – in this case, in the form of surrogate mothers. It will also be used to demonstrate the legal complications that can rise, and indeed are rising, from the lack of international consensus over, and regulation of, cross-border familial procreative movement, and the limits of global hypercapitalist forces, which apparently can be restricted by national bordering legislation.

Israel, with its pronatalist national and religious ideologies, holds almost all possible assisted reproduction techniques to be legal, including those that are restricted in many other countries due to moral or medical reservations, such as ova donation and freezing, posthumous sperm retrieval, and surrogacy.[45] It is also known for its advanced, high-quality fertility-related medical facilities. Moreover, there is no other country that

---

[44] A major motivation for the obsession with fertility in the Israeli legislature and government is the "demographic war" aimed at preserving Israel as the State of the Jewish people in the face of its ongoing conflict with Palestine. See also Chapter 5. Notwithstanding, Israel pronatalist legislation assists all its citizens, including Israeli-Palestinians. In addition, there is a Jewish religious command to procreate, which encourages the observant sector within Jewish Israeli society to bring large numbers of children into the world, including with the assistance of fertility technologies if needed. Finally, Israel is a familist society in which everybody is expected to become parents, whatever it takes. See Daphna Birenbaum-Carmeli, "Thirty-five Years of Assisted Reproductive Technologies in Israel," *Reproductive Biomedicine & Society Online*, 2 (2016), 16–23, available at: www.sciencedirect.com/science/article/pii/S2405661816300090.

[45] Birenbaum-Carmeli, "Thirty-five Years of Assisted Reproductive Technologies in Israel"; Yael Hashiloni-Dolev, *The Fertility Revolution* (Moshav Ben-Shemen: Modan, 2013) (Hebrew).

provides its citizens with such generous public financial support for fertility treatments. For example, Israeli women are eligible for state-funded in-vitro fertilization (IVF) until they give birth to two children, regardless of their marital status or sexual orientation, and until they reach the age of 45.[46] No wonder, then, that the use of assisted reproduction procedures per capita in Israel is the highest in the world.[47]

In addition, Israelis also take part in the global cross-border reproduction movement, including by using surrogates from different countries, including, until recently, India. In 2013, for example, 169 applications relating to babies born though international surrogacy were submitted to Israeli courts (in addition to 58 cases of local surrogacy), whereas 167 applications were submitted to British courts in relation to both local and international surrogacy. Although the numbers of applications in the UK do not necessarily represent the true scope of international surrogacy performed by British citizens, as some might not be reported to the authorities, this is still a staggering difference when taking into account that the British population is almost eight times larger than Israel's (8 vs. 63 million).[48] Although, in that year, 43 percent of international surrogacy initiated by Israeli intended parents took place in India, this dropped to only 6.5 percent in 2014, with Georgia (37 percent) and Thailand (28 percent) becoming the leading destinations,[49] due to dramatic regulative changes in India, detailed further on.

The surrogates used by Israelis are implanted, in most cases, with embryos produced with the intended mother's ova, or ova bought from a white woman, even if that means importing them from a third country, such as Ukraine, as most Israelis prefer to pay more to ensure a

[46] Daphna Hacker, "Single and Married Women in the Law of Israel – A Feminist Perspective," *Feminist Legal Studies*, 9(1) (2001), 29–56; Hashiloni-Dolev, *The Fertility Revolution*.

[47] Zvi Triger, "On the Regulation of Fertility Services in Israel," in Yishai Blank, David Levi-Faur, & Roy Kreitner (Eds.), *Regulation: Law and Policy* (Tel Aviv University, 2016), pp. 269–309 (Hebrew).

[48] Ruth Zafran & Daphna Hacker, "International Surrogacy – Israel, Final Report," February 2016, submitted to the Mission of Research for Law and Justice – the Ministry of Justice of the French Republic, "Filiation of Children Conceived Illegally (France, Belgium, UK, Israel)" (on file, with author).

[49] Zafran & Hacker, "International Surrogacy – Israel," at 13.

light-skinned child.[50] Hence, just as with the aforementioned popularity of Danish sperm, Israel–Global South surrogacy matchmaking has a racial dimension mitigated by imported "white ova".

Why would citizens of a country that legalizes surrogacy, such as Israel, turn to distant countries, such as India, for pregnancy services? The answer starts with Israeli surrogacy law, the first to be enacted worldwide. Although it allows surrogacy, it restricts it to heterosexual Israeli couples as intended parents. Hence, single and gay Israelis (as well as citizens of other countries) cannot use Israeli surrogates.[51] Furthermore, Israeli law imposes restrictions on the identity of Israeli surrogate mothers (they must not be married or be a relative of the intended parents) and on the sums they are allowed to be paid (costs and "reasonable compensation"),[52] hence lowering the availability of Israeli women who are allowed and are willing to be surrogates. Indeed, there are more Israelis who want to use a surrogate mother than Israeli women who are willing and eligible to fulfill the demand.[53]

Moreover, as Israeli parliamentary law does not regulate the use of surrogate mothers in other countries by Israelis, it opens the possibility for its citizens to use surrogacy-friendly countries that facilitate large-scale commercial surrogacy to noncitizens.[54] Finally, as the waiting period for adopting an Israeli child is five to six years, and since Israeli law discriminates against gay men in adoption of Israeli children,[55] and there are growing difficulties in international adoptions, as will be discussed in Chapter 6, the demand for international surrogacy among Israelis is on the rise.[56]

---

[50] Adi Moreno, "Crossing Borders: Remaking Gay Fatherhood in the Global Market," PhD Dissertation submitted to the University of Manchester (2016), at 169.

[51] Sharon Shakargy, "Israel" in Katarina Trimmings & Paul Beaumont (Eds.), *International Surrogacy Arrangements* (Oxford: Hart Publishing, 2013), pp. 231–46.

[52] Embryo Carrying Agreement (Agreement Authorization & Status of the Newborn Child) Law of 1996.

[53] Peled, "Surrogate Motherhood in Israel."

[54] Katarina Trimmings & Paul Beaumont, "General Report on Surrogacy" in Trimmings & Beaumont (Eds.), *International Surrogacy Arrangements*, at 443. Minimal regulation emerged in the form of unpublished governmental guidelines, see Zafran & Hacker, "International Surrogacy – Israel."

[55] Orna Hirschfeld, Renata Gorbatov, & Miri Ben Simhon, "Adopted Children and Adopting Families" in *Overview of Social Services* (2010), Ministry of Social Affairs and Social Services, pp. 247–63 (Hebrew).

[56] Orly Almagor Lotan, "Report on Surrogacy in Israel and Israelis' Surrogacy Abroad: Current Status and Changes Proposed by a Public Committee," Israeli Knesset (2012), available at: www.knesset.gov.il/mmm/data/pdf/m03065.pdf (Hebrew); Zafran & Hacker, "International Surrogacy – Israel."

In particular, during 2009–2013, the option of surrogacy in India had become attractive to Israeli singles and gays, as well as to heterosexual couples, since India's surrogacy industry provided immediately available surrogates (sometimes two surrogates were used for the same intended parents, to improve the chances of at least one successful birth), without the time-consuming bureaucracy involved in Israel even for those legally eligible to be intended parents. The surrogacy process in India was also cheaper than in other surrogacy-friendly countries.[57] For example, Israeli intended parents were required to pay $125,000–$200,000 for surrogacy in the United States to cover all direct and related expenses for the birth of one baby. Surrogacy in India, when it was available, on the other hand, cost only $60,000 or less per baby (depending on the origin of the ova).[58]

The appeal of Indian surrogate mothers for Israelis, as well as for people from other countries,[59] which turned India in those years into a hub for the multibillion dollar international surrogacy industry,[60] cannot be understood divorced from Indian law – most importantly, the lack of surrogacy regulation up until 2012. Although there were Indian National Guidelines and Ethical Guidelines related to surrogacy, they were not legally binding,[61] and so the market for surrogacy in India was almost completely governed by private clinics and intermediaries. In fact, the Indian government actively encouraged the industry, including through financial incentives to private clinics that performed surrogacy.[62]

---

[57] Zvi Triger, "A Different Journey: Experiences of Israeli Surrogacy Parents in India," *Theory and Criticism*, 44 (2015), 177–202 (Hebrew); Sharmila Rudrappa, "Working India's Reproduction Assembly Line: Surrogacy and Reproduction Rights?" *Western Humanities Review*, 66(3) (2012), 77–101, at 83.

[58] Triger, "A Different Journey"; Zafran & Hacker, "International Surrogacy – Israel," at 15.

[59] Sharvari Karandikar, Lindsay B. Gezinski, James R. Carter, & Marissa Kaloga, "Economic Necessity or Noble Cause? A Qualitative Study Exploring Motivations for Gestational Surrogacy in Gujarat, India," *Journal of Women and Social Work*, 29(2) (2014), 224–36.

[60] Rajendra Parsad Gunputh & Kartina Aisha Choong, "Surrogacy Tourism: The Ethical and Legal Challenges," *International Journal of Tourism Sciences*, 15(1–2) (2015), 16–21, at 17.

[61] Usha Rengachary Smerdon, "India" in Trimmings & Beaumont (Eds.), *International Surrogacy Arrangements*, pp. 187–217; Diksha Munjal & Yahita Munjal, "The 'Wanted' Child: Identifying the Gaps and Challenges in Commercial Surrogacy in India," *Asian Bioethics Review*, 6(1) (2014), 66–82.

[62] Maya Unnithan, "Thinking through Surrogacy Legislation in India: Reflections on Relational Consent and the Rights of Infertile Women," *Journal of Legal Anthropology*, 1(3) (2013), 287–313, at 292.

As the fascinating analysis of legal scholar Sharon Bassan reveals,[63] the available empirical data suggest that the outcomes of this deliberate regulatory vacuum for Indian surrogates were harsh. In many cases of international surrogacy, the contract with the surrogate mother was signed only after she became pregnant and at a stage at which she had no bargaining power. The contract, drafted by those representing the interests of the intended parents, the intermediary (an individual or agency), and the clinic, was in English, whereas many of the surrogates could not read English or were entirely illiterate. Meanwhile, the surrogates were not represented by a lawyer and in many cases received a very partial explanation of the medical procedure and the many risks involved, for which they were neither insured nor compensated (for example, Indian surrogates were implanted with up to five embryos, a large number that increases health risks).[64] In fact, in most cases the clinic and intermediary tried to avoid being part of the contract, so as to cover up their involvement and avoid any legal responsibility pertaining to the medical procedure and its outcomes.[65] What is more, whereas in many cases the husband of a married surrogate was required to sign the contract, to ensure he did not object, there was no legal procedure in place to ensure the woman was not coerced into surrogacy by her husband, which might have been the case, especially in second-time surrogacies.[66] Some contracts demanded that the surrogate mother be cut off from her family and community and live for the duration of the pregnancy in a dormitory provided by the clinic, with a supervised diet and medication. Although the intended parents were the other party in the contractual relationship, the surrogate mother typically knew nothing about their identity and had no say in the matter, and usually met them, if at all, only when they came to collect the baby. Moreover, most contracts, of which the surrogate might not even

---

[63] Sharon Bassan, "Cross-Border Reproductive Transactions in the Era of Globalization: Advancing Global Justice Through Shared Responsibility," PhD Dissertation, Tel Aviv University (2015).

[64] See Anu, Pawan Kumar, Deep Inder, & Nandini Sharma, "Surrogacy and Women's Right to Health in India: Issues and Perspective," *Indian Journal of Public Health*, 57(2) (2013), 65–70.

[65] Centre for Social Research, *Surrogate Motherhood – Ethical or Commercial* (2008), at 67, available at: www.womenleadership.in/Csr/SurrogacyReport.pdf.

[66] Sheela Saravanan, "An Ethnomethodological Approach to Examine Exploitation in the Context of Capacity, Trust and Experience of Commercial Surrogacy in India," *Philosophy, Ethics, and Humanities in Medicine*, 8(10) (2013), available at: http://peh-med.biomedcentral.com/articles/10.1186/1747-5341-8-10.

receive a copy, set the intended parents' legal system as the one governing any misunderstanding between the parties. With regard to payment, on average the surrogate mother received only about 10 percent of what the intended parents actually paid. The sum was set by the clinic and was paid only if a baby was born, which means that the surrogates bore all the costs of the many cases in which the treatments did not result in a pregnancy or the pregnancy did not result in a live baby. Finally, according to Indian law, the surrogate mother has no legal status vis-à-vis the baby, and so her existence was erased from all documents related to the child, as if she had had nothing to do with its coming into the world.[67]

Most of these conditions stand in sharp contrast to the relative power and protection enjoyed by surrogate mothers in countries that do not erase their basic human rights and liberties. Whereas there are inherent risks, complexities, and abusive elements in surrogacy procedures even in such countries, in the United States and in Israel, for example, the surrogate mother is involved in the drafting of the contract, she is allowed to go on with her regular life throughout the pregnancy though some restrictions in terms of smoking, diet, and travel might be agreed on, and she is paid between a third and a half of the overall sum paid by the intended parents.[68]

I would argue that all the aforementioned contractual practices, common in India until it closed its doors to international surrogacy, amounted to extreme legal objectification, in which the surrogate mothers were perceived by the other actors in the international surrogacy field as being *outside the law* as humans and *within the law* only as for-rent-baby-ovens. The contract signing, which we are used to perceiving as the epitome of mutual willingness between rational and free parties, was, in fact, a legally misleading ritual, a façade of a bilateral act, disguising the almost total governing of the situation by the intended parents, the clinic, and the intermediaries. Moreover, whereas some intended parents initiated contact with the surrogate mother and tried to overcome communication

---

[67] See also Alison Bailey, "Reconceiving Surrogacy: Toward a Reproductive Justice Account of Indian Surrogacy," *Hypatia*, 26(4) (2011), 715–41; Rudrappa, "Working India's Reproduction Assembly Line"; Daisy Deomampo, "Transnational Surrogacy in India: Interrogating Power and Women's Agency," *Frontier: A Journal of Women's Studies*, 34(3) (2013), 167–88; Vida Panitch, "Global Surrogacy: Exploitation to Empowerment," *Journal of Global Ethics*, 9(3) (2013) 329–43.

[68] Rudrappa, "Working India's Reproduction Assembly Line"; Trimmings & Beaumont, "General Report on Surrogacy," pp. 439–549; Panitch, "Global Surrogacy"; Nofar Lipkin & Etti Samama, *Surrogacy in Israel: Status in 2010 and Proposals for Legal Reforms*, Woman to Woman (2010), available at: http://isha.org.il/wp-content/uploads/2014/09/surrogacy_web-1.pdf (Hebrew); Peled, "Surrogate Motherhood in Israel," 94–5 (Hebrew).

barriers to keep in touch with her before and after the birth, others chose India precisely because it afforded them legal, physical, and emotional detachment from the surrogate.[69]

A tangible example of the deceptive contractual ritual that surrounded international surrogacy in India can be found in the excellent 2009 docu-film "Google Baby," directed by Zipi Brand Frank. This film follows an Israeli entrepreneur who, after experiencing an expensive surrogacy procedure in the United States, decides to open an agency that will mediate between Israelis and Indian surrogacy clinics. One of the clinics he contacts is that of Dr. Nayna Patal, an Indian surrogacy clinic owner and surgeon who enjoyed celebrity status, and who mentioned in many academic and media reports on surrogacy in India (leaving what was going on in the rest of the thousands of fertility clinics in India,[70] almost completely unexplored). The camera follows a woman signing a surrogate contract in Dr. Patal's clinic. The whole episode takes no more than a few minutes, in which the doctor explains to the woman and her husband that she will probably have to undergo a caesarean (the routine procedure in Indian surrogacy – to prevent complications of the precious delivery), that she will have to give up the baby straight away after the operation, and that she may lose her uterus and even die, with no responsibility on behalf of the clinic. The woman hardly speaks a word, and she and her husband sign the contract while the doctor talks about the house and the education of the couple's son that can be bought with the $6,500 the woman will receive for her service.[71]

The four-digit sums of dollars that were given to the Indian surrogates, which were usually lower than the sum mentioned by Dr. Patal in front of the camera,[72] were the reason they subjected themselves to the abusive and inhuman conditions posed by the intended parents, intermediaries, and clinics. In the literature, I found estimates of these sums as being equivalent to five and even twenty years of these women's usual annual salaries,[73] which is not surprising taking into consideration that most of them belong to the poorest segment of the world's population. Here it

---

[69] Triger, "A Different Journey."

[70] Anil Malhotra & Ranjit Malhotra, "All Aboard for the Fertility Express," *Commonwealth Law Bulletin*, 38(1) (2012), 31–41, at 32.

[71] Docu-film *Google Baby*, available at: www.youtube.com/watch?v=pQGlAM0iWFM.

[72] Panitch, "Global Surrogacy," at 332.

[73] Vida Panitch, "Surrogate Tourism and Reproductive Rights," *Hypatia*, 28(2) (2013), 274–89; Saravanan, "An Ethnomethodological Approach to Examine Exploitation in the Context of Capacity, Trust and Experience of Commercial Surrogacy in India."

is important to note Bassan's observation that although some empirical attention has been given to the motivations of Indian surrogates and their short-term experiences,[74] very little is known about the effects of their participation in the global reproduction market on their long-term physical, emotional, and economic wellbeing.[75] Bassan concludes, from the little that is known, that surrogacy is not necessarily a financially positive and life-changing choice for the women who provide the pregnancy and delivery services, and that most of them will continue to live in poverty.[76]

Hence, going back to the *bordered globalization* typology, the case of baby exportation from India by means of surrogacy – on a massive scale until very recently – is an example of a cooperative relationship, already termed by philosopher Vida Panitch as a kind of *mutually advantageous exploitation*.[77] Indian women cooperated with the global demand for surrogates in the hope of economically improving their and their family members' lives, whereas national, gender, and social-class borders added exploitative dimensions to this cooperation. This is why the yet-to-be-studied decision of the Indian authorities to shut down the international surrogacy industry, first in 2012 for gay couples,[78] and then in 2015 for all foreign intended parents,[79] is, in my opinion, quite extraordinary. It is a very rare example of an effective counter-reaction against global hyper-capitalism – in which a nation state reestablishes its borders, regardless of what seems to be a very high economic price for the state, for its private market, and even for the surrogates and their families.

Going back to the specific interrelation between India and Israel in the surrogacy context, it seems as if, in the first years of the *bordered globalization cooperative relations*, the Israeli authorities were more interested in the Indian surrogate mothers' legal subjectivity than the Indian

[74] Amrita Pande, "Not an 'Angel', Not a 'Whore': Surrogates as 'Dirty' Workers in India," *Indian Journal of Gender Studies*, 16(2) (2009), 141–73; Amrita Pande, "'It May Be Her Eggs but It's My Blood': Surrogates and Everyday Forms of Kinship in India," *Qualitative Sociology*, 32(4) (2009), 379–405; Amrita Pande, "'At Least I Am Not Sleeping with Anyone': Resisting the Stigma of Commercial Surrogacy in India," *Feminist Studies*, 36(2) (2010) 292–312; Amrita Pande, "Commercial Surrogacy in India: Manufacturing a Perfect 'Mother-Worker,'" *Signs: Journal of Women in Culture and Society*, 35(4) (2010), 969–92.
[75] Bassan, "Cross Border Reproductive Transactions in the Era of Globalization," Ch 1.
[76] See also Karandikar, Gezinski, Carter, & Kaloga, "Economic Necessity or Noble Cause?."
[77] Panitch, "Surrogate Tourism and Reproductive Right."
[78] Smerdon, "India," at 189.
[79] Government of India, Ministry of Home Affairs, *Foreign Nationals [Including Overseas Citizen of India (OCI) Cardholders] Intending to Visit India for Commissioning Surrogacy* (2015), available at: http://mea.gov.in/images/attach/surrogacy03112016.pdf.

authorities were. In an unpublished internal governmental regulation, the Israeli embassies and consulates were ordered not to start the bureaucratic and medical procedures of the DNA test required for granting a baby born through surrogacy abroad the status that would allow its emigration to Israel, unless the surrogate mother reported, in person, to the embassy or consulate, stating her wish that the baby be delivered to the Israeli intended parents.[80]

Notwithstanding, this procedure led to three unintended consequences, demonstrating the complexity of relations between two countries that had very different surrogacy regulations, and which were nevertheless entangled in the global surrogacy market. The first consequence was the potential additional physical and mental harm caused to the surrogate mother, who had to travel to the Israeli consulate very soon after delivery and meet the intended parents there even if she did not wish to.[81] The second unintended outcome was the blackmailing power that the surrogate and, more often, the intermediary, acquire. Zvi Triger, an Israeli legal scholar who experienced surrogacy in India as an intended parent, claims that intermediaries routinely took advantage of the Israeli demand that the surrogate personally come to the consulate, and tried to extort more money from the intended parents. The sums, which were much higher than could be regarded as suitable compensation to the surrogate for the ordeal of traveling to the embassy, were demanded at the exact point at which the intended parents were eager to return to Israel with the newborn. Hence, in the endeavor to ensure that the baby was the outcome of consensual surrogacy, Israel was unwittingly exposing its citizens to extortion at a profoundly vulnerable moment in life – in a faraway country, exhausted mentally and financially from a long surrogacy process, and desperate to take home the tiny baby they perceive to be theirs.[82] The third unintended consequence was the possible "no-one's child" scenario. If the Israeli authorities had not been convinced that the baby was the result of a voluntary surrogacy agreement and had not allowed the baby into Israel, then the baby would have had no parents and no citizenship, since according to Indian law the surrogate has no parental rights or obligations toward the

---

[80] Zvi Triger, "On the Regulation of Fertility Services in Israel"; Judith Meisels, "Reflections on the Centrality of Genetics in Parenting Following HCJ 566/11 Mamet v. Ministry of Interior Affairs," *Mivzakey Hearot Psika*, 28 (2014), 46–56, available at: www.colman.ac.il/sites/default/files/28_june_2014_5_meisels.pdf (Hebrew).

[81] Triger, "A Different Journey."

[82] Ibid.

baby, and the baby would not be a citizen of India as, legally, it was not born to an Indian.

Although such a situation has not occurred in relation to Israel's concern over the consent of the surrogate mother, it did happen in 2010, when an Israeli Family Court judge allowed his homophobic ideology to affect his judgment in the case of a gay couple assisted by two Indian surrogates (so each partner could be a genetic father of one set of twins carried by each surrogate). In order for the Israeli couple to bring the babies born through the surrogates to Israel, they would have had to obtain an Israeli court order for a genetic test that would establish their paternity, which would be followed by a court order to the Israeli authorities to recognize the babies as the children of their respective genetic fathers, and to issue the babies an Israeli passport that would allow them to travel to their country of citizenship. The Family Court Judge decided that because the babies were born in India and were still there, and because there was no proof that the petitioners were their parents, the Israeli Court had no jurisdiction over the case and could not order the genetic test that would establish such proof – hence locking the gay couple and the babies in India while an Indian Court determined their paternity. The judge argued further that, as homosexuals are not allowed to use surrogacy in Israel, to allow the petitioners parenthood through surrogacy in India would go against Israel's legal rationale that the best interests of the child demand a father and a mother, and not two fathers. So, as a result of this decision, the children were left, at least temporarily, stateless and parentless, as neither Israel nor India recognized them as children of their citizens. It took a petition to the Israeli District Court, and public protests with intense media coverage, to change this decision and allow the babies into Israel, as the Israeli children of Israeli citizens.[83]

Since that decision, Israeli authorities relaxed the bureaucratic barriers to international surrogacy even further. First, the nongenetic intended parent is now allowed to be registered as the baby's parent without an adoption procedure, demanded previously, and only based on a "public record," such as a birth certificate or a court order from the surrogate's country, or based on evidence of spousal relations and involvement in the surrogacy process with the genetic parent. This approach creates a new legal category within Israeli family law of legal parenthood via international or multinational surrogacy, marked by a *judicial*

---

[83] FC (Jerusalem) 14816-04-10 *Roe et al. v. District Attorney* (2010) (Israel); see also Moreno, "Crossing Borders," at 156–9.

parental order – a tool invented by the judiciary and found in Israeli legislation only in relation to internal surrogacy.[84] Second, even the demand for a genetic test for the biological parent has been recently relaxed, when the Family Court was willing to respect the wishes of a man (half of a gay couple that used a US surrogate) who was refusing to undergo a genetic test. He was allowed to use other evidence to be recognized as the father of the baby girl.[85] Although this tendency can be seen as an expression of moral familial pluralism and a recognition of gay people's right to form a family, it can also be perceived as part of the *familial globordered hypocrisy*, mentioned earlier in the context of abortion, because Israel allows surrogacy in other countries under conditions it does not allow within its own territory.

The relations with Israel were not the only ones to create complications within the context of the Indian involvement in international surrogacy.[86] Indeed, it was with countries that prohibit surrogacy altogether, such as Germany and France, that the entanglement of *families laws* (private international law, custody law, adoption law, citizenship law, and immigration law), discussed in Chapter 2, is most evident in the cross-border surrogacy context, with children at risk of being left stateless and parentless in the surrogate mother's country or with no citizenship status, even if permitted entry to the country of the intended parents.[87]

A thorough study is yet to be conducted on the motivations of India in abolishing the option of surrogacy for foreigners. Is it out of concern for the vulnerable surrogates? The wish to prevent possible no-one's children? Or, perhaps, the outcome of nationalist pride, damaged by the subordination of Indian wombs to outsiders' needs? These questions are still unanswered, and are becoming relevant to more and more countries that are, one by one, closing their doors to foreign intended parents.

Immediately after the 2012 Indian prohibition on international surrogacy for gays, Israeli mediating agencies and consumers reacted by searching for another surrogacy destination country, targeting Thailand as a preferred option. However, Thai law determines that the surrogate mother is the baby's legal mother. This, as well as more recent debates within Thailand regarding the legitimacy of surrogacy in general and of surrogacy for gay people in particular, has made the Thai surrogacy route

---

[84] Judith Meisels, "Reflections on the Centrality of Genetics in Parenting"; HCJ 566/11 *Mamet v. Ministry of Interior Affairs* (2014) (Israel).

[85] FC (TA) 32901-05-14 *Roe et al. v. District Attorney* (2016) (Israel).

[86] Smerdon, "India," pp. 187–217.

[87] Trimmings & Beaumont, "General Report on Surrogacy," at 503–10.

much riskier than the Indian option up to 2012. Indeed, after realizing that the Thai government objects to international surrogacy and might give the surrogate mother custody over the child, the Israeli government announced that, as of November 2014, Israelis would be prohibited from using Thai surrogates.[88] At the beginning of 2015, Thailand enacted a law prohibiting foreigners from paying for Thai surrogates or the services of agencies that promote surrogacy. Some journalists[89] argue that this new law is a response to problematic cases such as the alleged abandonment of a baby with Down syndrome by an Australian couple who were allowed to use a Thai surrogate despite the man having earlier been convicted of child molesting,[90] and a suspicion of multiple baby trafficking out of Thailand through surrogacy by a Japanese man.[91]

After realizing that Thailand was no longer an option, Israelis turned to Nepal, which prohibited its own citizens from being surrogates but allowed foreigners to use Indian surrogate mothers who gave birth in Nepal. However, shortly after commercial operations were set up in Nepal to manage this complex multinational surrogacy, the Nepalese Supreme Court and government decided in mid-2015 to freeze all international surrogacy procedures, interpreted by Israel and other countries as the end of cross-border surrogacy in Nepal.[92] Likewise, Mexico was explored by Israeli agencies as a possible destination for international surrogacy, until the enactment of a new law in late-2015 that prohibits surrogacy for gays and foreigners in the only Mexican state that previously allowed it.[93] Finally, the owner of a leading Israeli international surrogacy agency recently predicted that even Georgia, which is currently the major source of surrogates for Israelis, will probably close its doors. According to his analysis, the shortage in destination countries leads to mass interest from hopefuls looking to the very few permissive countries left, causing

---

[88] Zafran & Hacker, "International Surrogacy – Israel."

[89] For example, see "Thailand Bans Commercial Surrogacy for Foreigners," BBC News (February 20, 2015), available at: www.bbc.com/news/world-asia-31546717.

[90] Aine Hegarty, "Australian Father Who Abandoned Down Syndrome Baby was Convicted for Molesting a Child," The Mirror (August 5, 2014), available at: www.mirror.co.uk/news/world-news/australian-father-who-abandoned-downs-3993011#.U-dFc_mSx1A.

[91] Lessa Smith, "Foreign Minister Julie Bishop Calls on Thai Government to Allow a Transition Period before Banning Commercial Surrogacy the Day after Bangkok IVF Clinic Is Shut Down," Daily Mail Australia (August 9, 2014), available at: www.dailymail.co.uk/news/article-2720644/Great-concern-dozens-Australian-couples-popular-Thai-IVF-clinic-shuts-Gammy-saga-prompts-surrogacy-crackdown.html.

[92] Zafran & Hacker, "International Surrogacy – Israel."

[93] Associated Press, "Mexican State Votes to Ban Surrogacy for Gay Men and Foreign People," The Guardian (December 15, 2015).

an anxiety over exploitation, complications, and lack of control.[94] Such possible explanations should be thoroughly studied, yet a clear global isomorphic trend can already be detected: as developed countries are relaxing their regulation to allow intended parents to shop for surrogates abroad,[95] so are developing countries resisting the economic temptation embedded in providing surrogates for the global market by closing down this option.

The increasing legal, bureaucratic, and economic difficulties involved in obtaining cross-border surrogacy have led to an increasing pressure on the Israeli legislator to allow the use of Israeli surrogate mothers by single and gay Israelis. The former Israeli Minister of Health decided to promote a law reform that will equalize the right to use an Israeli surrogate among all Israelis wishing to do so, regardless of marital status or sexual orientation. However, she did not manage to do so before new elections put in her place an ultra-orthodox health minister who is unlikely to promote such pluralist legislation.[96] In my opinion, the shortage of Israeli surrogates and the relatively long bureaucratic procedure involved in Israel will leave cross-border surrogacy as an attractive option for Israelis, even if this equalizing initiative does materialize into a law. Still, just as in the case of abortion law in Ireland, events outside the nation state are pressuring it to change its reproduction law and relax its internal restrictive policy.

Israel's intense experience with multinational surrogacy made it one of the first countries to urge the international community to develop a multilateral response to the difficulties arising from the lack of consensus over surrogacy between different jurisdictions, for example by drafting an international convention on international surrogacy.[97] However, the lack of consensus is exactly what stands in the way of the much-needed multilateral action.[98] Whereas I cannot elaborate here on the recent scholastic

---

[94] Interview, conducted in Tel Aviv, by author and Ruth Zafran, June 23, 2016.

[95] See, for example, the ECtHR decisions that France should respect the rights of children born through international surrogacy in accordance with Article 8 of the ECHR: *Mennesson v. France* 65192/11 [2014] ECtHR and *Labassee v. France* 65941/11 [2014] ECtHR. By that, the court has diminished France's ability to prevent its citizens from purchasing surrogacy services (not allowed within French borders) abroad.

[96] Zafran & Hacker, "International Surrogacy – Israel".

[97] Hannah Baker, "A Possible Future Instrument on International Surrogacy Arrangements: Are There 'Lessons' to be Learned from the 1993 Hague Intercountry Adoption Convention?" in Trimmings & Beaumont (Eds.), *International Surrogacy Arrangements*, pp. 411–26, at 412.

[98] Yasmine Ergas, "Thinking 'through' Human Rights: The Need for a Human Rights Perspective with Respect to the Regulation of Cross-Border Reproduction Surrogacy" in Trimmings & Beaumont (Eds.), *International Surrogacy Arrangements*, pp. 427–34.

initiatives to offer national and international legal models for the regulation of cross-border surrogacy, I will note that most of them assume the persistence of the phenomenon. Even those who perceive cross-border surrogacy as a form of trafficking in women and children,[99] as abusing women,[100] or as harming children's human rights[101] adopt an allegedly realistic and pragmatic viewpoint and do not suggest the global abolishment of cross-border surrogacy. Instead, they propose national and international legislation to minimize the potential harm to the individuals involved in the transaction.[102] Hence, I could have ended this part by pointing to the elasticity of ethical borders between right and wrong in the face of global forces' exploitative cooperation with national, gender, and social-class borders. However, the recent developments in developing countries that used to be part of the international surrogacy market and effectively stopped playing the hypercapitalist global game prove that legal deliberations on cross-border reproduction services should not bend before global economic forces as if they were an immovable *fait-accompli*, but should, rather, insist on shaping their moral ground independently, while discussing the option of stopping international (and national) surrogacy as a realistic one.

Conclusion

Placing cross-border abortion alongside inter- and multinational surrogacy helps us see that globalization, just like borders, is not intrinsically evil or good, and that our moral stance toward the freedom of people to shop for reproduction services in other countries, or toward a state's attempts to prevent its citizens from carrying out certain reproduction actions across the border, is linked to our moral stance toward the national legislation that motivates or prevents this kind of global shopping. Moreover, both case studies make evident the mutually beneficial relationship between globalization and borders. It is not only that global capitalism benefits from the different national legal regimes that motivate transnational reproduction services;[103] it is also that the nation states

---

[99] John Henry Pascoe, "International Surrogacy: A New Kind of Trafficking?," a paper presented at LegalWise 2nd Annual International Family Law Conference, Cambodia, 2012, available at: http://tinyurl.com/hv42n2s.

[100] Bassan, "Cross Border Reproductive Transactions in the Era of Globalization."

[101] Ergas, "Thinking 'through' Human Rights, 427–34.

[102] For a detailed example, see Trimmings & Beaumont, "General Report on Surrogacy," at 531–49.

[103] Ulrich Beck & Elisabeth Beck-Gernsheim, *Distant Love* (Cambridge: Polity Press, 2014), Ch. 9.

benefit from their citizens' ability to perform *(im)moral outsourcing*[104] in the global sphere, which weakens external and internal political pressures to change existing national laws and the moral grounds they are based on. These mutually beneficial relations are possible, among other reasons, due to the current confusion, ambiguity, and disagreements within international law, as far as reproduction rights and obligations are concerned. Likewise, both case studies discussed in this chapter demonstrate the new challenge to sovereignty posed by bordered globalization – the weakening of the pragmatic ability of a country to stop its citizens from preventing parenthood or seeking it in another country. Notwithstanding, the developing countries' isomorphic new legislation that bans international surrogacy proves that national legislators can still, very effectively, control national borders if they are determined to do so. That is the case, even if they are placed within the less privileged stratum of the global hierarchy. Whether this new wall that currently prevents the use of surrogates in the Global South will be broken down again in the future, for example by illegal international surrogacy or by other developing countries entering the vacuum, is yet to be seen.

Moreover, although cross-border abortion and surrogacy could have been conceptualized as opposing one another – the former belonging to "death tourism,"[105] and the latter belonging to what can be perceived as "life-creation tourism" – the similarities arising from these two case studies support my argument that they should both be perceived as part of the global reproduction industry. In both cases, the central moral issue is reproduction autonomy – that of the pregnant woman who wants to abort and her intercourse partner (the latter, completely ignored by the literature), and that of the surrogate mother, the ova seller, and the intended parents. In both cases, women are at risk of being reduced to their wombs, being controlled during pregnancy for the sake of the fetus, in the case of abortion, and for the sake of the intended parents, in the case of surrogacy. In both cases we know too little about the experiences and outcomes of cross-border reproduction movement, not only those related to women but also those related to men as potential and actual fathers. Little is also known about the children touched by this movement: those who already exist (children of pregnant women who might be harmed if their mother is not allowed to terminate the pregnancy, and

---

[104] I thank my colleague Prof. Shai Lavi for suggesting this term.

[105] In that sense, cross-border abortion can be joined with "suicide tourism." See Daniel Sperling, *Suicide Tourism: Understanding the Legal, Philosophical and Socio-Political Dimensions* (Oxford University Press, forthcoming).

children of surrogate mothers who have to live without their mother for nine months or, in cases where they witness their mother's pregnancy, have to cope with the disappearance of their "sibling"); and those who come into the world unwanted because of restrictions on abortion, or who, due to advanced fertility technology and bordered globalization, are born with multiple parents (genetic, biological, and social) who belong to different nationalities, races, and cultures. In that sense, any current regulative proposal, be it national or international, is based on insufficient data. This is, of course, no excuse for the current regulation deficit of the phallocentric international law that already causes very evident extreme harm to women who cannot terminate their pregnancy safely and who are exploited as surrogates.

Finally, in both cases, we can see that the interrelations between borders and globalization are shaped not only by states, international bodies, and commercial entities, but also by individuals. Girls and women in Ireland who find themselves, unintentionally, in impossible and life-threatening situations, and a growing number of gay Israeli couples who are willing to do almost anything to have a genetic child, challenge national legal regimes and force their countries to reshape their jurisdictions in light of dynamically changing global options and pressures.

5

Familial Citizenship

Introduction

Citizenship of an affluent state is the most valuable resource of our era. The most significant divide of our times is not between those who have citizenship and the stateless[1] but, rather, between citizens of well-off democratic countries, which grant their citizens basic human and civil rights, including adequate standards of living,[2] and citizens of countries that fail to do so due to poverty, corruption, tyranny, violent conflicts, or some combination of these ills.

The rich literature on *citizenship* that has evolved over the last 20 years[3] has developed and expanded this analytical category to include a variety of concepts. They comprise territorial-based concepts such as *transnational citizenship* and *urban citizenship*; organizational-based concepts such as *industrial citizenship*; relational and identity-based concepts such as *cultural citizenship*, *sexual citizenship*, and *lived citizenship*; and concepts based on degree, such as *partial citizenship* and *virtual citizenship*.[4] In addition, these concepts are employed as descriptive or normative

---

[1] I refer here to the International Law definition of a stateless person as one who is not considered as a national by any state. See Article 1 of the Convention Relating to the Status of Stateless Persons 1954, available at: www.ohchr.org/EN/ProfessionalInterest/Pages/StatelessPersons.aspx. But see also Audrey Macklin's suggestion to broaden this definition to include citizens without a state, whom she defines as citizens of failed states. See Audrey Macklin, "Who Is the Citizen's Other? Considering the Heft of Citizenship," *Theoretical Inquiries in Law*, 8(2) (2007), 333–66.

[2] The right to an adequate standard of living is an internationally recognized human right. According to Article 25(1) of the Universal Declaration of Human Rights (UDHR) 1948: "Everyone has the right to a standard of living adequate for the health and wellbeing of himself and his family, including food, clothing, housing and medical care and necessary social services, and the right to security in the event of unemployment, sickness, disability, widowhood, old age or other lack of livelihood in circumstances beyond his control." Available at: www.un.org/en/universal-declaration-human-rights/index.html.

[3] Peter Nyers, "Introduction: Why Citizenship Studies," *Citizenship Studies*, 11(1) (2007), 1–4.

[4] Ruth Lister, "Inclusive Citizenship: Realizing the Potential," *Citizenship Studies*, 11(1) (2007), 49–61; Macklin, "Who Is the Citizen's Other?" at 334.

and even visionary, the latter leading, as political scientist Alexandra Dobrowolsky argues, to a widening gap between "citizenship-in-theory" and "citizenship-in-practice."[5]

This chapter addresses *familial citizenship*, which I define as the right of family members to be citizens of the same country, based on their family relations.[6] I situate the discussion of *familial citizenship* in the very basic, descriptive, legal, and national embedded definition of citizenship, as a "membership in a State".[7] Whereas the scope of *social citizenship* – that is, the "package of rights, responsibilities, entitlements, duties, practices and attachments that define membership in a polity"[8] – is contested philosophically and varies empirically from state to state, almost all countries attach to *legal citizenship* the unconditional right to enter and remain in the territory, and the right to have the rights[9] granted to all members of the specific state.[10] Hence, *legal citizenship* is not only part of the broader *social citizenship*, but also a precondition of its other components. And

---

[5] Alexandra Dobrowolsky, "(In)Security and Citizenship: Security, Im/migration and Shrinking Citizenship Regimes," *Theoretical Inquiries in Law*, 8(2) (2007), 629–61, at 630.

[6] In 2005, Nükhet Sirman coined the term "familial citizenship" to describe a situation in which a position within a particular familial discourse provides the person with a status within the national polity. Sirman analyzes the nation-building discourse in Turkey, which constructed the "ideal citizen" as the "sovereign husband and his dependent wife/mother." See Nükhet Sirman, "The Making of Familial Citizenship in Turkey" in Emin Fuat Keyman & Ahmet İçduygu (Eds.), *Citizenship in a Global World: European Questions and Turkish Experiences* (London: Routledge, 2005), pp. 147–72, at 148. Although I use the term *familial citizenship* in a more basic physical–legal sense, we will see that Sirman's relational and identity-based definition is also relevant to the cross-border context discussed in this chapter. I distinguish *familial citizenship* from the more general, yet relevant, term of *family citizenship* coined by Pierpaolo Donati in 1998: "family citizenship means that the family as such must enjoy its own set of rights-obligations, as a reality of solidarity, and not simply as the sum of the rights-obligations of its individual members." See Pierpaolo Donati, "The New Citizenship of the Family" in Koen Matthijs (Ed.), *The Family, Contemporary Perspectives and Challenges* (Leuven University Press, 1998), pp. 243–61, at 254. I am inspired here by the concept of *industrial citizenship* suggested by T.H. Marshall, to capture employees' rights to unite and struggle together for their labor rights. See Guy Mundlak, "Industrial Citizenship, Social Citizenship, Corporate Citizenship: I Just Want My Wages," *Theoretical Inquiries in Law*, 8(2) (2007), 719–48; and Nathan Lillie, "The Right Not to Have Rights: Posted Worker Acquiescence and the European Union Labor Rights Framework," *Theoretical Inquiries in Law*, 17(1) (2016), 39–62.

[7] Christian Joppke, "Transformation of Citizenship: Status, Rights, Identity," *Citizenship Studies*, 11(1) (2007), 37–48, at 38.

[8] Macklin, "Who Is the Citizen's Other?," at 334.

[9] On the conceptual connections between Hannah Arendt's famous dicta "the right to have rights," and "citizenship," see Alison Kesby, *The Right to Have Rights: Citizenship, Humanity, and International Law* (Oxford University Press, 2012).

[10] Macklin, "Who Is the Citizen's Other?," at 334.

so, although perceived by many as merely formal, it is, in fact, crucial and substantial.[11]

Although the era of bordered globalization is characterized by possible multiple memberships in supranational and subnational communities that can provide rights, obligations, identities, and relations, only states can grant citizenship as defined in this chapter.[12] Moreover, as there is no global power to enforce even the most basic human rights, let alone citizenship rights, there is a very limited meaning of citizenship talk beyond states' power.[13] Indeed, citizenship and the dramatic consequences of inequity attached to it are among the most significant evidence of the ongoing importance of nations and national borders.[14] Hence, I agree with those who argue that, in non-national contexts, citizenship can be employed only as a metaphor.[15]

There are two main ways of acquiring legal citizenship: to be born in the nation's territory, and to be born to a parent who is the nation's citizen. As will be discussed in the third part of this chapter, very few countries, including the United States, Canada, Brazil, and Guatemala,[16] grant citizenship to whoever is born on their soil, regardless of the citizenship status of the newborn's parents (*jus soli* – the law of the soil). Most countries, however, grant citizenship to children born within their borders only if at least one of their parents is a citizen (*jus sanguinis* – the law of blood). Hence, in the era of bordered globalization, we witness the growing phenomenon of *intergenerational denizenship*[17] – a situation in which immigrants who lack citizenship status transfer their resident-but-not-citizen status to their offspring who were born in the country of destination. The question of granting citizenship to children of citizens born outside the nation's

---

[11] Ibid., at 334–5.

[12] Ayelet Shachar, *The Birthright Lottery: Citizenship and Global Inequality* (Cambridge, MA: Harvard University Press, 2009), at 2.

[13] Gerald Delanty, "European Citizenship: A Critical Assessment," *Citizenship Studies*, 11(1) (2007), 63–72, at 65; Engin F. Isin & Bryan S. Turner, "Investigating Citizenship: An Agenda for Citizenship Studies," *Citizenship Studies*, 11(1) (2007), 5–17, at 12.

[14] Isin & Turner, "Investigating Citizenship"; Ayelet Shachar, "The Worth of Citizenship in an Unequal World," *Theoretical Inquiries in Law*, 8(2) (2007), 367–88, at 382.

[15] Shachar, *The Birthright Lottery*, at 2.

[16] Jon Feere, "Birthright Citizenship in the United States: A Global Comparison," Center for Immigration Studies (2010), at 15. Available at: www.cis.org/sites/cis.org/files/articles/2010/birthright.pdf.

[17] For an analysis of the current emergence of the concept of "denize" within immigration studies, see Meghan Benton "A Theory of Denizenship," PhD Dissertation, University College London (2010), available at: http://discovery.ucl.ac.uk/624490/1/624490.pdf.

borders, also becoming more and more relevant in our era, is like-wise complex, with different *jus soli* and *jus sanguinis* countries add-ing different tests such as the marital status of the parents,[18] how the parents acquired their citizenship,[19] and whether the child has another citizenship.[20]

In the era of bordered globalization, the ability to acquire legal citi-zenship of another country, and so to cross one's own national border and to stay in that country, might be critical to the ability to enjoy what globalization has to offer.[21] Acquiring citizenship through naturaliza-tion that follows immigration, however, is extremely rare compared to the territory- and blood-based routes.[22] As discussed in Chapter 1, we live in a world with harsh inequalities between states, hence, as Ayelet Shachar argues, citizenship – which is based almost entirely on "the lottery of birthright"[23] – is "the quintessential *inherited* entitlement of our time,"[24] functioning as the gatekeeper that allows the affluent to make sure their privileges will pass on only to their offspring. As such, it also functions as a Eurocentric and racist harmonizing mechanism, preventing the cultural and ethnic *other* from entering the allegedly white-enlightened part of the world.[25] Even international law does not challenge this global stratification and hierarchal legal mechanism and does not force states to allow entry to non-citizens, except in the very narrowly defined category of refugees.[26]

---

[18] The United States, for example, grants almost automatic citizenship to children born of US mothers outside of its soil, while making it much harder for children of US fathers to achieve citizenship. See Kristin A. Collins, "Illegitimate Borders: *Jus Sanguinis*, Citizenship and the Legal Construction of Family, Race, and Nation," *Yale Law Journal*, 123(7) (2014), 2167–206.

[19] For example, a child can be granted UK citizenship even if it was born outside its borders, if it was born to a UK citizen who secured his or her citizenship otherwise than through descent. See the British Nationality Act 1981, s. 2(1)(a).

[20] India, for example, prohibits dual citizenship, but in 2005 introduced the status of 'Overseas Citizenship of India' (OCI), which grants some, though not full, citizenship rights to people of Indian descent who live abroad and have non-Indian citizenship. The children of these people can also gain the OCI status. See "Frequently Asked Questions (FAQs) About OCI," Consulate General of India – Toronto, available at: www.cgitoronto .ca/content/faq-about-oci-0.

[21] Catherine Dauvergne, "Citizenship with a Vengeance," *Theoretical Inquiries in Law*, 8(2) (2007), 489–507, at 492.

[22] Shachar, *The Birthright Lottery*, at 11.

[23] Shachar, "The Worth of Citizenship," at 377.

[24] Ibid., at 371.

[25] Delanty, "European Citizenship," at 70.

[26] Shachar, "The Worth of Citizenship," at 375.

Supposedly, family relations constitute the golden key to developed nations' doors – a precious legitimate means of gaining citizenship through naturalization. Indeed, family immigration is today's single most important source of immigration to Europe, accounting for one-third of residence permits issued to immigrants from third-country nationals into the EU.[27] These permits can result in citizenship, dependent on the status of the family member in the destination country and this country's citizenship law, as well as the will of the family members involved.[28] Family relations are an even more significant justification for immigration visas to the United States,[29] accounting for two-thirds of documented immigration.[30] However, although this was also the case in Canada and Australia until the mid-1990s, in these two countries the category of family reunification currently gives way to the category of economic immigration.[31] Likewise, in Europe, the aforementioned one-third statistic of family-based immigration represents a drop from one-half, which was the figure at the beginning of the third millennium.[32]

[27] Anne Staver, "From Right to Earned Privilege? The Development of Stricter Family Immigration Rules in Denmark, Norway and the United Kingdom," PhD Dissertation, University of Toronto (2014), at 2, available at: https://tspace.library.utoronto.ca/bitstream/1807/68295/1/Staver_Anne_201411_PhD_thesis.pdf.

[28] There are significant differences in citizenship take-up rates in different European countries. For example, in the Netherlands and Sweden, around 80 percent of the foreign-born population is naturalized after at least ten years' residence, but in Germany and Switzerland the rate is as low as 35 percent. Maarten Peter Vink, Tijana Prokic-Breuer, & Jaap Dronkers revealed that this is so not only because of the differences in citizenship law but because of other variables, such as the country of origin of the resident. See Maarten Peter Vink, Tijana Prokic-Breuer, & Jaap Dronkers, "Immigrant Naturalization in the Context of Institutional Diversity: Policy Matters, but to Whom?," *International Migration*, 51(5) (2013) 1–20.

[29] US Department of State, *Immigrant and Nonimmigrant Visas Issued at Foreign Service Posts Fiscal Years 2010 – 2014* (2015), available at: http://travel.state.gov/content/dam/visas/Statistics/AnnualReports/FY2014AnnualReport/FY14AnnualReport-TableI.pdf.

[30] Catherine Lee, "Family Reunification and the Limits of Immigration Reform: Impact and Legacy of the 1965 Immigration Act," *Sociological Forum*, 30(S1) (2015), 528–48, at 529. Notwithstanding, since Asian and Latin immigrants started to dominate the family immigration category in the 1970s, this category has been constantly attacked in the public discourse also in the United States. See Bill Ong Hing, *Deporting Our Souls: Values, Morality, and Immigration Policy* (New York: Cambridge University Press, 2006), Ch. 3.

[31] Madine Vanderplatt, Howard Ramos, & Yoko Yoshida, "What Do Sponsored Parents and Grandparents Contribute?" *Canadian Ethnic Studies*, 44(3) (2012), 79–96, at 80; Australian Government – Department of Immigration and Boarder Protection, *Australia's Migration Trends 2013–14 at a Glance* (2014), at 2–3, available at: www.border.gov.au/ReportsandPublications/Documents/statistics/migration-trends13-14-glance.pdf.

[32] Helena Wray, Agnes Agoston, & Jocelyn Hutton, "A Family Resemblance? The Regulation of Marriage Migration in Europe," *European Journal of Migration and Law*, 16(2) (2014), 209–47, at 209–10.

Legal scholar Catherine Dauvergne argues that this shrinking in the relative significance of family-related immigration demonstrates a worldwide shift toward more scrutinizing and limiting immigration policies. Indeed, there is a general consensus that Western countries have toughened their citizenship laws since the beginning of the third millennium, and more so their immigration laws, including in relation to family reunification which, Dauvergne argues, are employed by the citizenship apparatus to do its "dirty work."[33] According to Dauvergne, the new immigration and citizenship polices in North America, Europe, and Australia, have two main goals. First, to fight the "illegals" – undocumented labor migrants and asylum seekers, and their family members – who are perceived as a burden on the market and on the state's resources. Second, to attract the "best and brightest" who can contribute to the national market with their particular skills, experience, education, and wealth.[34] I would add another goal, prominent in non-Western economically developed countries such as Taiwan, the Arab States of the Persian Gulf, and Israel,[35] of enabling cheap labor, by temporary working visas granted to unaccompanied migrants who are then sent away when the market's needs change, or even sooner, in order to prevent permanent settlement. Whereas one way of attracting the best and brightest is to allow them to immigrate with their family members, this last group of mainly agricultural workers, construction laborers, and carers is deprived of this privilege.

The sociologist Christian Joppke provides another illuminating explanation for the shrinking citizenship policies in Europe, including those related to family reunification. According to Joppke, the last third of the twentieth century witnessed a liberalization of access to citizenship for noncitizens and their offspring in Europe, "from discretionary anomaly to rule-based routine,"[36] leading to the transformation of the state "from ethnic nation-state, owned by 'its' people who could reject or accept newcomers as they saw fit, into post-national state, in which the principle of liberal democracy requires congruence between the subjects and

---

[33] Dauvergne, "Citizenship with a Vengeance," at 495.

[34] Catherine Dauvergne, "Globalization Fragmentation: New Pressures on Women Caught in the Immigration Law–Citizenship Law Dichotomy" in Seyla Benhabib & Judith Resnik (Eds.), *Migrations and Mobilities: Citizenship, Borders, and Gender* (New York University Press, 2009), pp. 333–55. See also Iseult Honohan, "Reconsidering the Claim to Family Reunification in Migration," *Political Studies*, 57(4) (2009), 768–87.

[35] Adriana Kemp, "Managing Migration, Reprioritizing National Citizenship: Undocumented Migrant Workers' Children and Policy Reforms in Israel," *Theoretical Inquiries in Law*, 8(2) (2007), 663–91, at 674.

[36] Joppke, "Transformation of Citizenship," at 39.

objects of rule."[37] Moreover, this period was also characterized by a move from understanding citizenship as belonging to a united welfare nation to perceiving it as peaceful coexistence of different groups that enjoy cultural autonomy within a neutral state. However, in the current millennium, a trend of raising the hurdles for naturalization in countries with a sizeable settled immigrant population can be observed, fueled by worries regarding Muslim terror and failing integration of the newcomers. An exclusionary discourse has emerged promoting the notion that "the liberal state is one for liberal people only,"[38] encouraging unity from within and rejecting the entry applications of so-called suspicious individuals who belong to certain groups perceived as a threat, be it at the level of culture or national security. It seems that the broadening of the option of naturalization has been followed by a backlash in the form of stricter national borders.

Joppke's culture-centered analysis, and Dauvergne's and my own economic-centered analyses, which, in my opinion, should be seen as complementary, suggest that our era is characterized by a convergence of hypercapitalist and ethno-nationalist interests that allows the cross-border movement of much-needed laborers, but, at the same time, prevents their settlement, and that of other aliens, in the host country – at least if they do not fit the profile of the desired newcomer who looks, thinks, and behaves like *us*. As Dauvergne concludes: "access to new citizenships is more and more closed for those with less, and more and more open to those with more."[39] Hence, at the same time that the scholastic discourse on *citizenship* expands the concept and includes calls for a world without borders, in practice citizenship becomes more bordered and excluding than ever before under the current policies of destination countries.[40] This chapter explores the impact of the convergence of hypercapitalist and ethno-nationalist interests, and its manifestation in law, on families – a relatively neglected exploration when compared to the political and academic immigration-related discussions which center on security and employment.[41]

---

[37] Ibid., at 40.

[38] Ibid., at 45.

[39] Dauvergne, "Citizenship with a Vengeance," at 506.

[40] See also Dobrowolsky, "(In)Security and Citizenship." Interestingly, and as will be explored in Chapter 6 in relation to remittances and international adoption, immigration-sending countries expand the concept of citizenship to allow and encourage continuing contact between those who leave for other countries and their motherland. See also Macklin, "Who Is the Citizen's Other?" at 363–4; Dauvergne, "Citizenship with a Vengeance," at 502.

[41] Audrey Holland, "The Modern Family Unit: Towards a More Inclusive Vision of the Family in Immigration Law," *California Law Review*, 96(4) (2008), 1049–91, at 1049.

The next part of the chapter deals with *spousal citizenship*, focusing on immigration and naturalization policies that affect spouses' ability to be citizens of the same country. It explores the *legal creativity* manifested by many developed countries in their attempt to minimize the significance of spousal citizenship, while allegedly respecting their citizens' right to family life. The last part of the chapter focuses on the outcomes of the lack of *parental citizenship* for many minor children and their noncitizen parents, who are not allowed to live together in the destination country. Many receiving countries strip labor migrants, refugees, and asylum seekers of their familial subjectivity, including by refusing the entry of their family members and by deportation that separates children from their parents. These practices are possible and common because the international community fails to establish a consensus over noncitizens' familial rights and because national immigration law and citizenship law defeat national family law.[42]

Taken as a whole, this chapter highlights the ongoing strength of national borders and the familial price paid by members of cross-border families due to their restricted access to citizenship. It also highlights the relevance of gender, economic status, ethnicity, and religion to people's ability to legally maneuver between globalization and borders in shaping their intersectional familial biographies.

Spousal Citizenship

At first glance it may seem that spousal citizenship is an obvious and undisputed form of familial citizenship. Recently, however, as legal scholar Helena Wray and her colleagues rightly argue: "In Europe, as elsewhere, many states find migration through marriage or equivalent relationship particularly problematic. Reconciling the desire to limit immigration, at least by certain types of immigrant, with the responsibilities to citizens who engage in transnational family life is a major preoccupation."[43] As this part of the chapter will demonstrate,

---

[42] Hence, this chapter, by and large, leaves out additional relevant categories, including spousal immigration of denizens, and other kinds of family relations affected by citizenship and immigration policies such as sibling relations and the relations between adult children and their parents. The latter is briefly discussed in Chapter 8.

[43] Wray, Agoston, & Hutton, "A Family Resemblance?" at 209. In Asia, spousal immigration is even more prevalent than in the West. See Hye-Kyung Lee, "Marriage Migration" in Immanuel Ness (Ed.), *The Encyclopedia of Global Human Migration* (Oxford: Wiley-Blackwell Publishing, 2013), available at: http://onlinelibrary.wiley.com/doi/10.1002/9781444351071.wbeghm353/abstract. However, as mentioned in the Introduction, several Asian countries have taken significant steps to minimize this phenomenon.

this preoccupation tilts the scales toward limiting immigration of undesired immigrants, even if they are the spouses of citizens of the limiting countries.

There are three main categories of citizens who might wish to bring a spouse from another country: labor immigrants who have gained citizenship in the host country and want to bring in their spouses who were left behind in the country of origin; naturalized offspring of immigrants who wish to bring new spouses from their ancestral country; and citizens who meet citizens of another country, in person or on-line, and wish to establish or continue spousal relations with them.[44] Hence, as immigration policy researcher Anne Staver observes, spousal citizenship is not only about the reunification of preexisting families, but also about family formation.[45] Moreover, as will be demonstrated in this section, each of these categories is constructed by gendered, economic, ethnic, and religious intersectionalities that affect and are affected by admission and integration regulation.

When considering spousal citizenship, a state must answer, by law, the following questions: (1) Is a citizen allowed to bring in a spouse? (2) If so, under what conditions? (3) Does the immigrating spouse receive immediate citizenship? (4) If not, what will his or her status be, and for how long? The first two questions are regulated by *immigration admission policy*, and the latter two by *immigration integration policy*, including the option of citizenship through naturalization.[46] The histories of the legislation that answers these questions in different countries reveal that the answers depend on: (1) the recognition of the right to family life by national and international policy-makers and legal bodies; (2) the state's interest in incoming emigration; (3) the state's interest in immigrants' assimilation; and (4) the state's perception of the family as an assimilation catalyst or as a risk to assimilation.[47] As we shall see, whether spousal citizenship policies are also genuinely affected by concerns over gender justice is debatable.

---

[44] Anne Staver, "Free Movement and the Fragmentation of Family Reunification Rights," *European Journal of Migration and the Law*, 15(1) (2013), 69–89, at 82. For example, in the Netherlands, see Saskia Bonjour & Betty de Hart, "A Proper Wife, a Proper Marriage: Constructions of 'Us' and 'Them' in Dutch Family Migration Policy," *European Journal of Women's Studies*, 20(1) (2013), 61–76, at 67.

[45] Staver, "Free Movement," at 82.

[46] Staver, "From Right to Earned Privilege?"

[47] For a fascinating example, providing a historical account of US familial citizenship and its changing rationale, see Kerry Abrams, "What Makes the Family Special?," *The University of Chicago Law Review*, 80(1) (2013), 7–27.

On the face of it, a citizen has a right to bring his/her spouse into his/her country, as part of the right to family life, the latter being recognized by International Law.[48] Clearly, the ability to exercise the right to be protected from arbitrary interference in one's family, to found a family, and to be protected as a family, all recognized by the Universal Declaration of Human Rights,[49] is crucially dependent on the ability to live together in the same country.[50] But this is where things get complicated, because the desire to control borders has led to a separation between the right to family life and the right to family life in one's country of citizenship.

The United States is an example of a country with immigration regulations that generously allow spousal visas, and in that sense, respect its citizens' interest to live together with their alien spouse on US soil.[51] However, even in the United States, there is a heated debate about whether this interest amounts to a protected constitutional right.[52] This is certainly not an *absolute* right, as demonstrated by the prohibition on family reunification with more than one spouse, relevant to polygamous families,[53] and the difficulties encountered by US citizens who establish spousal relations with an undocumented immigrant.[54]

---

[48] On international law's recognition of the right to family life, see Yuval Merin, "The Right to Family Life and Civil Marriage under International Law and its Implementation in the State of Israel," *Boston College International and Comparative Law Review*, 28(1) (2005), 79–147.

[49] Articles 12 and 16 of the Universal Declaration of Human Rights 1948.

[50] Honohan, "Reconsidering the Claim," at 771–2. This is not to say that all spouses must, or want to, share the same household. Indeed, data from Sub-Saharan Africa indicate that, in some cultures, family life does not necessitate cohabitation. In Senegal, Ghana, and DR Congo, marriage does not necessarily entail high levels of conjunctional interaction, and many couples live in different parts of the same town, in different parts of the same country, or in different countries. This cultural understanding of marriage is manifested also in the refusal of some of those who emigrated from these countries to Western countries to petition for family reunification. See Valentina Mazzucato, Djamila Schans, Kim Caarls, & Cris Beauchemin, "Transnational Families between Africa and Europe," *International Migration Review*, 49(1) (2015), 142–72.

[51] Liav Orgad, "Love and War: Family Migration in Time of National Emergency," *Georgetown Immigration Law Journal*, 23(1) (2008), 85–127, at 115–19.

[52] *Kerry v. Din*, 135 S Ct 2128 (2015).

[53] Nora V. Demleitner, "How Much Do Western Democracies Value Family and Marriage?: Immigration Law's Conflicted Answers," *Hofstra Law Review*, 32(1) (2003), 273–311, at 274.

[54] April M. Schueths, "'Where Are My Rights?' Compromised Citizenship in Mixed-Status Marriage: A Research Note," *Journal of Sociology & Social Welfare*, 39(4) (2012), 97–109; Evelyn Haydee Cruz, "Because You're Mine, I Walk the Line: The Trials and Tribulations of the Family Visa Program," *Fordham URB Law Journal*, 38(1) (2010), 155–81.

Likewise, in other jurisdictions, it is not at all clear that the right to family life includes the right to live with one's spouse in the country of which one is a citizen. The ECtHR, for example, acknowledges that the right to family life, recognized by the ECHR,[55] includes the right of binational couples to live together but does not acknowledge the right of the spouses to choose in which of the two countries of origin the living together will take place. According to the Court, a state can refuse the alien spouse's entrance or can deport that spouse, and expects its citizen to emigrate to the alien's home country, not only if the alien spouse is residing in the state illegally[56] but also if the citizen has connections with the spouse's home country.[57] Indeed, as Staver argues,[58] it seems that many Western countries have developed strategic regulations to overcome family immigration, converting it from a right to a privilege governed by national interests.[59] In what follows, I will detail what I perceive as the five main clusters of these strategic regulations that destination countries use in their attempt to evade their liberal obligation to respect the right to family life of their citizens who choose a spouse from another country.

The Second-Class-Citizenship Strategy

One way in which states try to minimize spousal citizenship is by creating a form of second-class citizenship, which excludes the right to family reunification. One such example, stemming from the analysis of legal scholar Betty de Hart, is that of the British Immigration Rules of 1980.[60] These rules introduced stricter conditions for husbands to join their wives settled in the UK than for the wives of settled men. Even in cases in which the settled wife became a UK citizen, her spouse was not allowed to enter or stay in Britain, and the wife was expected to leave for her husband's home country. Hence, the British authorities not only discriminated against women citizens compared to men, perceiving their relations with foreign men "as

---

55 Article 8 of the European Convention on Human Rights 1950, available at: www.echr.coe.int/Documents/Convention_ENG.pdf.

56 For accounts of the difficulties of US citizens who have a non-US citizen spouse, especially in cases where the spouse is an 'illegal' immigrant, caused by the current immigration and citizenship policies, see Schueths, "'Where Are My Rights?'"; Cruz, "Because You're Mine, I Walk the Line."

57 Betty de Hart, "Love Thy Neighbour: Family Reunification and the Right of Insiders," *European Journal of Migration and the Law*, 11(3) (2009), 235–52.

58 Staver, "From Right to Earned Privilege?"

59 See, for example, the United States. Lee, "Family Reunification," at 545.

60 de Hart, "Love Thy Neighbour."

a more serious threat to restrictive immigration policies,"[61] but also created a status of second-class citizens: citizens through naturalization were lesser citizens as far as their right to be united with their spouse in the UK was concerned. Although the UK had to change its gender-based discriminatory policy due to the interference of the ECtHR,[62] it was undisturbed in doing so by taking away men's right to be joined by their wives.[63] Hence, the ECtHR left open the option of a gender-neutral second-class-citizenship strategy available for member states.

Another example of the second-class-citizenship strategy can be found in Israeli law. Since 2003, Israel has imposed extreme restrictions on the possibility of reunification of Israeli citizens with their spouses from the Occupied Territories (the West Bank and Gaza).[64] Although theoretically these restrictions affect all Israeli citizens, in practice they deny the Arab Palestinian Israeli citizens from realizing their right to family life because they are those who find spouses from within the Palestinians living in these areas.[65] Moreover, Israeli male citizens are less restricted in bringing over a Palestinian spouse than female citizens because the law allows some discretion to the Ministry of Interior in allowing entry from the Occupied Territories of female spouses above the age of 25, but of male spouses only over 35.[66]

The Israeli Supreme Court concluded that the law imposing these restrictions violated the right to family life and the right to equality, and forced the legislator to introduce some proportionality changes. However, overall, the majority of the Supreme Court judges accepted the state's argument that the restrictive law was justified as the right to family reunification of Israeli citizens was abused by a number of Palestinians from the Occupied Territories who entered Israel and became involved in terrorist activity.[67] Several scholars, however, argue that the security threat justification is not empirically convincing and is aimed at covering the

---

[61] Ibid., at 251.

[62] *Abdulaziz et al. v. United Kingdom* (1985) 7 EHRR 471.

[63] de Hart, "Love Thy Neighbour," at 239.

[64] These restrictions were broadened in 2007, to include spouses from Iran, Iraq, Syria, and Lebanon, which are all considered by Israel as enemy states. See Ruth Lapidoth & Ofra Friesel, "Some Reflections on Israel's Temporary Legislation on Unification of Families," *Israel Law Review*, 43(2) (2010), 457–567.

[65] Ibid.

[66] The Citizenship and Entry into Israel Law (Temporary Provision) 5763 – 2003, Article 3, Unofficial Translation, available at: http://knesset.gov.il/laws/special/eng/citizenship_law .htm.

[67] The State of Israel argued that in 2001–2010, 54 Palestinians who had entered Israel through family reunification were involved in terrorist activity, 28 of whom were involved

true motivation of the State of Israel in preventing family reunification of its Palestinian citizens, which is to preserve the demographic dominance of the Jewish population.[68]

Hence, whereas in Britain the second-class-citizenship strategy was aimed at preventing newcomers from bringing in more so-called aliens, in Israel it is used by the Jewish majority to block the Palestinian indigenous population from uniting with spouses across the border that was created as an outcome of the conflict between the Jewish and Palestinian nations. Interestingly, in both cases, the policy was tailored in a way that privileges male citizens, because alien female spouses are perceived as less of a threat than alien male spouses. Finally, although in both cases courts tried to modify the policies so they were less restrictive or discriminatory, legitimation to limit the right to spousal citizenship in the name of a nation's right to guard its borders is judicially granted.

The Illegitimate Spouse Strategy

The only broadening tendency that can be identified in recent years in relation to spousal citizenship is that of the expansion of the definition of a spouse. Whereas in the past only married heterosexual bi-national couples were allowed to unite, today more and more jurisdictions allow the reunification of spouses belonging to one or more of these categories: same-sex married couples, heterosexual registered couples, same-sex registered couples,[69] heterosexual cohabitants, and same-sex cohabitants.[70]

---

in planned or executed terrorist attacks. See HCJ 466/07 *MK Zehava Galon (Meretz-Yahad) v. Attorney General* (2012) (Israel), at 7–8.

[68] For example, Yoav Peled, "Citizenship Betrayed: Israel's Emerging Immigration and Citizenship Regime," *Theoretical Inquiries in Law*, 8(2) (2007), 603–28; Aeyal M. Gross, "In Love with the Enemy: Justice, Truth, Integrity and Common Sense between Israel and Utopia in the Citizenship Law Case," *Hamishpat*, 23 (2007), 79–85 (Hebrew); Guy Davidov, Jonathan Yovel, Ilan Saban, & Amnon Reichman, "State or Family? The 2003 Amendment to the Citizenship and Entrance to Israel Law," *Mishpat Umimshal*, 8 (2005), 643–99 (Hebrew).

[69] While cohabitation is usually legally established by criteria such as a shared household, several jurisdictions allow cohabitants to register themselves as a "registered partnership," also called "civil partnership," to avoid misunderstandings between themselves and between them and the state. In some countries, registered partnership yields the same rights and obligations as marriage, and in some it does not. For example, see the legal ramifications of these different categories in the Netherlands – "Marriage, registered partnership and cohabitation agreements," Government of the Netherlands, available at: www.government .nl/issues/family-law/marriage-registered-partnership-and-cohabitation-agreements.

[70] For a discussion of the implications of the recent recognition of same-sex marriages by the US Supreme Court on US immigration and citizenship policies, see Benjamin P. Edwards,

Still, for many unmarried couples and same-sex spouses the option of spousal citizenship does not exist because immigration policies do not even grant the alien spouses residency or work permits, let alone allow them citizenship though naturalization. Within the thirty countries of the European Economic Area (EEA),[71] for example, as of 2014 only nine recognize the right to spousal reunification of registered partners, eight recognize cohabitants' right, and eight grant same-sex spouses the same reunification rights that they give to heterosexual spouses.[72] Hence, many spouses are illegitimate spouses in the eyes of immigration and citizenship law due to their sexual orientation or spousal formal status.

Moreover, recent policies push at further narrowing the definition of a legitimate spouse in order to limit the ability of aliens to seek citizenship on the grounds of their spousal relations with a citizen. The most prominent new policy within the illegitimate spouse strategy denies citizenship based on "sham marriage," "fraudulent marriage," "fictive marriage," or "marriage of convenience." These terms refer to cases in which the state argues that the marriage or partnership between its citizen and the alien was contracted with the sole or primary purpose of enabling the alien to enter the country or reside in it. The alien, as constructed by this policy, is not a legitimate spouse but a manipulative and exploitative one – or not a spouse at all.

The 2004 Citizens Directive of the EU, for example, allows member states to restrict the right of their citizens to live with their spouse, in cases of "abuse of rights or fraud, such as marriages of convenience."[73] Indeed, most of the EEA states have laws that restrict their citizens from uniting with a spouse if the sole, exclusive, primary, or main purpose of the relationship is to gain entry to, or residence of, the alien in their territory.[74] These countries have developed indicators to expose marriages of convenience, including noncohabitation, no shared language, and significant age difference.[75] Likewise, in the United States "fraudulent

---

"Welcoming A Post-Doma World: Same-Sex Spousal Petitions and Other Post-Windsor Immigration Implications," *Family Law Quarterly*, 47(2) (2013), 173–89.

[71] Currently, the EEA includes the twenty-seven EU countries and Iceland, Norway, and Lichtenstein.

[72] Wray, Agoston, & Hutton, "A Family Resemblance?," at 236–38.

[73] European Parliament and Council Directive 2004/38/EC of 29 April 2004, Article 35, available at: http://eur-lex.europa.eu/LexUriServ/LexUriServ.do?uri=OJ:L:2004:158:0077 :0123:en:PDF.

[74] Wray, Agoston, & Hutton, "A Family Resemblance?," at 239.

[75] Ibid., at 240–1; Betty de Hart, "Introduction: The Marriage of Convenience in Europe Immigration Law," *European Journal of Migration and Law*, 8(3–4) (2006), 251–62.

marriages are taken extremely seriously by the CIA," which, to detect such marriages, adds to the European cohabitation, age, and language criteria, the unawareness of family and friends of the marriage, the spouse being a friend of the family, or the marriage being arranged by a third party.[76]

An interesting exception to the general trend of revealing and sanctioning those perceived as illegitimate spouses is the UK, which has revoked its primary-purpose rule that allowed a spousal immigration permit only if the primary purpose of the alien spouse was marriage and not immigration. The government abolished this rule in 1997, arguing that it was "arbitrary, unfair and ineffective and has penalized genuine marriages, divided families and unnecessarily increased the administrative burden on the immigration system".[77] This reform was followed by a significant increase in approvals for spousal settlement, from 30,190 in 1994 to 57,390 in 2008.[78] However, the proportion of spousal-related settlement approvals among the overall settlement approvals dropped from 59 percent in 1995 to 39 percent in 2008. This can be explained by other related immigration policies,[79] as well as by Wray's argument that the UK authorities use the test of the intention of each spouse to "live permanently with the other" in "subsisting" marriage, left in the law after the 1997 reform, as a gate-keeping substitute to the revoked primary-purpose test. Immigration officers become, through this test, and much as they did in the era of the primary-purpose test, "engaged in deciding whether the marriage is 'credible', a process that often collapses into a judgment upon the parties' conduct or even the advisability of the marriage."[80]

Whereas sham marriages no doubt exist in the era of bordered globalization, precisely because spousal citizenship is one of the only available routes to legal emigration to, and naturalization in, a developed

---

[76] Nicole Lawrence Ezer, "The Intersection of Immigration Law and Family Law," *Family Law Quarterly*, 40(3) (2006), 339–66, at 347–8.

[77] Staver, "From Right to Earned Privilege?," at 208.

[78] Katharine Charsley, Brooke Storer-Church, Michaela Benson, & Nicholas van Hear, "Marriage-Related Migration to the UK," *International Migration Review*, 46(4) (2012), 861–90, at 864.

[79] These policies include the 2003 raising of the probationary period between spousal entry and settlement from one to two years, and the demand for "knowledge of life in the UK." See ibid., at 865.

[80] Helena Wray, "An Ideal Husband? Marriages of Convenience, Moral Gate-Keeping and Immigration to the UK," *European Journal of Migration and Law*, 8(3–4) (2006), 303–20, at 312.

country, there are no reliable statistics on their scale and characteristics.[81] What is clear from available research is that immigration officers and marriage registrars find it hard to distinguish between sham and genuine marriages, and that this distinction ignores the complex and plural meaning of marriage, which often includes a mixture of motivations.[82] Rather than successfully detecting sham marriages, this and similar tests under the illegitimate-spouse strategy enable states to create an imaginary border between love and economic motivations in marriage and to translate it into an undeclared geo-political bordering policy and practice that refuse entry and deport undesirable aliens. As with the second-class-citizenship strategy, these undesirable aliens are mainly men from the South and East.[83] Undesirable female aliens are more often prevented entry through the next strategy of consensual marriage.

The Consensual-Marriage Strategy

Another strategy adopted by developed countries in relation to spousal citizenship is to limit it to consensual relations and marriages. Under the current immigration policy of a number of countries, spousal relations that are perceived by the state as involuntary or forced do not yield the right to unification and naturalization.[84] This strategy is particularly interesting and challenging as it is the outcome not only of national

---

[81] Wray, "An Ideal Husband?," at 314.

[82] Sara L. Friedman, "Determining the 'Truth' at the Border: Immigration Interviews, Chinese Marital Migrants, and Taiwan's Sovereignty Dilemmas," *Citizenship Studies*, 14(2) (2010), 167–83; Lee Ann Wang, "'Of the Law, but Not Its Spirit': Immigration Marriage Fraud as Legal Fiction and Violence against Asian Immigrant Women," *UC Irvine Law Review*, 3(4) (2013), 1221–50; Marie-Claire Foblets & Dirk Vanheule, "Marriage of Convenience in Belgium: The Punitive Approach Gains Ground in Migration Law," *European Journal of Migration and Law*, 8(3–4) (2006), 263–80; Jaeeun Kim, "Establishing Identity: Documents, Performance, and Biometric Information in Immigration Proceedings," *Law & Social Inquiry*, 36(3) (2011), 760–86.

[83] Wray, "An Ideal Husband?," at 319 (UK); Johanna Leinonen & Saara Pellander, "Court Decisions over Marriage Migration in Finland: A Problem with Transnational Family Ties," *Journal of Ethics and Migration Studies*, 40(9) (2014), 1488–506 (Finland); Bonjour & de Hart, "A Proper Wife, a Proper Marriage" (The Netherlands). But on the disproportional impact of the US Immigration Marriage Fraud Amendment of 1986 on Asian Women, See Wang, "'Of the Law, but Not Its Spirit.'"

[84] One can argue that the regulation against the importation of mail-order brides is also part of national strategies developed to allow only "consensual marriage," especially if the phenomenon of mail-order brides is perceived as connected to women and sex trafficking. See Chapter 7, fn. 23.

economic and cultural interests, which some see as blunt racism,[85] but also of feminist activism from within the majority society in the country of destination,[86] as well as from within minority groups living in that country.[87]

Although, as argued in Chapter 3, forced marriage is recognized in international law as a gross violation of human rights, it has triggered moral panic in countries such as Denmark, the UK, and Norway only in the context of immigration and spousal citizenship.[88] In Denmark, for example, this moral panic has been expressed in the form of legislation that does not allow spousal residence permits to aliens in cases in which one of the spouses is under the age of 24;[89] if there is a suspicion of the marriage being arranged "by someone other than the spouse";[90] and in the case of marriages between first and second cousins.[91] Hence, common marital practices of many non-Western communities, such as marrying at a relatively young age, arranged marriage, and marriage between

---

[85] For example, Eileen Muller Myrdahl, "Legislating Love: Norwegian Family Reunification Law as a Racial Project," *Social & Cultural Geography*, 11(2) (2010), 103–16.

[86] For example, the contribution of Hege Storhaug, a feminist and anti-Islam journalist, to the debate over forced marriage and immigration in Norway. See Staver, "From Right to Earned Privilege?," at 148–50.

[87] For example, the contribution of the secular Muslim feminists in Germany to the perception of anti-forced-marriage immigration policy as a moral way to save women. See Doris Urbanek, "Forced Marriage vs. Family Reunification: Nationality, Gender and Ethnicity in German Migration Policy," *Journal of Intercultural Studies*, 33(3) (2012), 333–45, at 336–7.

[88] Staver, "From Right to Earned Privilege?," at 145–6. Other areas in which forced marriage could have been addressed, if the moral panic were not actually about restricting incoming immigration from non-Western countries, include education of the general population, dialogue with communities in which this practice is more common, and assistance to victims of forced marriage. See Khatidja Chantler, Geetanjali Gangoli, & Marianne Hester, "Forced Marriage in the UK: Religious, Cultural, Economic or State Violence?," *Critical Social Policy*, 29(4) (2009), 587–612; Anne Phillips & Moira Dustin, "UK Initiatives on Forced Marriage: Regulation, Dialogue and Exit," *Political Studies*, 52 (2004), 531–51; Urbanek, "Forced Marriage vs. Family Reunification," at 340.

[89] Section 9 of the Danish Aliens (Consolidation) Act of 2009, available at: www.nyidanmark. dk/NR/rdonlyres/2A42ECC8-1CF5-4A8A-89AC-8D3D75EF3E17/0/aliens_consolidation_act_863_250613.pdf. In Denmark, as well as in the other seven countries within the EEA that introduced age limitation to international marriages, the minimum age of national marriages is not above 18. See Wray, Agoston, & Hutton, "A Family Resemblance?," at 222–4.

[90] Staver, "From Right to Earned Privilege?," at 89.

[91] Garbi Schmidt, "Troubled by Law: The Subjectivizing Effects of Danish Marriage Reunification Laws," *International Migration*, 52(3) (2014), 129–43, at 129. See also "Forced marriages," New to Denmark – the Official Portal for Foreigners, available at: www.nyidanmark.dk/en-us/coming_to_dk/familyreunification/spouses/forced_marriages.htm.

cousins, are treated by the Danish legislator as forced marriages, which are, of course, also explicitly prohibited.[92]

Likewise, in the Netherlands, age and income limitations were introduced into immigration law, allegedly, to prevent any kind of involuntary marriage. As the analysis of Saskia Bonjour and Betty de Hart exposes, the Dutch political discourse uses "forced marriage," "arranged marriage," and "marrying off" interchangeably, portraying real marriages as only those entered into freely by individual and autonomous spouses. Freedom of partner choice has emerged in this discourse as "a core value of the Netherlands," creating a cultural border between *us* – the "true" Dutch people – and *them* – second-generation Muslim labor immigrants who have not adopted the Western notion of romantic love as the only legitimate base for spousal relations.[93]

Whereas there are no data pointing at the exact impact of such consensual marriage policies on the phenomenon of forced marriage, there are indications that they have had both intended and unintended consequences. For example, in Denmark they have resulted in "a substantial drop in the number of people of immigrant background who marry a person from abroad." Such marriages hardly exist among people under 23, while prior to the age-limitation legislation 60 percent of married people from immigrant backgrounds aged 20–23 married a person from their country of origin. Moreover, the new legislation resulted in a 900 percent increase in the emigration of ethnic minority youth from Denmark to Southern Sweden, where they are able to marry a person from a third country in circumstances prohibited in Denmark.[94] This is the outcome of the anomaly created by the mismatch between national and EU legislation, labeled by scholars as *reverse discrimination* – the situation in which "citizens living in their own country (who are subject to national legislation) are disadvantaged with regard to family reunification vis-à-vis mobile Europeans living in the same place (who are subject to EU free movement legislation)".[95] The Danish citizen who is prohibited from uniting with a third-country national in Denmark, according to Danish law

---

[92] "Spouses and cohabiting partners," New to Denmark – the Official Portal for Foreigners, available at: www.nyidanmark.dk/en-us/coming_to_dk/familyreunification/spouses/spouses.htm.

[93] Bonjour & de Hart, "A Proper Wife, a Proper Marriage." For similar arguments portraying the forced marriage regulation in Norway as a cultural "demarcation between those citizens who are seen as nationals whose presence in the nation is naturalized, and those citizens who are seen as neither nationals nor fully present in the nation," see Myrdahl, "Legislating Love," at 114.

[94] Schmidt, "Troubled by Law," at 131, 140.

[95] Staver, "Free Movement," at 70.

(for example because the spouse is under 24), is able to do so in Sweden where he is considered a mobile EU citizen, entitled to family reunification according to the Citizens' Directive of 2004, which does not have any such age limitation.[96] As Staver argues, citizens in states with restrictive reunification regulations are "forced to move freely" to be united with their spouses.[97] Finally, as the analysis of five qualitative datasets conducted by Garbi Schmidt reveals, at the same time that some young people of immigrant descent benefit from the Danish consensual marriage policy because it allows them to escape forced marriage and resist marrying at a young age, many others suffer from the stigma it creates and feel anger, exclusion, and the diminishment of freedom.[98]

The Cultural Strategy

In addition to the three strategies detailed here, which all have an undeclared cultural bias, states develop integration policies even more bluntly directed against the cultural *other*. As Staver observes, whereas, in the past, family reunification was considered a way of securing immigrants' integration, today, integration tests are a precondition of family reunification.[99] These policies include new or harder language tests and tests to establish the applicant's knowledge of the society, culture, history, and law of the destination country, which can be introduced prior to entry or as part of the permanent residence and naturalization stages.[100] Some states demand that newcomers and alien spouses who want to enter their borders take courses that will prepare them for these tests, which in some cases last a year or even two years.[101]

---

[96] European Parliament and Council Directive 2004/38/EEC of 29 April 2004.

[97] Staver, "Free Movement," at 88.

[98] Schmidt, "Troubled by Law," at 131–2. See also Geetanjali Gangoli & Khatidja Chantler, "Protecting Victims of Forced Marriage: Is Age a Protective Factor?," *Feminist Legal Studies*, 17(3) (2009), 267–88.

[99] Staver, "From Right to Earned Privilege?," at 16.

[100] Wray, Agoston, & Hutton, "A Family Resemblance?" at 226; Natalia Banulescu-Bogdan, "Shaping Citizenship Policies to Strengthen Immigrant Integration," Migration Policy Institute (August 2, 2012), available at: www.migrationpolicy.org/article/shaping-citizenship-policies-strengthen-immigrant-integration.

[101] Council of Europe – Parliamentary Assembly, *Integration Tests: Helping or Hindering Integration?* (2014), available at: http://assembly.coe.int/nw/xml/XRef/X2H-Xref-ViewPDF.asp?FileID=19772&lang=en; Christian Joppke, "Do Obligatory Civic Integration Courses for Immigrants in Western Europe Further Integration?," *Focus Migration*, Policy Brief No. 8 (2007), available at: www.hwwi.org/uploads/tx_wilpubdb/PB08_IntegrationCourses_02.pdf.

France, for example, has introduced a new preentry language test for spouses. If the spouses fail the test, they must attend a two-month course in the country of origin. If they fail the test again, they may still enter France but only on the condition they undertake additional courses and tests. Moreover, all non-EU immigrants to France, including spouses of citizens, must sign an 'integration contract' (*contract d'accueil et de l'integration*) that demands not only language skills but also knowledge of "the principles that constitute the French Republic," including its "family life values."[102] Spouses, who in the past had the right to a ten-year residence visa, now only receive a renewable temporary visa for one year, and will be granted a ten-year visa only after two additional years and the fulfillment of the integration-contract conditions.[103]

The Netherlands provides another example of the growing tendency of European countries to use the cultural strategy to prevent immigration. Tineke Strik, the Rapporteur of the Council of Europe Committee on Migration, Refugees and Displaced Persons, and herself from the Netherlands, has described the development there.[104] She notes that up until the 1980s there was no integration policy in the Netherlands, because "guest workers" were expected to return to their country of origin at some point. When they did not, and asked instead to be united with their families, a "minorities policy" was developed, recognizing settled labor migrants' right to family reunification. This policy included a language test to the potential newcomers, who had to prove they could conduct a short conversation with a municipal official. An increase in naturalization rates was followed by a more demanding integration test. In 1988 a new legal requirement was introduced, whereby newcomers were obliged to participate in free integration courses with a language test at the end, based on standardized linguistic competency measures developed by the CoE.[105] Despite the fact that 60 percent of the newcomers failed to participate in these courses, they were rarely sanctioned. In 2003, a naturalization test was introduced by law, examining oral and written

---

[102] Wray, Agoston, & Hutton, "A Family Resemblance?" at 227; Joppke, "Do Obligatory Civic Integration Courses for Immigrants in Western Europe Further Integration?," at 2–3; Council of Europe, *Integration Tests*, at 8.

[103] European Migration Network, *Ad-Hoc Query on Marriage: Rights to Entry and Permanent Residence* (2011), at 11–2, available at: http://tinyurl.com/j3hgzek.

[104] Council of Europe, *Integration Tests*.

[105] Brian North, Neus Figueras, Sauli Takala, Piet van Avermaet, & Norman Verhelst, "Relating Language Examinations to the Common European Framework of Reference for Languages: Learning, Teaching, Assessment (CEFR)," Council of Europe (2009), available at: www.coe.int/t/dg4/linguistic/Source/ManualRevision-proofread-FINAL_en.pdf.

language skills as well as knowledge of the Dutch society, and costing €260. Some 40 percent of those taking the test failed it, and the rate of naturalization in the Netherlands dropped by 50 percent. Following the 9/11 terrorist attacks and the rise of anti-immigration political discourse, a new law was enacted in 2007, establishing the test as a precondition for entry, permanent residence, and naturalization, and sanctioning failure with possible deportation. The courses and tests are no longer funded by the state, except in the case of refugees.[106]

As Strik observes, there are mixed empirical findings about the effectiveness of these integration courses and tests in promoting social integration.[107] But, what *is* certain is that such policies are effective in diminishing rates of family reunification requests and access to family-based naturalization[108] and are discriminatory toward citizens who wish to be united with spouses from non-Western countries or whose spouses are relatively uneducated or poor.[109] This discrimination is further reinforced by the last strategy I will discuss, which centers on economic resources.

The Economic Strategy

Many destination countries have developed entry and residence requirements that are part of a strategy to prevent their poorer citizens from uniting with their alien spouses. These requirements include sponsorship, accommodation, and fees.

A sponsorship requirement on behalf of citizens who wish to bring in an alien spouse has been adopted by many countries. Some impose it as a condition for the spouse's entry into the country, and some as a condition against deportation. The sponsorship requirement is based on the available income of the citizen spouse, with the minimum acceptable income varying from country to country. It ranges from the citizen simply being eligible for social allowance (Italy and Luxemburg),[110] earning 125 percent of the amount constituting the poverty line (US)[111] or being independent

---

[106] Council of Europe, *Integration Tests*, at 7, 18–19.

[107] Ibid., at 12.

[108] Council of Europe, *Integration Tests*, at 8.

[109] Ibid.; Human Rights Watch, *The Netherlands: Discrimination in the Name of Integration, Migrants' Rights Under the Integration Abroad Act* (2008), available at: www.hrw.org/sites/default/files/reports/netherlands0508.pdf.

[110] Wray, Agoston, & Hutton, "A Family Resemblance?" at 230.

[111] Department of Homeland Security, *Form I-864P – 2016 HHS Poverty Guidelines for Affidavit of Support* (2016), available at: www.uscis.gov/sites/default/files/files/form/i-864p.pdf.

of public assistance (Denmark),[112] to earning the minimum wage (the Netherlands),[113] earning 120 percent of the minimum wage (Belgium),[114] and earning up to the much-debated 150 percent of the minimum wage in the UK.[115]

Sponsoring income is not the only policy within the economic strategy employed by Western countries to limit spousal citizenship. Many add an accommodation requirement, according to which the citizen has to prove a "suitable," "adequate," "normal," "sufficient," or set "minimal size" family dwelling.[116] In addition, many states charge fees for processing the admission, residence, and citizenship of the alien spouse, as well as fees for language and integration tests, document administration, stamp duties, and medical examinations, which are mandatory within the immigration process.[117] The UK stands out for its relatively high fees, including £1,195 for initial entry,[118] £1,622 for a spousal leave-to-remain permit,[119] and £1,005 for naturalization.[120]

Whereas some might argue that the discriminatory outcomes of the consensual marriage strategy are balanced by the advancement of gender equality that is harmed by forced marriage, it is hard to ignore the harsh discriminatory outcomes of the economic strategy. This strategy actually discriminates women citizens as they, on average, earn less and have fewer resources than men to sponsor a spouse.[121] Of course, it also

---

[112] Wray, Agoston, & Hutton, "A Family Resemblance?," at 231.

[113] Ibid., at 230.

[114] Ibid.

[115] See Home Office, *Immigration Directorate Instructions* (2016), Ch. 8, Appendix FM (family members), section FM 1.7 Financial Requirement, available at: www.gov.uk/government/uploads/system/uploads/attachment_data/file/420154/Appendix_FM_Annex_1_7_Financial_Requirement.pdf. The relatively high income demand in the UK has been disputed and litigated, and reached UK Supreme Court in February 2016. See *R (on the application of MM (Lebanon)) v. Secretary of State for the Home Department* [2015] UKSC 0011.

[116] Wray, Agoston, & Hutton, "A Family Resemblance?" at 225.

[117] Ibid., at 232–4.

[118] "Apply to Join Family Living Permanently in the UK," Government of the UK, available at: www.gov.uk/join-family-in-uk.

[119] UK Visa & Immigration, *Application for Leave to Remain in the UK on the Basis of Your Family Life as a Partner or Parent or on the Basis of Your Private Life in the UK and for a Biometric Immigration Document* (2016), available at: www.gov.uk/government/uploads/system/uploads/attachment_data/file/524252/FLR_FP__Version_05-16.pdf.

[120] "Home Office Immigration & Nationality Charges 2015/2016," Visas and Immigration Operational Guidance: Fees and Forms, available at: www.gov.uk/government/uploads/system/uploads/attachment_data/file/419449/fees_table_for_website_2015_03_30.pdf.

[121] Demleitner, "How Much Do Western Democracies Value Family and Marriage?," at 284.

discriminates against poorer citizens in general and citizens of other vulnerable groups, such as the offspring of immigrants and people of color, who are overrepresented in the lower deciles in Western countries.[122] Sponsorship, accommodation, and fees are all part of a blunt strategy that turns the right to family life into a privilege of the relatively wealthy.

The five strategies detailed here demonstrate the common trend among destination countries to limit immigration of the non-Western and the poor, as presented in the introduction to this chapter. As spousal relations become one of the very few remaining routes to naturalization for the undesired immigrants, they also become the target of isomorphic restrictive regulation.[123] This legal drift, while allegedly focused on the spouses outside the border, actually targets citizens from within. The citizenship of those who choose an alien spouse is compromised – they are constructed as second-class citizens, not only through direct discrimination as a result of the first strategy, but also through all the other four strategies: their choice of spouse is portrayed as naïve (as they are allegedly manipulated by their alien spouse) or as a crime (when thought to be conspiring with the alien to manipulate the state); as coerced (when marriages are arranged by their parents) or as coercing (when the immigrating spouse is under 24); as a threat to the allegedly homogenous cultural fabric of the nation (if their spouse cannot speak the language); and as an economic risk in terms of burdening the state (if the citizen cannot provide a large enough family dwelling).

Hence, the spousal outcomes of globalization constitute a force that, at the same time, weakens national borders by allowing immigration in, and strengthens them by new and more restrictive immigration and naturalization regulation. Most importantly, the five strategies detailed here show that border panic leads nation states to compromise the most basic concept of their *raison d'être* – citizenship. Legal citizenship is no longer a stable concept embodying the unconditional right to stay in the territory and to have equal rights. Citizens attaching their familial biography to an alien spouse might be expected to leave the territory if they wish to be

---

[122] Schueths, "'Where Are My Rights?,'" at 100; María E. Enchautegui & Cecilia Menjívar, "Paradoxes of Family Immigration Policy: Separation, Reorganization, and Reunification of Families under Current Immigration Laws," *Law & Policy*, 37(1–2) (2015), 32–60, at 43.

[123] Legal (mimetic) isomorphism is a process by which states imitate each other and adopt similar laws. This process is clear in Western Europe within the spousal citizenship context, as well as in other immigration-related policies. See Wray, Agoston, & Hutton, "A Family Resemblance?."

with their spouse or may face legal restrictions and burdens not imposed on citizens who choose a fellow citizen as their spouse.

Interestingly, as explained earlier, the EU created an anomaly in which noncitizens may enjoy greater freedom in fulfilling their right to family life than citizens. However, in most other parts of the world the restrictions on the family life of citizens, detailed earlier, pale in comparison to the infringement of the right to family life of noncitizens residing in a country as labor migrants or asylum seekers. In the next and final part of this chapter we will look at these particularly vulnerable groups, focusing on their right to live together with their children.

Parental Citizenship

The UN Convention on the Rights of the Child (CRC), ratified by all 195 nations of the world with the exception of the United States, places extreme importance on the right of minor children to live with their parents. It states that:

> 9(1). States Parties shall ensure that a child shall not be separated from his or her parents against their will, except when competent authorities subject to judicial review determine, in accordance with applicable law and procedures, that such separation is necessary for the best interests of the child.

In the following Article, the Convention adds an obligation very relevant to cross-border families:

> 10(1). In accordance with the obligation of States Parties under article 9, paragraph 1, applications by a child or his or her parents to enter or leave a State Party for the purpose of family reunification shall be dealt with by States Parties in a positive, humane and expeditious manner. States Parties shall further ensure that the submission of such a request shall entail no adverse consequences for the applicants and for the members of their family.[124]

Recent family law reforms in the Western world express a deep commitment to the obligation stated in Article 9(1) to allow children to grow up in the presence and care of both their parents. The abolition of the tender years doctrine with its maternal custody preference, and the promotion of joint legal and physical custody, recognize the importance of both

---

[124] Convention on the Rights of the Child, 20 November 1989, United Nations Treaty Series, vol. 1577, p. 3, available at: www.ohchr.org/en/professionalinterest/pages/crc.aspx.

parents, and not just the mother, in their children's lives.[125] The growing restrictions on parental relocation, mentioned in Chapter 3, limit the most basic right of freedom of movement in order to guarantee the child ongoing contact with both parents, which is perceived as crucial for both child and nonrelocating parent.[126] Moreover, courts in Western countries enforce what legal scholars Gaia Bernstein and Zvi Triger critically term "intensive parenting norms," expecting parents to actively cultivate their children, to acquire sophisticated knowledge of best child-rearing practices, and to utilize this knowledge to closely monitor the child's development and daily activities.[127] As for Article 10(1), in some cases the notion that children have a right to know and to be cared for by both their parents, and that parents have a right to live with their children and to be a significant part of their everyday lives, trickles down to safeguard children's relationship with their noncitizen parents. An extreme example of this trickling-down process can be found in the 2013 decision of the ECtHR in the case of *Udeh v. Switzerland*.[128]

Kinsley Chike Udeh was born in Nigeria in 1972 and left for Switzerland when he was 21. There is no information in the court decision about how he managed to stay there for so long and not be deported, but we do know that in 2001, under a false identity and age, he was convicted of possessing a small quantity of cocaine and given a four-month suspended prison sentence by an Austrian court. Later that year, the Swiss authorities dismissed his asylum request, which had also been submitted on a false identity. However, he was not deported. In 2003, Udeh married a Swiss citizen shortly after she had given birth to their twin girls. By virtue of his marriage, he was formally granted leave to stay in Switzerland. In 2006, Udeh was arrested in Germany for attempting to import cocaine by concealing it inside his body (bodypacking).

---

[125] Vivienne Elizabeth, "Child Custody" in Constance L. Shehan (Ed.), *The Wiley Blackwell Encyclopedia of Family Studies* (2016), available at: http://onlinelibrary.wiley.com/doi/10.1002/9781119085621.wbefs107/abstract?userIsAuthenticated=false&deniedAccessCustomisedMessage; J. Herbie DiFonzo, "Dilemmas of Shared Parenting in the 21st Century: How Law and Culture Shape Child Custody," *Hofstra Law Review*, 43(4) (2015), 1003–24; Anna Singer, "'Active Parenting or Solomon's Justice?' Alternative Residence in Sweden for Children with Separated Parents" in Katharina Boele-Woelki (Ed.), *Debates in Family Law around the Globe at the Dawn of the Twenty-First Century* (Oxford: Intersentia, 2009), pp. 55–81.

[126] Christina G. Jeppesen De Boer, "Parental Relocation, Free Movement Rights and Joint Parenting" in Boele-Woelki (Ed.), *Debates in Family Law*, pp. 107–20.

[127] Gaia Bernstein & Zvi Triger, "Over-Parenting," *UC Davis Law Review*, 44(4) (2010), 1221–79.

[128] *Udeh v. Switzerland* 12020/09 [2013] ECtHR 328.

He was sentenced to 42 months' imprisonment by a German court. In 2007, the Swiss migration authority annulled Udeh's residence permit on the grounds of his absence. The migration office also decided that a new residence permit should not be issued, due to his criminal activity and his family's inability to sponsor him (his wife and children were living on social benefits at the time). An appeal on this decision to the Swiss Federal Court was denied. In 2009, Switzerland ordered Udeh, who had by then been granted early release from the German prison, to leave the country. He, his wife, and two daughters appealed to the ECtHR. In 2010, he was officially declared to have disappeared, probably in an attempt to avoid his deportation. He was later found, arrested, and banned by Swiss authorities from reentering Switzerland until 2020. The ECtHR was later informed that Udeh had divorced his wife and fathered a third baby girl with another Swiss citizen whom he intended to marry. He still had little knowledge of the German language, was unemployed, and sick with tuberculosis.

The application to the ECtHR was based on Article 8 of the ECHR, which states:

> 1. Everyone has the right to respect for his private and family life, his home and his correspondence.

> 2. There shall be no interference by a public authority with the exercise of this right except such as is in accordance with the law and is necessary in a democratic society in the interests of national security, public safety or the economic wellbeing of the country, for the prevention of disorder or crime, for the protection of health or morals, or for the protection of the rights and freedoms of others.

There was no controversy around the fact that the Swiss decision to deport Udeh, and to refuse his reentry until 2020, "had sufficient legal basis and pursued legitimate aims." The applicants, however, argued that the Swiss actions were "not necessary in a democratic society" and were hence in violation of Article 8. The Court reiterated that the Convention does not guarantee the right of an alien to enter or to reside in a particular country, even if he is a family member of a citizen, as discussed in the previous part of this chapter, and that states may deport aliens convicted of criminal offences. However, when the alien has family members who are citizens, the state power is restricted by Article 8, and a balance must be struck between the need to protect national borders for legitimate interests mentioned in Article 8, and the right of family members to family life. The Court detailed a list of considerations that national courts must take into account when balancing such conflicting interests and rights, including the seriousness of the criminal offences, the length of stay of the alien in the destination country and his contacts with his country of origin, his family situation including number and age of children, and the likely wellbeing of the children if they were to immigrate to the alien's country of deportation.[129]

As the Swiss court and government did not call into question the fact that Udeh "had genuine and close relations with his ex-wife and the children they had together," the ECtHR concluded that these relations should prevent his deportation. The Court reasoned that "it is in the daughters' best interest to grow up with both parents and, as the latter are now divorced, the only way for regular contact to be maintained between the first applicant and his two children is to authorize him to remain in Switzerland, given the mother could not be expected to follow him to Nigeria with their two children." The Court chose to minimize the significance of Udeh's past behavior and predicted "positive evolution in the future" based on the fact that only one offence was serious and that his subsequent conduct was "irreproachable." Hence, Switzerland was forced by a transnational court to let Udeh stay, despite the fact that he had presented himself in Europe on a false identity, traded in cocaine, was in prison while his daughters were 3–5 years old, escaped the authorities, divorced the mother of his daughters to immediately establish a new family, and lived on social benefits while suffering from a contagious disease.[130] What is more, based on what we learn from the court decision of the actual everyday relations between Udeh and his twin daughters, it seems that the visitation schedule set after the divorce was "limited to one afternoon at least every two weeks,"[131] suggesting very limited paternal daily care and involvement.

Although Europe is indeed relatively generous in its recognition of children's right to live with their parents in the same national territory, including when one of the parents is not a citizen of any European state, even in Europe this right is not absolute. The ECtHR allows member states to refuse the reunification of parents with their left-behind children, if, for example, there are other relatives that can care for the children in the country of origin; and it allows the deportation of a noncitizen parent, and hence his/her separation from the child that will remain in

[129]   Ibid., para. 45.
[130]   Ibid.
[131]   Ibid., para. 19.

the host country with its other citizen parent, if, for example, the child was conceived when the parents would have known the noncitizen parent might be deported.[132] This is why, in the Udeh case, the ECtHR refused to take into consideration the relationship he had with his third child. Moreover, and most importantly, the mere existence of immigration screening polices in Europe, lead to illegal immigration, in which parents leave their children behind so as not to jeopardize them by taking them on a risky journey to the unwelcoming *Fortress Europe* and by an illegal stay there. By that, Europe, like all privileged parts of the world, takes in parents from the underprivileged parts and separates them from their children, who are thus left behind while their parents search for a better future for all family members.

Indeed, in other parts of the world, receiving countries are even more restrictive than Europe in recognizing parental citizenship – that is, the right of parents and children to live in the same national territory.[133] I will focus here on two examples. The first is Israel, which offers an extreme case of a destination country that invites migrant workers to perform jobs undesired by its citizens, while stripping them of their familial subjectivity. Although extreme, Israel is not alone in its antifamily policies applied only to aliens; such policies can be found in several other countries.[134] The second example is the United States, which is rare in that it grants citizenship to children born in its territory even if both their parents are non-US citizens. Alas, this seeming generosity in the citizenship realm does not guarantee these children's right to family life, and often they are brutally separated from their parents.

---

[132] Francesca Ippolito, "(De)Constructing Children's Vulnerability under European Law" in Francesca Ippolito & Sara Iglesias Sánchez (Eds.), *Protecting Vulnerable Groups: The European Human Rights Framework* (Oxford: Hart Publishing, 2015), pp. 23–47; Daniel Thym, "Respect for Private and Family Life Under Article 8 ECHR in Immigration Cases: A Human Right to Regularize Illegal Stay?," *International and Comparative Law Quarterly*, 57(1) (2008), 87–112.

[133] See also the related discussion on remittances and children's needs, in Chapter 6.

[134] For example, in the Arab States of the Persian Gulf (Kuwait, Saudi Arabia, Bahrain, Qatar, Oman, and the United Arab Emirates), the monthly minimum salary to qualify for a family visa is so high that many labor immigrants cannot afford it. This, and the high cost of living, result in a huge immigrating bachelor population. See Andrew M. Gardner, "Gulf Migration and the Family," *Journal of Arabian Studies*, 1(1) (2011), 3–25, at 17. In South-East Asia, several countries employ thousands of female migrant caregivers, while restricting their familial rights. In Singapore, for example, migrant domestic workers are not allowed to live with a local spouse, are required to undergo pregnancy tests every six months, and are forced to leave if they are found to be pregnant. See Nicole Constable, "Migrant Workers, Legal Tactics, and Fragile Family Formation in Hong Kong," *Oñati Socio-Legal Series*, 3(6) (2013), 1004–22, at 1011.

Israel

Israel is a small country of about 8 million citizens, which defines itself as a Jewish and democratic state, hence not concealing its excluding ethnocentric nature. Since the 1990s, Israel has actively recruited substantial numbers of overseas migrant workers, in particular to the agriculture, construction, and elderly- and disability-care sectors.[135] These migrants receive a time-limited working visa[136] with no family reunification entitlements attached to it.[137] Moreover, no work permit will be issued to a person who already has a close family member (spouse, child, parent) who is a guest worker in Israel.[138] Hence, if migrant workers have children in the country of origin, they cannot live together as long as the parent stays and works in Israel. Only a marriage to an Israeli spouse might change this legal reality and create an opportunity for the immigrant to bring left-behind children.[139]

This antifamilial labor migration policy is one of the regulative mechanisms Israel developed to prevent the settlement of non-Jewish immigrants, perceived as a threat to the Jewish national endeavor.[140] It is extreme not only in comparison to other countries, such as the members of the EU, but also in comparison to the Israeli socio-legal attitude toward the rights of Israelis to parenthood and to family life.[141] Unlike Western

[135] The increase in the number of migrant workers in the 1990s was the outcome of the Israeli government's plan to replace Palestinian laborers in construction and agriculture with labor migrants, following the Palestinian uprising in 1987, known as the First Intifada. See Kemp, "Managing Migration, Reprioritizing National Citizenship," at 671. At its peak, it is estimated that documented and undocumented migrant workers comprised about 10 percent the Israeli labor force. See Gilad Nathan, "Migrant Workers and Victims of Human Trafficking: The Government's Policy and Activity of the Immigration Authority," The Knesset Research and Information Center (2009), available at: www.knesset.gov.il/mmm/data/pdf/me02294.pdf.

[136] On the Israeli visa regime, see Daphna Hacker & Orna Cohen, *Research Report: The Shelters in Israel for Survivors of Human Trafficking* (2012), Section 3.8 (section written by Idan Halili), available at: www2.tau.ac.il/InternetFiles/news/UserFiles/The%20Shelters%20in%20Israel.pdf.

[137] Kemp, "Managing Migration, Reprioritizing National Citizenship," at 674.

[138] Hila Shamir & Guy Mundlak, "Spheres of Migration: Political, Economic and Universal Imperatives in Israel's Migration Regime," *Middle East Law and Governance*, 5(1–2) (2013), 112–72, at 123–4.

[139] See Norly's case, in Daphna Hacker, "From the Moabite Ruth to Norly the Filipino: Intermarriage and Conversion in the Jewish Nation State" in Hanna Herzog & Ann Braude (Eds.), *Gendering Religion and Politics: Untangling Modernities* (New York: Palgrave Macmillan, 2009), pp. 101–24.

[140] Shamir & Mundlak, "Spheres of Migration."

[141] Tali Kritzman-Amir, "Iterations of the Family: Parents, Children and Mixed-Status Families," *Minnesota Journal of International Law*, 24(2) (2015), 245–311.

countries, and as mentioned before, Israel is a familist country with relatively high rates of marriage and childbirth and low rates of divorce, supported by an extreme pronatalist legislation and broad legal recognition of the importance of the family.[142] As Tally Kritzman-Amir argues, this profamily ideology retreats in the face of the anti-non-Jewish immigration apparatus.[143] What is considered to be the absolute truth for Israeli children and parents is questionable, contingent, and silenced when it comes to labor migrants and their minor children.

Whereas the children of labor migrants are excluded from outside of the national border, it is much harder to stop labor migrants, as well as asylum seekers,[144] from conceiving children while they stay within the borders of Israel. Indeed, the estimations refer to several thousand children born in Israel to labor migrants and asylum seekers.[145]

The State of Israel tried to prevent the procreation of labor migrants by issuing a directive stipulating that a documented migrant worker who

---

[142] Ibid.; Sylvie Fogiel-Bijaoui, "Familism, Postmodernity and the State: The Case of Israel," *Journal of Israeli History: Politics, Society, Culture*, 21(1–2) (2002), 38–62.

[143] Kritzman-Amir, "Iterations of the Family."

[144] During 2010–2013, tens of thousands of asylum seekers from Africa entered Israel through its southern border. This flow of unauthorized immigration diminished substantially only after Israel constructed a wall along its border with Egypt. See Noga Tarnopolsky, "Israel Built a New Border Wall to Prevent Migrants from 'Smuggling in Terror'," *Global Post* (December 5, 2013), available at: www.globalpost.com/dispatch/news/regions/middle-east/131204/israel-new-border-wall-egypt-terrorism-immigration-project-hourglass. Israel faces difficulties in deporting these newcomers, as it does not have diplomatic relations with the countries many of them come from. See Shamir & Mundlak, "Spheres of Migration," at 124–30. According to the Ministry of Interior, there are, as of 2016, 41,477 asylum seekers (who are termed "infiltrators"), 81,438 documented labor migrants, 15,284 undocumented labor migrants, and 91,000 people who entered on tourist visas that were not extended. See "Compiled Data Regarding Aliens in Israel – 2/2016," Population, Immigration and Border Authority – Piba (2015), available at: www.gov.il/BlobFolder/reports/foreign_workers_report_q2_2016/he/q2_2016.pdf (Hebrew).

[145] According to the Israeli National Council for the Child, in 2015 some 61,349 children with no legal status lived in Israel; see National Council for the Child, "Data Collection – Children in Israel Yearbook 2015," available at: www.children.org.il/Files/File/SHNATON/Leket2015.pdf (Hebrew). However, other estimations of the number of children with no legal status whose parents are labor migrants who reside in Israel illegally, or asylum seekers who entered Israel illegally, are much lower. See Jonah Newman, "Whose Home? The Role of Jewish Identity in Israel's Policy towards the Children of Foreign Workers," *Washington University International Review*, 1 (2012), 42–54; Israel State Comptroller, *Treatment of Minors without Civil Status in Israel, Review under section 21 (a) of the State Comptroller Law, 5718–1958* (2014), available at: www.mevaker.gov.il/he/Reports/Report_121/380533ec-c59b-4ae3-ada9-de763f2386de/2013-200.pdf (Hebrew). These figures do not include migrant workers' and asylum seekers' children who were granted citizenship due to the fact that their other parent is an Israeli citizen.

gives birth in Israel must leave the country with the newborn within ninety days. She may then return to Israel, without the baby, and work until her work permit expires, but for no more than two years. In 2005, five NGOs petitioned the Israeli Supreme Court, arguing that this directive violates (1) female labor migrants' right to gender equality as it means they cannot enjoy the full time period allowed under the terms of their work permit just because they give birth, and (2) their rights to family and parenthood, recognized by Israeli law as part of the human rights to dignity and to privacy. The Ministry of Interior, for its part, argued that this directive is necessary to secure Israel's borders from immigrants wishing to illegally settle in the country. The Ministry argued that these immigrants cause unemployment of the socio-economically weaker Israelis and create "social and moral problems."[146]

It took the Israeli Supreme Court six years to hand down its decision, which accepted the petition and suggested to the Ministry of Interior ways to amend the directive so it would proportionally balance between the legitimate interest of the state to secure its borders and the right of female migrant workers to gender equality and family life.[147] In light of the court's guidelines, the directive was changed. Today, a female migrant worker can choose to take her baby out of Israel and come back without it, or to live with it in Israel for the whole duration of her initial work permit (granted for sixty-three months), on the condition that she is "practically able to combine her employment duties and the need to care for the child, and that there is a way for such combination in her working place." Moreover, to rule out any misunderstanding regarding possible naturalization of mother or child, the new directive clearly states that the permission to stay in Israel with the baby does not grant any additional rights over and above those granted by the work permit. If the baby is born while the worker works on an extended permit (after sixty-three months), the mother might return to Israel if her employer wishes her to, but without the baby. Finally, the directive states that if the father of the newborn is also a noncitizen living in Israel, and the child is to stay in Israel with one of the parents, the other parent must leave the country.[148]

---

[146] HCJ 11437/05 *Kav LaOved v. Ministry of the Interior* (2011) (Israel).

[147] Ibid.; Shamir & Mundlak, "Spheres of Migration."

[148] Population and Immigration Authority, *Directive 5.3.0023 – Procedure for Treatment of a Pregnant Foreign Migrant Worker, and a Migrant Worker Who Gave Birth in Israel* (updated on 20.5.2013), available at: www.gov.il/he/Departments/policies/procedure_pregnant_foreign_worker_in_israel_2013 (Hebrew).

Of course, this directive is far from recognizing documented migrant workers' right to family life. In particular, and as will be elaborated in Chapter 8, since most female migrant workers in Israel are employed around the clock as caregivers for the elderly or the disabled and are expected to live in at their employer's house without the freedom to choose another kind of job, the condition, set by the new directive, of being able to combine employment duties with caring for the child is extremely hard to fulfill. Although some of the care recipients allow the migrant worker to live with the child at their house, in most other cases the child is sent to the mother's country of origin while the mother returns to work in Israel, and occasionally the mother stays in Israel with the child to work in a job that allows her to practice active parenthood, while losing her legal status and risking deportation.[149]

Although Israel somewhat modified its regulation to recognize documented female labor migrants' limited right to family life in Israel, migrants who entered Israel illegally, or whose legal permit has expired, as well as asylum seekers who are not recognized as refugees,[150] are left at risk of deportation. This is so even if they are the parent of a child who holds Israeli citizenship. According to Israeli law, a child born in Israel to mixed-status parents can be recognized as an Israeli, but the non-Israeli parent has no secured right to stay with the child in Israel.[151] As the study of Kritzman-Amir shows, the courts refuse to recognize (1) the right of these children to live with both their parents in Israel, (2) the right of the alien parent to live in Israel with the Israeli child, and (3) the right of the Israeli citizen parent not to be left to care for the child as a single parent. The courts reaffirm the government's policy that an alien parent can be granted a permanent status in Israel based on his or her child's citizenship only in rare humanitarian cases.[152]

---

[149] E-mail correspondence between the author and Adv. Oded Feller, Director of the Human Rights in Israel Department, The Association for Civil Rights in Israel (August 12, 2015); E-mail correspondence of the author with Rotem Ilan, Director of the Immigration and Status Unit, The Association for Civil Rights in Israel (August 16, 2015). See also Nicole's story, detailed in Chapter 8.

[150] Israel hardly ever recognizes asylum seekers as refugees. See Shamir & Mundlak, "Spheres of Migration," at 127–8; as of July 2016, some 14,644 asylum requests are awaiting reply. During April–July 2016, 1,090 applications were denied, and not a single one was granted. See Ilan Lior, "Nearly 15,000 Asylum Requests Still Pending – Israel Yet to Approve Single One in 2016," Haaretz (July 21, 2016), available at: www.haaretz.com/israel-news/.premium-1.732150.

[151] Kritzman-Amir, "Iterations of the Family."

[152] Ibid.

As Kritzman-Amir demonstrates, the fact that the cases of possible deportation of noncitizen immigrating parents of Israeli children are decided by the Ministry of Interior officials and by Administrative Courts is of great significance. Unlike the specialized Israeli Family Courts, trained to hold the best interests of the child at the center of deliberations, these legal bodies are trained in immigration law, and their habitus centers on securing the Israeli borders from aliens – not on evaluating and appreciating family relations.[153] Moreover, these bodies' decisions can contradict decisions of the Family Court in relation to the custody, visitation, and child-support rights and obligations of the alien parent, or can even lead to the deportation of the parent before such decisions can be reached, hence creating a legal maze and familial crisis that harms not only the alien but also the Israeli family members involved.

Interestingly, two governmental decisions, from 2006 and 2010, temporarily created a situation of reverse discrimination in which noncitizen children with two noncitizen parents were granted greater familial rights than Israeli children with one Israeli parent and one noncitizen parent. In these two decisions, the State of Israel allowed children whose parents resided in Israel illegally, and who "integrated into the Israeli society," to acquire the status of permanent residency. These were ad hoc decisions that did not permanently change the immigration and citizenship policies as a rule, but rather opened a narrow time window for such requests (two-and-a-half months in the first decision, and three weeks in the second). The extent of integration was mainly determined on the basis of the children's age (younger than 14 in the first decision, and younger than 13 in the second), their having lived in Israel for several years (at least six in the first decision, and five in the second), their ability to speak Hebrew, and their attendance at an Israeli school.[154] If the request for permanent residency for the child was approved, these children's parents and siblings were granted temporary residency permits, if they shared the same household with the child. When these integrated children reach the age of 21, they are able to apply for Israeli citizenship, and their parents and

---

[153] Ibid. See also Daphna Hacker, "Strategic Compliance in the Shadow of Transnational Anti-Trafficking Law," *Harvard Human Rights Journal*, 28(1) (2015), 11–64.

[154] Government Decision No. 156 of June 18, 2006, "Temporary Arrangement for the Grant of Status to Children of Persons Staying Illegally in Israel, their Parents and Siblings Present in Israel – Amendment of Decision," available at: www.pmo.gov.il/Secretary/GovDecisions/2006/Pages/des156.aspx (Hebrew); Government Decision No. 2183 of August 1, 2010, "Temporary Arrangement for the Grant of Status to Children of Persons Staying Illegally in Israel, Their Parents and Siblings Present in Israel," available at: www.pmo.gov.il/Secretary/GovDecisions/2010/Pages/des2183.aspx (Hebrew).

siblings for permanent residency. About 1,500 children and their families were allowed to stay in Israel, thanks to these two governmental deci-sions,[155] and to escape the deportation awaiting other 'illegal' immigrants, including noncitizen parents of Israeli children.

Several studies try to explain these surprising governmental decisions, which do not correlate with the overall ethno-based Israeli immigration and citizenship policy. They point to the role played by specific Interior Ministers, active NGOs, and supportive media attention, in creating a dis-course that objects to the deportation of the integrated children, on the basis that they should not be punished for their parents' illegal acts and as they know no other country but Israel. While legal scholars Hila Shamir and Guy Mundlak view this discourse as universal–humanitarian,[156] Jonah Newman points to its "Jewishness," manifested in claims that "true Jewish" values demand protection of these children.[157] All researchers agree that these two decisions were highly controversial within the Israeli parliament and general public, and that they were accompanied by other policies aimed at increas-ing the overall deportation of aliens,[158] including, since 2012, of children.[159] Hence, these ad hoc decisions were a temporary triumph of a child-centered discourse that relaxed borders and distinctions between *us* and *them*, and that usually gives way to the economic and ethnic discourses that strengthen borders and enhance exclusion. Notwithstanding, these decisions provide evidence that even a state that declares itself to be an ethno-democracy, intolerant of non-Jewish *others*, finds it hard to completely ignore the human and familial rights of the unwelcome who are nevertheless present.

The United States

The United States is a superpower of about 322 million people. Each year, it receives approximately a million immigrants, the highest number within the members of the Organization of Economic Co-operation and Development (OECD).[160] Currently, about 30 percent of children living in

---

[155] E-mail correspondence of the author with Rotem Ilan (August 16, 2015). See also Kritzman-Amir, "Iterations of the Family," at 277.

[156] For example, Shamir & Mundlak, "Spheres of Migration."

[157] Newman, "Whose Home?."

[158] Ibid.; Kemp, "Managing Migration, Reprioritizing National Citizenship"; Shamir & Mundlak, "Spheres of Migration."

[159] Shamir & Mundlak, "Spheres of Migration," at 149.

[160] Adam Ozimek, "Is the U.S. the Most Immigrant Friendly Country in the World?," *Forbes* (November 18, 2012), available at: www.forbes.com/sites/modeledbehavior/2012/11/18/is-the-u-s-the-most-immigrant-friendly-country-in-the-world/#66e576ac1bad.

the United States are of Hispanic or Asian origin, and it is estimated that this percentage will only grow in light of future immigration trends.[161]

Whereas other countries that used to grant citizenship based on the *jus soli* principle changed their law so as not to grant citizenship to the children of noncitizens, the United States and Canada are the only advanced Western economies that continue to do so.[162] In the United States, *jus soli* citizenship, also called *birthright citizenship*, is guaranteed by the Constitution as a civil right,[163] and so is more immune than other immigration and naturalization policies. Notwithstanding, calls to abolish this right are part of the current American debate over immigration, but remain, for now, in the minority.[164] Meanwhile, each year, 300,000–400,000 children born to parents who reside in the United States illegally are granted citizenship, creating a reality in which millions of families in the United States are of parent–child mixed citizenship status.[165] At first glance, it seems that this socio-legal reality places the United States at the other end of the parental citizenship spectrum from Israel. However, although the citizenship the United States grants to every child born on its soil implies a child-centered approach, the reality of US parental citizenship in the era of toughened border security policy is much more complex.

When it comes to children's citizenship, it seems self-evident that it should include the right of the child to be cared for by its parents in its homeland. However, what is taken for granted in the case of US-citizen children with US-citizen parents, is not guaranteed at all when it comes to

---

[161] Federal Interagency Forum on Child and Family Statistics, *America's Children: Key National Indicators of Well-Being, 2015* (2015), available at: www.childstats.gov/pdf/ac2015/ac_15.pdf.

[162] Feere, "Birthright Citizenship."

[163] U.S. Const. Amend. XIV, Sec. 1, available at: www.usconstitution.net/xconst_Am14.html.

[164] Ibid. However, Donald Trump has made the call to end the birthright citizenship of children of undocumented immigrants, as part of his presidential election campaign. See Stephen Braun (Associated Press), "Trump: Deport Children of Immigrants Living Illegally in US," YAHOO – News (August 16, 2015), available at: http://news.yahoo.com/trump-deport-children-immigrants-living-illegally-us-192747863.html. There is an ongoing debate about whether the constitutional recognition of birthright citizenship includes children of immigrants who reside in the United States illegally, as it is interpreted today. The US Supreme Court has not yet been asked to settle this controversy. See Jessie M. Mahr, "Protecting Our Vulnerable Citizens: Birthright Citizenship and the Call for Recognition of Constructed Deportation," *Southern Illinois University Law Journal*, 32(3) (2008), 723–47, at 728.

[165] Feere, "Birthright Citizenship," at 1; Mahr, "Protecting Our Vulnerable Citizens," at 723; Jeffrey S. Passel," Number of Babies Born in U.S. to Unauthorized Immigrants Declines," Pew Research Center (September 11, 2015), available at: www.pewresearch.org/fact-tank/2015/09/11/number-of-babies-born-in-u-s-to-unauthorized-immigrants-declines/.

the 4.5 million US-citizen children of undocumented immigrants.[166] The numbers of US-citizen children whose parents are deported from the United States are staggering. For example, between July 1, 2012 and September 30, 2013, alone, over 200,000 parents of US-citizen children were deported.[167] Nearly one out of every four deportations from the United States involves a parent of a US-citizen child.[168] It seems that, just as in Israel, the deportation apparatus usually triumphs over all other considerations.

In many of the cases of deportation of an undocumented parent of a US-citizen child, the parent faces an impossible dilemma – to take the child with her/him to a country the child has never known and where its chances of an adequate standard of living are relatively low, both immediately and in the future, or to leave the child behind in the care of distant relatives or strangers. Social work and public policy researchers Luis Zayas and Mollie Bradlee argue that by putting the parent in this dilemma the US government condemns its child citizens to exile or orphanhood.[169] Legal scholar Jessie Mahr adds that children of noncitizens are discriminated against compared to children whose parents are US citizens, when put at risk of losing their country or their parents.[170] Public health and legal scholar Jacqueline Bhabha observes that the discourse on illegal immigration usually ignores the children involved, and treats them as "parcels that are easily movable across borders with their parents without particular cost to them." According to Bhabha, the children of undocumented immigrants suffer from "citizenship deficit," because, although they are US citizens, they lack an enforceable right "to initiate family reunion or resist family separation where a family is divided by national borders."[171]

In some cases, the noncitizen parent is deprived even of the limited autonomy to make the difficult choice of taking the child to the deportation destiny or leaving it behind in the United States. Because the child is a US citizen, the US welfare system can legally step in when it perceives that the child is at risk and strip the parent of all parental rights. The case of the adoption of Carlos Bail, now named Jamison Moser, is an example of such

---

[166] Luis H. Zayas and Mollie H. Bradlee, "Exiling Children, Creating Orphans: When Immigration Policies Hurt Citizens," *Social Work*, 59(2) (2014), 167–75, at 168.
[167] Ibid.
[168] Sarah Rogerson, "Lack of Detained Parents' Access to the Family Justice System and the Unjust Severance of the Parent-Child Relationship," *Family Law Quarterly*, 47(2) (2013), 141–72, at 141.
[169] Zayas & Bradlee, "Exiling Children, Creating Orphans," at 169.
[170] Mahr, "Protecting Our Vulnerable Citizens," at 729.
[171] Jacqueline Bhabha, "The Citizenship Deficit: On Being a Citizen Child," *Development*, 46(3) (2003), 53–9, at 55–6.

a scenario that received critical judicial, activist, and media attention – none of which prevented the separation of the child from his mother.

Encarnación Bail Romero, an undocumented immigrant from a small village in Guatemala, entered the United States pregnant and gave birth to Carlos on October 15, 2006. Carlos's father was never a part of his life. Encarnación and her son lived with Encarnación's brother, who was also an undocumented immigrant, and his nuclear family, in very poor conditions, and were assisted to a limited degree by a Ms. Davenport, a parent-educator.[172] On May 22, 2007, when Carlos was seven months old, the United States Department of Homeland Security – Immigration and Customs Enforcement – conducted a raid on the poultry processing plant where Encarnación was working. She was arrested in the raid, together with more than 100 other undocumented workers. Encarnación was charged with aggravated identity theft because she worked under false identity at the plant, pleaded guilty, and was sentenced to two years in prison followed by deportation.[173]

After Encarnación's arrest, her brother gave Carlos to their sister, who, like him and their imprisoned sister, was an undocumented immigrant. However, the aunt soon realized she could not take proper care of her nephew because she had two toddlers of her own and she and her spouse worked full time. Ms. Davenport suggested Jennifer and Oswaldo Velazco, a local clergy couple, for babysitting services. Soon, Carlos was left in the constant care of the Velazcos. On September 9, 2007, Ms. Davenport visited Encarnación in jail to suggest Carlos's adoption – a suggestion the mother refused. Soon after, the Velazcos took it on themselves to ask Seth and Melinda Moser, a childless couple, if they wished to adopt Carlos. They did, and on October 5, 2007, the Mosers filed a petition at the Circuit Court of Jasper County for transfer of custody, termination of the mother's parental rights, and adoption. Twelve days later, the court held a hearing, at which Encarnación was not present, but with a guardian *ad litem* appointed for Carlos. At this first and only hearing, the court granted Seth and Melinda Moser custody over the little boy. On October 28,

---

[172] Ms. Davenport worked on behalf of a program run by the non-profit organization Parents as Teacher, funded by the State of Missouri. See John H. Tucker, "In a Tiny Town Just outside Joplin, a Landmark Adoption Case Tests the Limits of Inalienable Human Rights," *Riverfront Times* (October 20, 2011), available at: www.riverfronttimes.com/2011-10-20/ news/encarnacion-bail-carlos-jamison-moser-adoption-carthage-missouri-supreme-court/.

[173] 18 U.S. Code § 1028A ("Aggravated Identity Theft"), available at: www.law.cornell.edu/ uscode/text/18/1028A.

2007, Encarnación, who by then had been transferred to a federal prison, sent the Mosers' attorney a letter stating that she did not want her child adopted but rather placed in foster care, with her having visitation rights. A year later, in a short hearing – at which, once more, Encarnación was not present and where she was represented instead by her lawyer who was paid by the Mosers – the court granted the adoption request, stating that the mother's consent was not necessary because she had willfully abandoned the child.

Supported by the Guatemalan Embassy and several NGOs and university legal clinics,[174] Encarnación successfully appealed, first and foremost because the Velazcos had "absolutely no legal authority" to place Carlos for adoption in the first place,[175] only to find herself facing a decision by the Supreme Court of Missouri to resend the case to a new adoption trial. In their decision of January 2011, more than two years after the adoption order, all the Supreme Court judges agreed that the case was "a travesty in its egregious procedural errors, its long duration, and its impact on Mother, Adoptive Parents, and, most importantly, Child." However, despite their agreement on the nature of the case, they were unable to reach a consensus about the solution. Whereas the dissenting judges thought that Encarnación should regain parental rights immediately, the majority were of the opinion that a re-adoption trial was mandatory by law.[176]

Two years later, when Carlos was almost six years old and had been separated from his mother for more than five years, the Judge at the new adoption trial decided he should stay in the custody and care of the Mosers, and that they be allowed to adopt him. That ruling was upheld by the Missouri Court of Appeals in a unanimous decision in October 2013. This time, the same court that had portrayed Encarnación in 2010 as the victim of "serious failures" on behalf of the trial court, depicted her in harsh terms as a bad mother before, during, and after incarceration: she endangered Carlos while pregnant by crossing the border illegally, and did not care well enough for his health after birth; and while in jail, "... despite access to a phone, ability to write letters, individuals providing [her with] money at her request, cellmates to translate on her

---

[174] Brief of the Young Center for Immigrant Children's Rights et al. as *Amici Curiae* in Support of Appellant, *S.M. and M.M. v. E.M.B.R. (In Re Adoption of C.M.B.R.)*, SD32228 (Mo App 2013), available at: http://theyoungcenter.org/wp-content/uploads/2013/01/Young-Center-Amicus_FINAL.pdf; Tucker, "In a Tiny Town."

[175] *S.M. and M.M. v. E.M.B.R. (In Re Adoption of C.M.B.R.)*, 2010 Mo App LEXIS 976 (Mo App 2010).

[176] *S.M. and M.M. v. E.M.B.R. (In Re Adoption of C.M.B.R.)*, SC91141, 332 SW 3d 793 (Mo. 2011).

behalf, knowledge of where Child was living, funds to call Child, funds and ability to send support to Child, and constant communication with her family, [she] expressed and/or showed no interest in Child."[177] After release from prison, the court continued "... although working, Mother made no attempt to contact Child [...] or provide support for Child. [...] It was not until July 30, 2010, that Mother requested visitation with Child. At this point, Mother had not seen Child for over three years."[178] Encarnación was also portrayed by the court as a bad mother to her two children left behind in Guatemala: "When questioned about her other children in Guatemala, Mother could not remember their birthdays. She testified she had no plans to see them, and knew her children wanted to see her, but she would rather be in the U.S."[179] The Court also implied that Encarnación might send Carlos to Guatemala, whereas she preferred to stay in the United States.[180] Hence, the appeal court reaffirmed the trial court's conclusion that Encarnación was an unfit parent and that Carlos's best interest would be to be adopted by the Mosers. Appeal attempts on behalf of Encarnación, to the Missouri Supreme Court and later to the US Supreme Court, were unsuccessful.[181] I have been unable to find out if Encarnación was subsequently deported from the United States.

Reading the 2013 Appeal Court decision left me speechless. Nothing remains of the reflection in the 2011 decision of the Supreme Court of Missouri regarding the contribution of the US authorities, including its legal system, to the past conditions in which Encarnación could not perform her maternal duties and the subsequent state of affairs in which the best interest of Carlos was deemed to be to stay with the only parents he ever really knew. Instead, there is a narrative portraying Encarnación as a monstrous mother who is a serial child deserter. Furthermore, the decision imposes maternal expectations that ignore the harsh objective circumstances of a single mother from a remote village in a poor country, who finds herself behind bars in a foreign and hostile country. It sets a maternal standard inspired by the Western *good-mother* ideal and by practices afforded by privileged mothers (that is white, middle-class citizens),

---

[177] *S.M. and M.M. v. E.M.B.R. (In Re Adoption of C.M.)*, SD32228, 414 SW 3d 622, 642 (Mo App 2013).

[178] Ibid., at 644.

[179] Ibid.

[180] Ibid.

[181] Susan Redden, "U.S. Supreme Court Declines to Consider Area Adoption Case," *The Joplin Globe* (July 1, 2014), available at: www.joplinglobe.com/news/local_news/u-s-supreme-court-declines-to-consider-area-adoption-case/article_3479fa7a-11a9-5d87-a08b-613608d32e45.html.

just to label the colored poor immigrant an unfit mother. Finally, this court decision does not question the all-or-nothing policy of the welfare services that advocated closed adoption as the only solution for Carlos. Other possible solutions, such as open adoption with visitation rights granted to the birth mother, are not even mentioned, let alone considered.

Needless to say, the judges in the Encarnación and Carlos case do not mention the CRC, with its fundamental obligation not to separate children from their parents. Indeed, this case, which hopefully will attract the scholastic attention it deserves for further normative analysis,[182] demonstrates why the United States cannot ratify this Convention without dramatically changing its immigration policy and deportation practices. This case is but one of hundreds of thousands in which US-citizen children are separated from their parents for months, years, and sometimes for life when the parents are detained, jailed, or deported. These harsh outcomes have been condemned by activists and researchers as creating "shattered families,"[183] "impossible families,"[184] "deporting our souls,"[185] and harming the US's "forgotten citizens."[186]

Indeed, many scholars have criticized the deficiencies in the US legal system when it comes to the rights of US-citizen children to be cared for by their noncitizen undocumented immigrant parents.[187] Elizabeth Hall, for example, argues that state courts do not follow the Supreme Court constitutional framework for termination of parental rights, and terminate the parental rights of undocumented immigrants without sufficient evidence that they are unfit. Among other deficiencies, courts perceive the incarceration of the parent as a demonstration of unfitness and are influenced by their cultural bias in preferring American parents. Hall

---

[182] On the ramification of the lack of proper legal aid in this case, see, Mary O'Neill, Parisa Bagheri, & Alexis Sarnicola, "Forgotten Children of Immigration and Family Law: How The Absence of Legal Aid Affects Children in the United States," *Family Court Review*, 53(4) (2015), 676–97.

[183] Seth Freed Wessler, "Shattered Families – The Perilous Intersection of Immigration Enforcement and the Child Welfare System," Applied Research Center (2011), available at: www.sph.sc.edu/cli/word_pdf/ARC_Report_Nov2011.pdf.

[184] Jane Lilly López, "'Impossible Families': Mixed-Citizenship Status Couples and the Law," *Law and Policy*, 37(1–2) (2015), 93–118.

[185] Hing, *Deporting Our Souls*.

[186] Luis Zayas, *Forgotten Citizens: Deportation, Children, and the Making of American Exiles and Orphan* (Oxford University Press, 2015).

[187] For example, ibid.; Rogerson, "Lack of 'Detained Parents' Access to the Family Justice System"; Elizabeth C. Hall, "Where Are My Children … and My Rights? Parental Rights Termination as a Consequence of Deportation," *Duke Law Journal*, 60(6) (2011), 1459–504.

also points to the fact that prison conditions in the United States render maintaining parent–child relations during detention and imprisonment difficult. Not only are there no special facilities that enable children to live with their detained parent, but phone calls and face-to-face visits are a practical challenge both due to prison conditions and also lack of cooperation on the part of those who care for the child.[188] Social work and legal scholar Sunny Harris Rome harshly criticizes the laws enacted in 1996 which prohibit the reentry of those deported for up to ten years while eliminating defense opportunities that were open in the past to prevent deportation, including the existence of family ties in the United States.[189] Legal scholar Sara Rogerson adds that because immigration law, including the resulting detention and deportation, is understood as part of civil law and not criminal law, the family members involved are not granted due process protections, such as the right to counsel, the right to a speedy trial, protection against cruel and unusual punishment, and disproportionate sentencing. As Rogerson observes, without these protections, "detained-immigrant parents face innumerable hurdles to defending any challenge to their parental rights in family courts."[190]

Although no legal steps were taken to address these deficiencies, and after his administration deported a record number of two million noncitizen immigrants,[191] in November 2014 President Barack Obama endeavored to use his authority to "fix our broken immigration system" while bypassing congressional approval.[192] Although much of Obama's reform was about toughening the borders, it did include very good tidings to the approximately 3.6 million parents residing in the US illegally and their US-citizen or legally permanent-resident children.[193] According to the Deferred Action for Parents of Americans and Lawful Permanent Residents (DAPA), included in Obama's reform, such parents can ask for

---

188 Hall, "Where Are My Children … and My Rights?"
189 Sunny Harris Rome, "Promoting Family Integrity: The Child Citizen Protection Act and Its Implications for Public Child Welfare," *Journal of Public Child Welfare*, 4(3) (2010), 245–62.
190 Rogerson, "Lack of Detained Parents' Access to the Family Justice System," at 141.
191 "Border Enforcement Policies Ensnare Parents of US Citizen Children," Human Rights Watch (January 8, 2015), available at: www.hrw.org/news/2015/01/08/border-enforcement-policies-ensnare-parents-us-citizen-children.
192 "Fixing the System – President Obama Is Taking Action on Immigration," The White House (November 21, 2014), available at: www.whitehouse.gov/issues/immigration/immigration-action.
193 "Data Hub – Unauthorized Immigrant Population Profiles," Migration Policy Institute (MPI), available at: www.migrationpolicy.org/programs/us-immigration-policy-program-data-hub/unauthorized-immigrant-population-profiles.

a deferred action for three years, which will prevent their deportation and allow them to work legally, if they have lived in the United States continuously since January 1, 2010 and are not a threat to national security (due, for example, to their criminal behavior).[194]

Whereas this dramatic development could have been a significant signal that the United States was adopting the concept of parental citizenship, even if in a limited manner, the majority of states challenged Obama's reform in court. In February 2015, in a 123-page decision, Judge Andrew S. Hanen of the Federal District Court for the Southern District of Texas blocked the reform by a preliminary injunction. The judge ruled that "The DHS [Department of Homeland Security] has adopted a new rule that substantially changes both the status and employability of millions. These changes go beyond mere enforcement or even nonenforcement of this nation's immigration scheme. It inflicts major costs on both the states and federal government. Such changes, if legal, at least require compliance with the APA [Administrative Procedure Act]."[195] The United States Court of Appeals for the Fifth Circuit, in New Orleans, denied a request from Justice Department lawyers to allow DAPA to go into effect pending appeal.[196] As the Administration decided not to appeal this decision to the Supreme Court, it means that while the issue is appealed, which might take months, eligible undocumented immigrants will be unable to apply for the program, which is designed to allow them to live with their children in the United States.[197] How these recent developments and, more so, the recent election of President Donald Trump, will affect the rate of incarceration and deportation of parents of US-citizen children remains to be seen.

Both the Israeli and the United States case studies, then, demonstrate the weakness of international law in promoting parental citizenship and

---

[194] "Executive Actions on Immigration," U.S. Citizenship and Immigration Services – Official Website of the Department of Homeland Security, available at: www.uscis.gov/immigrationaction#2. DAPA was an expansion of the Deferred Action for Childhood Arrivals (DACA), which the Obama administration initiated in 2012, to allow undocumented immigrants who entered the United States before their sixteenth birthday and before June 2007 to receive a renewable two-year work permit and exemption from deportation. This initiative affected the lives of hundreds of thousands. See Guillermo Cantor, "Who and Where Are the Actual and Potential Beneficiaries of DACA?," Immigration Impact (August 12, 2015), available at: http://immigrationimpact.com/2015/08/12/who-and-where-are-the-actual-and-potential-beneficiaries-of-daca/.

[195] *Texas v. United States*, Memorandum opinion and order (Civil No. B-14–254/Case No. 1:14 cv 00254), at 112, 86 F Supp 3d 591, 671 (SD Tex 2015).

[196] *Texas v. United States*, 787 F 3d 733 (5th Cir 2015).

[197] Jordan Fabian, "Obama Holds off on Immigration Appeal to the Supreme Court," The Hill (May 27, 2015), available at: http://thehill.com/homenews/administration/243253-justice-dept-wont-seek-stay-for-immigration-ruling.

protecting children's right to live with their parents. Whereas the former ratified the CRC but does little to follow the obligations stated in Articles 9 and 10, the latter did not even ratify this Convention and indeed separates its citizen children from their noncitizen parents. Likewise, the International Convention on the Protection of the Rights of All Migrant Workers and Members of Their Families, which was drafted in 1990, has so far been ratified only by immigration-sending and not immigration-receiving countries.[198] This Convention aims to secure basic rights for all documented and undocumented migrant workers and their families, and in relation to the former even includes the duty of states' parties "to take measures that they deem appropriate and that fall within their competence" to facilitate the reunification of migrant workers with their spouses and minor dependent unmarried children.[199] Hence, many of the advanced economies rely on immigration, including the undocumented, because their populations shrink due to low birthrates and their citizens' refusal to take on unskilled or low-paid jobs,[200] while dehumanizing these immigrants and their children as familial subjects.[201]

Conclusion

This chapter demonstrates the partiality and distortion created by the common conceptualization of citizenship only in individualist terms. Citizenship should also be perceived in relational terms, and discussion over it, as well as over immigration policies, should acknowledge the centrality of family relations to individuals' lives and wellbeing. As sociologist Jane Lilly López recently observed: "By legally privileging certain interpersonal relationships while simultaneously limiting status and rights to the individual, the law itself generates the contradictions that lead to the dissimilation of citizens married to [or parented by] immigrants and result in some families becoming "impossible".[202]

---

[198] International Convention on the Protection of the Rights of All Migrant Workers and Members of their Families, available at: https://treaties.un.org/Pages/ViewDetails .aspx?chapter=4&clang=_en&mtdsg_no=IV-13&src=TREATY.

[199] Article 44(2) of the International Convention on the Protection of the Rights of All Migrant Workers and Members of their Families, December 18, 1990, United Nations Treaty Series, vol. 2220, p. 3, available at: https://treaties.un.org/Pages/ViewDetails .aspx?src=TREATY&mtdsg_no=IV-13&chapter=4&lang=en.

[200] Isin & Turner, "Investigating Citizenship," at 10.

[201] See also Chapters 6 and 8, for further discussion of the neglect of familial subjectivity of migrant workers.

[202] López, "'Impossible Families,'" at 114.

Indeed, it seems that this is exactly what nation states try to achieve – to make families that challenge the geo-political, as well as the cultural, religious, and economic borders, impossible. The discussion of familial citizenship highlights the ongoing power of national borders and the antagonist relations between them and between global forces – both legal and social. Receiving countries manage to resist international law's efforts to force them to recognize spousal and parental citizenship as rights that must be respected within their territory. Although there is a general agreement that familial life depends on the ability to live in the same country, citizen family members are not guaranteed the right to live with their alien spouse, parent, or child, and may well be required to follow their family member to another country or to live apart from them. Receiving countries employ a legal–bureaucratic–security apparatus to detect the unwelcome *others* and to prevent their entry or deport them. This is so, even if they are family members of citizens or of other people living in the country lawfully. The current hostility toward immigration from developing countries creates a paradox in which family relations, which are supposed to be valued and promoted for their intimacy and care, become highly regulated and open to public scrutiny and suspicion. This paradox is created precisely because family relations constitute the only remaining legitimate route for citizenship in a developed country for those who are not considered the best and brightest.

However, as discussed in Chapter 2, borders are never immune from infiltration. First, because, developing countries actively reject global forces associated with immigration and with immigrants' familial rights, but, simultaneously, they also embrace and indeed depend on cross-border movement of laborers. Many of those who want to unite with family members who are currently at the other side of the border or who are present illegally within the country are immigrants or the descendants of immigrants who were invited to the industrial countries to compensate for workforce shortages in undesired jobs and to be used and abused as cheap labor. In the much-quoted words of Swiss writer Max Frisch: "we asked for workers, and we got people."[203] Second, the current misery in parts of South America, Africa, the Middle East, and Asia is such that people keep trying to cross borders in search of a potential better future for themselves and for their families. Many times, they fail, with increasing numbers paying with their lives. But at times they succeed, rarely by cheating the border apparatus to believe they are family members, and

[203] Constable, "Migrant Workers," at 1018.

more often by smuggling themselves over the border, assisted by professional smugglers or on their own, or by entering on a temporary visa and staying on after it expires. These undocumented immigrants become a *human fact*, which truly liberal and democratic countries must find hard to ignore. Part of the humanity of this fact is that the unwelcome immigrants may go on to establish families. As we saw in relation to parental citizenship, this human tendency leads to anomalies and suspensions in the overall excluding immigration and citizenship policies, in the shape of reverse discrimination and ad hoc governmental decisions, aimed at addressing the familial needs of those who, although unwelcome, are present. Finally, in some cases, national borders do surrender to transnational law, as is the case of the EU, with its Conventions, Directives, and ECtHR decisions that force member states to grant immigrants familial citizenship even in circumstances in which it is denied to citizens, and, in cases such as the *Udeh* case, in which there is a compelling reason not to. Hence, focusing on familial citizenship reveals the simultaneous pull-and-push movement between bordered nation states and global forces, and the paradoxical and inconsistent outcomes this yields.

Of course, the hardest questions stemming from this chapter are the normative ones: should familial citizenship be recognized as a basic human right? And, if so, in what circumstances and on what conditions should it be protected or restricted? Whereas a comprehensive discussion of these questions goes beyond the scope of this chapter,[204] I will conclude it by pointing to what I perceive as essential normative food for thought on this point.

In my opinion, the answer to the first question is yes – the centrality of familial relations to people's wellbeing should elevate familial citizenship to a basic human right, as is already the case in several regional and international conventions, including the CRC. However, like almost all human rights, this is not an *absolute* right, making the questions relating to the circumstances and conditions of its protection or restriction more difficult than the general acknowledgment.

As I accept individuals' right to self-determination via political group frameworks, among other reasons due to the conflicting religious and secular norms around family and gender described in Chapter 3, and as I currently see no better or more effective organizing frame to fulfill this right than the nation state, I must accept the

---

[204] See, for example, Linda Bosniak, *The Citizen and the Alien: Dilemmas of Contemporary Membership* (Princeton, NJ: Princeton University Press, 2006); Colin Grey, *Justice and Authority in Immigration Law* (Oxford: Hurt Publishing, 2015).

latter's right to control its border.[205] Such border control is, by definition, excluding. This excluding power might be used in a legitimate and justified way, for example, when refusing to acknowledge familial citizenship of those who practice antiliberal familial relations, such as forced marriage, as well as of those who entered the country illegally. However, even this legitimate excluding apparatus must be performed in the least damaging way to familial relations, and, for example, must not allow the separation of a mother from her baby, as was the case for Encarnación and Carlos.

Moreover, I am intrigued by arguments that challenge the privileging of the nuclear family in immigration and citizenship policies. Matthew Gibney, the Deputy Director of the Refugee Studies Centre at Oxford University, for example, argues that humanitarian considerations should lead to a higher priority being placed on refugees' immigration over family immigration, given that residence in liberal democratic states is a scarce good.[206] I would add that, when it comes to economic migration, which is likely to remain limited by certain quotas imposed by developed countries, distributive justice considerations might justify an approach in which needy families from developing countries are each permitted to nominate one *immigrating representative* to start a new life in a developed market and support them via remittances (discussed in Chapter 6). This could provide a much more sustainable outcome than family reunification, which results in a much smaller number of families being assisted by remittances from developed countries. This *representative immigrant* would be allowed to establish a family in the destination country but not to bring family members from the country of origin. Legal scholar Kerry Abrams raises another interesting doubt in relation to familial immigration and citizenship polices with regard to the common prioritization of unification over reunification. She argues that it might be more justified to favor the latter as it values existing family relations – such as in the case of a sibling or the parent of a shared child – rather than the former, which values spousal import that is often not based on substantial relations.[207] Finally, legal scholar Nora Demleitner adds that the prioritization of the nuclear family found

---

[205] For cutting-edge writing on national sovereignty, see the articles in *Theoretical Inquiries in Law*, 16(2) (2015).

[206] Matthew Gibney as referred to in Honohan, "Reconsidering the Claim," at 768.

[207] Abrams, "What Makes the Family Special?"

in Western immigration and citizenship policies is culturally biased, because many people from the Global South and East might prefer a reunification with an extended family member, such as a sibling.[208]

These reservations should be a part of internal discussions on immigration and citizenship within each receiving country, as well as part of the urgently needed international discussion on the allocation of the burdens resulting from the masses who wish, or are forced, to emigrate to the developed parts of the world. This dialogue should involve not only normative and economic arguments but also empirical investigation on the familial aspects of immigration from poor or violent areas, and the intersectionality of these aspects with different cultural understandings and practices of familiality. Such research, while emerging, is still far from shedding enough light on the contextual familial constraints and preferences of documented and undocumented immigrants from different parts of the world (and those of their joining or left-behind family members) and on the familial outcomes of this immigration.[209]

The national and international discussions should also respond to what legal scholar Kari Hong recently called "Famigration": "the field in which family law doctrines, principles, and statutes are employed to critically examine the ways in which immigration law is recognizing families."[210] This field is developed by scholars who criticize the separation between family law and immigration law that is created by the disregard, on the part of legislators, of basic family law principles (such as the best interests of the child, when it comes to entry and deportation rules) and by the separation between the family court system and the immigration tribunals, with the latter's lack of sensitivity to family relations and needs.[211] As this chapter demonstrates, immigration and citizenship have much to

---

[208] Demleitner, "How Much Do Western Democracies Value Family and Marriage?," at 292–3. See also Mazzucato, Schans, Caarls, & Beauchemin, "Transnational Families between Africa and Europe," and text in supra note 50 in this chapter.

[209] One of the few relevant phenomenon that did receive substantial empirical attention is that of mixed-status families of US citizens and noncitizens originally from a South American country. See, for example, the recent collection: April Schueths & Jodie Lawston (Eds.), *Living Together Living Apart, Mixed Status Families and US Immigration Policy* (Seattle: University of Washington Press, 2015).

[210] Kari E. Hong, "Famigration (Fam Imm): The Next Frontier in Immigration Law," *Virginia Law Review Online*, 100 (2014), 63–81, at 63.

[211] For example, Kerry Abrams & R. Kent Piacenti, "Immigration's Family Values," *Virginia Law Review*, 100(4) (2014), 629–709; Holland, "The Modern Family Unit." See also, Hong, "Famigration."

do with familial relations, hence they should not be regulated without the integration of family law's theories, protections, and special courts. This integration will not produce a magic solution to the problems created by harsh world inequalities, but it will promote the humanization of all people, whether citizens, denizens, undocumented immigrants, refugees, or asylum seekers. *Familyzing* the *other* makes it much harder to treat her or him as an *it*.

6

Feeding Children

Introduction

In their book, "Hungry World: What the World Eats," photographer Peter Menzel and writer Faith D'Aluisio present their fascinating project in which they documented families from all over the world together with the food they typically eat. We learn who the family members are, where they live, how much money they spend on food weekly, and what their favorite foods are. One generic picture brilliantly captures each family in its particular dwelling, surrounded by a week's-worth of groceries.[1]

Viewing the photographs, one gets a glimpse of the differences in family composition and diet around the world. Whereas most families are nuclear families of two adults and their minor children, some are extended families, with three generations or several siblings and their off-spring sharing the same household, and several are polygamous families, while others are headed by only one parent. The difference in the amount of food and the money spent on it is no less marked. The Natomo family from Mali, for example, eats mostly grains, with hardly any fruits, vegetables, or meat. No processed food is seen in the picture. The Natomos spend $26 per week on groceries, which feeds one man, three women (two are the man's wives and one is his sister-in-law), and eleven children aged 4 months to 18 years.[2] The Afro-American Revis family from North Carolina, consisting of two parents and their two teenage sons, spend more than ten times that amount ($342 per week or 50 times more per family member), and their table is piled with junk food, including ready-made pizzas, hamburgers, snacks, and soft drinks.[3] The Glad Ostensen family from Norway spends more than twice as much as the Revis family

---

[1] Peter Menzel & Faith D'Aluisi, *Hungry World: What the World Eats* (Napa, CA: Material World Books, 2005).

[2] Ibid., at 206–7.

[3] Ibid., at 266–7.

($731 per week or 107 times more per person than the Natomo family), although they share the same family composition. Their diet is impressively varied and healthy.[4] The strength of these visual images lies in their making so very clear the fact that more money buys more food and allows access to more varied and healthier nutrition. These pictures also provide a highly visual example of what seems to be a global paradox, of the poorest having the highest birth rate despite barely being able to feed their offspring, whereas the most privileged have a negative birth rate, with no or very few children.[5]

This documentary project highlights the dietary outcomes of the global inequalities discussed in Chapter 1. According to the World Food Programme, there are 795 million hungry people in the world, 98 percent of whom live in developed countries.[6] According to United Nations International Children's Emergency Fund (UNICEF), in the poorer parts of the globe, every 3.6 seconds a person dies of starvation – and usually it is a child under the age of five.[7] Some 156 million children are stunted – that is, they are underdeveloped for their age due to lack of adequate nutrition. This is a significant improvement, compared to the 255 million children suffering from stunting, reported in 1990.[8] In the rich parts of the world, many children have unlimited access to food, whereas the relatively poor suffer from unhealthy, cheaper diets. The

---

[4] This family is not presented in the book, but their story can be found, among those of other families, in "Hungry Planet: What The World Eats," *Time* (Sep. 20, 2013), available at: http://world.time.com/2013/09/20/hungry-planet-what-the-world-eats/photo/nor_130531_334_x/.

[5] Globally, see United Nations, *World Population Prospects: Key Findings & Advance Tables* (2015), available at: https://esa.un.org/unpd/wpp/Publications/Files/Key_Findings_WPP_2015.pdf. This is also true, in many cases, nationally. See, for example, the United States, "Birth Rate in the United States in 2010, by Family Income," Statista, available at: www.statista.com/statistics/241530/birth-rate-by-family-income-in-the-us/. Exploring this paradox goes beyond the scope of this chapter. For a review of relevant research from within the field of evolutionary demography, see Rebecca Sear, David W. Lawson, Hillard Kaplan, & Mary K. Shenk, "Understanding Variation in Human Fertility: What Can We Learn from Evolutionary Demography?" *Philosophical Transactions of the Royal Society B: Biological Sciences,* 371 (2016), 20150144, available at: http://rstb.royalsocietypublishing.org/content/roytb/371/1692/20150144.full.pdf.

[6] "Who Are the Hungry?" World Food Programme, www.wfp.org/hunger/who-are.

[7] "Millennium Development Goals: Eradicate Extreme Poverty and Hunger," UNICEF, available at: www.unicef.org/mdg/poverty.html.

[8] UNICEF, *Levels and Trends in Child Malnutrition* (2015), available at: http://data.unicef.org/corecode/uploads/document6/uploaded_pdfs/corecode/JME-2015-edition-Sept-2015_203.pdf.

surplus in food and access to processed food in developed countries have led to unprecedented rates of obesity.[9] A radical example is the United States, where one-third of the population is clinically obese and another third overweight.[10] Hence, while millions of children do not have enough food to survive, millions of others have too much for their own good.

This chapter looks at three of the ways suggested in our era to address the challenge of feeding children in the impoverished parts of the world: remittances, child labor, and intercountry adoption. All of these very different solutions take part within the framework of bordered globalization and cannot be fully understood or thoroughly debated without it.

The first part of the chapter discusses remittances sent by labor migrant parents back to their home country. The discussion will move away from the national economic dimensions of this phenomenon, which are widely covered in the literature, to highlight its familial dimensions and in particular the impact of parental immigration on children, which is a relatively neglected research area. The second part of the chapter looks at the tension between international legal attempts to abolish child labor, and the reality in certain countries where it might be needed to secure children's survival and fulfill their basic needs. The third part of the chapter presents four case studies of intercountry child adoption, and its pros and cons, to ask whether this diminishing solution to children at risk should be revived.

The joint discussion of these three different topics will allow readers to develop an overarching understanding of the familial, communal, national, and international efforts needed to secure children's basic right to a minimal standard of living. This discussion also illuminates the challenges embedded in the aspiration to secure this right in the era of bordered globalization, in ways that would not jeopardize children's familial rights.

---

[9] According to UNICEF, 41 million children were overweight in 2014. This is 10 million more than in 1990. See ibid.

[10] Ironically, the rates of obesity in the United States are higher among the relatively poor, as they consume more fat and processed foods and exercise less, due to lack of leisure time, money to spend on sports activities, and access to safe public outdoor facilities. See James A. Levine, "Poverty and Obesity in the U.S.," *Diabetes*, 60 (2011), 2667–8. See also "Adult Obesity Facts," Centers for Disease Control and Prevention, available at: www.cdc.gov/ obesity/data/adult.html. Globalization is also bringing obesity to other parts of the world, with rising rates of obesity now found in countries such as China and India, due to their economic boom and the replacement of a traditional diet with the Western one. For an example on China, see H. Wang & F. Zhai, "Programme and Policy Options for Preventing Obesity in China," *Obesity Reviews*, 14 (2013), 134–40.

Parental Remittances

According to the World Bank, remittance flow to developing countries in 2014 stood at $427 billion.[11] In the same year, official development assistance flow from developed to developing countries amounted to less than a third of that sum – $137.2 billion.[12] These statistics are part of what Carol Adelman, an expert in international economics, calls "the privatization of foreign aid" – the process through which a growing share of the foreign aid provided to poorer parts of the world is the outcome of donations of private entities and of remittances sent back home by immigrating individuals, [13] rather than the donations of foreign governments and international official bodies.[14]

The magnitude of the remittances phenomenon has resulted in much policy debate and academic attention, both of which center on its contribution to "growth and development" on the national or household scales. Interestingly, the very basic question of whether remittances have a positive impact on the economic growth of the nations to which they are sent is still empirically debated, with some researchers finding positive impact and others finding no significant or negative, impact. The recent study of economics scholars Uwaoma Nwaogu and Michael Ryan, for example, found that remittance flow had no effect on country-level growth in Africa and a positive, yet not robust, impact on country-level growth in Latin America and the Caribbean. These researchers suggest that although remittances reduce poverty in developing countries, their positive effect might dissolve due to the loss of highly skilled, active workers to their home countries' economy, and the use of money by the recipients in ways that do not encourage long-term growth.[15] Indeed, on the

---

[11] The World Bank, *Migration and Remittances: Recent Developments and Outlook, Migration and Development Brief 25* (2015), at 4, available at: http://pubdocs.worldbank.org/pubdocs/publicdoc/2015/10/102761445353157305/MigrationandDevelopmentBrief25.pdf.

[12] OECD, *Final Official Development Assistance Figures in 2014* (2015), available at: www.oecd.org/dac/stats/final-oda-2014.htm.

[13] In this part I refer to remittances as money and goods sent by emigrating individuals to their families back home in the country of origin. For discussions of other kind of remittances, including social remittances, technological remittances, political remittances, and collective remittances, see Luin Goldring, "Re-Thinking Remittances: Social and Political Dimensions of Individual and Collective Remittances," CERLAC Working Paper Series, York University (2003).

[14] Carol C. Adelman, "The Privatization of Foreign Aid: Reassessing National Largesse," *Foreign Affairs*, 82(6) (2003), 9–14.

[15] Uwaoma G. Nwaogu & Michael J. Ryan, "FDI, Foreign Aid, Remittance and Economic Growth in Developing Countries," *Review of Development Economics*, 19(1) (2015), 100–15. On the macro-economic level, additional possible negative impacts of labor

household level, there is an empirical consensus that remittances are of short-term positive economic value as they are used for immediate consumption, including to meet the basic need for food, clothing, and housing, as well as for health and education services. But the long-term impact of the economic mobilization created by remittances is doubtful, as very little is saved or invested in projects that might protect the current or next generation from poverty.[16]

What I find striking in the scholastic and international policy debates over remittances is the relative absence of child-centered deliberations. Although gender has become a central theme in the last decade of policy and academic discussions over remittances – after being a nontopic within the emerging discourse on remittances during the 1990s[17] – children, and their interests and rights, as well as the construction of childhood in an era in which parents might leave for another country for long periods, are still very much missing from this discourse. The few studies that look at the impact of parental immigration on children's wellbeing suffer from one or more methodological deficiencies, including a small sample, lack of comparison to the child's wellbeing prior to parental immigration and to the wellbeing of children in intact families, and reliance on parental or caregiver reports rather than on direct evidence from the child.[18] Even the basic statistics of how many children are left behind

---

migrants who send money home are those borne by the countries of destination, such as higher unemployment and lower working conditions of the working poor among their citizens. See Jeffrey H. Cohen, "Remittance Outcomes and Migration: Theoretical Contests, Real Opportunities," *Studies in Comparative International Development*, 40(1) (2005), 88–112, at 92. Nevertheless, Ernesto Castañeda argues that labor migration "produce[s] more development in the host communities than in the remittance-receiving ones," See Ernesto Castañeda, "Living in Limbo: Transnational Households, Remittances and Development," *International Migration*, 51(s1) (2012), e13–e35, at e27, available at: http://onlinelibrary.wiley.com/wol1/doi/10.1111/j.1468-2435.2012.00745.x/full.

[16] Cohen, "Remittance Outcomes and Migration," at 93–9; Castañeda, "Living in Limbo."

[17] Rahel Kunz, "'Moneymaker and Mother from Afar': The Power of Gender Myths" in Ton van Naerssen, Lothar Smith, Tine Davids, & Marianne H. Marchand (Eds.), *Women, Gender, Remittances and Development in the Global South* (London: Routledge, 2016), pp. 207–28.

[18] Valentina Mazzucato & Djamila Schans, "Transnational Families and the Well-Being of Children: Conceptual and Methodological Challenges," *Journal of Marriage and Family*, 73(4) (2011), 704–12 at 705–6. For a literature review of the impact of parental immigration on children in Asia and South America, see Theodora Lam, Brenda S. A. Yeoh, & Lan Anh Hoang, "Transnational Migration and Changing Care Arrangements for Left-Behind Children in Southeast Asia: A Selective Literature Review in Relation to the CHAMPSEA Study," Working Paper Series No. 207, Asia Research Institute, National University of Singapore (2013).

by one or both parents are missing. In Romania, for example, according to official statistics, 80,000 children are left behind, with more than 25 percent living without either parent. However, a study conducted by UNICEF suggests that the numbers are much higher and amounted in 2007 to 350,000 children, with a third deprived of any parental care as both parents were away in another country.[19] Likewise, it is known that millions of children are left behind in the major immigration-sending countries, such as the Philippines and Mexico, but exact numbers and data on the division between those children left behind by one or by both parents are missing.[20]

The basic and taken-for-granted assumption is that when parents emigrate for work and leave their children behind, it is "in search of better wages to send as remittances to their children".[21] The departure of the parent is framed as a necessary and responsible act, benefiting the children and made for their sake.[22] This assumption and the literature on remittances more generally ignore the common cases in which the emigration of the parent does not result in any improvement of the economic situation of the family left behind. The difficulties in returning loans taken to enable the costs of emigration and in securing a job at the host country, abusive employment conditions, imprisonment of the parent due to lack of legal status, and high living costs in the host country are several of the reasons, largely ignored by researchers and policy makers,[23] that can lead to the inability of the parent to advance the economic wellbeing of the children left behind. For example, a third of transnational parents who

[19] Bertha Sănduleasa & Aniela Matei, "Effects of Parental Migration on Families and Children in Post-Communist Romania," *Revista de Stiinte Politice* 46 (2015), 196–207, at 201–2.

[20] In several immigration-sending countries, approximately 25 percent of children have at least one parent abroad. See Mazzucato & Schans, "Transnational Families and the Well-Being of Children," at 705. For the Philippines, see UNICEF, *Children and Women Left Behind in Labour Sending Countries: An Appraisal of Social Risks* (2008), at 11, available at: www.unicef.org/policyanalysis/files/Children_and_women_left_behind(2).pdf.

[21] Leisy J. Abrego, *Sacrificing Families: Navigating Laws, Labor, and Love Across Borders* (CA: Stanford University Press, 2014), at 2.

[22] This perception is also shared by parents. For example, in a survey conducted among transnational parents who emigrated from Romania, only a fifth considered separation from children as an argument against the idea of emigrating for paid work. See Sănduleasa & Matei, "Effects of Parental Migration on Families and Children," at 201–2.

[23] For a rare ethnographic account of the familial conflicts that may arise when the immigrants fail to send the expected remittances back home due to difficulties faced in the destination country, see Galia Sabar, "African Migrant Workers in Israel: Between Extended Family, Money and a Sense of Evil" in Ehud R. Toledano (Ed.), *African Communities in Asia and the Mediterranean: Between Integration and Conflict* (London: Africa World Press, 2012), pp. 255–84.

emigrated from Romania report no improvement in the economic condition of the family they left behind.[24]

Moreover, the vast majority of the calculations in relation to the contribution of remittances to "growth and development" are made according to the state, region, or household units, with no statistics on how much money is spent on the children left behind, as opposed to the money spent on their caregiver and on other family members of the migrant parent.[25] The only study published in English I found, which analyzes remittances according to family relation with the provider, was based on data from five South-American countries extracted in 2003. It found that children received only 11 percent to 16 percent of remittances, whereas siblings of the migrant worker received 28 percent to 42 percent, parents 19 percent to 29 percent, and spouses 6 percent to 13 percent.[26] However, because this survey did not include information about the parental status of the provider, it is unclear if these statistics represented a reality in which most labor migrants were single and childless, or a phenomenon of parental remittances not necessarily spent on children. One of these countries was El Salvador, in which 15 percent of remittances went to the provider's children. In this case, we have further evidence that supports the second interpretation. Quantitative data reveal that 10 percent of children and adolescents with migrant parents do not receive remittances at all.[27] Likewise, in a qualitative study conducted by sociologist Leisy Abrego among 130 transnational El Salvadorian families, about 15 percent described a state of economic deprivation among the left-behind children, in spite of, or because of, parental immigration. A further 37 percent described a state of "surviving," in which the children left behind have food and go to school, but have no money for clothes or higher education. Only 48 percent of the interviewees claimed that the parental emigration and family separation was "paying off," allowing the children to thrive, with enough money for food, schooling, some luxuries, and savings. On this point, Abrego warns her readers not to think that half of transnational El Salvadorian families are thriving. She explains that her sample is not representative but is aimed at highlighting the disparity between

[24] UNICEF Romania 2008 survey, as reported in Sănduleasa & Matei, "Effects of Parental Migration on Families and Children," at 202.

[25] Mazzucato and Schans, "Transnational Families and the Well-Being of Children," at 704.

[26] Manuel Orozco, "Remittances to Latin America and the Caribbean: Issues and Perspectives on Development," Organization of American States (2004), at 6, available at: www.rrojasdatabank.info/iadbremit/orozco04.pdf.

[27] Abrego, Sacrificing Families, Ch. 6, fn. 6.

left-behind children who have three pairs of shoes and those who barely survive – the latter, she claims, representing the majority of cases.[28]

Some anecdotal evidence suggests that this might also be the case in other countries, and that the common assumption that children are saved from poverty if their parents emigrate to work abroad is overoptimistic. In an interview I conducted with a woman who had emigrated from the Philippines to work in Israel when her daughter was 6 years old, she told me of the suffering of her child. As the father was never a part of the daughter's life, she was left at the care of her grandmother and other extended family members. Though the mother sent a significant amount of money to the Philippines over the years, to ensure that the needs of her daughter would be met and a house bought for the family, in fact her relatives spent the money on themselves, no house was bought, and the daughter lived in what the interviewee described as "a tiny wreck," neglected by the relatives. When the daughter became a teenager, she talked to her mother over the phone countless times, describing her despair and begging her to take her to Israel. The mother decided to do all that she could to save her child. She converted to Judaism, married an Israeli, and had two sons. Her husband then managed to adopt her daughter and bring her to Israel so she could live with them. Even so, the interviewee said, she hoped to go back to work once her two sons were a little older, to earn her own money again and send it to her mother – on a regular basis, not only on the holidays as she now did. She explained her philosophy thus: "With us [the Filipinos], the money of one person is the money of the whole family. It does not matter if your family did something wrong, you still need to respect the parents and family."[29] Hence, the remittances are understood as a family resource, not necessarily, or primarily, designated to the children of the provider.

The story of this interviewee demonstrates that although there is a common norm of sending remittances to be shared by the left-behind household members,[30] conflicts can arise about the exact way of sharing – that

---

[28] Ibid., at 135–51.

[29] Interview conducted by author, July 10, 2005. For more details and findings from this study, see Daphna Hacker, "From the Moabite Ruth to Norly the Filipino: Intermarriage and Conversion in the Jewish Nation State" in Hanna Herzog & Ann Braude (Eds.), *Gendering Religion and Politics: Untangling Modernities* (New York: Palgrave Macmillan, 2009), pp. 101–24.

[30] Interestingly, Ron Peleg found that the sum of remittances sent by Filipino immigrants working in Israel is not affected by their being parents or not, but by the number of family members in the household to which the remittances are sent. See Ron Peleg, "Filipina in the Holy Land: Remittances and their Uses," MA Thesis, Tel Aviv University (2011), at 31. For a recent study on the familial dynamics emerging over the norm of remittances

is, the relative sums provided to each family member and the goods and services to be purchased. However, very little is empirically known about these conflicts[31] or how they affect children left behind. In particular, I could not find any study of legal conflicts over remittances, to shed light on questions such as: are the remittances sent by a parent with minor children left behind understood – by the individuals involved, as well as by the national legal system in the country of origin – as a salary to the caregiver, as child support, as support to the extended family, or as a gift to be used by the adult who receives them as they see fit? Are there contractual deliberations between the parent and the child's caregiver in relation to sums and use of remittances? Are any such deliberations understood as legally binding? What happens when the parent does not send any or enough money to support the child? What happens if the caregiver fails to adequately care for the child? Are these questions answered differently in different immigration-sending countries? Are there differences due to the parents' or child's gender, caregiver's identity, or other variables or circumstances? The lack of socio-legal studies aimed at answering these questions might suggest that remittances are not conceptualized by the parties involved in legal terms, and that conflicts over remittances are never resolved in litigation or legal mediation. Alternatively, this scholastic lacuna might simply be another manifestation of the general neglect around the study of immigration's outcomes in sending countries (as opposed to the intense study of its outcomes in receiving countries)[32] and in particular, as I argue, around the study of its outcomes for children.

A recent study conducted in Nigeria identified the research lacuna of "the implications remittance has on intrahousehold conflicts in immigrants' households." The study attempted to address this research gap by interviewing 37 Nigerians who had emigrated to developed countries and who were currently on holiday back in Nigeria.[33] Every

---

in Vietnam, see Hung Cam Thai, *Insufficient Funds: The Culture of Money in Low-Wage Transnational Families* (CA: Stanford University Press, 2014).

[31] The conflicts can become extremely intense when the immigrant is unable to send any money home. See Sabar, "African Migrant Workers in Israel."

[32] Ernesto Castañeda & Lesley Buck, "A Family of Strangers: Transnational Parenting and the Consequences of Family Separation due to Undocumented Migration" in Lois Ann Lorentzen (Ed.), *Hidden Lives and Human Rights in America: Understanding the Controversies and Tragedies of Undocumented Immigration* (Santa Barbara, CA: Praeger, 2014), pp. 175–202.

[33] Adediran Daniel Ikuomola, "Unintended Consequences of Remittance: Nigerian Migrants and Intra-Household Conflicts," *SAGE Open*, 5(3) (2015), 1–8, available at: http://sgo.sagepub.com/content/spsgo/5/3/2158244015605353.full.pdf.

interviewee had at least one grievance in relation to how remittances were shared and utilized. The providers were critical of their relatives for spending the remittances on luxuries or diverting money that was intended for a specific family member or for a specific purpose to other people or purposes, or for not progressing on the promised building of a house with the funds sent. Female interviewees in particular felt that their male family members were trying to take control over the remittances they sent and created family conflicts. Unfortunately, this study did not focus on remittances sent for left-behind children, although it seems that most interviewees were parents who had immigrated without their children. Still, it is very clear from this study that the immigrants sending remittances faced difficulties in controlling the identity of the recipients and the uses to which the money they sent home was put, including the share and use of the money in relation to their children. One particular example stands out: one interviewee accused her husband of using the money she sent on himself, on other women, and on alcohol, while sending the children to low-quality schools and leaving them in the care of elderly and incapable family members. The outcomes were devastating: "... for five years I was sending money directly to my husband for the upkeep of the family, only to return in 2008 for the first time, seeing my only daughter pregnant at fifteen. I was not informed. Her two brothers were also not doing well in school. They have grown stubborn under the control of their father and other extended family members. This situation completely strained my relationship with their father and I had to seek for divorce in 2009. A lot had gone wrong in my absence."[34]

This story sheds light not only on the possibility that the common presumption that all left-behind children benefit economically from their parent's immigration is too optimistic, but also on the emotional costs for children, which are not necessarily compensated by the remittances sent by their parents.[35] This is another relatively neglected aspect within the research and policy debates over remittances.[36] As sociologist Ernesto Castañeda and clinical social worker Lesley Buck recently argued: "The literature on migration and development also often ignores the human drama and the social and psychological effects that family separation has on the members of transnational households."[37]

[34] Ibid., at 6.
[35] Castañeda & Buck, "A Family of Strangers."
[36] Sănduleasa & Matei, "Effects of Parental Migration on Families and Children," at 198–9.
[37] Castañeda & Buck, "A Family of Strangers."

Sociologist Rhacel Salazar Parreñas was among the first to point to the "care crisis" created by parental immigration from developing countries.[38] She was also a pioneer in interviewing the children left behind, once they reached young adulthood, giving them voice and presenting their narratives – so absent from the discourse on labor migration and remittances.[39] Salazar Parreñas's study was conducted in the Philippines, a country that views labor migration of its citizens as a major export industry. In 2013, more than 10 million Filipinos worked abroad (about 10 percent of the entire population),[40] with a ratio of 67/100 male/female immigrants.[41] In her study, the mothers were living without their children for an average of 11.42 years, and saw them during this long period just 4.4 times, for an average length of 5.39 weeks per visit. The fathers were absent for an average of 13.79 years, visiting 9.81 times, for 7.57 weeks each time.[42] As in other countries, parental immigration is very often not temporary, even if planned as such, and parents can spend very long periods abroad – sometimes for most of their children's childhoods.[43] Salazar Parreñas revealed the gendered narratives of left-behind children in her study. When referring to an immigrating father, the children described a "gap" – "a sense of discomfort, unease, and awkwardness" they felt toward him, the difficulties they faced in openly communicating with him, and the ambivalence they felt over his absence, wishing for his return, but not immediately – reflecting their unfamiliarity with him.[44] Children of immigrating mothers, on the other hand, reported that they had ongoing contact with their mother and that she was still very much involved in their lives from afar. These children also reported inadequate care received by caregivers, a sense of abandonment, and the commodification of the tie with their

---

[38] Rhacel Salazar Parreñas, "The Care Crisis in the Philippines: Children and Transnational Families in the New Global Economy" in Barbara Ehrenreich & Arlie Russell Hochschild (Eds.), *Global Woman: Nannies, Maids, and Sex Workers in the New Economy* (New York: Henry Holt and Company, 2004), pp. 39–54.

[39] Rhacel Salazar Parreñas, *Children of Global Migration: Transnational Families and Gendered Woes* (CA: Stanford University Press, 2005).

[40] "Yearly Stock Estimation of Overseas Filipinos," Office of the President of the Philippines, Commission on Filipinos Overseas, available at: http://www.cfo.gov.ph/program-and-services/yearly-stock-estimation-of-overseas-filipinos.html.

[41] "Statistical Profile of Registered Filipino Emigrants," Office of the President of the Philippines, Commission on Filipinos Overseas, available at: http://www.cfo.gov.ph/downloads/statistics/statistical-profile-of-registered-filipino-emigrants.html.

[42] Parreñas, *Children of Global Migration*, at 32.

[43] Castañeda, "Living in Limbo," at e23–e24.

[44] Parreñas, *Children of Global Migration*, Ch. 4.

mother.[45] Salazar Parreñas argues that these reports are not necessarily because children with immigrant mothers are less cared for at home, but because of the traditional gendered perceptions of parenthood prevalent within Filipino society affecting their subjective experience. Finally, out of the sixty-nine children interviewed by Salazar Parreñas, thirteen lived without either of their parents. These children were more likely to drop out of school and to suffer from poor guardianship.[46]

Feelings of sadness, loneliness, and abandonment, were also reported by Abrego in her study of left-behind children in El Salvador, mentioned earlier.[47] Likewise, sociologist Joanna Dreby reports feelings of resentment and sadness among left-behind children in Mexico.[48] Both researchers found evidence that these sentiments correlate with the amount of remittances sent – the more the child feels that the parent succeeds in securing their economic wellbeing, the more successful the child is in overcoming the sadness of separation. This finding is part of other evidence that points to the process of the commodification of parental love resulting from the growing phenomenon of parental immigration. As it becomes more common, children are learning to expect their parents to leave and to conceptualize parental love as the willingness to travel abroad and send remittances.[49] Indeed, remittances are sometimes conceptualized within the literature as a "product of love"[50] and as a communicative "bridge"[51] between a loving parent and loving children, all suffering the pain of separation. Still, when reading the children's testimonies in the very few studies, referred to earlier, that make left-behind children the center of attention, it becomes clear that those whose economic situation

---

[45] Ibid., Ch. 5–6.

[46] Ibid., at 153. But see the quantitative study of Elspeth Graham & Lucy P. Jordan, which found no evidence of poorer psychological wellbeing among Filipino children in transnational families, compared to children with no immigrant parent, while finding negative effects of parental immigration on children's wellbeing in other Southeast Asian countries. See Elspeth Graham & Lucy P. Jordan, "Migrant Parents and the Psychological Well-Being of Left-Behind Children in Southeast Asia," *Journal of Marriage and Family,* 73(4) (2011), 763–87.

[47] Abrego, *Sacrificing Families,* at 151.

[48] Joanna Dreby, "U.S. Immigration Policy and Family Separation: The Consequences for Children's Well-being," *Social Science & Medicine,* 132 (2015), 245–51, at 248. But recent quantitative data suggest no impact of parental absence on psychological distress among Mexican youth. See Juyoung Jang, Veronica Deenanath, & Catherine A. Solheim, "Family Members' Transnational Migration, Community Contexts, and Psychological Distress in Mexican Families," *Family Science Review,* 20(2) (2015), 94–112.

[49] Cati Coe, "What Is Love? The Materiality of Care in Ghanaian Transnational Families," *International Migration,* 49(6) (2011), 7–24.

[50] Castañeda & Buck, "A Family of Strangers."

[51] Paolo Boccagni, "Migration and the Family Transformations It 'Leaves Behind': A Critical View From Ecuador," *The Latin Americanist,* 57(4) (2013), 3–24, at 13–14.

changes significantly for the better and, further, those who manage to join the emigrating parent in the host country, are more likely to appreciate the parent's departure, whereas the others often voice a preference for their family to have stayed together, even at the price of economic wellbeing. The children's narratives echo sociologist Paolo Boccagni's observation in relation to transnational families in which children are separated from their parents: "while most of the care activities that are typical of proximate families ... can be enacted even from afar, some cannot. This crucially applies to that kind of 'personal support' that requires a sensorial perception of the other's co-presence (hence some physical contact), access to the same life spaces, or the simple staying together."[52]

One unique case study that most radically blurs the boundaries between emotional and material parental care is that of left-behind children in Ghana. In this study, the children were less concerned about the absence of the migrant parent, and more concerned about the remittances sent. The researchers suggest that to comprehend these responses one must see them as the outcome of two cultural characteristics of Ghanaian society: the understanding that love is a willingness to provide the necessities of life, not an emotion detached from material giving; and the common practice – unrelated to globalization, though enhanced by it – of sending children away from their parents to live with an adult who can better provide for them.[53]

The Ghanaian case study and the evidence from other countries are a reminder that parenthood is a social and cultural construct. As such, the emotional wellbeing of children is not affected only by the actual separation from a parent, but also by the presence of other adults who *parent* the child and by the overall social attitude toward the connection between emotional and material care, and such care and parental physical presence or absence.[54] Notwithstanding, coming from a family-law perspective, I find it interesting to compare the current socio-legal discursive themes prevalent in the West in relation to parental divorce in developed countries, and the discursive assumptions, shared by receiving and sending immigration countries, in relation to parental emigration from developing countries.[55] I have summarized these themes in Table 6.1.

---

[52] Ibid., at 19.
[53] Coe, "What Is Love?"
[54] Mazzucato & Schans, "Transnational Families and the Well-Being of Children," at 707.
[55] See also related difference between current socio-legal discursive themes prevalent in the West in relation to parental divorce in developed countries, and these countries' disregard of the importance of noncitizen parents to the lives of their children who were born in the destination country, as discussed in Chapter 5.

Table 6.1. *Discursive Comparison: Parental Divorce and Parental Emigration*

Parental Divorce (in developed countries)	Parental Emigration (from developing countries)
Best interests of the child – the paramount consideration – at the center of discourse.[a]	Best interests of the child – missing from most policy and scholastic discussions.[b]
The negative consequences of divorce for children are explored and highlighted.[c]	The negative consequences of parental emigration for children are ignored.[d]
Best interests of the child are best served by intense involvement of both parents.[e]	Parental emigration is a necessary evil, needed for the economic wellbeing of the children.[f]
Fathers are as important to children as their mothers.[g]	Maternal immigration might harm the children. The impact of paternal immigration on children is ignored.[h]
Joint physical custody or broad visitation is promoted, including by legislators, to secure both parents' day-to-day involvement.[i]	Parents are expected to emigrate, for long periods, and are even encouraged to do so by their own government.[j]
Policies are developed to target and address the needs of children within post-divorce families.[k]	No policies are developed within migrant-sending countries to target and address the needs of left-behind children.[l]
Growing limitation on parental freedom to relocate, both within and outside the country, in the name of the children's right to have contact with both parents and in the name of both parents' right to be involved in their children's lives.[m]	Receiving countries' immigration policies separate parents from their children – harsh restrictions on family unification, and difficulties imposed on home visits. Children's right to be cared for by their parents and parents' right to be physically present in their children's lives are ignored.[n]
Parental love is distinct and separate from parental obligation to economically support the child.[o]	Parental love is manifested, and hence can be substituted, by remittances.[p]
Parents are excessively evaluated and judged in pursuit of the best post-divorce parental plan for their children.[q]	Fear among researchers of patronizing and demonizing emigrating parents leads to the negative impact of parental immigration on children being empirically overlooked.[r]
Children should participate in shaping post-divorce familial arrangements – programs are developed to secure children's participation in legal divorce procedures.[s]	Apparently, children are not consulted on the decision of their parent's immigration,[t] and their exclusion is also apparent in the general discourse on parental migration.

a June Carbone, "Legal Applications of the 'Best Interest of the Child' Standard: Judicial Rationalization or a Measure of Institutional Competence?," *Pediatrics*, 134 (2014), S111–20.

b Arlie Russell Hochschild, "Love and Gold" in Ehrenreich & Hochschild (Eds.), *Global Woman*, pp. 15–30.

c For example, see Joan B. Kelly & Robert E. Emery, "Children's Adjustment Following Divorce: Risk and Resilience Perspectives," *Family Relations*, 52(4) (2003), 352–62.

d Mazzucato & Schans, "Transnational Families and the Well-Being of Children," at 707.

e For example, see Robert Bauserman, "Child Adjustment in Joint-Custody Versus Sole-Custody Arrangements: A Meta-Analytic Review," *Journal of Family Psychology*, 16(1) (2002), 91–102.

f Castañeda & Buck, "A Family of Strangers."

g Significant fathers' movements influenced legislation in various countries such as the United States, Australia, and Canada. For example, see Reg Graycar, "Family Law Reform in Australia, or "Frozen Chooks Revisited Again?" *Theoretical Inquiries in Law*, 13(1) (2012), 241–69. See also articles in the *Canadian Journal of Women and the Law*, "Men's Groups: Challenging Feminism," 28(1) (2016).

h For example, in the Philippines, see Parreñas, *Children of Global Migration*; in Ecuador, see Boccagni, "Migration and the Family Transformations It 'Leaves Behind'," at 8.

i See Chapter 5, fn. 125.

j See, for example, the Philippines, as discussed earlier. See, more generally, Collette V. Browne & Kathryn L. Braun, "Globalization, Women's Migration, and the Long-Term-Care Workforce," *The Gerontologist*, 48(1) (2008), 16–24, at 19.

k For example, Rebecca Love Kourlis, Melinda Taylor, Andrew Schepard, & Marsha Kline Pruett, "Iaals' Honoring Families Initiative: Courts and Communities Helping Families in Transition Arising from Separation or Divorce," *Family Court Review*, 51(3) (2013), 351–76.

l Mazzucato & Schans, "Transnational Families and the Well-Being of Children," at 709.

m Ayelet Blecher-Prigat, "The Costs of Raising Children: Toward a Theory of Financial Obligations Between Co-Parents," *Theoretical Inquiries in Law*, 13(1) (2012), 179–207, at 200–2.

n See also Chapters 5 and 8 in this book; Castañeda & Buck, "A Family of Strangers"; Mazzucato & Schans, "Transnational Families and the Well-Being of Children," at 709.

o Paul R. Amato, "More than Money? Men's Contributions to Their Children's Lives" in Alan Booth & Ann C. Crouter (Eds.), *Men in Families: When Do They Get Involved? What Difference Does It Make?* (New York: Psychology Press, 1998), pp. 241–78.

p Castañeda & Buck, "A Family of Strangers"; Boccagni, "Migration and the Family Transformations It 'Leaves Behind'," at 13–4.

q Gaia Bernstein & Zvi Triger, "Over-Parenting," *UC Davis Law Review*, 44(4) (2011), 1221–79.

r Castañeda & Buck, "A Family of Strangers."

s Tamar Morag, Dori Rivkin, & Yoa Sorek, "Child Participation in the Family Courts – Lessons from the Israeli Pilot Project," *International Journal of Law, Policy and the Family*, 26(1) (2012), 1–30.

t For example, Sănduleasa & Matei, "Effects of Parental Migration on Families and Children," at 201.

Although both discourses, presented in Table 6.1, relate to a similar situation of children not being able to continue sharing the same household with both their parents, they construct a border between two extreme archetypes of children: on the one hand, children in the West are constructed as the center of the family, in need of intense contact with both parents. Legal reforms are advanced to secure the fulfillment of this need, even by restricting the parents' freedom of movement (by limiting their ability to relocate). The pursuit of both parents' involvement in the child's life is so jealous that it ignores studies showing that joint physical custody might harm children,[56] and the disempowering outcomes of these reforms for mothers (who must surrender to paternal custody demands and suffer the resultant loss of child support).[57] On the other hand, children of the South and East are constructed by the Western immigration discourse, as well as by several sending countries, as nonchildren or the children of no-one. At best, they are beings who do not need parenting, at least by their biological parents, and at worst, they are transparent. These children's separation from their parents is taken for granted, and even encouraged or demanded. When the children are taken into account, they are usually perceived as an indistinct part of the household or nation, and their understudied emotional wellbeing and long-term development[58] are often understood only in economic terms.

The conceptual framework of bordered globalization can help to point at the possible motivations behind the discursive construction of these two dramatically different archetypes of children. As discussed in the previous chapter, and as will be further discussed in Chapter 8, developed countries are eager to receive working hands with no

---

[56] Jennifer McIntosh, Bruce Smyth, Margaret Kelaher, Yvonne Wells, & Caroline Long, "Post-Separation Parenting Arrangements: Patterns and Developmental Outcomes for Infants and Children," collected reports prepared for the Australian Government Attorney General's Department (2010), at 9, available at: www.ag.gov.au/FamiliesAndMarriage/ Families/FamilyViolence/Documents/Post%20separation%20parenting%20 arrangements%20and%20developmental%20outcomes%20for%20infants%20and%20 children.pdf.

[57] Susan S. Boyd, "Autonomy for Mothers? Relational Theory and Parenting Apart," *Feminist Legal Studies*, 18(2) (2010), 137–58; Daphna Hacker & Ruth Halperin Kaddari," The Ruling Rules in Custody Disputers – On the Dangers of the Parental Sameness Illusion in a Gendered Reality," *Mishpat and Mimshal*, 15 (2013), 91–170. (Hebrew).

[58] I could not find studies looking at the long-term effect of parental separation on left-behind children, except that they tend to become immigrants themselves. See, for example, Parreñas, *Children of Global Migration*.

following family members. In particular, these countries are in desperate need of paid care to replace their "liberated" female citizens – who are no longer able or willing to devote themselves to the care of children, the elderly, or the sick and disabled – and their male citizens, who hardly ever perform caring as a central role.[59] This need explains the current feminization of immigration, which leaves more and more children in poor countries without the gendered parental care, and at times without the physical care of either parent.[60] Moreover, both immigration-receiving and -sending countries cooperate with the "privatization of aid" to the poorer parts of the world, mentioned earlier. It seems to me that private remittances release rich countries from monetary solidarity and compensation for wrongs committed in the past (under colonialism) and the present (such as exploitation of resources and human capital). At the same time, the remittance flow creates an illusion within poor countries of national sovereignty, independence, and control of their citizens and economy. These assertions cannot be developed here, and are offered only as food for further thought and study, yet what this part of the chapter highlights is the lack of concern for children within the abusive alliance between labor immigration-receiving and -sending countries.

Several solutions are offered, by the very few scholars who do not ignore these children, to cope with the negative consequences of parental labor emigration, including: reunification policies of receiving countries; securing economies in poor countries so their citizens can enjoy the right to not have to emigrate; and developing policies within immigration-sending countries to assist left-behind children and educate parents about the possible harsh outcomes of their immigration.[61] Another way a family can try to prevent parental emigration is by sending the child to work. We turn now to child labor as a possible answer to children's poverty.

Working Children

The relative neglect of a child-centered approach within the discussions over remittances stands in sharp contrast to the intense international

---

[59] Hochschild, "Love and Gold."
[60] Ibid.
[61] Abrego, *Sacrificing Families*, at 198; Mazzucato & Schans, "Transnational Families and the Well-Being of Children."

preoccupation[62] with the millions of children who work.[63] When it comes to child work,[64] the dichotomy between children of the global North and 'other' children, so evident from the comparison of the discourse on parental emigration and the discourse on parental divorce, captured in Table 6.1, is replaced by an imagined global consensus on the best interests of all the world's children.[65]

By the beginning of the twentieth century, international conventions had already been drafted to limit child work.[66] Current international

---

[62] In 2001, William E. Mayers argued that "Child Labor has in recent years been perhaps the most visible single issue generating discussion about how children's rights are to be defined and observed in an era of globalization." See William E. Mayers, "The Right Rights? Child Labor in a Globalizing World," *Annals of the American Academy of Political and Social Science*, 575 (2001), 38–55, at 39. Although several other issues have developed since, such as refugee children and genital mutilation, child labor is still an outstanding example of global children's rights discourse.

[63] According to the ILO, between 2008 and 2012 about 264 million children aged 5–17 worked, 158 million of whom suffered working conditions classed as illegal according to the ILO standards. This represents a significant drop, from 222 million and 215 million, respectively, in 2008. See Yacouba Diallo, Alex Etienne, & Farhad Mehran, "Global Child Labour Trends 2008 to 2012," International Labour Organization (2013), available at: www.ilo.org/ipecinfo/product/download.do?type=document&id=23015; However, statistics on working children should be approached with caution as they are often inaccurate, partial, and biased. See Smolin, "Strategic Choices in the International Campaign against Child Labor," at 950–6.

[64] Because the term *child labor* is burdened by negative connotations and by moral judgment, I prefer the terms *child work* and *working children*, which include all kinds of work done by children, including legitimate and beneficial work. These terms also include nonpaid work, which the term *child employment*, also offered in the literature, does not capture. See Karl Hanson, Diana Volonakis, & Mohammed Al-Rozzi, "Child Labour, Working Children and Children's Rights" in Wouter Vandenhole, Ellen Desmet, Didier Reynaert, & Sara Lembrechts (Eds.), *Routledge International Handbook of Children's Rights Studies* (London: Routledge, 2015), pp. 316–30, at 323; David M. Smolin, "Strategic Choices in the International Campaign against Child Labor," *Human Rights Quarterly*, 22(4) (2000), at 942–88.

[65] Roland Pierik & Mijke S. Houwerzijl, "Normative Political Theory in an Era of Globalization. The Case of Child Labor," paper presented at the annual meeting of the American Political Science Association (August 28, 2002). Yoshie Noguchi, for example, argues that the abolishment of child labor, which he defines as work that is likely to cause negative consequences, is "an internationally accepted principle." See Yoshie Noguchi, "20 Years of the Convention on the Rights of the Child and International Action against Child Labour," *The International Journal of Children's Rights*, 18(4) (2010), 515–34, at 516, 525.

[66] The driving force behind these conventions was the ILO, an international organization currently comprising 186 member states devoted to "promoting social justice and internationally recognized human and labor rights." See "Mission and Impact of the ILO," International Labour Organization, www.ilo.org/global/about-the-ilo/mission-and-objectives/lang-en/index.htm. The early conventions were drafted not only in the name

standards in this area are embedded in three international conventions: (1) The Minimum Age Convention of 1973 was drafted by the International Labour Organization (ILO) in an attempt to abolish child work by setting a universal standard of a minimum age of 15 for working children. It is currently ratified by 168 countries;[67] (2) The 1989 UN Convention on the Rights of the Child (CRC), ratified by almost all countries of the world. This convention obliges states parties to "recognize the right of the child to be protected from economic exploitation and from performing any work that is likely to be hazardous or to interfere with the child's education, or to be harmful to the child's health or physical, mental, spiritual, moral or social development." The CRC also recognizes "the right of the child to rest and leisure, to engage in play and recreational activities appropriate to the age of the child";[68] and (3) Worst Forms of Child Labour Convention, drafted by the ILO in 1999 and ratified with unusual speed by 180 states. This convention targets child slavery, trafficking, prostitution, pornography, and other illicit activities such as those related to drug dealing. It demands that states parties act immediately and effectively to prohibit and eliminate these phenomena, as well as to prohibit and eliminate the much broader category of "work which, by its nature or the circumstances in which it is carried out, is likely to harm the health, safety or morals of children."[69] Unlike the Minimum Age Convention, which does not aim at protecting young people over 15 and does not target informal and unpaid labor, the last two Conventions define a child as any person under 18, and relate also to unpaid work – that is, work done within the household or in the informal labor sector.

Although these three Conventions differ in scope, definitions, and economic and cultural sensitivities,[70] they are perceived by many as part of a

---

of children's wellbeing, but also in an attempt to prevent economic advantage to countries that allowed child labor within the growing global economy. See Trevor Buck, *International Child Law*, 3rd edn. (London: Routledge, 2014), at 241.

[67] Minimum Age Convention 1973, available at: www.ilo.org/dyn/normlex/en/f?p=NORML EXPUB:12100:0::NO::P12100_ILO_CODE:C138.

[68] Articles 31(1) & 32 of the Convention on the Rights of the Child 1989, available at: www .ohchr.org/en/professionalinterest/pages/crc.aspx.

[69] Articles 1 & 3 of the Worst Forms of Child Labour Convention 1999, available at: www .ilo.org/dyn/normlex/en/f?p=NORMLEXPUB:12100:0::NO:12100:P12100_ILO_ CODE:C182.

[70] For a detailed analysis of these Conventions, see Smolin, "Strategic Choices in the International Campaign against Child Labor"; Buck, *International Child Law*, at 242–57; R. A. Mavunga, "A Critical Assessment of the Minimum Age Convention 138 of 1973 and the Worst Forms of Child Labour Convention 182 of 1999," *Potchefstroom Electronic Law Journal*, 16(5) (2013), 121–68, available at: http://papers.ssrn.com/sol3/papers.cfm?abstract_id=2427729;

unified Western attempt to globally enforce Western and privileged perceptions of childhood on all the nations of the world, regardless of their poverty level and culture. This attempt includes media coverage, NGO campaigns, and transnational boycott threats,[71] all portraying child labor as an absolute evil that must be abolished, with no attention to differing circumstances and to the possible benefits of work for children.[72] These efforts are condemned by many as imperialist, ahistorical, patronizing, and demeaning.[73] Moreover, their opponents argue that the true motivation of industrialized countries in limiting child labor is to limit the economic competiveness of developing countries.[74] Finally, the wall-to-wall signing of the anti-child labor international conventions, according to their critics, is the outcome of diplomatic pressures and strategies rather than shared norms and interests in relation to working children.[75] Indeed, the debate between those who object to child participation in economic activities and those who support it is a powerful example of the ongoing existence and significance of economic and cultural borders, which resist what seem to be universally shared theories and norms, because these do not correspond with lived realities.[76]

Millions of children will continue to work in the foreseeable future, for two main reasons: poverty and cultural understandings of childhood.[77]

Noguchi, "20 Years of the Convention on the Rights of the Child and International Action against Child Labour."

[71] The famous example, often cited in the literature, is the Child Labor Deterrence Act proposed to the US Congress in 1992 by Senator Tom Harkin (the Harkin Bill). The Harkin Bill aimed to prohibit the importation of any manufactured or mined goods into the United States that were produced by children under the age of 15. Although the Harkin Bill was not passed, it led the exporting clothing manufacturing industries in Bangladesh to dismiss about 55,000 working children. A follow-up study by ILO-UNICEF found that none of these children had enrolled in school as a result, and that many had ended up working in less rewarding and safe workplaces. See Ben White, "Globalization and the Child Labor Problem," *Journal of International Development,* 8(6) (1996), 829–39.

[72] Michael Bourdillon, "Children and Work: A Review of Current Literature and Debates," *Development & Change,* 37(6) (2006), 1201–27; Smolin, "Strategic Choices in the International Campaign against Child Labor"; Sarada Balagopalan, "Memories of Tomorrow: Children, Labor, and the Panacea of Formal Schooling," *Journal of the History of Childhood and Youth,* 1(2) (2008), 267–85; Lorenza B. Fontana & Jean Grugel, "To Eradicate or to Legalize? Child Labor Debates and ILO Convention 182 in Bolivia," *Global Governance,* 21(1) (2015), 61–78.

[73] Bourdillon, "Children and Work"; Mayers, "The Right Rights?"

[74] Smolin, "Strategic Choices in the International Campaign against Child Labor," at 957.

[75] Tendai Charity Nhenga-Chakarisa, "Who Does the Law Seek to Protect and from What? The Application of International Law on Child Labour in an African Context," *African Human Rights Law Journal,* 10(1) (2010), 161–96, at 189–92.

[76] White, "Globalization and the Child Labor Problem."

[77] Bourdillon, "Children and Work."

With regard to poverty, the sad reality in many parts of the world is that children work to survive and to contribute to the survival of their family.[78] If these children's countries are too poor to provide a minimal standard of living – and in many cases they are – then withdrawing children from work is against their best interests,[79] unless the richer parts of the world are willing to feed them and their families. Not only is this not the case, as we saw from the statistics on foreign aid in the previous part of this chapter, but those who support child work argue that the rich countries are *contributing* to child poverty in the poor countries. Through the mechanisms of the global economy, they alter and weaken local markets and encourage cheap labor. These trends increase adult unemployment and increase child participation in the labor sector.[80] Finally, the anti-child-labor movement ignores the reality of many children left alone in the world due to catastrophes such as the AIDS epidemic and war. These children, who will be discussed also in the next part of this chapter in relation to intercountry adoption, must work to support themselves and often also their younger siblings.[81]

Interestingly, globalization is also responsible for a growing "subjective poverty," which, according to Ben White, an anthropologist specializing in child work in rural areas, pushes children to work even if they do not objectively need to in order to survive. Exposure to global media not only makes children in the poor countries aware of their relative poverty when compared to children in the privileged parts of the world, but also sells them the Western lifestyle as a desired ideal, making them want to earn money to buy products such as Coca-Cola, Nike sportswear, and mobile phones.[82]

Even if a minimal standard of living is provided by parents, community, or state, for many children, working, at least part-time, seems to serve their best interests as there are no better alternatives. In particular, if there are no schools, or they are far away or expensive, or they provide

---

[78] Nehaluddin Ahmad, "Child Labour: Ground Realities of Indian Labour Laws," *Commonwealth Law Bulletin*, 37(1) (2011), 61–74.

[79] Bourdillon, "Children and Work."

[80] Manfred Lieble, in Bourdillon, "Children and Work," at 1210.

[81] Bourdillon, "Children and Work," at 1206.

[82] White, "Globalization and the Child Labor Problem," at 830–1. For an ethnography of child work in mines in Congo that reveals the family dynamics over children's wishes to earn money independently (at times against their parents' will, and at times while refusing to share their earning with their family, so as to be independent consumers), see Géraldine André & Marie Godin, "Child Labour, Agency and Family Dynamics," *Childhood*, 21(2) (2014), 161–74.

poor quality or irrelevant education, then acquiring skills, experience, and connections in the labor force might be the best available option for the child.[83] Putting an age limit on employment channels these already underprivileged underage children toward the unofficial and less protected sector, prevents them from paying for school,[84] or punishes them indirectly by sending them into substandard educational institutions with little practical or other value. None of these scenarios serves their best interests.[85]

But poverty and lack of better options do not tell the whole story. The debate over child work is also embedded in competing perceptions of childhood.[86] In the Global North, as the canonical study of prominent sociologist Viviana Zelizer explores, a rapid revolution occurred in the late nineteenth century, in which children were transformed from wage-earners to the emotional raison-d'être of the nuclear family.[87] Ever since, in this part of the world, childhood has been perceived as a unique and separate life period. Children are no longer understood as small adults but as vulnerable, innocent, precious beings who should be protected and nurtured. According to this notion, children should be supported by their parents and kept far-removed from the labor market, so their childhood is completely dedicated to learning and leisure.[88] In this paradigm, parents who send their children to work are regarded, at best, as short-sighted as they fail to understand that it is in their children's long-term best interests to be educated,[89] and, at worst, as abusive parents who victimize their

---

[83] See, for example, Indian schools, established to keep children out of the labor force, while not providing true schooling and harming poor children by exposing them to the experience of failure and shame, see Balagopalan, "Memories of Tomorrow." See also Bourdillon, "Children and Work"; Smolin, "Strategic Choices in the International Campaign against Child Labor," at 960.

[84] For an ethnography of children mining gold in Ghana, revealing that many of them work to earn the money needed for their education, and manage to combine work and school, see Samuel Okyere, "Are Working Children's Rights and Child Labour Abolition Complementary or Opposing Realms?," *International Social Work*, 56(1) (2013), 80–91.

[85] Smolin, "Strategic Choices in the International Campaign against Child Labor," at 961; Mavunga, "A Critical Assessment," at 152–4; Fontana & Grugel, "To Eradicate or to Legalize?," at 70.

[86] Bahira Sherif Trask, *Globalization and Families: Accelerated , Systematic Social Change* (New York: Springer, 2010), Ch. 6.

[87] Viviana A. Zelizer, *Pricing the Priceless Child: The Changing Social Value of Children* (Princeton, NJ: Princeton University Press, 1994).

[88] Bourdillon, "Children and Work"; Balagopalan, "Memories of Tomorrow."

[89] Jessica Selby, "Ending Abusive and Exploitative Child Labour through International Law and Practical Action," *Australian International Law Journal*, 15 (2008), 165–80, at 175.

children and use them for their own self-interest.[90] A recent example of this antiparental suspicion is the response of UNICEF to the new amendments of the Indian law that governs child labor. In particular, UNICEF voiced its concern regarding the amendment that allows children to work to help the family or family enterprise, even though this is allowed only if the labor is not hazardous, and only after school hours and during vacations.[91] UNICEF strongly recommends that India remove this amendment, to "protect children from being exploited in invisible forms of work, from trafficking, and from boys and girls dropping out of school due to long hours of work."[92] India can indeed be criticized for not introducing any age limit to child work within the family, yet UNICEF's response is extremely problematic as it portrays all families assisted by their children as potential child traffickers and abusers, and offers an unrealistic overarching prohibition.

The more recent discourse on children's rights, that somewhat challenges the paternalistic perception of children,[93] nevertheless still does not impose duties on children nor expect them to become part of the demanding world of adults. Even according to the children's rights discourse, children are free of responsibilities except for attending school. Parents, on the other hand, are responsible "for the upbringing and development of the child," are demanded to consider their children's best interests as their basic concern,[94] and are expected to ensure that the childhood period of their offspring will be the "best years of life."[95]

In the Global South, however, childhood and adulthood are understood as part of a continuum, rather than as distinct and separated periods of life. According to this perception, while children should be supported and cared for, they should also be gradually integrated

---

[90] Kaushik Basu, "Child Labor: Cause, Consequence, and Cure, with Remarks on International Labor Standards," *Journal of Economic Literature*, 37(3) (1999), 1083–119, at 1084, 1095.

[91] Section 5 of The Child Labour (Prohibition and Regulation) Amendment Act No. 35 (2016), available at: http://bombayhighcourt.nic.in/libweb/actc/yearwise/2016/2016.35 .pdf.

[92] "UNICEF Concerned about Amendments to India's Child Labour Bill," UNICEF (July 26, 2016), available at: www.unicef.org/media/media_92021.html.

[93] Michael Freeman, "Article 3: The Best Interests of the Child" in André Alen, Johan Vande Lanotte, Eugeen Verhallen, Fiona Ang, Eva Berghmans, & Mieke Verheyde (Eds.), *A Commentary on the United Nations Convention on the Rights of the Child* (Leiden: Brill, 2007), pp. 1–74.

[94] Article 18 of the Convention on the Rights of the Child 1989.

[95] Nhenga-Chakarisa, "Who Does the Law Seek to Protect and from What?," at 174.

into the world of adults, in accordance with their developing competence. Work, both paid and unpaid, is part of this integration.[96] Work is also a manifestation of a collectivist perception of family and society, according to which kinship is granted extreme importance and each individual, whether young or grown up, is expected to contribute for the benefit of the group. From infancy, children must learn the familial reciprocal aid relationships, which include rights and duties and which demand the ability to live in harmony with others, work for collective goals, participate in social activities, and obey authority.[97] Hence, parents are granted discretion regarding the work their children need to do, as they have the best interests of their children in mind and are in the best position to judge the situation contextually.[98] In many cases, this perception is accompanied by a strict gender division, in which girls are expected to perform housework and care for younger siblings, and boys are expected to work in the fields or tend to the livestock.[99]

A manifestation of this perception can be found in the 1990 African Charter on the Rights and Welfare of the Child (ACRWC). This Convention, ratified by forty-one countries and signed by a further nine out of the fifty-four African countries, shares the CRC prohibition on exploitive and hazardous child labor, as well as on any work that is "likely... to interfere with the child's physical, mental, spiritual, moral, or social development."[100] At the same time, it states that in addition to rights and freedoms, children have duties toward their family, society, community, and state, and to the international community. Among these, a "child, subject to his age and ability," has "the duty: to work for the cohesion of the family, to respect his parents, superiors and elders at all times and to assist them in case of need;" and "to serve his national community by placing his physical and intellectual abilities at its service."[101]

---

[96] Bourdillon, "Children and Work."

[97] Nhenga-Chakarisa, "Who Does the Law Seek to Protect and from What?," at 169.

[98] Balagopalan, "Memories of Tomorrow," at 270.

[99] Nhenga-Chakarisa, "Who Does the Law Seek to Protect and from What?," at 170. This, and the difficulty in documenting work within the family, might explain the higher rates of males reflected in statistics of child labor. See Diallo, Etienne, & Mehran, "Global Child Labour Trends," at 4.

[100] Article 15(1) of the African Charter on the Rights and Welfare of the Child 1990, available at: www.achpr.org/instruments/child/.

[101] Ibid., Article 31.

Another example of the different perception of childhood and child work that can be found in the global South is the Bolivian Code for Children and Adolescents, enacted in 2014. Like the ACRWC, it includes a list of rights, as well as a list of duties children have, including the duty to take care of their life and health and to respect their parents. As for child work, like the aforementioned recent Indian law amendments, it aims to affirm Bolivia's opposition to the abolitionist stance of international law and to promote the rights of working children instead. It was drafted with the participation of working children's organizations, and it permits child work within the family with no age limit, whereas work for an employer is restricted to a starting age of 14 with limited exceptions. Furthermore, when the work is for an employer, the consent of the child is mandatory, in addition to the consent of one of the parents.[102]

I would argue that the Western neglect of children's duties, in general – and of their duty to work, in particular – might harm children in the long run in the Global North, as well as in the South. Children will eventually become adults, and sheltering them from adult realities means not preparing them well for the rest of their lives. Work, at home and in the paid labor force, is a significant and crucial part of adult life. Without developing this understanding, together with self-discipline, diligence, and awareness of the needs of others, children can grow up to be confused, lazy, spoiled, or narcissist adults, in shock at the demands imposed on them as adults. With no participation in housework or paid light work during childhood, they may find it hard to establish and maintain familial relations and employment as adults. There is already preliminary evidence that current "intensive-parenting," common in the Global North, which treats the child as the center of the family, in need of constant nurturing and shielding from the world of adults, is harmful in the long run. These overprotected children (known as the Millennials or Generation Y) delay adulthood into their 30s, continue to be dependent on their parents, and find it hard to relate to others' feelings and to perform with confidence and decisiveness.[103]

Even if confined to the discourse of children's rights, rather than children's duties, I believe child work should be recognized, allowed, and

---

[102] Manfred Liebel, "Protecting the Rights of Working Children Instead of Banning Child Labour: Bolivia Tries a New Legislative Approach," *The International Journal of Children's Rights*, 23(3) (2015), 529–47.

[103] Bernstein & Triger, "Over-Parenting," at 1275–77.

applauded, so long as it is not coerced, abusive, or harmful. Indeed, even in the developed countries, many children (including my 16-year-old daughter and 14-year-old son, who, for several years now, have worked diligently during school vacations in their father's business to earn their own money) work for reasons other than survival. Exact figures do not exist, but in 2007 it was estimated that, in the EU, 21 percent of the 17 million children aged 15–17, and an additional 3–3.5 million younger children, work for pay, profit, or family gain. These figures do not include children's chores within the household, but in general, children are expected to help at home.[104] As the anthropologist Olga Nieuwenhuys[105] and the legal scholars Karl Hanson and Arne Vandaele[106] argue, ignoring, devaluing, and prohibiting the work children do – in developing and developed countries, at home and in the paid sector – is to deny their agency, their contribution to the familial and social economy, and their legal rights, including their right to work and their right to participate. The perception of children as individual human beings and legal subjects, capable of voicing an opinion and taking action, does not correspond with the "denial of their capacity to legitimately act upon their environment by undertaking valuable work" that dominates the abolitionist stand against child work in which children are portrayed as dependent and passive.[107] As the Bolivian working children's organizations claim, the call for abolishing child work, regardless of competence and will, constitutes, in itself, age-based discrimination.[108]

Notwithstanding the two decades of deep controversy between those who call for the abolition of child labor and those who recognize children's right, need, and duty to work,[109] I perceive the discussion over working children as an opportunity for constructive dialogue in which

---

[104] Ricardo Rodríguez, Helmut Hägele, Herman Katteler, Gianni Paone, & Richard Pond, "Study on Child Labour and Protection of Young Workers in the European Union: Final Report," The European Commission (2007), available at: http://ec.europa.eu/social/BlobS ervlet?docId=4200&langId=en.

[105] Olga Nieuwenhuys, "The Paradox of Child Labor and Anthropology," *Annual Review of Anthropology*, 25(1) (1996), 237–51.

[106] Karl Hanson & Arne Vandaele, "Working Children and International Labour Law: A Critical Analysis," *The International Journal of Children's Rights*, 11(1) (2003), 73–146.

[107] Nieuwenhuys, "The Paradox of Child Labor," at 238.

[108] Fontana & Grugel, "To Eradicate or to Legalize?" at 70.

[109] Sharon Bessell, "Influencing International Child Labour Policy: The Potential and Limits of Children-Centered Research," *Children and Youth Services Review*, 33(4) (2011), 564–68, at 565.

different cultures learn from each other and develop a richer understanding of childhood. I believe there is a way to develop a broad consensus around child work that is "neither the embrace of an artificial and sterile universalism nor the acceptance of an ultimately self-defeating cultural relativism."[110] In Table 6.2, I present the basic arguments of both sides, and the third column points to the shared understandings that can already be traced in the theoretical discussions and international, regional, and national legal norms, as well as those that can – and in my opinion, should – be developed.

The current discourse on child labor, discussed in this part of the chapter and summarized in the two left-hand columns of Table 6.2, seems to center on imagined strict, clear dichotomies: Adult/Child; Work/Labor; North/South; Hazardous/Beneficial; Rights/Duties; Individualism/Collectivism; Family Work/Paid Work; Working/ Learning; Parental Authority/ Parental Abuse; Universalism/ Relativism. I hope that the right-hand column in Table 6.2 demonstrates the potentially constructive challenge to these dogmatic dichotomies if a pluralist and contextual continuum approach can be developed and adopted. Such an approach suggests that we should view children as individuals embedded in relationships, whose best interests are unavoidably and rightly interwoven with those of their caregivers, communities, and societies;[111] childhood as a unique period of life that should be dedicated to learning and developing, including by working; children as full-time workers in need of survival as a failure on the part of global, national, community, or familial forces; and the protection of the rights of children as working subjects, when they need or want to work, as the proper mission of child-centered national and international labor law.

We now turn to the third and last option discussed in this chapter as a possible answer to the need to feed children on our hungry planet. Much like the issue of child labor, intercountry adoption is highly contested, attracting dogmatic and conflicting perceptions, often detached from diverse national, communal, and familial context and from children's actual needs.

---

[110] Philip Alston, as cited in Mayers, "The Right Rights?" at 43.

[111] Barbara Bennett Woodhouse, "A World Fit for Children Is a World Fit for Everyone: Ecogenerism, Feminism, and Vulnerability," *Houston Law Review*, 46 (2009), 818–65.

Table 6.2. *Child Work: Thesis, Anti-Thesis, Synthesis*

Thesis: Anti-Child Work[a]	Anti-Thesis: Pro-Child Work[b]	Synthesis: Actual and Possible Shared Understandings
Work is harmful to children.	Work is beneficial to children.	1 – Children should not be exposed to exploitive, hazardous, or illegal labor, paid or unpaid, within the family or outside the family.[c] 2 – Full-time child work has long-term negative developmental and economic effects on the child and his/her society.[d] 3 – Work can be beneficial to any child, regardless of economic need, because, when appropriate to age and competence, it can stimulate physical, cognitive, economic, and social development.[e] 4 – Work within the family can be performed at a younger age than work for an external employer, because it is part of familial and cultural socialization and is more protective.[f]
Children should attend school regularly.	There are circumstances in which work serves children's interests better than school.	1 – Working has a learning value.[g] 2 – Children have a right to education, and their working should not infringe this right.[h] 3 – The right to education is fulfilled by schooling only if the schools are accessible and the education level is adequate.[i] 4 – Children can go to school *and* work (flexible schooling and part-time work).[j]
Children do not have a duty to work. They are bearers of individual rights, with no legal obligations.	Children have a duty to work. They are part of the collective and must contribute as they can.	1 – Children are individuals whose lives are embedded in relations with others. In particular, children's best interests and wellbeing cannot be separated from the wellbeing of their families and cultural group. Cultures that expect children to work are legitimate, as long as the basic rights of the child are protected and her chances of fulfilling her potential are promoted.[k] 2 – Children should take part in shaping their culture, including in relation to child work, as part of their right of participation.[l]

| No child, no matter the circumstances, should work. | Poor children must work. | 1 – International, national, community, and familial efforts should be made so children do not have to work for survival.[m] |
| | | 2 – As much as possible, child work should not interfere with children's schooling, to increase the chances that the poverty cycle will be broken in the long run.[n] |

[a] For prominent examples of this stand, see Noguchi, "20 years of the Convention on the Rights of the Child and International Action against Child Labour"; Selby, "Ending Abusive and Exploitative Child Labour through International Law and Practical Action."

[b] For prominent examples of this stand, see Nhenga-Chakarisa, "Who Does the Law Seek to Protect and from What?"

[c] White, "Globalization and the Child Labor Problem"; Smolin, "Strategic Choices in the International Campaign against Child Labor," at 961–5. It is important to emphasize that what constitutes exploitative or hazardous work is debatable (see Fontana & Grugel, "To Eradicate or to Legalize?" at 74) and that there are insufficient data on the actual risks of different kinds and circumstances of child labor, see Nhenga-Chakarisa, "Who Does the Law Seek to Protect and from What?".

[d] Elena Samonova, "Socioeconomic Impacts of Child Labour," *Journal of Education, Psychology and Social Sciences*, 2(1) (2014), 50–4.

[e] Nhenga-Chakarisa, "Who Does the Law Seek to Protect and from What?," at 180.

[f] As mentioned earlier, UNICEF takes an opposite stand that regards work within the family as highly suspect. Even those who, like me, support child work within the family, must be aware that such work can disproportionally harm girls. See White, "Globalization and the Child Labor Problem." Hence, child work within the household should be governed by the rule of respect to the right to education, like any other kind of work. See also Smolin, "Strategic Choices in the International Campaign against Child Labor," at 965–7.

[g] Nhenga-Chakarisa, "Who Does the Law Seek to Protect and from What?," at 186.

[h] Smolin, "Strategic Choices in the International Campaign against Child Labor," at 977.

[i] Balagopalan, "Memories of Tomorrow."

[j] Bourdillon, "Children and Work."

[k] Hanson & Vandaele, "Working Children and International Labour Law."

[l] Ibid., at 80.

[m] Faraaz Siddiqi & Harry Anthony Patrinos, "Child Labor: Issues, Causes and Interventions," Human Capital Development and Operations Policy, Working Paper No. 56 (1995).

[n] Ibid., at 9.

Intercountry Adoption

One of the world's most famous ex-couples, the Hollywood actors Angelina Jolie and Brad Pitt, are also famous for their intercountry adoptions. Of their six children, three are adopted from overseas. In 2002, Jolie adopted her first child, a seven-month-old baby boy, from an orphanage in Cambodia. Although the US Government suspected, at the time, that adoptions from Cambodia amounted to child trafficking (Jolie's adoption facilitator was later convicted of visa fraud and money laundering in relation to other cases),[112] the adoption was approved. Three years later, Jolie adopted a six-month-old baby girl from an orphanage in Ethiopia. The baby was initially believed to be an orphan as a result of her birth mother dying of AIDS – but the mother later came forward in the media and said she was happy the poor baby girl she had abandoned had been adopted by Jolie. Pitt was formally recognized as the co-adoptive father of Jolie's two adopted children soon after becoming her spouse in 2006, the year they also became parents of their first biological child. A year later, Jolie adopted a three-year-old boy from an orphanage in Vietnam. She applied for adoption as a single parent, because Vietnam's adoption regulations do not allow unmarried couples to co-adopt. After their return to the United States, Pitt co-adopted the boy.[113] In 2008, Jolie and Pitt became the biological parents of twins, and rumors just before the couple seperated suggested they had plans to adopt another child from Syria[114] or Cambodia.[115]

At first glance, it may seem that intercountry adoption is an answer to the pressing needs of many of the millions of hungry, abandoned, or orphaned children in poorer parts of the world.[116] Indeed, during 2000–2010 at least 410,000 children were internationally adopted. However, the

[112] "Adoption Scammer Gets 18 Months in Jail," ABC News (November 19, 2004), available at: http://abcnews.go.com/WNT/story?id=267559.

[113] See Wikipedia, *Angelina Jolie: Children*, https://en.wikipedia.org/wiki/Angelina_Jolie#Children (as of April 24, 2016).

[114] Chelsea Peng, "Angelina Jolie and Brad Pitt Are Reportedly in the Process of Adopting another Child," *Marie Claire* (September 22, 2015), available at: www.marieclaire.com/celebrity/news/a13283/angelina-jolie-and-brad-pitt-adopt-child/.

[115] Rachael Moon, "Angelina Jolie and Brad Pitt 'have adopted Cambodian baby boy from slums," *Mirror* (January 12, 2016), available at: www.mirror.co.uk/3am/celebrity-news/angelina-jolie-brad-pitt-have-7165395.

[116] According to UNICEF, in 2005 there were 13 million children who had lost both their parents. Most of them lived with their extended family. See "Orphans," UNICEF, available at: www.unicef.org/media/media_45279.html. There are no official statistics on the number of children living in institutions, with the estimations ranging from 2 to 8 million. The vast majority of these children are not orphans, but were abandoned by their parents due

two major sending countries during this period were China and Russia – by no means the poorest countries in the world. As will be detailed here, most adopted children from these two countries were "social orphans" deserted or neglected by their (very much alive) biological parents. During the same period, Ethiopia was the only African country sending a significant number of children for intercountry adoption, although Africa is the continent with the highest rate of hungry children[117] and the highest number of orphans.[118] Hence, intercountry adoption is not the simple story of adoptive parents from developed countries rescuing starving children whose parents died due to war, disease, or hunger in developing ones, as some portray it.[119] Moreover, the dramatic decline of intercountry adoption in recent years demonstrates the ongoing controversies over this practice and the growing reservations among both sending and receiving countries.[120] The United States, for example, which is the leading receiving country, with more than 20,000 adoptees per year at the beginning of the third millennium,[121] received just 5,648 adopted children in 2015.[122] Of this total, 2,354 were adopted from China, a country that sent more than three times this number to the United States just a decade earlier.[123]

to poverty, disability, or gender (mainly in the Global South), or were taken away from abusive parents (mainly in the Global North). See *Lumos, Children in Institutions: The Global Picture* (2015), available at: http://wearelumos.org/sites/default/files/1.Global%20 Numbers_2_0.pdf.

[117] "Hunger Map," World Food Programme, available at: http://documents.wfp.org/stellent/ groups/public/documents/communications/wfp275057.pdf. Africa is the only continent in which the number of stunted children is rising, see UNICEF, *Levels and Trends in Child Malnutrition* (2015).

[118] UNICEF, *Africa's Orphaned Generations* (2003), available at: www.unicef.org/sowc06/ pdfs/africas_orphans.pdf.

[119] See, for example, Simon and Alstein's claim that intercountry adoption has evolved into "a story of global relations, where non-White, free-for-adoption Third World children are adopted by White families living in the West," quoted in Indigo Willing, Patricia Fronek, & Denise Cuthbert, "Review of Sociological Literature on Intercountry Adoption," *Social Policy and Society*, 11(3) (2012), 465–79, at 467.

[120] Robert L. Ballard, "Introduction" in Robert L. Ballard, Naomi H. Goodno, Robert F. Cochran, & Jay A. Milbrandt (Eds.), *The Intercountry Adoption Debate* (NewCastle upon Tyne, UK: Cambridge Scholars Publishing, 2015), pp. 1–4, at 1.

[121] Peter Selman, "Global Statistics for Intercountry Adoption: Receiving States and States of Origin 2003–2013" (2015), available at: https://assets.hcch.net/docs/3bead31e-6234-44ae-9f4e-2352b190ca21.pdf.

[122] Bureau of Consular Affairs at the U.S. Department of State, *FY 2015 Annual Report on Intercountry Adoption* (2016), available at: https://travel.state.gov/content/dam/aa/pdfs/ 2015Annual_Intercountry_Adoption_Report.pdf.

[123] "Statistics," Bureau of Consular Affairs at the U.S. Department of State, available at: https:// travel.state.gov/content/adoptionsabroad/en/about-us/statistics.html.

Although much of the literature on intercountry adoption presents its global trends, noting a peak of more than 45,000 adoptions in 2004 and a constant and sharp decline ever since,[124] and treats it as a global phenomenon that should be discussed in universal terms of rights and wrongs,[125] I find it to be primarily a national, bordered – and bordering – phenomenon that calls for highly contextual normative deliberation. Hence, in what follows, I will center on four significant adoptee-sending countries (China, Russia, Guatemala, and Ethiopia) to demonstrate my argument of the importance of borders and contextualization in the understanding and regulating of intercountry adoption. These case studies reveal the limited role played by the international legal mechanism developed to regulate intercountry adoption – namely, the 1993 Hague Convention on Protection of Children and Co-operation in Respect of Intercountry Adoption (HCIA).[126] National law, national diplomatic interests, local cultural familial perceptions, and local norms regarding adoption, gender, and disability within the sending countries, play no less a significant a role in shaping the recent rise and fall of intercountry adoption than international regulation.[127]

China started to unofficially allow intercountry adoption during the 1980s, and in 1992 passed a special law to legalize this option. For almost two decades it was the leading sending country, with over 133,000 children sent for adoption to other countries in 1998–2013.[128] This legitimization and legalization of intercountry adoption

---

[124] Selman, "Global Statistics for Intercountry Adoption: Receiving States and States of Origin 2003–2013."

[125] For example, Elizabeth Bartholet, "International Adoption: The Child's Story," *Georgia State University Law Review*, 24(2) (2007), 333–79.

[126] See also Marijka Breuning, "Samaritans, Family Builders, and the Politics of Intercountry Adoption," *International Studies Perspectives*, 14(4) (2013), 417–35. For a legal analysis of this Convention, and other relevant conventions, see Kerry O'Halloran, *The Politics of Adoption: International Perspectives on Law, Policy and Practice*, 3rd edn. (Dordrecht: Springer, 2015), Ch. 5.

[127] Alexandra Young acknowledges the heterogeneity of intercountry adoption that poses a challenge to any "global" discussion of the practice. Nevertheless, she offers a fascinating temporal typology of the development of intercountry adoption from 1945 to the present. See Alexandra Young, "Developments in Intercountry Adoption: From Humanitarian Aid to Market-Driven Policy and beyond," *Adoption & Fostering*, 36(2) (2012), 67–78.

[128] Peter Selman, "Global Trends in Intercountry Adoption: 2001–2010," National Council For Adoption (2012), available at: www.adoptioncouncil.org/images/stories/documents/NCFA_ADOPTION_ADVOCATE_NO44.pdf; Selman, "Global Statistics for Intercountry Adoption: Receiving States and States of Origin 2003–2013."

is attributed to China's enforcement of the one-child policy (modified to a two-children policy only recently)[129] and to the cultural preference for a male child, which led to the abandonment of many baby girls. These abandoned babies had little chance of being adopted internally because Chinese law allowed internal adoption only by childless parents over 35, to prevent it from becoming a loophole to overcome the one-child policy.[130] The Chinese government was also motivated to prefer intercountry over domestic adoptions because of the foreign funds involved, as foreign adoptive parents were obliged to pay $3,000 to the orphanage, which assisted the government in maintaining the orphanage system.[131] This mandatory payment also led to child trafficking, with hundreds of babies being kidnapped or bought with the involvement of orphanage personnel.[132]

China signed the HCIA only in 2000, and ratified it in 2005. The first year after ratification was also the year that the decline in intercountry adoption from China started. This case study and others, suggest that this Convention had a chilling effect and that the new international regulation, aimed at ensuring coordinated and safe adoption for children with no adequate alternatives, turned out to be a deterring device, for both sending and receiving countries.[133] But it seems that the downward trend in the case of China has much to do with internal changes, and that those might be of even more significance than the international convention. Legal scholar David Smolin suggests that the relaxation of the one-child policy, as well as increasing individual incomes, increasing domestic adoptions, a shortage in girls produced by the many years of an imbalanced sex ratio, and the availability of sex-selection abortions, all led to a decline in the availability of baby girls for intercountry adoption. Indeed, not only did the numbers of intercountry adoptions from China dropped, but the characteristics of adoptees also changed, with more of them being older

---

[129] Tom Phillips, "China Ends One-Child Policy after 35 Years," *The Guardian* (October 29, 2015), available at: www.theguardian.com/world/2015/oct/29/china-abandons-one-child-policy.

[130] Kay Johnson, "Politics of International and Domestic Adoption in China," *Law & Society Review*, 36(2) (2002), 379–96.

[131] Ibid.

[132] Patricia J. Meier & Xiaole Zhang, "Sold into Adoption: The Hunan Baby Trafficking Scandal Exposes Vulnerabilities in Chinese Adoptions to the United States," *Cumberland Law Review*, 39(1) (2008), 87–130.

[133] Elizabeth Bartholet, "The Hague Convention: Pros, Cons and Potential" in Ballard, Goodno, Cochran, & Milbrandt (Eds.), *The Intercountry Adoption Debate: Dialogues across Disciplines*, pp. 239–44.

male children and children of both sexes with disabilities.[134] Moreover, internal legislation, introduced soon after the ratification of the HCIA, changed the authorized profile of adopting parents from abroad, allowing only married heterosexual couples to adopt, with limited exceptions for single women who may adopt children with special needs.[135]

Russia provides another fascinating example of the interrelations between globalization and borders that shape intercountry adoption in a unique way in different countries. Although Russia also signed the HCIA in 2000, it never ratified it, despite the fact that during the first decade of this millennium it was the second sending country after China, with more than 56,000 children adopted overseas in 2003–2013.[136] This is explained by the relatively high number and percentage of "social orphans" in Russia, who, as in China, are children who are not cared for by their parents although they have at least one living biological parent. In 2009, for example, there were over 700,000 such children in Russia (2.79 percent of the total child population). However, the Russian social orphanhood phenomenon is very different from that produced by the Chinese one-child policy, and is the outcome of poverty, widespread alcoholism, the absence of a supportive parental welfare system, the abandonment of disabled children, the absence of a foster-care system, and the rarity of local adoption.[137]

Like most other sending countries, Russia witnessed a recent sharp decline, from a peak of 9,453 children in 2004 to just 1,834 in 2013. This is despite the fact that about 128,000 children still occupy Russian orphanages[138] and that many of these children suffer from neglect and abuse within these underbudgeted institutions.[139] The political drama behind this story of decline is reflected in the following figures: 5,865 Russian

---

[134] David M. Smolin, "Child Laundering and the Hague Convention on Intercountry Adoption: The Future and Past of Intercountry Adoption," *University of Louisville Law Review*, 48(3) (2010), 441–98, at 464–66, 471–3.

[135] Peter Selman, "Intercountry Adoption of Children from Asia in the Twenty-First Century," *Children's Geographies*, 13(3) (2015), 312–27, at 318.

[136] Selman, "Global Statistics for Intercountry Adoption: Receiving States and States of Origin 2003–2013."

[137] Anna Jane High, "Pondering the Politicization of Intercountry Adoption: Russia's Ban on American 'Forever Families'," *Cardozo Journal of International & Comparative Law*, 22(3) (2014), 497–560, at 518–520.

[138] Cynthia Hawkins DeBose & Ekaterina DeAngelo, "The New Cold War: Russia's Ban on Adoptions by U.S. Citizens," *Journal of the American Academy of Matrimonial Lawyers*, 28(1) (2015), 51–77, at 52.

[139] Ibid., at 68.

children were adopted by US citizens in 2004,[140] yet in 2015 not a single child made the adoption journey from Russia to the United States.[141] These figures are the outcome of a Russian law passed in December 2012 that prohibits Americans from adopting Russian children. This law is known colloquially by two different names, revealing two alternative explanations to this radical legislative act. The first is the Dima Yakovlev Bill – named after a little boy who tragically died of hypothermia three months after arriving in the United States from Russia, due to the negligence of his adoptive father who unintentionally left him in the car. The swift acquittal of the father of involuntary manslaughter received much attention in Russia and harsh criticism by the Russian Ministry of Foreign Affairs.[142] The case of Dima Yakovlev, which happened in 2008, was one of nineteen documented cases of Russian children who died due to abuse or neglect after being adopted by Americans.[143] In addition to these deaths, there was a relatively large number of failed adoptions, with Russian adoptees – more than children adopted by US citizens from other countries – being hospitalized, re-adopted, or sent to foster care or an institution.[144] Although some of these failures were the outcome of neglect or abuse at the hands of the adoptive parents and the inadequacy of the American adoptive parental screening system, they were also the result of incomplete disclosure of the special needs of the adoptees, and lack of training and support to the adoptive parents to help them fully cope with these needs.[145] Indeed, there was a relatively high risk that children from Russia might have special needs because these might have been the reason they were abandoned by their biological parents in the first place, or because of their institutionalization period within deficient Russian orphanages.[146] The ban on American adoption led to hundreds of adoption procedures

---

[140] Selman, "Global Trends in Intercountry Adoption: 2001–2010"; Selman, "Global Statistics for Intercountry Adoption: Receiving States and States of Origin 2003–2013."

[141] Bureau of Consular Affairs at the U.S. Department of State, *FY 2015 Annual Report on Intercountry Adoption* (2016).

[142] High, "Pondering the Politicization of Intercountry Adoption," at 499–502.

[143] Christina Champenois, "Does the Russian Adoption Ban Violate International Law?," *Brigham Young University International Law & Management Review*, 11(2) (2015) 29–54, at 40.

[144] High, "Pondering the Politicization of Intercountry Adoption," at 523.

[145] Ibid., at 527.

[146] Russian adoptees are relatively old compared to adoptees from other countries. For example, between 1993 and 2005, 52 percent of Russian adoptees to the United States were between one and four years old, and 21 percent were five years and older, see High, "Pondering the Politicization of Intercountry Adoption," at 515.

being halted, including those of children with special needs whose chance to be adopted locally were extremely low, and who, in extreme cases, could die for lack of appropriate treatment.[147]

Yet, because the case of Dima Yakovlev took place four years before the law banning intercountry adoptions by US citizens was enacted, it is very hard to believe the ban was motivated first and foremost by the wish to protect Russian children from abusive American adoptive parents.[148] After all, this ban resulted in harm being done to many abandoned and orphaned Russian children, and a special bilateral agreement between Russia and the United States on cooperation in relation to intercountry adoption was even signed just two months before the blanket ban. Indeed, the second name given to the Russian law that bans adoptions by US citizens – the 'anti-Magnitsky law' – suggests a very different motive: political retaliation.[149] Sergei Leonidovich Magnitsky was imprisoned in a Moscow jail, without trial, for almost a year, after exposing a tax fraud among Russian officials. He died in prison in November 2009. Although international and national investigations, which took several years, concluded that Magnitsky had suffered under prison conditions that amounted to a breach of the right to life, no one was convicted of his death.[150] In November 2012, the United States adopted the Sergei Magnitsky Rule of Law Accountability Act, which allows Russian human rights violators to be denied visas to enter the United States, and any of their assets in the United States to be frozen.[151] A month after the passing of this Act, the Russian Parliament and President approved the law banning adoption to the United States, which many interpret as a form of retaliation for the Magnitsky Act.[152] As legal scholar Christina Champenois shows, this retaliation was also an opportunity to recover Russian national pride, harmed by its failure to take care of its own children – a failure characterizing the poorest countries in the world rather than strong, developed nations such as Russia. This motivation is clear in the response to the ban of the Russian Children's Ombudsman, Pavel Astakhov, who said that "it is shameful to export children," that "we as a State and society are ready to take care of our children and help our families," and that "Russia, same as any loving mother, wants to bring up its

---

[147] Champenois, "Does the Russian Adoption Ban Violate International Law?"
[148] See also ibid., at 39–41.
[149] High, "Pondering the Politicization of Intercountry Adoption."
[150] Champenois, "Does the Russian Adoption Ban Violate International Law?" at 37.
[151] Ibid., at 34.
[152] Ibid., at 37–8.

children."[153] The concern, voiced by several scholars, is that Russia is in fact unable, at least in the short term, to properly care for the thousands of the children it holds in institutions, and that the ban on US adoptions condemns many of these children to a miserable childhood and long-term difficulties.[154]

The third example I wish to present of the importance of contextualizing intercountry adoption, is the case of Guatemala. This is one of the poorest countries in Latin America, with high levels of poverty, malnutrition, and child mortality.[155] In 2003–2008, Guatemala was a major sending country, only after China and Russia in numbers, despite being much smaller than these two giants.[156] At its peak, the almost unbelievable figure was that one out of one-hundred Guatemalan children was sent for intercountry adoption to the United States.[157] Indeed, whereas other Latin American countries limited intercountry adoption after realizing the difficulties associated with preventing related ills such as child abduction, profiteering, and corruption, Guatemala allowed it – despite suffering from these problems.[158] Likewise, the United States was one of the only countries permitting intercountry adoption form Guatemala, whereas other countries refused to allow in Guatemalan children as adoptees due to severe allegations of child trafficking. An intercountry adoption industry evolved between Guatemala and the United States, with an average of $30,000 paid per child by American adoptive parents and most of the money going to American agencies and Guatemalan lawyers, which, in some cases, cooperated with criminals who stole and sold babies.[159]

In 2000, a UN Special Rapporteur published a harsh report on the illegal conducts accompanying international adoption from Guatemala.[160] In 2002, Guatemala joined the HCIA by ascension, which was later

---

[153] See ibid., at 42.

[154] Ibid.; High, "Pondering the Politicization of Intercountry Adoption"; DeBose & DeAngelo, "The New Cold War."

[155] David M. Smolin, "Child Laundering: How the Intercountry Adoption System Legitimizes and Incentivizes the Practices of Buying, Trafficking, Kidnapping, and Stealing Children," *Wayne Law Review,* 52(1) (2006), 113–200, at 164.

[156] Selman, "Global Statistics for Intercountry Adoption: Receiving States and States of Origin 2003–2013."

[157] Smolin, "Child Laundering and the Hague Convention on Intercountry Adoption," at 468.

[158] Smolin, "Child Laundering: How the Intercountry Adoption System Legitimizes and Incentivizes the Practices of Buying, Trafficking, Kidnapping, and Stealing Children," at 163.

[159] Ibid., at 164–5.

[160] Ibid., at 165–7.

overruled by its Supreme Court as an unconstitutional procedure. Although the Guatemalan government did not consider itself to be bound by the Convention after the Supreme Court's decision,[161] the United States did consider the Guatemalan ratification valid, and after ratifying the Convention itself in 2007, it could no longer receive children from Guatemala without a drastic reform to bring it within the conditions of the HCIA.[162] As Guatemala failed to introduce such a reform, a sharp decline occurred in 2009, with very few Guatemalan children being adopted overseas ever since.[163]

The last case study I wish to present is that of Ethiopia (the second sending country since 2009, after China), which sends children of different ages to a variety of countries.[164] Paradoxically, because Ethiopia has not signed the HCIA, receiving countries that have ratified it, including the United States, Spain, France, and Belgium, which receive the highest numbers of Ethiopian adoptees,[165] can do so, even if Ethiopia does not comply with the Convention's conditions. In fact, it has a negative incentive to ratify the Convention, as intercountry adoption is the main funding source of its child welfare system. It demands "AIDS Relief & Humanitarian Services' Fees" from intercountry adoption agencies, amounting, for example, to $14 million in 2010.[166] However, in 2011 Ethiopia did acknowledge its inability to control the rapid growth in intercountry adoption, and decided to reduce the numbers of adoptees to prevent fraud and corruption in the adoption process.[167] Indeed, the numbers for 2013 were less than half of those for 2010: 4,368 and 2,005,

---

[161] Ibid., at 167.

[162] Smolin, "Child Laundering and the Hague Convention on Intercountry Adoption," at 477–80.

[163] For example, in 2013, only twenty-six children were adopted internationally from Guatemala. See Selman, "Global Statistics for Intercountry Adoption: Receiving States and States of Origin 2003–2013."

[164] Ibid. In 2015, for example, 335 Ethiopian children were adopted by Americans, with more than half of them three years old or older, of which 83 were between five and twelve years old. See "Statistics," Bureau of Consular Affairs at the U.S. Department of State.

[165] Selman, "Global Trends in Intercountry Adoption: 2001–2010."

[166] Kristen Cheney, "'Giving Children a Better Life?' Reconsidering Social Reproduction, Humanitarianism and Development in Intercountry Adoption," European Journal of Development Research, 26(2) (2014), 247–63, at 259.

[167] Peter Selman, "The Global Decline of Intercountry Adoption: What Lies Ahead?" Social Policy & Society, 11(3) (2012), 381–97, at 388; "Ethiopia to Cut Foreign Adoptions by Up to 90 Percent," Voice of America (March 3, 2011), available at: www.voanews.com/content/article–ethiopia–to–cut–foreign–adoptions–by–up–to–90–percent–117411843/157582.html.

respectively.[168] This step brings Ethiopia closer to the norm of preferring local solutions to orphaned and abandoned children, manifested in both the CRC and the ACRWC, both of which it ratified in 1999. Unlike the HCIA, which allows intercountry adoption if the sending country finds that it is in the best interests of the child after considering "possibilities for placement of the child within the State of origin,"[169] the CRC and the ACRWC allow intercountry adoption only as an "alternative means" (the CRC) or as "a last resort" (the ACRWC), and only "if the child cannot be placed in a foster or adoptive family or cannot in any suitable manner be cared for in the child's country of origin,"[170] which can be understood as including adequate institutional care.[171]

Although the four case studies detailed here demonstrate the diversity of circumstances, motivations, and dynamics of intercountry adoption – dependent, first and foremost, on the specific circumstances of the particular sending country and its relations with other countries and with the international community – most participants in the normative debate over the desirability of intercountry adoption tend to generalize and homogenize it, as if it were a unified phenomenon that can be discussed and regulated on the basis of abstract notions such as the best interests of the child and the right to identity, and on interests and characteristics of *generic* sending and receiving countries. I offer a summary of these controversies in Table 6.3.

Although at the extremes we can find those who argue that any child who is not raised by her/his birth parents should be considered for intercountry adoption,[172] and those who argue that international adoption should never be considered,[173] several scholars have offered different suggestions to mitigate between the benefits and risks of this option. Some

---

[168] Selman, "Global Statistics for Intercountry Adoption: Receiving States and States of Origin 2003–2013."

[169] Article 4 of the Hague Convention on Protection of Children and Co-operation in Respect of Intercountry Adoption 1993, available at: www.hcch.net/en/instruments/conventions/full-text/?cid=69.

[170] Article 21(b) of the Convention on the Rights of the Child 1989; Article 24 of the African Charter on the Rights and Welfare of the Child 1990.

[171] Benyan Dawit Mezmur, "Acting Like a Rich Bully: Madonna, Mercy, Malawi, and International Children's Rights Law in Adoption," *International Journal of Children's Rights*, 20(1) (2012), 24–56, at 37.

[172] Bartholet, "International Adoption: The Child's Story"; Elizabeth Bartholet, "International Adoption: A Way Forward," *New York Law School Law Review*, 55 (2010/2011), 687–99.

[173] Romania is an example of a country that passed a law that prohibits intercountry adoption, but by the relatives of a child, after being a major sending country during the 1990s and in response to allegations of child trafficking, See Neagu, "Children by Request."

Table 6.3. *Support of, and Opposition to, Intercountry Adoption*

Issue	Support of Intercountry Adoption	Opposition to Intercountry Adoption
The best interests of the child	1. International adoption serves the interests of children better than homelessness and orphanages.[a] 2. Studies show that the vast majority of intercountry adoptees are doing well.[c] 3. The best interests of the child can be defined and should be the paramount consideration.[e]	1. Children's best interests are better served, in the vast majority of cases, within their own country.[b] 2. There are cases of abuse, neglect, and pedophilia perpetrated by intercountry adoptive parents.[d] 3. The best interests of the child is a vague and contested concept that should be deliberated together with the rights and interests of the biological parents.[f]
Child trafficking	Regulated international adoption diminishes child trafficking caused by the 'black market'.[g]	1. Intercountry adoption leads to children being taken away from their birth parents without the latter's voluntary consent,[h] and to children being stolen and sold.[i] 2. Some poor parents place their children in institutions, with the intention of maintaining family ties. Sending these children for intercountry adoption is child trafficking.[j]
Identity	1. The child's right to identity is less important than other basic human rights of which adoptable children are deprived.[k] 2. Identity can be preserved following an intercountry adoption.[m] 3. Studies show that interracial adoptees are well-adapted.[o]	1. The child's right to identity is very important.[l] 2. Identity cannot be preserved after intercountry adoption.[n] 3. Interracial adoptions place the children at risk within intolerant receiving societies.[p]
Political considerations	Children are not 'owned' by their country or group of origin and so any group-based argument is illegitimate.[q]	Intercountry adoption is contaminated by imperial abuse of developing countries and nationalist abuse of ethnic minority groups.[r]
Local arrangements	1. In some countries, local adoption rates are low and cannot supplement intercountry adoption.[s] 2. There is empirical evidence suggesting that orphaned children are discriminated-against in extended family settings.[u] 3. Intercountry adoption is increasingly serving disabled, sick, and older children, unattractive to local adopters and at harm in institutionalized settings.[w]	1. Local adoptions should be preferred over intercountry adoptions.[t] 2. Care via extended family members, foster care, or institutionalization (but not to the detriment of parental and familial ties), are adequate care options.[v] 3. The intercountry adoption of disabled, sick, and older children would not happen if restrictions on intercountry adoption that limit intercountry adopters' access to babies were relaxed.[x]

Economic considerations	Intercountry adoption saves sending countries the high costs of orphanages.[y]	1. The investment that would have allowed the child's biological family to stay intact, or paid for the care of the child within the community of origin, is lower than the sums spent on the child's adoption.[z] 2. Cost-saving considerations are illegitimate as a justification for a child's international adoption.[aa]
International regulation	1. The HCIA's narrow interpretation prevents the intercountry adoption of children who need it.[bb] 2. The HCIA can be implemented to ensure safe and legal intercountry adoption.[dd] 3. The HCIA is ratified by 96 of the world's countries and so represents a broad consensus.[ff]	1. The HCIA fails to protect children from trafficking.[cc] 2. Weak countries do not have the resources to enforce international intercountry adoption norms.[ee] 3. The HCIA centers on Western notions of what constitutes familial care, and is biased against familial arrangements common in non-Western societies.[gg]

(continued)

[a] Bartholet, "International Adoption: The Child's Story"; Rebecca Worthington, "The Road to Parentless Children Is Paved with Good Intentions: How the Hague Convention and Recent Intercountry Adoption Rules are Affecting Potential Parents and the Best Interests of Children," *Duke Journal of Comparative & International Law*, 19(3) (2009), 559–86, at 569–71; High, "Pondering the Politicization of Intercountry Adoption," at 554.

[b] Richard Carlson, "Seeking the Better Interests of Children with a New International Law of Adoption," *New York Law School Law Review*, 55(3) (2011), 733–79.

[c] Jesús Palacios, "Crisis in Intercountry Adoption, Crisis in Adoptive Families," *Family Science*, 6(1) (2015), 43–9, at 45–6.

[d] David M. Smolin, "Child Laundering as Exploitation: Applying Anti-Trafficking Norms to Intercountry Adoption under the Coming Hague Regime," *Vermont Law Review*, 32 (2007), 1–55.

[e] Bartholet, "International Adoption: The Child's Story."

[f] Claudia Fonseca, "Transnational Influences in the Social Production of Adoptable Children: The Case of Brazil," *The International Journal of Sociology and Social Policy*, 26(3/4) (2006), 154–71.

[g] Worthington, "The Road to Parentless Children Is Paved with Good Intentions," at 562–3.

[h] Veronica S. Root, "Angelina and Madonna: Why All the Fuss? An Exploration of the Rights of the Child and Intercountry Adoption within African Nations," *Chicago Journal of International Law*, 8(1) (2007), 323–54, at 343.

[i] Smolin, "Child Laundering and the Hague Convention on Intercountry Adoption."

[j] Mahsa Farid, "International Adoption: The Economics of the Baby Industry," *Whittier Journal of Child and Family Advocacy*, 12(1) (2012), 81–103, at 90.

[k] Worthington, "The Road to Parentless Children Is Paved with Good Intentions," at 564.

[l] Root, "Angelina and Madonna," at 345.

[m] For relevant empirical review, see Selman, "Intercountry Adoption of Children from Asia in the Twenty-First Century," at 321.

[n] Root, "Angelina and Madonna," at 345.

Table 6.3 (*continued*)

o Carlson, "Seeking the Better Interests of Children with a New International Law of Adoption," at 746–7.

p Root, "Angelina and Madonna," at 344–6.

q Bartholet, "International Adoption: The Child's Story."

r See arguments presented in Carlson, "Seeking the Better Interests of Children with a New International Law of Adoption," at 747–52.

s Worthington, "The Road to Parentless Children Is Paved with Good Intentions," at 572

t Elizabeth Bartholet, "International Adoption" in Lori Askeland (Ed.), *Children and Youth in Adoption, Orphanages, and Foster Care* (London: Greenwood Press, 2006), pp. 63–78.

u Worthington, "The Road to Parentless Children is Paved with Good Intentions," at 571–2.

v Willing, Fronek, & Cuthbert, "Review of Sociological Literature on Intercountry Adoption."

w Worthington, "The Road to Parentless Children is Paved with Good Intentions," at 573.

x Ibid.

y Elizabeth Bartholet, "The International Adoption Cliff: Do Child Human Rights Matter?" in Ballard, Goodno, Cochran, & Milbrandt (Eds.), *The Intercountry Adoption Debate: Dialogues across Disciplines,* pp. 193–202.

z Smolin, "Child Laundering: How the Intercountry Adoption System Legitimizes and Incentivizes the Practices of Buying, Trafficking, Kidnapping, and Stealing Children," at 181; Cheney, "Giving Children a Better Life?," at 256.

aa Mariela Neagu, "Children by Request: Romania's Children between Rights and International Politics," *International Journal of Law, Policy and the Family*, 29(2) (2015), 215–36, at 232.

bb Bartholet, "The Hague Convention."

cc Smolin, "Child Laundering and the Hague Convention on Intercountry Adoption," at 482.

dd Worthington, "The Road to Parentless Children is Paved with Good Intentions," at 585.

ee David M. Smolin, "The Two Faces of Intercountry Adoption: The Significance of the Indian Adoption Scandals," *Seton Hall Law Review*, 35(2) (2005), 403–93.

ff "Status Table: Convention of 29 May 1993 on Protection of Children and Co-operation in Respect of Intercountry Adoption," The Hague Conference on Private International Law, available at: www.hcch.net/en/instruments/conventions/full-text/?cid=69.

gg Willing, Fronek, & Cuthbert, "Review of Sociological Literature on Intercountry Adoption," at 473.

suggestions center on minimizing the circumstances that lead to the need for intercountry adoption, including encouragement of internal adoption, support for extended family care, and legitimization and support of unmarried mothers so they have no need to abandon their child.[174] Other suggestions center on the adoption procedure, and include: foreign aid to support sending countries in enforcing international regulation of adoption to prevent child trafficking;[175] enforcement of internal adoption standards on intercountry adoption, including matching the child to the family, a trial period, and postadoption monitoring;[176] the preservation of the child's citizenship of origin, and the encouragement of annual visits, to preserve his or her identity;[177] prohibition on any kind of financial transfer, and the transformation of intercountry adoption into a bilateral public service;[178] and the exploration of open intercountry adoption and intercountry foster care as alternative options that do not cut the child's ties with the birth family as closed adoption does.[179]

However, I have not integrated into Table 6.3 a third synthesis column, in contrast to Table 6.2, because I believe that the case studies described here prove that such a synthesis is impossible, and even dangerous. The relative value and risk of international adoption are dependent on many contextual variables that are shaped by national and cultural borders and that yield different options and constraints in relation to poverty, gender, disability, health, race, and family. These variables include: the reasons that children are defined as adoptable (war, plague, poverty, illegitimate single motherhood, abandonment of disabled children, or other special circumstances); the availability of alternatives in the country of origin (care by extended family, internal adoption, foster care, institutions), and their quality; the quality of local law enforcement aimed at preventing related child trafficking; and the familial and social conditions within the receiving country (eligibility of adoptive parents and racial tolerance of receiving country).

Moreover, as in the case of remittances discussed at the beginning of this chapter, most of the empirical attention in relation to adoption is focused on the Northern part of the globe, with its emphasis on the adoptees and

---

[174] Selman, "Intercountry Adoption of Children from Asia in the Twenty-First Century," at 323.
[175] Bartholet, "The Hague Convention."
[176] Neagu, "Children by Request," at 230–1.
[177] Ibid., at 231.
[178] Ibid.
[179] Selman, "Intercountry Adoption of Children from Asia in the Twenty-First Century," at 323.

the adopters, whereas very little is known about the biological parents and communities that lose children to adoption overseas[180] or about the children who might need intercountry adoption and are deprived of it.[181] Without such knowledge, grounded in each and every relevant country, definitive normative conclusions are irresponsible.

Notwithstanding, I would suggest a minimal standard that, in my opinion, can be carved out based on current available knowledge and experience: under the conditions that (1) it can be assured that the option of international adoption will not lead to child kidnapping from their family and (2) that the child consents, if of relevant age and capacity,[182] intercountry adoption should be allowed in cases of parentless or institutionalized children who have no active and significant familial ties that can secure their ongoing care and no realistic prospect for local adoption or adequate foster care, as it serves their best interests. In my opinion, institutional care in the home country can be considered as better serving the child's interest only if the child is a teenager and only if the institution is of a very high quality, which is rarely the case.

Moreover, perhaps somewhat provocatively, I would like to end this part of the chapter by portraying an alternative hypothetical HCIA. This hypothetical convention will differ from the current one in several crucial elements. First, it will allow intercountry open adoption, guardianship, and foster care. Second, these more moderate options will be permitted also for children who have identifiable and loving parents, but who still suffer from extreme poverty that deprives them of a minimal standard of living. The cross-border movement of these children will be allowed only with the consent of the parents and child (if capable of voicing an opinion). Third, the biological parents will be allowed to accept a significant amount of money from the adoptive parents/guardians/foster care family (receiving parents) in return for the privilege granted to the latter to care for the child. The payment will promote the chances that the semi-adoptive child will not only be saved from deprivation, but also that his/her siblings will enjoy a minimal standard of living. The receiving family

---

[180] Willing, Fronek, & Cuthbert, "Review of Sociological Literature on Intercountry Adoption."

[181] Sarah Dillon in Carlson, "Seeking the Better Interests of Children with a New International Law of Adoption," at 736.

[182] As mentioned earlier, today, more so than in the past, some of the adoptees are relatively old. Hence, the right to participation becomes more relevant and must include children's informed consent for the removal from their country, an issue mentioned in Article 4(3) of the Hague Convention on Protection of Children and Co-operation in Respect of Intercountry Adoption 1993, but ignored in the literature.

will also be committed by the convention to maintain ongoing contact with the child's biological family, according to a multiparental plan that will be signed by the parties. A sum will be deposited by the receiving parents at the state of origin's intercountry adoption authority to secure their contact obligation according to the parental plan.

At first glance, this hypothetical international regulative scenario looks outrageous – pure trafficking and commodification of poor children, based on the use of the child as an object and a means rather than a subject and a human being.[183] But the tragic reality of hungry children – at the heart of this chapter – suggests that this reaction might be completely misguided, and that a child-centered approach that treats children as subjects must lead to radical measures that will secure their most basic rights, even if that means the geographic separation of the migrating child from the biological family and birth nation, and payment for the parents that will enable the rest of the family to escape famine.[184] Moreover, other, already existing, harsh familial cross-border phenomena discussed in this book lead to some very challenging questions and comparisons. In what sense is this option more of a child trafficking and commodification than international surrogacy, discussed in Chapter 4? Is this option more harmful and morally wrong than the long-term separation of labor migrant parents from their left-behind children, as discussed in the first part of this chapter? Is this option not a safer institutionalized and supervised framework to govern the existing phenomenon of children sent by their parents as *parachute children* or *unaccompanied minors*, as mentioned in the Introduction? In what way is this a worse option than the common practice in several Global South societies, mentioned in Chapter 3, of poor

---

[183] The critics of this hypothesis might compare it to the known controversial thesis of Landes and Posner on the desirability of a private market of babies. See Elisabeth M. Landes & Richard A. Posner, "The Economics of the Baby Shortage," *Journal of Legal Studies,* 7(2) (1978), 323–48. However, it is very different, first and foremost as it will not be governed by the private market but by government bodies and international law, and because it is not motivated to secure "white babies" for white parents.

[184] The suggestion presented here can be seen as corresponding with Dwyer's thesis on children's moral right "to the best available caregiver." See James G. Dwyer, "Diagnosing and Dispelling Denialism Regarding Children" in Ronald Moerland, Hans Nelen, & Jan C. M. Willems (Eds.), *Denialism and Human Rights* (Cambridge: Intersentia 2016), pp. 49–68. However, I do not believe children, or adults, have such a right, and completely disagree with Dwyer's individualistic perception of children's rights that ignores parents' and other family members' rights and interests. If my suggestion were to be followed, poverty-based intercountry adoption would be allowed only in extreme cases of deprivation, only with the consent of the parents, and only in a way that would not detach the connection between the child and the biological family.

parents sending their children to be "fostered" in a household that can offer them a better chance of survival? This option can also be viewed as a development of the *representative-immigrant* possibility introduced in Chapter 5. Under this scenario, the child, who will have ongoing contact with his/her biological family, will grow up in a developed country and have a better chance than an adult immigrant of integrating into a well-paid position in the labor market, and thus be able to send remittances or reimmigrate back and contribute to his/her homeland's economy and society.

In a globalized world with widening inequities, perhaps it is time to imagine a new kind of transnational family – a family composed of two families with ongoing contact, united by a child who came into the world thanks to one, is cared for by another, and who might want, and manage, to care for the former as an adult. This book demonstrates that this is not as radical a proposal as it may sound, and in many respects is only a small stretch of existing familial arrangements.

This suggestion, of course, has its potential risks, such as that desperate poor people will bring babies into the world solely with the aim of selling them. Sadly, even if this and other potential risks were overcome, it is hard to imagine that the alternative HCIA I suggest would succeed in assisting but a fraction of the 156 million stunted children of the world. The numbers are so high that, even if the hypothetical suggestion is normatively desirable, especially relatively to other options, it is not realistic as an overarching solution. Even at its peak, intercountry adoption has served fewer than half a million children over ten years. The answer to children's extreme poverty must be found without a reshuffling of the world's hungry minors across borders. Until this answer is found, and as long as intercountry adoption is allowed – in its current traditional form or under a more radical framework, as the one suggested here – a basic normative guideline must be preserved. All such cross-border movement of children should always be only about children who need a family that can feed and nurture them, and not about Western adults' need for children (even if they are among the world's most famous celebrities).

Conclusion

This chapter by no means aims at discussing the reasons for the acute and complex problem of our unevenly hungry planet or the overall solution to it. Rather, I have chosen to place side-by-side three specific, apparently feasible, partial solutions, as I believe they highlight the relevance and importance of familial practices and perceptions, often ignored in the discourse on global economic inequities. Parental remittances, child labor, and international adoption, discussed through the lens of families laws, force us to focus on the children involved and to be honest about our familial ideology.

Discussing these three options together reveals the problematic Western tendency to ignore the familial ties of children in the poorest parts of the world. Parental immigration is understood as inherently good for poor children who arguably enjoy parental remittances, as if these children, unlike children in the West, did not need ongoing physical and emotional care from their biological parents; child labor is conceptualized as an evil that should not be governed by parental authority and diverse cultural understandings of childhood, but by universal anti-child-labor norms; and intercountry adoption is, at times, accepted even if it generates child trafficking or the separation of children from their functioning families of origin. This tendency to overlook the 'other' children's and families' needs and voices correlates with Western interests of dehumanizing labor migrants, reducing global market competiveness among poor countries, and having babies made available for adoption to meet demand.

Notwithstanding, this analysis suffers from Western bias itself. It ignores the agency of parents who choose to leave their children behind or give them up for intercountry adoption for the chance of a better economic future. It also overlooks the adaptability of children to a variety of familial arrangements, and the role of extended family members and other adults in caring for children. The focus of this chapter on children in poor countries, moreover, marks them, and their parents, as 'a problem,' while masking concerns over the impact of globalization on children and parental care in the West, due to scenarios including: parental intense travel abroad for business; children who are raised by nannies who might be deported; children who are sent to boarding schools, at times overseas; and children who are forced to relocate to another country with both their parents, or with one of them after divorce.

It is clear from my analysis and emphasis in this chapter that I believe children and parents have a natural right to enjoy a sphere of joint familial emotional care and intimacy. This sphere includes economic dimensions, although I believe it should not be minimized to these. Although care and intimacy can be created for children by extended family members and other adults, and although biological parents can fail painfully in providing adequate care, as will be discussed in Chapter 7, I conclude from current empirical knowledge that biological parental care is the kind most likely to serve children's interests. However, current knowledge on families and children's need for parental care is Westernized itself, and the voices of those to whom parental remittances, child labor, and intercountry adoption are most relevant are still absent or marginalized.

Although much in this chapter underlines the importance of contextualization and multiculturalism, I refuse to translate the criticism of Westernized interests and perceptions into relativism or to antiliberalism. I would insist on a vision – sadly still challenging and far from realization – that should guide international and national policy makers, of a globordered world in which children's right to a minimal standard of living is guaranteed while so too is their – and their biological parents' – right to family life.

7

Familial Violence

Introduction

This book relies on the premise that families, at their best, can, and should, provide a unique and essential source of nurturing and support that benefits their members. As a minimal standard, families must provide a secure physical and emotional space in which each family member is kept safe from abuse. However, the reality is that families can be, and too often are, a locus of physical, sexual, emotional, and economic violence.[1] Indeed, it is the very privacy, intimacy, and dependency of familial ties that often foster even harsher and more persistent violence than can be found among strangers.

Although it might seem that the common terms *family violence* and *domestic violence*, and also the term used here, *familial violence,* are clear and carry the same meaning all over the globe, they are, in fact, heatedly contested. *Marital rape* and *corporal punishment* are but two examples that demonstrate that what might be perceived in one culture as family violence, might be considered in another as a natural marital prerogative or as parental responsible care.[2] In this chapter, I define familial violence as any act by a family member against another family member, of omission or commission, which harms the latter's physical, sexual, emotional, or economic wellbeing.[3] As we shall see in what follows, it is at not at all clear that all forms of familial violence should be illegal. Indeed, I chose this broad definition, which deliberately does not include an element of intent, as it allows us to question the circumstances in which the law, both national and international, should interfere in family life and protect family members from other members, and those in which it should restrain

---

[1] Ola W. Barnett, Cindy L. Miller-Perrin, & Robin D. Perrin, *Family Violence across the Lifespan: An Introduction*, 3rd edn. (Thousand Oaks, CA: Sage, 2011), Ch. 1.
[2] Ibid., at 22.
[3] On the question of defining family violence, see ibid., Ch. 1.

itself in the name of multiculturalism, or the victim's overall wellbeing, or the realization that the perpetrator is, in fact, the victim.

The most pervasive kinds of familial violence are spousal violence perpetrated by men against women (often termed 'domestic violence') and parental violence perpetrated by fathers and mothers against their children. But familial violence also occurs in many other circumstances, such as among same-sex couples, among siblings, against a wife by her in-laws, and by grown children against their elderly parents.[4] Furthermore, as this chapter will demonstrate, severe harm can be inflicted on one family member by another by means of brutal acts such as circumcision or abduction, even though such acts are rarely conceptualized within the law or in the literature as family violence.

This chapter explores this dark side of familial life through the lens of several legal controversies particularly relevant to families affected by bordered globalization. The first part of the chapter discusses domestic violence perpetrated by men against their female spouse, and focuses on the legal questions arising when the victim of spousal violence is a non-citizen. It will show the positive impact of the global assimilation of the anti-domestic-violence norm, on the one hand, and its limits caused by national borders and laws, on the other. The second part of the chapter discusses parental violence by focusing on the international and national legal debates over female genital mutilation and male circumcision, common in some cultures and communities. This part reveals the complexities arising from the intersection of children's rights and multiculturalism in the global and national spheres, and the impact of these complexities on communal identity, parental authority, and children's gendered lives. It will also discuss child beauty pageants and the lack of regulation in this area, to highlight the cultural biases and phobias embedded in the global discourse opposing violence against children. The third part of the chapter looks at international child abduction as another kind of familial violence, increased by globalization, and at the international attempts to prevent it, which are well coordinated yet limited in their effectiveness. This part will further complicate the discussion by pointing at the possible link between child abduction and spousal or parental violence on the part of the parent from whom the child is abducted.

Together, the three parts of this chapter highlight the significant impact and further potential of the law in combating violence within the family

---

[4] Harvey Wallace & Cliff Roberson, *Family Violence: Legal, Medical and Social Perspectives*, 7th edn. (London: Routledge, 2016).

in the era of bordered globalization, as well as the new risks of violence that is *heightened* by bordered globalization – and the limitations of the law in addressing these risks.

Spousal Violence

Spousal violence of men against women is one of the most common kinds of violence. For many women, the home is far from being a safe haven. According to the World Health Organization (WHO), worldwide, almost a third of women who have been in a spousal relationship report having been physically or sexually assaulted by their partner, and 38 percent of all women who are murdered die at the hands of an intimate partner.[5] Whereas the phenomenon of spousal violence is affected by individual variables such as male alcohol abuse and personality disorder, and by the quality of the spousal relations, it is also significantly impacted by social and cultural variables. It is more common in poor communities and in societies that suffer from an armed conflict or high levels of crime, for example. It is also more common within cultures that hold to traditional, patriarchal gendered norms that justify violence against women and that encourage marriage at a young age and a high number of childbirths. Finally, women suffer more domestic violence in countries that do not prosecute violent spouses or provide shelters for their victims.[6] Hence, although spousal violence is so prevalent as to constitute a risk to women from all varieties of social, cultural, and economic backgrounds, it is undoubtedly more prevalent in some societies than in others. For example, whereas 15 percent of Japanese women report suffering physical or sexual violence perpetuated by an intimate partner, 71 percent of Ethiopian women report being the victims of such violence.[7] According to the WHO, the prevalence rate of physical and/or sexual violence perpetrated by an intimate partner among ever-partnered women is 23 percent in North America and West Europe, and rises to 30 percent in South

---

[5] "Violence against Women," World Health Organization – Media Center, available at: www .who.int/mediacentre/factsheets/fs239/en/.

[6] Sarah Bott, Andrew Morrison, & Mary Ellsberg, "Preventing and Responding to Gender-Based Violence in Middle and Low-Income Countries: A Global Review and Analysis," World Bank Policy Research Working Paper 3618 (2005), 1–61, at 15, Figure 1.4.

[7] "Violence against Women," World Health Organization. While relying on the rate of report is problematic when assessing the scope of domestic violence, as much of it is not reported, there is no reason to assume that Japanese women are more reluctant to report domestic violence than Ethiopian women.

America and approximately 37 percent in Africa, the Middle East, and South-East Asia.[8]

Outrageously, the Convention on the Elimination of All Forms of Discrimination against Women (CEDAW) does not include an explicit prohibition on violence against women.[9] Fortunately, although in the late 1970s, when this convention was drafted, an anti-domestic-violence international norm was yet to exist,[10] such a norm has since evolved. In 1992, the CEDAW Committee issued a General Recommendation according to which "the definition of discrimination includes gender-based violence, that is, violence that is directed against a woman because she is a woman or that affects women disproportionately," thereby prohibiting gender-based violence.[11] Under this Recommendation, the 189 states parties[12] are demanded to implement a number of measures to "overcome family violence," including: "Criminal penalties where necessary and civil remedies in cases of domestic violence"; "Services to ensure the safety and security of victims of family violence"; and "Rehabilitation programmes for perpetrators of domestic violence."[13] As eminent legal anthropologist Sally Engle Merry demonstrates, although this General Recommendation, like CEDAW and many other international conventions and declarations, constitutes "law without sanctions," the CEDAW Committee manages – through its monitoring and shaming review process (based on periodical state and shadow reports) – to place violence against women, including within the family, high on the anti-gender-discrimination agenda.[14]

In 1993, the UN General Assembly adopted the Declaration on the Elimination of Violence against Women, stating that "violence against

---

[8] World Health Organization, *Global and Regional Estimates of Violence against Women: Prevalence and Health Effects of Intimate Partner Violence and Non-Partner Sexual Violence* (2013), at 17–18, available at: http://apps.who.int/iris/bitstream/10665/85239/1/9789241564625_eng.pdf.

[9] Siobhan Mullally, "Domestic Violence Asylum Claims and Recent Developments in International Human Rights Law: A Progress Narrative?" *International and Comparative Law Quarterly*, 60(2) (2011), 459–84, at 461.

[10] Sally Engle Merry, "Constructing a Global Law – Violence against Women and the Human Rights System," *Law & Social Inquiry*, 28(4) (2003), 941–77, at 952.

[11] Convention on the Elimination of All Forms of Discrimination against Women, General Recommendation No. 19, Article 6, available at: www.un.org/womenwatch/daw/cedaw/recommendations/recomm.htm.

[12] Convention on the Elimination of All Forms of Discrimination against Women, available at: www.un.org/womenwatch/daw/cedaw/states.htm.

[13] Convention on the Elimination of All Forms of Discrimination against Women, General Recommendation No. 19, Article 24(r)(i) (iii) and (iv), available at: www.un.org/womenwatch/daw/cedaw/recommendations/recomm.htm.

[14] Merry, "Constructing a Global Law."

women is an obstacle to the achievement of equality, development and peace ... [and] constitutes a violation of the rights and fundamental freedoms of women and impairs or nullifies their enjoyment of those rights and freedoms."[15] Importantly, the Declaration rejects multiculturalism as a justification of violence against women, including spousal violence,[16] noting that "states should condemn violence against women and should not invoke any custom, tradition or religious consideration to avoid their obligations with respect to its elimination."[17] This universalist anti-domestic-violence norm was further adopted by other UN bodies, as well as by regional treaties and tribunals, including in South America and Africa[18] and the Arab world.[19] Moreover, most countries of the world now have specific laws prohibiting spousal violence, with only two dozen still failing to adopt a nationwide anti-spousal-violence stance.[20] This is a very dramatic, rapid, and impressive global legal isomorphic shift, considering that only fifty years ago spousal violence was widely perceived as a private matter, unworthy of the intervention of state law,[21] and that CEDAW was originally silent on the matter.

This intense international and national anti-spousal-violence regulation provides a powerful example of the new global commitment to gender equality.[22] This commitment extends to altering the meaning of "the family," which is no longer perceived as the domain of the patriarch who can rule his wife physically, sexually, emotionally, and economically. Sadly, the existing regulation is also an example of the possible gap between law on the books and socio-legal realities. This gap, while evident from the ongoing prevalence of domestic violence in all social contexts and reflected in

---

[15] UN Resolution A/RES/48/104 of 20 December 1993 on the Elimination of Violence against Women, available at: www.un.org/documents/ga/res/48/a48r104.htm.

[16] Ibid., Article 2(a).

[17] Ibid., at Article 4.

[18] Mullally, "Domestic Violence Asylum Claims," at 464–5.

[19] Marianne D. Blair, Merle H. Weiner, Barbara Stark, & Solangel Maldonado, *Family Law in the World Community: Cases, Materials and Problems in Comparative and International Family Law*, 2nd edn. (Durham, NC: Carolina Academic Press, 2009), at 350.

[20] Charlotte Alfred, "These 20 Countries Have No Law against Domestic Violence," *The World Post* (March 10, 2014), available at: www.huffingtonpost.com/2014/03/08/countries-no-domestic-violence-law_n_4918784.html.

[21] Nina Rabin, "At the Border between Public and Private: U.S. Immigration Policy for Victims of Domestic Violence," *Law & Ethics of Human Rights*, 7(1) (2013), 109–53, at 116.

[22] Generally, on global isomorphism of gender equality norms, see Nitza Berkovitch, *From Motherhood to Citizenship: Women's Rights and International Organizations* (Baltimore: Johns Hopkins University Press, 1999).

the WHO data, is especially acute when it comes to noncitizen victims. It is yet another example of the ongoing resilience of national borders and an important reminder of their impact on familial power relations. The interrelation between spousal violence and bordered globalization will be discussed here regarding two groups: immigrant women who experience spousal violence in the destination country, and women who seek asylum based on the spousal violence they suffered in their country of origin.

Immigrant Women

Although there is no evidence to suggest that immigrant women are more at risk of domestic violence than native women, studies are consistently teaching us that immigration intensifies domestic violence in the sense that it traps the victim in the abusive relationship. It is important to understand the role of the law in contributing to this intensification. Research shows that the intersection between family law and immigration law uniquely shapes migratory domestic violence. First, since a spousal visa is a major route to naturalization in a developed country, as discussed in Chapter 5, alien women are motivated to marry a citizen of such a country, even if he is abusive.[23] Moreover, it has been found that violent male spouses use immigration law to weaken their alien spouses' positions, such as by convincing them to enter the destination country on a tourist visa although they are eligible for spousal visas, by not submitting a request for their naturalization, or by controlling their access to the documents needed for reassuring the immigration authorities.[24] All this makes alien wives citizenship status more fragile than it needs to be, and adds to the abusers' power over their migrant spouses. Moreover, there is

---

[23] The most-discussed manifestation of this motivation is the phenomenon of mail-order brides. Several sending and receiving countries have legislated special laws to minimize the risk of this practice being used for sex-trafficking and involuntary servitude, including by prohibiting advertisements featuring mail-order brides, regulating related mediating agencies, and limiting the age of the bride and the age discrepancy between her and the groom. See Roxanne Sims, "A Comparison of Law in the Philippines, the U.S.A., Taiwan and Belarus to Regulate the Mail Bride Industry," *Akron Law Review*, 42(2) (2009), 607–37; Donna R. Lee, "Mail Fantasy: Global Sexual Exploitation in the Mail-Order Bride Industry and Proposed Legal Solutions," *Asian Law Journal*, 5 (1998), 139–79; Kathryn A. Lloyd, "Wives for Sale: The Modern International Mail Order Bride Industry," *Northwestern Journal of International Law & Business*, 20(2) (2000), 341–67.

[24] Giselle A. Hass, Nawal Ammar, & Lesley Orloff, "Battered Immigrants and U.S. Citizen Spouses," Legal Momentum (2006), available at: http://iwp.legalmomentum.org/reference/additional-materials/research-reports-and-data/research-US-VAIW/copy_of_BB_RSRCH_ImmVictims_Battered_Imm.pdf/at_download/file.

empirical evidence that domestic violence increases around immigration-specific activities, such as entering the country, filing immigration papers, and undertaking the necessary periodic reporting to the immigration authorities. Likewise, violent spouses very often use immigration status to terrorize their victims and force their will upon them. They threaten to report their spouses' illegal immigration status, interrupt the naturalization process, or take away the children and deny the mothers custodial rights.[25] For women with an unsecured immigration status, these threats are subordinating speech-acts based on the terrifying option of deportation and separation from their children.

The lack of citizenship status is joined by other factors that lead to the intensification of domestic violence due to its intersection with immigration. Researchers who have interviewed immigrants who are victims of domestic violence repeatedly cite a range of difficulties these individuals face in leaving an abusive spouse. Among the more common factors identified are: language barriers, isolation from the family of origin and from friends left in the home country, a cultural and legal background in the country of origin that justifies domestic violence, economic dependency on the violent spouse, ignorance of the law, and mistrust of the police.[26] These findings are at the heart of a typology, recently suggested by legal scholars Hadar Dancig-Rosenberg and Nomi Levenkron, of the barriers that immigrant women face in their endeavors to extricate themselves from domestic violence. This typology includes: (1) the cultural–psychological barrier, which is the immigrant's personality shaped by her culture of origin and its attitude toward domestic violence. In cases in which the women come from a society that legitimizes domestic violence, they might find it harder to blame their spouses and seek assistance; (2) the social barrier, which includes the lack of social support in the destination country and the language barrier that make the violent spouse the victim's only bridge to the world outside, as well as the economic constraints that might include debts to immigration agencies, the need to send remittances, or unemployment and economic dependency on the violent spouse; and (3) the state barrier, which includes the legal and bureaucratic

---

[25] Edna Erez, Madelaine Adelman, & Carol Gregory, "Intersections of Immigration and Domestic Violence: Voices of Battered Immigrant Women," *Feminist Criminology*, 4(1) (2009), 32–56; Hadar Dancig-Rosenberg & Naomi Levenkron, "Migratory Violence," *Tel Aviv University Law Review*, 37(2) (2015), 341–88, at 372–74 (Hebrew).

[26] Cecilia Menjívar & Olivia Salcido, "Immigrant Women and Domestic Violence, Common Experiences in Different Countries," *Gender & Society*, 16(6) (2002), 898–920; Erez, Adelman, & Gregory, "Intersections of Immigration."

mechanisms of the destination country that place significant power in the hands of the violent spouses by creating a legal dependency on the part of the abused immigrant spouses.[27] Indeed, although the universalistic anti-domestic-violence norm became so central as to make several destination countries sensitive to the special vulnerability of spousally abused immigrant women, their laws, nevertheless, constitute what Dancig-Rosenberg and Levenkron call "migratory violence" in which the state sustains, even if unintentionally, the violent spousal relationship.[28]

The UK provides an example of "migratory violence" notwithstanding regulation aimed at assisting immigrant victims of domestic violence. In 2002, the UK changed its immigration system to offer those non-European Economic Area (EEA) nationals in the UK on spousal visas the possibility of being granted the right to remain in the UK independently of their spouses if they suffered domestic violence. This Domestic Violence Rule is crucial as, without it, victims of domestic violence might be reluctant to report the abuse and leave their spouses, for fear of deportation. However, it is applicable only if the victim's spouse is British or settled, and gives no escape route to those married to violent temporary workers, foreign students, asylum seekers, or immigrants who reside in the UK illegally.[29] Indeed, a study conducted by an NGO in Northern Ireland found that only a third of the immigrant women who were seeking refuge from domestic violence at the time of the research would have been eligible to remain in the UK according to this rule.[30] Another barrier to an independent residency visa, so vital for immigrant women who want to leave their violent spouses, is the need to prove that they are the victims of domestic violence. A study conducted by political scientist Sundari Anitha found that the high rejection rate of applications under the Domestic Violence Rule is largely due to unrealistic proof requirements.[31] Moreover, the lack of access to public funding among non-EEA nationals who did not enter the UK on spousal visas, yet suffer domestic violence in the UK, effectively bars these immigrants and their children from shelters for victims of domestic violence, assistance with housing,

---

[27] Dancig-Rosenberg & Levenkron, "Migratory Violence."
[28] Ibid.
[29] Monica McWilliams, Priyamvada N. R. Yarnell, & Molly Churchill, "Forced Dependency and Legal Barriers: Implications of the UK's Immigration and Social Security Policies for Minoritized Women Living in Abusive Intimate Relationships in Northern Ireland," *Oñati Socio-Legal Series*, 5(6) (2015), 1536–56, at 1544.
[30] McWilliams, Yarnell, & Churchill, "Forced Dependency," at 1544.
[31] See as reported in ibid., at 1545.

and a minimal allowance that can help prevent dire poverty in the case of leaving the violent spouses. Whether the 2013 CEDAW recommendation that the UK extend the access to public funding to all victims of domestic violence, regardless of their immigration status (including asylum seekers), will make the UK lift this bar is yet to be seen.[32] Finally, the study conducted by the activist scholars Monica McWilliams, Priyamvada Yarnell, and Molly Churchill reveals that even battered wives from the EEA are exposed to legal and bureaucratic barriers to freedom in the UK, because the Child Benefit, which could have assisted in leaving the violent spouses, is usually granted to the father, and because they face racism by officials when seeking help.[33]

The UK is not alone in its failure to protect victims of domestic violence who have an insecure immigration status. Taiwan, for example, conditions any assistance to an immigrant victim of domestic violence on her being the mother of a Taiwanese child.[34] Israel offers an independent visa to immigrant victims of domestic violence under certain circumstances, but this visa is always temporary and, as such, only delays the deportation rather than ensuring the right to stay permanently in Israel. This policy, therefore, forces immigrant women to choose between two evils: to stay in their violent relationships until their spousal-based naturalization is finalized (a process that can take between five and seven years) or to be deported at some stage.[35]

Even the United States – which goes a long way to assist migrant victims of domestic violence by providing them with an independent route to a work permit, green card, and eventually citizenship – offers this kind of support only to those who are married to a US citizen or a lawful permanent resident.[36] Furthermore, those eligible for this escape route must overcome a heavy evidentiary burden, including in relation to the immigration status of the violent spouse, the bona fide nature of the marriage, and the domestic abuse suffered.[37] In 2000, the United States established a special kind of visa for crime victims, including immigrant

---

[32] Ibid., at 1553.

[33] Ibid., at 1547–50.

[34] Sara L. Friedman, "Adjudicating the Intersection of Marital Immigration, Domestic Violence, and Spousal Murder: China–Taiwan Marriages and Competing Legal Domains," *Indiana Journal of Global Legal Studies*, 19(1) (2012), 221–55, at 227.

[35] Dancig-Rosenberg & Levenkron, "Migratory Violence."

[36] Katerina Shaw, "Barriers to Freedom: Continued Failure of U.S. Immigration Laws to Offer Equal Protection to Immigrant Battered Women," *Cardozo Journal of Law & Gender*, 15 (2009), 663–89, at 674.

[37] Ibid., at 674–8.

women suffering violence at the hands of their spouse who could not use the independent route open to those whose abuser was a US citizen or permanent resident. The U Visa, which can lead to permanent residency, depends on the ability to prove substantial physical or mental abuse as a result of a criminal act (such as domestic violence, robbery, or involuntary servitude), along with certification from a law enforcement official or judge stating that the victim has been, or is being, helpful or is likely to be helpful in investigating or prosecuting the crime.[38] However, many domestic violence victims do not apply for the U Visa option, for fear of being deported if their request is denied, or in case the authorities refuse to issue the necessary certification confirming their cooperation with the investigation or prosecution.[39] Hence, as the study by criminologist Edna Erez and her colleagues reveals, although living in the United States leads immigrants to perceive domestic violence as wrong even if coming from cultures in which it is regarded as a legitimate and private matter, many of its victims are still trapped in violent relations under the fear of deportation.[40] Needless to say, in countries that do not offer such significant, though imperfect, escape routes as the United States, the chances that a woman with no secured immigration status who suffers domestic violence will report it and leave her abusive spouse are even tragically lower.

Asylum Seekers

The second group that provokes debate over destination countries' legal obligation toward noncitizens who are victims of domestic violence is that of women who seek asylum based on the domestic violence they have suffered in their country of origin. This is an even tougher demand to impose on the nation state than in the case of the first group, because it calls for the state to demonstrate responsibility toward victims of acts that did not take place on its soil.

The question of the responsibility of country A toward victims of human rights violations taking place in country B is central within the evolving field of transnational human-rights law. One of the most interesting recent theses within this field is that developed by legal scholar Eyal Benvenisti.[41] Benvenisti argues that, in our global era, the concept of sovereignty should

---

[38] Rabin, "At the Border," at 122.

[39] Show, "Barriers to Freedom," at 679.

[40] Erez, Adelman, & Gregory, "Intersections of Immigration."

[41] Eyal Benvenisti, "Sovereigns as Trustees of Humanity: On the Accountability of States to Foreign Stakeholders," *American Journal of International Law*, 107(2) (2013), 295–333.

be modified to allow – and even oblige – states to take the interests of foreigners into account. He argues that, rather than a "solipsistic" notion of sovereignty, which centers on the concept of full overlap between the nation state, the people it affects, and its authority, one should adopt a global perception of sovereignty, stemming from the understanding that, in our era, states are embedded in a global order, affecting and affected by actions taking place in other states. The current global order, which allows collectives to be organized as sovereign nation states, should simultaneously oblige each nation state to contribute to the protection of all the world's citizens under the overarching canopy of universal basic human rights, recognized in international law. According to Benvenisti, although nation states should primarily be committed to their own citizens, they should, at the same time, act as "trustees of humanity." As such, all states, but particularly powerful ones that enjoy an exclusive large part of the earth's resources, have a responsibility toward all human beings.[42]

One of the earliest manifestations of the understanding that country A has obligations toward citizens of country B was the 1951 UN Refugee Convention. This Convention, stemming from the horrors of World War II, obliges states' parties to provide asylum to refugees, defined as anyone who, "by reason of a well-founded fear of persecution for reasons of race, religion, nationality, membership in a particular social group or political opinion," is outside of his or her country and is unable, or fears, to return to it.[43] Gender was not recognized as a basis for "persecution" at the time the Convention was drafted, and nor was it added at a later stage. In 2002, the UN Refugee Agency issued guidelines acknowledging that "[h]istorically, the refugee definition has been interpreted through a framework of male experiences, which has meant that many claims of women and of homosexuals have gone unrecognized".[44] Nevertheless, the Agency insists that "there is no need to add an additional ground to the 1951 Convention definition" because "[t]he refugee definition, properly interpreted ... covers gender-related claims."[45] However, the

---

[42] This should be so, according to Benvenisti, at least until a robust global constitutional system that ensures an equal and effective voice for all stakeholders is established. Ibid.

[43] The UN Refugee Agency, The 1951 Refugee Convention, *Conference of Plenipotentiaries on the Status of Refugees and Stateless Persons: Summary Record of the Thirty-Fourth Meeting*, Article 1- Definition of the Term "Refugee," available at: www.unhcr.org/en-us/protection/travaux/3ae68cdf0/conference-plenipotentiaries-status-refugees-stateless-persons-summary.html.

[44] The UN Refugee Agency, *Guidelines on International Protection* (2002), at Section II.A.5, available at: www.unhcr.org/3d58ddef4.html.

[45] Ibid., Section II.A.6.

history of refugees' claims as victims of domestic violence and of other gender-related human rights violations demonstrates that women pay a high price for this gendered omission, which forces them to attempt to fit into androcentric legal categories that were not created with them in mind.[46] As legal scholar Melanie Randall demonstrates, the omission of gender as a category of persecution is also apparent in the national legislation that emerged out of the international commitment to aid refugees. Whereas a few countries, such as South Africa and the Republic of Ireland, added gender to their refugee laws, major immigration receiving countries, such as the United States and Canada, did not.[47]

Canada is an interesting case, because it is perceived by many as an example to be followed for its gender-sensitive refugee law, including in relation to domestic violence. However, its current legal position vis-à-vis victims of spousal violence who seek asylum is not the outcome of *hard law* but, rather, of administrative guidelines and judicial interpretations.[48] The Canadian Immigration Board Guidelines recognize that spousal violence can amount to persecution, but only if "it is imposed on account of any one, or a combination, of the statutory grounds for persecution," which do not include gender.[49] It was the Canadian Supreme Court that, in an obiter comment, opened the door in 1993 for the recognition of

---

[46] Talia Inlender, "Status Quo or Sixth Ground? Adjudicating Gender Asylum Claims" in Seyla Benhabib & Judith Resnik (Eds.), *Migrations and Mobilities: Citizenship, Borders and Gender* (New York University Press, 2009), pp. 356–79.

[47] Melanie Randall, "Particularized Social Groups and Categorical Imperatives in Refugee Law: State Failures to Recognize Gender and the Legal Reception of Gender Persecution Claims in Canada, the United Kingdom, and the United States," *Journal of Gender, Social Policy & the Law*, 23(4) (2015), 529–71, at 532. In 2014, the CEDAW Committee issued General Recommendation No. 32, that encourages states parties "to add sex and or gender as an additional grounds for refugee status in their national legislation." See UN Committee on the Elimination of Discrimination against Women, General Recommendation No. 32, at Section 30, available at: www.refworld.org/docid/54620fb54.html.

[48] Randall, "Particularized Social Groups," at 537–43; Canada's decision not to change its parliamentary refugee law but to be satisfied with administrative guidelines was criticized by the Canadian legal scholar Constance MacIntosh as "inconsistent with the position that Canada has taken in other contexts, where we have voluntarily and proudly explicitly bound ourselves by law to protecting women against wrongful treatment on the basis of their gender." See Constance MacIntosh, "Domestic Violence and Gender Based Persecution: How Refugee Adjudicators Judge Women Seeking Refuge from Spousal Violence – and Why Reform is Needed," *Refuge*, 26(2) (2010), 147–64, at 149.

[49] Immigration and Refugee Board of Canada, *Chairperson Guidelines 4: Women Refugee Claimants Fearing Gender-Related Persecution* (1996), at Section A.I.3. available at: www.irb-cisr.gc.ca/Eng/BoaCom/references/pol/GuiDir/Pages/GuideDir04.aspx#note2.

gender as independent grounds for persecution claims.[50] This comment, together with the Guidelines, was later developed by judges to recognize domestic violence victims who are not protected by their home state as belonging to a "particular social group" and hence classified as refugees deserving protection by Canada.[51] This legal development was applauded as shifting refugee law from political law to human rights law. It was also commended for expanding refugee law's substantive eligibility grounds and extending refugee status to embrace "countless claimants previously denied protection, many of them women."[52]

Two studies, nevertheless, reveal the complex outcomes of not including gender as a sixth category of persecution within Canadian refugee law and of leaving spousal violence victims to the mercy of broad administrative discretion. The first study, conducted by Constance MacIntosh, analyzed 135 published cases involving spousal violence, handed down by the Canadian Refugee Protection Division (RPD) of the Immigration and Refugee Board (IRB) in 2005–2009. Since most RPD decisions are not published, this is not a representative sample but still a very enlightening one. The striking finding is that, although the RPD recognizes physical spousal violence as a form of persecution,[53] it nevertheless rejected 98 percent of the spousal violence-based applications covered in its published decisions. In the years 2005–2008, not one single published decision of the IRB was of an approved application. Significantly, 67 percent of the published rejections were based on the inability of the women to prove that their home country could not protect them from the domestic violence they suffered. This was so although many of them came from countries acknowledged as having very high rates of domestic violence. In 34 percent of the cases studied, the RPD was not convinced that the woman suffered domestic violence in her home country. Other reasons for rejection (some claims were rejected on multiple grounds) were that the woman could have relocated within her own country to escape the violence (11 percent) and that the woman's delay in seeking protection

---

[50] Interestingly, this was in a case of a male claimant. See discussion of *Ward v. Canada*, in Randall, "Particularized Social Groups," at 539–40.

[51] Efrat Arbel, "The Culture of Rights Protection in Canadian Refugee Law: Examining the Domestic Violence Cases," *McGill Law Journal*, 58(3) (2013), 729–71, at 745.

[52] Arbel, "The Culture of Rights Protection," at 738–40.

[53] No cases based on psychological or economic domestic violence were traced in the database, suggesting that the immigration authorities do not acknowledge these kinds of domestic violence, regardless of growing international awareness of the harm they inflict on women. See MacIntosh, "Domestic Violence and Gender," at 153.

proved that she did not fear the alleged abuse (12 percent).[54] Another striking finding is that 44 percent of reported appeals to the Federal Court against RPD rejection decisions in relation to spousal violence were accepted. In 39 out of the 89 decisions, "the Federal Court found that the RPD adjudicator either had the law or an element of procedural fairness wrong, or else had reached indefensible conclusion on factual matters."[55] This intense interference on behalf of the Federal Court might explain the high rates of acceptance of claims based on alleged spousal violence persecution (reported by the IRB to Efrat Arbel, who conducted the second study) of more than 40 percent in 2002–2012. According to the IRB, in this period, of the 9,839 such claims submitted and decided, 4,493 were accepted.[56] Another explanation about the gap found between the very low rate of acceptance in the published decisions and the overall acceptance rate, found in both studies,[57] is that for some reason the IRB chooses to publish a highly unrepresentative proportion of its decisions, focusing principally on rejections. As the IRB does not publically report the overall high rates of acceptance, I dare suggest that its publication of rejecting decisions is perhaps an attempt to deter potential spousal violence-based applications.[58]

Indeed, one of the fears behind states' reluctance to recognize alien spousal violence victims as refugees is that doing so could "open the floodgates." Taking into consideration the magnitude of the phenomenon of spousal violence, allowing women entry because their spouse is violent toward them is potentially a *de jure* invitation for millions of women from all over the world. Yet Karen Musalo, who specializes in

---

[54] Ibid., at 152–3.

[55] Ibid., at 161.

[56] These data are not routinely published, but were handed to Efrat Arbel in response to her request under the Access to Information Act. See Arbel, "The Culture of Rights Protection," at 746–7.

[57] In her study of 528 RPD decisions related to domestic violence, defined broader than in this chapter and in MacIntosh's study to include "familial physical violence, sexual violence, and spousal or familial rape," Arbel found a 20 percent rate of claims acceptance. See Arbel, "The Culture of Rights Protection."

[58] A lack of transparency of immigration-related decisions and the power of immigration adjudicators in shaping law in action in relation to domestic violence and refugee claims were also observed in the United States. Blaine Bookey studied sixty-seven unpublished decisions, handed in the year following the precedential decision of the US Immigration Board in 2014 recognizing domestic violence as a basis for asylum. Bookey found that notwithstanding this precedent, immigration judges continue to issue contradicting and arbitrary decisions, leaving many victims without the protection they need. See Blaine Bookey, "Gender-Based Asylum Post-Matter of A-R-C-G: Evolving Standards and Fair Application of the Law," *Southwestern Journal of International Law*, 22 (2016), 1–19.

gender and refugee law, points to the Canadian experience to rebut this fear.[59] Indeed, going back to the data provided to Arbel by the Canadian IRB, on average, fewer than 1,000 women seek domestic-violence-based asylum per year, and fewer than 500 are granted it, in a country known for being more generous than most in this respect. Musalo offers several explanations about why incorporating spousal violence into refugee law as a basis for persecution claims is unlikely to result in a deluge of applications. Women who suffer domestic violence in countries that do not provide them with protection, and who therefore might be eligible for refugee status in countries such as Canada, very often lack the basic rights and resources that will allow them to escape their country. With no access to capital and with restrictions on their movement, victims are trapped within their own nation state. Musalo adds that in most cases these women are the primary caregivers to their children and other family members. Hence, they are faced with the horrible dilemma of leaving family behind or exposing loved ones to the risks of the escape journey,[60] and, as we shall see in the last part of this chapter, to prosecution for child abduction.

Legal scholar Jessica Marsden argues that "excluding an entire class of asylees simply because there may be too many of them is unprincipled and unjust."[61] She also reassures against the "floodgates" anxiety by reminding us that, even according to the most generous refugee legislation, many domestically abused women will not be eligible for asylum. The claimant has to prove that the level of violence she suffered in the past and is likely to suffer in the future constitutes persecution, which is a high standard of harm. She also has to prove that her home country is unwilling or unable to protect her, most typically by demonstrating that she filed a complaint to the local authorities and was refused, and was unable to relocate internally away from the abuser.[62] Taking the social barriers in the home country and the legal barriers in the destination country into account, Marsden argues that the problem is not that there are too many

---

[59] Karen Musalo, "Protecting Victims of Gendered Persecution: Fear of Floodgates or Call to (Principled) Action?" *Virginia Journal of Social Policy & the Law,* 14(2) (2007), 119–43, at 133.

[60] Ibid.

[61] Jessica Marsden, "Domestic Violence Asylum after Matter of L-R," *The Yale Law Journal,* 123(7) (2014), 2512–57, at 2553. Interestingly, Marsden mentions that the 'floodgates' anxiety did not stop the United States from offering asylum to women at risk due to the one-child policy in China.

[62] See also Mullally, "Domestic Violence Asylum Claims."

who seek asylum due to spousal violence, but that there are, and probably will continue to be, too few.[63]

I perceive spousal-violence asylum to be both an international and national law victory *and* an international and transnational legal failure. The asylum solution resembles that of shelters for domestic violence survivors, found in countries striving to combat this phenomenon internally. Shelters might be a solution in dire times, but not one that should be celebrated, as they punish the victims rather than the abusers. It is the woman who has to face the upheaval of leaving her home, workplace, friends, and family, whereas the abuser carries on with his life in his habitual environment. Her children, if allowed entry to the shelter, are also torn away from their environment and exposed to life conditions that in many cases do not suit children's needs. Furthermore, in many cases there is not enough room at the shelters to accommodate all the women who request them (and their children), and in many more cases women are afraid to even try to escape to a shelter, among other reasons for fear of retaliation and poverty.[64] Likewise, in many cases, domestic violence asylum is not only a blessing but also a punishment of coerced exile and separation. Women should not be forced to leave behind everything they hold most dearly and seek help in a foreign country, in a foreign language, among strangers, and in many cases in detention conditions until their applications are handled. In addition, as explained earlier, for many women, escaping to another country is not even a viable option. Hence, relying only on asylum is as bad as relying only on shelters. The international community, as well as superpowers such as the United States, should develop effective pressure mechanisms that strongly encourage states to take educational, economic, and punitive measures to prevent spousal violence and ensure women's safety (in their private home and, more broadly, in the nation they call home).[65] The urgency in providing women such safety, and the

---

[63] Marsden, "Domestic Violence Asylum," at 2555–6.

[64] For a review of different intervention strategies to assist women suffering spousal violence, including the option of placement in a shelter, see articles in Albert R. Roberts (Ed.), *Battered Women and Their Families: Intervention Strategies and Treatment Programs*, 3rd edn. (New York: Springer, 2007).

[65] This is especially urgent in the face of a global backlash trend of misogynous men's groups arguing that there is no such phenomenon as domestic violence against women, that women submit false complaints, and that men suffer domestic violence at similar rates to those of women. See Molly Dragiewicz, *Equality with a Vengeance: Men's Rights Groups, Battered Women, and Antifeminist Backlash* (Lebanon, NH: Northeastern University Press, 2011). A model for such transnational intervention may be the US effort to battle human trafficking globally. Although there are downsides to the "sheriff" role played by the United States in its anti-trafficking transnational pressure, it has nevertheless managed to

international measures that should be taken when women are vulnerable to the mercy of their violent spouses, are also relevant to the last part of this chapter that deals with international child abduction. Before turning to this phenomenon, the second part centers on violence against children through the discussion of female genital mutilation, male circumcision, and child beauty pageants.

Parental Violence

Children all over the world are exposed to physical, sexual, and emotional violence inflicted on them by those who are supposed to be their protecting guardians: their parents.[66] The UN Convention on the Rights of the Child (CRC) reflects a global consensus that parental violence is wrong and should be illegal. Article 19(1) clearly states: "States Parties shall take all appropriate legislative, administrative, social, and educational measures to protect the child from all forms of physical or mental violence, injury or abuse, neglect or negligent treatment, maltreatment or exploitation, including sexual abuse, while in the care of parent(s), legal guardian(s) or any other person who has the care of the child."

However, even this universal norm is both contested in practice, since many parents continue to abuse their children, and also debated theoretically as different perceptions of parental authority collide. To explore some of the issues surrounding parental violence and point out the relevance of bordered globalization to their regulation, I have chosen to focus on three phenomena in this part of the chapter: female genital mutilation (FGM), male circumcision (MC), and child beauty pageants (CBPs). The discussion here will center only on FGM and MC performed on children, by far the most widely affected group.[67] Although discussions on the rights of adults are important in this regard (the right to undergo FGM or MC themselves, the right of the medical professions to cooperate with such practices on children or their obligation

---

pressure countries to effectively act against it. See Daphna Hacker, "Strategic Compliance in the Shadow of Transnational Anti-Trafficking Law," *Harvard Human Rights Journal*, 28(1) (2015), 11–64.

[66] Barnett, Miller-Perrin, & Perrin, *Family Violence across the Lifespan*, Ch. 3–5.

[67] FGM is usually performed on girls aged 4–12. See Population Reference Bureau, *Female Genital Mutilation/Cutting: Data and Trends* (2014), at 2, available at: www.prb.org/pdf14/fgm-wallchart2014.pdf; MC is performed on newborns or on children around the age of seven. See Rhona Schuz, "The Dangers of Children's Rights' Discourse in the Political Arena: The Issue of Religious Male Circumcision as a Test Case," *Cardozo Journal of Law & Gender*, 21 (2015), 347–91, at 354–5.

to refuse, and the right of adults to participate in beauty pageants), they do not involve the question of family violence that interests us here.[68] It is the power of parents to potentially cause harm to their children by exposing them to such practices that makes their regulation part of the discussion around legalized families.

I think it is very useful to place these phenomena side by side, and ask if they amount to parental violence that should be prohibited by law. These comparisons are helpful in producing a rational discussion and consistent regulation in relation to the boundaries of parental authority over children's bodies and souls. The need for such rational discussion and consistent regulation is ever more pressing in the era of bordered globalization. Both immigration, which brings to the same national territory different cultural perceptions of parental violence, and international law, which aims at advancing a shared global understanding of the limits of parental authority, increase the risk of biased, inconsistent, and harmful legislation. I offer, in what follows, a normative model that I believe minimizes this risk by revealing the cultural biases and phobias embedded in current discourse and legislation on parental violence.

Female Genital Mutilation

Female genital mutilation, female genital cutting, and *female circumcision* are three terms describing a traditional practice in some parts of the world that involves the removal of some or all of the external female genitalia for nonmedical reasons.[69] My choice of the term *female genital mutilation* already exposes my stance that this phenomenon is harmful and wrong – and more so than MC.

The WHO has classified FGM into four categories: Type I – partial or total removal of the clitoris and/or the prepuce (clitoridectomy); Type II – partial or total removal of the clitoris and the labia minora, with or without excision of the labia majora (excision); Type III – narrowing of the vaginal orifice by creating a covering seal by cutting and appositioning the labia minora and/or the labia majora, with or without excision of the clitoris (infibulation); and Type IV – all other harmful procedures to the female genitalia for nonmedical purposes, for example: pricking,

---

[68] When performed on adults, I would place the discussion of FGM and MC in the broader context of medical and nonmedical cosmetic surgery and practices.

[69] Rigmor C. Berg & Eva Denison, "Interventions to Reduce the Prevalence of Female Genital Mutilation/ Cutting in African Countries," *Campbell Systematic Reviews*, 8(9) (2012), 1–155.

piercing, incising, scraping, and cauterizing.[70] Most of the 3.6 million FGM acts currently performed on girls each year[71] are of Types I and II, but in several countries, including Somalia, Eritrea, and Senegal, the most severe type of FGM which includes the sewing of the genitalia is still performed on more than one in five of the girls cut.[72]

Over the last three decades, a universal legal consensus has emerged, according to which girls should be protected from FGM, even when their parents insist it should be carried out. Article 24(3) of the CRC, which was drafted during 1979–1981, demands that "States Parties shall take all effective and appropriate measures with a view to abolishing traditional practices prejudicial to the health of children." Though not mentioning the term, this article was particularly and deliberately targeting FGM.[73] CEDAW later published a General Recommendation specifically on "female circumcision," calling states parties to take appropriate and effective measures to eradicate it.[74] Four years later, in 1994, the UN launched a Plan of Action, endorsed by the WHO, UNICEF, and the United Nations Population Fund (UNFPA), to eliminate "harmful traditional practices," meaning first and foremost FGM.[75] Recently, the 193 UN member states agreed to include the elimination of FGM as part of the 2030 Agenda for Sustainable Development.[76]

It seems that Africa shares this legal consensus even though almost all the countries with the highest rates of FGM are located in this continent. In 2003, 36 African countries ratified the Protocol to the African Charter on Human and Peoples' Rights on the Rights of Women in Africa, which obliges them to "prohibit and condemn all forms of harmful practices

---

[70] "Classification of Female Genital Mutilation," World Health Organization, available at: www.who.int/reproductivehealth/topics/fgm/overview/en/.

[71] UNICEF, *Female Genital Mutilation/Cutting: What Might the Future Hold?* (2015), at 3, available at: www.unicef.org/media/files/FGM-C_Report_7_15_Final_LR.pdf.

[72] UNICEF, *Female Genital Mutilation/Cutting: A Statistical Overview and Exploration of the Dynamics of Change*, available at: www.unicef.org/media/files/FGCM_Brochure_Lo_res.pdf.

[73] Michael Freeman, "The Morality of Cultural Pluralism," *The International Journal of Children's Rights*, 3 (1995), 1–17, at 6; Patricia Wheeler, "Eliminating FGM: The Role of the Law," *The International Journal of Children's Rights*, 11 (2004), 257–71, at 260.

[74] Convention on the Elimination of All Forms of Discrimination against Women, General Recommendation No. 14, available at: www.un.org/womenwatch/daw/cedaw/recommendations/recomm.htm.

[75] Wheeler, "Eliminating FGM," at 257.

[76] UN Sustainable Development Summit 2015, *Sustainable Development Goals* (2015), Article 5.3, available at: www.who.int/mediacentre/events/meetings/2015/un-sustainable-development-summit/en/.

which negatively affect the human rights of women and which are contrary to recognised international standards." The Protocol demands that
states' parties take all necessary legislative and other measures to eliminate
such practices, including the "prohibition, through legislative measures
backed by sanctions, of all forms of female genital mutilation, scarification, medicalisation and para-medicalisation of female genital mutilation and all other practices in order to eradicate them."[77] Indeed, a recent
review found that 18 of the 28 African countries in which FGM is most
common had enacted laws banning it, with one further country having
provincial laws, two countries working on draft laws, and one having a
general law that can be used to criminalize FGM.[78] Finally, as FGM began
to enter the Global North as a result of immigration, regional resolutions
and national laws were passed in Europe and North America with the aim
of combating and eliminating the practice wherever it takes place.[79]

It would appear that this international, regional, and national anti-FGM
legal commitment is bearing fruit. According to the most recent UNICEF
estimation, based on surveys conducted in nineteen countries in which
FGM is practiced, whereas, on average, in 1985, 51 percent of girls aged
15–19 had undergone FGM, by 2015 the rate had dropped to 37 percent.[80]
However, due to population growth in the nations in question, even if
the current rate of decline were to persist, the number of girls mutilated
each year would increase, from 3.6 million today to 4.1 million in 2050.[81]
Indeed, as in the case of spousal violence, the regulation against FGM
is only a partial success story. Whereas some countries demonstrate the

---

[77] African Commission on Human and Peoples' Rights, *Protocol to the African Charter on
Human and Peoples' Rights on the Rights of Women in Africa* (2003), Article 5. available
at: www.achpr.org/instruments/women-protocol/#5.

[78] Jane Muthumbi, Joar Svanemyr, Elisa Scolaro, Marleen Temmerman, & Lale Say, "Female
Genital Mutilation: A Literature Review of the Current Status of Legislation and Policies
in 27 African Countries and Yemen," *African Journal of Reproductive Health*, 19(3)
(2015), 32–40.

[79] See, for example, "European Parliament Resolution of 14 June 2012 on Ending
Female Genital Mutilation," available at: www.europarl.europa.eu/sides/getDoc.
do?type=TA&reference=P7-TA-2012-0261&format=XML&language=EN; Female Genital
Mutilation Act 2003, available at: www.legislation.gov.uk/ukpga/2003/31/contents; and 18
U.S. Code S. 116 – Female Genital Mutilation, available at: www.law.cornell.edu/uscode/
text/18/116. This includes recognizing the fear of being exposed to FGM in the home
country as a basis for asylum claims, along similar lines to the domestic violence claims
discussed in the previous part of this chapter. See Randall, "Particularized Social Groups."

[80] UNICEF, *Female Genital Mutilation/Cutting: A Global Concern*, available at: www.unicef
.org/media/files/FGMC_2016_brochure_final_UNICEF_SPREAD.pdf.

[81] UNICEF, *Female Genital Mutilation/Cutting: What Might the Future Hold?*.

ability and will to legislate and enforce anti-FGM policies, others allow
the practice to continue undisturbed, regardless of the international and
regional outcry against it.[82]

Egypt is an interesting example of the latter, being one of the three countries contributing the highest numbers of FGM, together with Indonesia
and Ethiopia.[83] According to UNICEF, 87 percent of females aged 15–49
living in Egypt underwent FGM.[84] However, there has been a major shift
in recent years in the way in which FGM is managed in Egypt. The practice continues to be widespread, yet it is now highly medicalized. Indeed,
Egypt has the highest rate of FGM medicalization in Africa, with 77 percent of the procedures performed by healthcare professionals.[85] Yet interestingly, in the case of Egypt, the *how* of FGM has provoked significant
debate in its own right. Although the Egyptian Ministry of Health issued
a decree prohibiting FGM as long ago as 1959, a 1994 decree allowed
it if performed by doctors in governmental hospitals. Just a year later,
the government then banned hospitals from performing it, re-allowed
it for both governmental and private hospitals in 1996, and re-banned it
in 2007 after the deaths of two girls who had undergone the procedure
under medical care.[86] This legislative instability echoes internal debates
between religious leaders who seek to ban FGM and those who encourage it,[87] and between doctors who accept and perform it[88] and medical
scholars who strongly oppose it.[89] The repeated legislative change of
heart, together with a very poor enforcement record,[90] also reflects the
support for FGM among the majority of Egyptians and the high social
costs awaiting any parents who would choose not to send their daughter
to undergo it. The daughters themselves also face heavy social sanctions

[82] Muthumbi, Svanemyr, Scolaro, Temmerman, & Say, "Female Genital Mutilation."
[83] UNICEF, *Female Genital Mutilation/Cutting: A Global Concern.*
[84] Ibid.
[85] Muthumbi, Svanemyr, Scolaro, Temmerman, & Say, "Female Genital Mutilation," at 37.
[86] Ibid.
[87] Ronan van Rossem, Dominique Meekers, & Anastasia J. Gage, "Women's Position and
Attitudes towards Female Genital Mutilation in Egypt: A Secondary Analysis of the Egypt
Demographic and Health Surveys, 1995–2014," *BMC Public Health,* 15(2015), 874–87,
at 874–5.
[88] Muthumbi, Svanemyr, Scolaro, Temmerman, & Say, "Female Genital Mutilation," at 37.
[89] See, for example, G. I. Serour, "Medicalization of Female Genital Mutilation/Cutting,"
African Journal of Urology, 19 (2013), 145–9.
[90] Only in January of 2015 was the first sentence under the 2007 banning regulation handed
against a doctor who performed FGM. See Massoud Hayoun, "Egypt Court Jails Doctor
in 'Historic' FGM Prosecution," *Aljazeera America,* available at: http://america.aljazeera
.com/articles/2015/1/26/egypt-sentences-doctor-father-in-fgm-case-equality-now.html.

including loss of status, fewer marriage opportunities, and social exclusion.[91] Indeed, it is vital to remember that, in communities that practice FGM, girls and women are harmed not only if undergoing it, but also if not. In the latter scenario, their body is left intact, but their social position can be severely damaged and their chances of establishing a family substantially reduced. In this light, we must understand the observation of sociologist Ronan van Rossem and his colleagues: "Often mothers have little control over the decision whether their daughters will be cut. They may oppose having their daughters cut, but neither be willing nor able to influence this decision."[92] This group of researchers found that opposition to FGM among Egyptian women is positively correlated with education level, literacy, and participation in the labor market.[93] Hence, the low gender equality in Egypt (ranked 131 by the UN out of 188 countries),[94] and the growing political power of the conservatives leave very little hope for decisive and effective state actions against FGM in the near future or for a substantial and effective resistance on the part of mothers. The Egyptian case is also an example of the lack of effective international pressure in relation to FGM. For instance, the fact that the vast majority of Egyptian women undergo FGM does not stop the United States from providing the country with substantial foreign aid, nor has it prevented Egypt from being a powerful leading force within Africa as well as the Arab world.

Interestingly, the universal law-in-the-books consensus against FGM is challenged not only by the lack of enforcement that exposes millions of girls to this practice every year, but also by academics. The practice has become one of the most hotly debated issues between feminists, on the one hand, and post-colonialists and multiculturalists, on the other.

Since the mid-1970s, FGM has been conceptualized by feminists as an extreme example of women's oppression. For most feminists, FGM is a clear case of a tradition that must be completely and immediately eliminated, regardless of respect for cultural differences or contextual narratives.[95] The feminist discourse on FGM emphasizes its short- and

---

[91] Van Rossem, Meekers, & Gage, "Women's Position and Attitudes," at 875.

[92] Ibid., at 877.

[93] Ibid., at 881.

[94] United Nations Development Programme, *Human Development Reports* (2015), at Table 5, available at: http://hdr.undp.org/en/composite/GII.

[95] See Susan Moller Okin's canonical essay mentioning female genital cutting as an example for her overall argument that group cultural rights should never trample over individual rights. Susan Moller Okin, "Is Multiculturalism Bad for Women?" in Joshua Cohen, Matthew Howard, & Martha C. Nussbaum (Eds.), *Is Multiculturalism Bad for Women?* (Princeton, NJ: Princeton University Press, 1999), pp. 7–26.

long-term, empirically proven, physical, and psychological risks and harms.[96] These include, among others, pain, bleeding, urine and menstrual disorders, genital infection, decreased sexual desire and pleasure, pain during sex, obstetric complications, psychological post-trauma disorders, and even death.[97] The feminist discourse also discusses the roots of FGM, arguing that it symbolizes women's lower social status because it stems from the wish to control women's sexuality and from patriarchal notions of the female body as in need of reshaping to ensure aesthetics and cleanliness.[98]

As the study of sociologist Lisa Wade shows, this abolitionist feminist stance was very soon attacked within academic circles as ethnocentric, imperialist, patronizing, demonizing, unproven, discriminatory, and simplistic. By the mid-1990s this line of critique dominated the literature.[99] This is interesting because no such claims materialized in relation to the feminist battle against spousal violence, discussed earlier, although I would argue that it is just as much a cultural practice as FGM. It seems that both the conceptualization of spousal violence as a nontraditional practice[100] and its prevalence in most societies, as opposed to the definition of FGM as a traditional practice and its prevalence in Africa, singled out feminist efforts in relation to the latter as suspicious and problematic.

As Wade demonstrates, this postcolonial and multicultural attack homogenized the feminist discourse, although, in fact, it varies substantially. Whereas some feminist writers do, indeed, speak from a Westernized and patronizing perspective (because they regard those who practice FGM as inferior, ignorant, cruel, and inhuman), others are much more

---

[96] For example, Shelley Simms, "What's Culture Got to Do With It? Excising the Harmful Tradition of Female Circumcision," *Harvard Law Review*, 106(8) (1993), 1944–61.

[97] "Health Risks of Female Genital Mutilation," World Health Organization, available at: www .who.int/reproductivehealth/topics/fgm/health_consequences_fgm/en/; Ellen Gruenbaum, *The Female Circumcision Controversy: An Anthropological Perspective* (Philadelphia: University of Pennsylvania Press, 2001), pp. 4–7; Peggy Mulongo, Sue McAndrew, & Caroline H. Martin, "Crossing Borders: Discussing the Evidence Relating to the Mental Health Needs of Women Exposed to Female Genital Mutilation," *International Journal of Mental Health Nursing*, 23(4) (2014), 296–305; Armelle Andro, Emmanuelle Cambois, & Marie Lesclingand, "Long-Term Consequences of Female Genital Mutilation in a European Context: Self-Perceived Health of FGM Women Compared to Non-FGM Women," *Social Science & Medicine*, 106 (2014), 177–84.

[98] See Okin, "Is Multiculturalism Bad for Women?"

[99] Lisa Wade, "Learning from 'Female Genital Mutilation': Lessons from 30 Years of Academic Discourse," *Ethnicities*, 12(1) (2011), 26–49.

[100] Moira Dustin, "Female Genital Mutilation/Cutting in the UK," *European Journal of Women's Studies*, 17(1) (2010), 7–23, at 8.

responsive to cultural meanings and differences, and aware of the dangers of imposing feminist ideas top-down. They call for a much more nuanced and contextualized understanding of the practice, for the empowerment of women from the relevant communities to bring gradual change from within, and for feminist interpretation of religious texts that would base anti-FGM arguments on its religious unnecessity.[101]

An inspiring example of reflexive feminism, which embraces the post-colonial and multicultural critique while insisting on the need to eliminate FGM, is the recent paper by scholar and educator Jennifer Wanjiku Khamasi.[102] As a woman raised in a Nigerian community that celebrated female circumcision, and as a feminist researcher who monitors cultural changes in relation to female and male circumcision in Kenya, she finds herself "sandwiched between the circumcised and the uncircumcised."[103] Based on her personal and professional experiences, and in light of feminist and hermeneutic theories – which emphasize the subjective standpoint as a source of objective knowledge, the need to understand the other's viewpoint in the historical, social, and cultural context of power relations, and the need to develop a critical consciousness – Wanjiku Khamasi calls for a dialogue between anti-FGM activists and the women within the communities in which it is practiced. The dialogue can then be widened to include the men from these communities. This exchange, she emphasizes, should be based on conversations of the activists *with* the parents and the circumcisers, rather than monologues directed *at* them. The conversations should include "truth telling," in which the legal narrative is not privileged over personal narratives, and women are invited to take part and share their personal histories and beliefs, including feelings of pride and happiness at their cutting, as well as shame, victimization, or sadness at being circumcised or uncircumcised. Finally, she asserts, these conversations should avoid "othering" and, instead, represent a mutual journey toward new solutions, such as alternative rites of passage that are not harmful for girls. I see in Wanjiku Khamasi's insights an important reminder that outlawing FGM can only be the start or endpoint of an internal cultural change. Without dialogue, education, and alternatives

---

[101] Wade, "Learning from 'Female Genital Mutilation.'"

[102] Jennifer Wanjiku Khamasi, "Transcending Female Circumcision: A Call for Collective Unmasking" in Chia Longman & Tamsin Bradley (Eds.), *Interrogating Harmful Cultural Practices: Gender, Culture and Coercion* (London: Routledge, 2015), pp. 99–110.

[103] Ibid., at 100.

within the relevant communities, FGM will probably go on openly, as is the case in Egypt, or underground, as is the case in Nigeria and other countries and communities in the Global South[104] and Global North,[105] and will harm both circumcised and uncircumcised girls and women. Notwithstanding, national laws and police and welfare services should voice a clear message, in harmony with international law, that FGM is wrong and unacceptable, and in particular should provide assistance to parents and potential victims who wish to resist it.[106]

Male Circumcision

MC is performed on millions of baby boys and male children around the world,[107] and involves the removal of some, or all, of the foreskin from the penis.[108] Recently, a heated debate has evolved around this practice, first among academics, and then legislators and jurists, calling to abolish it. Among those who take an anti-MC stance, we often find the argument that FGM and MC are very similar and therefore should both be prohibited. In response, several scholars argue that these two practices are so different that there are no grounds for comparison between them and no lessons to be learned from discussing them together.

Sami Aldeeb Abu-Sahlieh, who heads the Center of Arab and Islamic Law in Switzerland, was among the first voices within the current anti-MC movement. He compares FGM and MC and comes to the conclusion that "both are mutilations of healthy sexual organs of non-consenting

---

[104] Longman & Bradley, *Interrogating Harmful Cultural Practices*; Gruenbaum, *The Female Circumcision Controversy.*

[105] Dustin, "Female Genital Mutilation."

[106] For example, FGM has been a criminal offense in the UK since 1985. In 2003, it also became a criminal offence for UK nationals or permanent residents to take their child abroad to undergo FGM. In 2015, the law was further amended to allow FGM protection orders, which can be obtained through a civil procedure within the Family Court. The request for the order can by submitted by the potential victim, a relevant third party such as the local authority, or others if permitted by the court, such as teachers and other family members. See "Female Genital Mutilation (FGM): Legislation, Policy and Guidance," NSPCC, available at: www.nspcc.org.uk/preventing-abuse/child-abuse-and-neglect/female-genital-mutilation-fgm/legislation-policy-and-guidance/.

[107] In some parts of the world, including the Middle East, North and West Africa, and Central Asia, MC is almost universal. In several other parts, including North America, it is very common. See World Health Organization, *Neonatal and Child Male Circumcision: A Global Review* (2010), at Section 2.3, available at: www.who.int/hiv/pub/malecircumcision/neonatal_child_MC_UNAIDS.pdf.

[108] Ibid.; David L. Gollaher, *Circumcision: A History of the World's Most Controversial Surgery* (New York: Basic Books, 2000).

children. There is no justification for such mutilations. If the foreskin were useless, Nature would not have made it. It is imperative in any case to leave the child intact until the age of 18 when he will have the freedom to decide for himself whether he wants to be circumcised or not."[109] He shows that both FGM and MC are not required in the Koran, and argues that, in any case, "a God who demands that his believers be mutilated and branded on their genitals the same as cattle, is a God of questionable ethics."[110] In his later work, he argues that, just like FGM, MC provides no health benefits. Moreover, he claims, while the risks of FGM are exaggerated, the risks of MC are ignored.[111]

Interdisciplinary researcher Brian Earp follows a similar line of argument in several of his many recent articles devoted to MC.[112] He argues that the harms of FGM can be minimized, and even eliminated, by a transition toward its less invasive forms coupled with medicalization. According to Earp, the argument that FGM harms women's sexuality is valid, though exaggerated, as studies show that different women react sexually differently to the cutting they have experienced. "These same considerations apply to male circumcision," he claims. Like FGM, MC is not monolithic, and includes more and less harmful practices, depending on factors such as the amount of skin removed, the age of the child, and whether he is awake or under some kind of anesthetic. Again like FGM, MC can result in pain, damage to the genitals, infections, and decreased sexual pleasure, and can even be life-threatening.[113] On the symbolic level, Earp argues that the main motivation for both male and female circumcision in Africa is cultural perceptions of cleanliness. Moreover, in Judaism, circumcision symbolizes the inferiority of females, as it is only men that carry on their body the sacred covenant between God and Avraham, the primordial patriarch of the Jewish nation. The motivation to control male sexuality through circumcision, Earp observes, is evident both in

---

[109] Sami A. Aldeeb Abu-Sahlieh, "To Mutilate in the Name of Jehovah or Allah: Legitimization of Male and Female Circumcision," *Medicine and Law*, 13(7–8) (1994), 575–622, at 610.

[110] Ibid., at 612.

[111] Sami A. Aldeeb Abu-Sahlieh, "Male and Female Circumcision: The Myth of the Difference" in Rogaia Mustafa Abusharaf (Ed.), *Female Circumcision: Multicultural Perspectives* (Philadelphia: University of Pennsylvania Press, 2006), pp. 47–74, at 60–1.

[112] Oxford Academia website, Brian D. Earp, available at: https://oxford.academia.edu/BrianDEarp.

[113] Brian D. Earp, "Female Genital Mutilation and Male Circumcision: Toward an Autonomy-Based Ethical Framework," *Medicolegal and Bioethics*, 5 (2015), 89–104. See also Brian D. Earp, "Between Moral Relativism and Moral Hypocrisy: Reframing the Debate on FGM," *Kennedy Institute of Ethics Journal*, 26(2) (2016), 105–44.

Judaism and in the Victorian period, the latter bringing this practice to Christian audiences. Hence, he argues, the similarity between FGM and MC is such that "the ordinary distinctions that *are* maintained [between them], including by powerful decision-making bodies with considerable influence on a global scale, are morally inconsistent."[114] And so, if Western societies wish to allow MC as long as it does not cross "an arbitrary threshold of 'harm'" they should allow "similar alteration to the genitals of little girls."[115] Because it is hard to define "harm" and enforce this definition, and because both girls and boys have a right to bodily integrity, Earp argues that it is better to prohibit FGM and MC on infants, and allow them only when the subjects are mature enough to give their free informed consent.

Recent social and legal changes reflect the arguments and concerns of both Aldeeb Abu-Sahlieh and Earp. Among Christians in the Global North, for whom circumcision was always based on medical considerations rather than being a religious obligation or cultural ritual, a decline in the practice is being witnessed, as more parents than before opt out of it.[116] Moreover, there are growing calls by activists and policy makers in the Global North – not yet successful – to completely ban it by law.[117]

On the opposite side of the debate, we find those who argue that FGM and MC are so different that comparing them must inevitably lead to the conclusion that the former must be eradicated, whereas the latter must be allowed. For example, according to Michael Freeman, one of the world's leading experts on children's rights, FGM and MC are "radically different."[118] Unlike FGM, which is one of the most harmful traditional practices for children,[119] MC is not an act of violence as it does not cause injury, he argues. Freeman's argument can be supported by medical evidence gathered by the WHO that MC "is generally a safe procedure when conducted by trained and experienced providers in hygienic conditions,"[120]

---

[114] Earp, "Female Genital Mutilation," at 98.

[115] Ibid.

[116] For example, in Australia and New Zealand, see The Royal Australasian College of Physicians, *Circumcision of Infant Males* (2010), available at: www.ccyp.vic.gov.au/childsafetycommissioner/downloads/male_circumcision.pdf; In Canada, see Todd S. Sorokan, Jane C. Finlay, & Ann L. Jefferies, "Newborn Male Circumcision," *Paediatrics & Child Health*, 20(6) (2015), 311–5.

[117] Johanna Schiratzki, "Banning God's Law in the Name of the Holy Body: The Nordic Position on Ritual Male Circumcision," *The Family in Law*, 5 (2011), 35–53.

[118] Michael D. A. Freeman, "A Child's Right to Circumcision," *BJU International*, 83(1) (1999), 74–8, at 74.

[119] Freeman, "The Morality of Cultural Pluralism," at 6.

[120] World Health Organization, *Neonatal and Child Male Circumcision*, at 55.

and by the results of the systemic review conducted by medical experts Brian Morrison and Jon Krieger. This review showed that MC, as currently performed in both medicalized and nonmedicalized settings, does not have any adverse effect on sensitivity or on sexual function, sensation, or satisfaction.[121]

According to Freeman, not only should MC be allowed, but, in the case of Jewish babies and Muslim children, they have a right to circumcision as part of their internationally recognized right to cultural heritage and identity. To decree that children must be old enough to give their informed consent is only to expose them to greater physical and emotional distress than if the procedure is carried out in infancy. Jewish and Muslim parents should be allowed to give "future-oriented-consent" on behalf of their children to be circumcised, because for their sons "cultural and religious identity, the sense of belonging to a group, is of greater significance than minor invasive treatment administered when they were unaware of it."[122] Mark Swatek-Evenstein adds another reason for questioning the validity of comparing FGM and MC – namely, the medical benefits associated with MC and lacking in FGM.[123] Indeed, the WHO has reviewed available medical evidence and concluded that MC reduces the risk of several urinary tract infections, reduces the risk of heterosexually-acquired HIV infection in men by 50–60 percent, and reduces the risk of several reproductive tract infections, which also lowers the chances of the female partners of circumcised men being infected.[124]

As a feminist secular Jewish mother who cooperated with the circumcision of her son, I find the comparison between FGM and MC enlightening. This cross-cultural comparison made me question my absolute opposition to FGM alongside my perception that parents should be allowed to circumcise their boys. I believe this comparison teaches us that, contrary to Freeman's claim, MC *is* a violent act, as it cuts the boy's body, inflicts pain, and in rare cases causes harms, such as infection, sexual dysfunction, and even death from excessive bleeding.[125] As a parental violent act, it should be justified or otherwise prohibited. The justification should be

[121] Brian J. Morris & John N. Krieger, "Does Male Circumcision Affect Sexual Function, Sensitivity, or Satisfaction? – A Systematic Review," *Journal of Sexual Medicine*, 10(11) (2013), 2644–57.
[122] Freeman, "A Child's Right to Circumcision."
[123] Mark Swatek-Evenstein, "Limits of Enlightenment and the Law – On the Legality of Ritual Male Circumcision in Europe Today," *Merkourios*, 29(77) (2013), 42–50, at 45.
[124] World Health Organization, *Neonatal and Child Male Circumcision*, Section 7.5.
[125] Ibid., Section 6.

strong, as the basic assumption should be that violence against the child harms the child's best interests, is inflicted without the child's consent, and violates the child's right to bodily autonomy and integrity. Like FGM and any other parental violent acts, I believe MC should be judged according to a normative model of three parameters: the proven harms and risks, the proven benefits, and the cultural meaning as perceived by the family members and their community. If there are significant benefits and profound cultural meaning, then parental violence that does not cause harsh damage might be tolerated by the law.

To make such a judgment requires, first and foremost, knowledge of the physical, psychological, and social outcomes of the act, and an open discussion around its history and cultural meaning. Like the WHO, I am convinced by the available data on the physical and psychological risks and benefits of FGM and MC, and primarily on this basis believe that the former should be outlawed but the latter allowed.[126] Notwithstanding, just as in the case of vaccination, parents of male babies should be granted full information about the risks and benefits of MC, including in relation to the different degrees of foreskin removal and the child's age. I can testify that in Israel, for example, discussing the risks of MC is almost a taboo,[127] and even the medical benefits are ignored. Most Israeli parents, therefore, do not truly grant their *informed* "future-oriented-consent" on behalf of their children, but rather an uninformed consent rooted in unquestioned social conventions. Furthermore, parallel to the search for less harmful alternatives to FGM, so should the risks of MC be minimized. This can be achieved by allowing it only if performed by circumcisers certified according to evidence-based regulations,[128] and by conducting more research on the least harmful MC procedure possible. Finally, unlike FGM, MC is a religious practice which, for observant Jews, amounts to a divine commandment, and which holds positive symbolism for its male subjects. As such, it is more fundamental to culture than nonreligious traditions, and not symbolically demeaning to the children undergoing it. Nonetheless, it should not be trivialized and should be openly debated.

---

[126] See also Schuz, "The Dangers of Children's Rights' Discourse in the Political Arena."

[127] In recent years there have been several NGOs promoting an anti-MC agenda in Israel and weakening the social and religious taboo of discussing MC's risks and harms. See, for example, the Ben Shalem Foundation website, available at: www.britmila.org.il/; and the Group of Parents of Complete Children website, available at: www.kahal.org/ (Hebrew).

[128] Germany and Sweden have already legislated laws that subject MC to medical standards. See Reinhard Merkel & Holm Putzke, "After Cologne: Male Circumcision and the Law. Parental Right, Religious Liberty or Criminal Assault?" *Journal of Medical Ethics*, 39 (2013), 444–9; Schiratzki, "Banning God's Law."

Another lesson that can be usefully drawn, in my opinion, from the comparison between FGM and MC is that part of the anti-MC discourse may possibly be a pretext for Islamophobia, anti-Semitism, and the *othering* of immigrants and non-Western cultures. Just as in the case of religious tribunals, discussed in Chapter 3, although Jews have circumcised their male babies for centuries and have been persecuted over this practice in different historical periods, the current anxiety over this practice emerged only after significant numbers of Muslim immigrants arrived at the Global North. Moreover, the lack of debate over Western patriarchal practices that affect minors' bodily integrity (including the new trends among female teenagers, of genital trimming for cosmetic reasons and the removal of all pubic hair by waxing or laser)[129] raises the suspicion of a double standard on the part of Western scholars and activists. To explore this potential double standard further, I would like to end this part of the chapter by focusing on CBPs, which, unlike FGM and MC, are a phenomenon neglected by the legal discourse, despite having global patriarchal effects and, in my opinion, being based on unjustifiable parental violent acts. Hence, I would argue, CBPs should be outlawed.

Child Beauty Pageants

CBPs constitute a flourishing multibillion dollar industry in the United States that is growing faster than its adult counterpart. Each year about 5,000 child beauty contests are held around the United States, involving millions of participants.[130] The media plays an important role in transforming this industry into a global one, with several American reality shows (such as *Toddlers & Tiaras* and *Here Comes Honey Boo Boo*) documenting the family lives of CBP contestants, and different broadcasters and YouTube bringing this phenomenon to millions of homes around the world. Indeed, CBPs are now also organized in countries such as Australia,[131] the UK,[132] and

---

[129] See Roni Caryn Rabin, "More Teenage Girls Seeking Genital Cosmetic Surgery," *The New York Times* (Apr. 25, 2016), available at: http://well.blogs.nytimes.com/2016/04/25/increase-in-teenage-genital-surgery-prompts-guidelines-for-doctors/?_r=0.

[130] Lucy Wolfe, "Darling Divas or Damaged Daughters? The Dark Side of Child Beauty Pageants and an Administrative Law Solution," *Tulane Law Review*, 87 (2012), 427–55; Lindsay Lieberman, "Protecting Pageant Princesses: A Call for Statutory Regulation of Child Beauty Pageants," *Journal of Law and Policy*, 18(2) (2010), 739–74.

[131] Australian Royalty Pageants website: http://arpageants.com.au/.

[132] "Children Beauty Pageants UK," Facebook, available at: www.facebook.com/childrenbeautypageant/?fref=nf.

Canada,[133] and their growing global popularity has led some national and local jurisdictions, such as in France[134] and in Russia,[135] to limit or ban them by law.

In these contests, little girls[136] compete for a crown and a monetary prize by presenting themselves on stage in sportswear, evening gowns, and bathing suits – mimicking the adult beauty contest – while singing and dancing. Unlike genuine talent shows and sporting competitions, the CBPs are not really about celebrating special singing or dancing prowess, but rather about showcasing contestants' feminine physical appearance.[137] Although these are very young girls, they are sexualized in their adult-like poses, costumes, cosmetics and flirtatious behavior, on which they are judged.[138] These girls' parents spend thousands of dollars – money they do not always have[139] – on entry fees, travel and accommodation, wigs and hair extensions, false eyelashes, teeth-whitening products and fake teeth, expensive clothes, manicures, pedicures, body tanning, professional hair stylists, make-up artists, and coaches.[140]

A recent example was reported in the online version of the popular UK newspaper, the *Daily Mail*. The article featured a 23-year-old mother, Jas Sullivan, who turns her 22-month-old daughter, Minnie-Beau, into a "beauty queen." This British single parent, who still lives with her mother, has invested £20,000 in 300 costumes, including bikinis, and gold jewelry so her daughter can compete in CBPs. It is clear she derives enormous

[133] Miss All Canadian Pageant Website: http://www.allcanadianpageants.com/.

[134] "French MPs Ban Beauty Contests for under-13s," *The Local fr* (January 27, 2014), www .thelocal.fr/20140127/beauty-contests-ban-france-mini-miss-pageants.

[135] Lydia Smith, "Russia Calls to Ban Child Beauty Pageants: Should We Do the Same?" *International Business Times* (February 18, 2014), available at: www.ibtimes.co.uk/ russia-calls-ban-child-beauty-pageants-should-we-do-same-1436946.

[136] There are also competitions for boys, though they are not common. Some of the competitions include babies. See Lieberman, "Protecting Pageant Princesses."

[137] For a rare sociological study of CBPs, see Martha Heltsley, "From Lollipops to Lolita: The Making of the Pageant Child," PhD Dissertation, Southern Illinois University at Carbondale (2003), available at: http://search.proquest.com/docview/288361158/.

[138] Tisha Dejmanee, "Nursing at the Screen: Post-Feminist Daughters and Demonized Mothers on Toddlers and Tiaras," *Feminist Media Studies*, 15(3) (2015), 460–73, at 465; Lieberman, "Protecting Pageant Princesses," at 745.

[139] Elisabeth Blumer Thompson, "Trailer Park Royalty: Southern Child Beauty Pageants, Girlhood and Power," PhD Dissertation, Georgia Southern University (2007), available at: http://digitalcommons.georgiasouthern.edu/cgi/viewcontent.cgi?article=1471&conte xt=etd.

[140] Lieberman, "Protecting Pageant Princesses," at 744–5.

personal satisfaction from preparing her little girl for these competitions and seeing her dressed to adult standards. Minnie-Beau's ears were pierced when she was just four months old (so she can now wear adult-style hoop earrings), and for every one of the competitions she has taken part in since she was 18-months old, her mother has made her wear make-up including false eyelashes, hair extensions, and painted nails. If the toddler gets cranky during preparations, she is "bribed" with ice cream. Though she still cannot talk, she already knows how to dazzle the pageant judges with her dances, kisses, and pouting. Although the article mentions that Minnie-Beau won eight titles, it does not say if these included any monetary prizes.[141]

Although not yet systematically studied,[142] there are clear indications that the CBP industry, and the parents (predominantly the mothers)[143] who feed and cooperate with it, expose the participating girls to physical and psychological risks, and cause generalized social damage to girls and women. The physical risks include: immediate pain experienced during the intense bodily preparations for the contests (for example in the process of applying and removing hair extensions, eyebrow waxing, and even cosmetic surgery); exposure to potentially dangerous chemicals and cosmetic procedures (for example during full-body artificial tanning and gluing of artificial eyelashes); and the consumption of unhealthy amounts of caffeine and sugar needed to withstand the long hours of the competition.[144] The psychological risks include stress, eating disorders, low self-esteem, and difficulties in forming positive relations with other children.[145] On

---

[141] Phoebe Jackson-Edwards, "Mother Spends £20,000 Turning her 22-Month-Old Baby into a Beauty Queen," Mail Online (October 16, 2015), available at: www.dailymail.co.uk/femail/article-3275764/Mother-spent-20-000-turning-22-month-old-baby-beauty-queen-complete-makeup-hair-extensions.html.

[142] There are hardly any empirical studies on the outcomes of CPB, and those that exist are based on very small samples. For example, one study include twenty-two women, eleven who participated in CBPs and eleven who did not. Significant correlation was found between participating in CBPs and increased body dissatisfaction, difficulty trusting interpersonal relationships, and greater impulsive behaviors. There were no significant differences between the two groups on measures of bulimic behavior, body perception, depression, or self-esteem. See Anna L. Wonderlich, Diann M. Ackard, & Judith B. Henderson, "Childhood Beauty Pageant Contestants: Associations with Adult Disordered Eating and Mental Health," *Eating Disorders* 13(3) (2005), 291–301. Although I am already convinced that the harms of CBPs outweigh their benefits, it is important to conduct more studies to allow evidenced-based regulation, as suggested by my three-parameters model.

[143] Dejmanee, "Nursing at the Screen."

[144] Wolfe, "Darling Divas," at 431–4; Lieberman, "Protecting Pageant Princesses," at 754–6.

[145] Wolfe, "Darling Divas," at 434–7; Lieberman, "Protecting Pageant Princesses," at 752–4.

the social level, this phenomenon feeds patriarchal notions of girls and women as sex objects, judged and loved only according to their stereotypically feminine physical appearance. Some also argue that the sexualization of such young girls encourages pedophilia and child pornography.[146] One example of the possible wider social effects of the CBP industry is the growing popularity of birthday parties for young girls that center on providing adult-style clothes, make-up, and hairstyles for the birthday girl and her friends.[147]

Interestingly, although CBPs are gaining popularity and supportive public exposure through the global media, this industry is simultaneously heavily criticized by educators, health professionals, and journalists in relation to the harms it causes to the young competitors as well as to girls and women in general.[148] Even the behind-the-scenes reality shows about CBPs are critical of the mothers of the contestants, demonizing them as poor parents who, selfishly, push their daughters to undergo painful and harmful practices against their will.[149] Notwithstanding this critical awareness, this industry is completely unregulated in most places.[150] Likewise, despite the awareness of many of the parental failure involved, parents are not restricted or punished in any way for the voluntary exposure of their children to the industry's hazards.[151]

Among the very few legal scholars who have paid attention to this phenomenon, there is an agreement that some state intervention is in order. Lindsay Lieberman suggests granting child pageants the same protection as granted by US law to child actors. A state regulatory scheme should include safe working conditions; psychological and emotional training and examinations; financial counseling; limited hours of practice, preparation, and performance; limitation on the excessive use of appearance-altering techniques and adult-like costumes (especially on younger participants); licensing the organizers allowed to work with children; and limiting the minimum age requirement for participants to two weeks (!).[152] Lucy Wolfe, writing after Lieberman, proposes a much milder intervention by US legislator, based on administrative programs to train

---

[146] Wolfe, "Darling Divas," at 437–41.
[147] Lieberman, "Protecting Pageant Princesses," at 750. For example, see the Cozy's Cuts for Kids website (Parties & Events): http://cozyscutsforkids.com/parties/.
[148] Lieberman, "Protecting Pageant Princesses."
[149] Dejmanee, "Nursing at the Screen."
[150] Lieberman, "Protecting Pageant Princesses." See, for exceptional legislative interventions, supra fn. 134–135.
[151] Wolfe, "Darling Divas."
[152] Lieberman, "Protecting Pageant Princesses."

the organizers, educate the parents, and urge the industry to regulate itself so the wellbeing of the young participants is protected. According to Wolfe: "Congressionally authorized regulation is an extreme remedy, and one that should only be approached after other, less invasive, methods have been exhausted."

I disagree with both scholars and argue that CBPs should be outlawed. I perceive sending young girls to beauty contests, while sexualizing their bodies and performance and subjecting them to painful and harmful cosmetic treatments, as physical and mental violence, abuse, maltreatment, and exploitation – all of which are prohibited by the CRC. Moreover, going back to the three parameters model I suggested earlier to judge whether parental violence can be justified, there are no worthwhile benefits to the children who participate in these competitions. Although some win prizes, most do not, and even the winners do not benefit as their parents have often invested more in participating in the first place, or will gamble the prize money on winning the next competition.[153] Moreover, whereas the industry pushes for these contests to be viewed as harmless fun and even as spaces of "girl power" in which the participants affirm their subjectivity through pleasure and agency,[154] I find these arguments ridiculous when it comes to babies, toddlers, and young girls. Babies just a few weeks or months old, and girls aged two, four, and even eight, should not be experiencing "girl power" but rather a protected childhood, as discussed in Chapter 6 – and certainly should not be expected to perform, with sexualized undercurrents, during their pre-sex-life period for the entertainment of adults. Finally, as for cultural meaning, these contests are far from an age-old tradition that defines a cultural or religious group. Hence the multicultural justifications for them, stemming either from the public–collectivist–dogmatic or the private–individualist–pluralistic conception of the family (detailed in Chapter 2) are irrelevant. CBPs are the outcome of greedy businesses that strive for profit while perpetuating the most stereotypically feminine features that are at the base of Western patriarchy and exploiting many disadvantaged parents who gamble their meager resources and children's welfare on a fantasy of wealth and glamour.[155] Hence, there is

---

[153] Ibid.

[154] Dejmanee, "Nursing at the Screen."

[155] See also Christine Renee Bagley "Pint-Sized Spectacles: American Youth Beauty Queens and the Power(Ful) Dynamic of the Institutionalized Pageant," MA Thesis, George Washington University (2010), available at: http://media.proquest.com/media/pq/classic/doc/2058638851/fmt/ai/rep/NPDF?_s=yjO%2BH2cCRwF3IWhDB%2FXvYqsFFsQ%3D.

no justification at the governmental level for tolerating the violence and abuse to which the "pageant princesses" are exposed.

Trying to protect these girls through labor law regulation of child actors, as Lieberman suggests, is to legitimize the industry and even grant it artistic value. To settle for administrative educational programs, as Wolfe suggests, is too little too late. The industry should be outlawed, as is the industry of child pornography. Pageant organizers should be prohibited from accepting competitors who cannot truly grant their informed consent. Taking parental pressure and the *beauty myth* social pressure into consideration, I would argue that such informed consent cannot be granted before the age of 16.[156] Likewise, broadcasting bodies should be prohibited from promoting the phenomenon by showing such competitions and producing related reality shows.[157] Furthermore, should this industry be outlawed as I propose, although in general I would refrain from prosecuting the parents involved (as I perceive them as victims of the industry and of patriarchy), in extreme cases that fall under existing criminal codes prohibiting parental abuse, neglect, exploitation, and pornography,[158] I believe they should be prosecuted. Finally, in cases of substantial individual damages, tort claims on behalf of the child-participants against their parents should be allowed, with a delayed limitation clause. The law should reflect the understanding that parental authority does not grant parents the right to treat their daughters as dolls, sex objects, or gambling chips.

Outrageously, although the United States, the initiator and leading country in the field of CBP, took part in the drafting of the CRC and signed it, it did not ratify it. Moreover, the United States grants broad authority to parents, including in cases that are interpreted in other parts of the world as parental abuse and, therefore, illegal. For example, whereas many countries prohibit parental corporal punishment and view it as illegitimate and harmful violence against children,[159] all the states in the

---

[156] The French legislator prohibits CBPs for girls under 13, and conditions them for girls aged 13–16 years by special permission. See Article 58 of the Law for Real Equality between Women and Men (LOI n° 2014–873 du 4 août 2014 pour l'égalité réelle entre les femmes et les hommes), available at: www.legifrance.gouv.fr/affichTexte.do?cidTexte=JORFTEXT 000029330832&categorieLien=id.

[157] Although I am fully aware of the radical American pro-freedom-of-speech stance, such broadcasting should be conceptualized as commercial speech, requiring a high level of scrutiny in the name of the best interests of the specific children involved and female children in general.

[158] Wolfe, "Darling Divas," at 442.

[159] Nathalie duRivage, Katherine Keyes, Emmanuelle Leray, Ondine Pez, Adina Bitfoi, Ceren Koç, Dietmar Goelitz, Rowella Kuijpers, Sigita Lesinskiene, Zlatka Mihova, Roy Otten, Christophe Fermanian, & Viviane Kovess-Masfety, "Parental Use of Corporal Punishment

United States allow it.[160] At the very least, if the United States allows CBPs to continue, it should refrain from judging and interfering in parental and cultural violent acts against children occurring in other parts of the world, as it does not have the necessary moral ground to play the global sheriff in this respect.

Child Abduction

The last part of this chapter is devoted to international child abduction, because this can be considered both "a form of domestic violence" and "a response to domestic violence," relevant to both cross-border parental and spousal violence.[161] On the one hand, abducting the child – that is, one parent taking the child to another country without the consent of the other parent – is a violent act toward the child and toward the other parent. Indeed, it is criminalized by many jurisdictions,[162] and perpetrated, in many cases, by abusive spouses as a continuum of their pattern of violent behavior.[163] On the other hand, in many abduction cases, it is the abused spouse who crosses the international border with the child without the other parent's (or court's) permission, in an attempt to escape the violent spouse, who is, in some cases, also a violent parent.[164] Hence, jurists committed to aiding victims of domestic violence must struggle with the tension between the need to prevent child abduction and the need to allow it.

The 1980 Hague Convention on the Civil Aspects of International Child Abduction (CCA), now signed by 94 countries,[165] was drafted with the

in Europe: Intersection Between Public Health and Policy," *Plos One Journal*, 10(2) (2015), available at: www.ncbi.nlm.nih.gov/pmc/articles/PMC4326463/.

[160] Global Initiative to End All Corporal Punishment of Children, *Country Report for USA: Summary of Law Reform Necessary to Achieve Full Prohibition* (2016), available at: www.endcorporalpunishment.org/progress/country-reports/usa.html.

[161] Hague Conference on Private International Law, Domestic and Family Violence and the Article 13 "Grave Risk" Exception in the Operation of the *Hague Convention of 25 October 1980 on the Civil Aspects of International Child Abduction:* A Reflection Paper (2011), at 7, available at: https://assets.hcch.net/upload/wop/abduct2011pd09e.pdf.

[162] Buck, *International Child Law*, Ch. 5.

[163] Robert L. Snow, *Child Abduction: Prevention, Investigating and Recovery* (Westport, CT: Praeger, 2008), Ch. 5.

[164] Merle H. Weiner, "International Child Abduction and the Escape from Domestic Violence," *Fordham Law Review*, 69(2) (2000), 593–706, at 602; Taryn Lindhorst & Jeffrey L. Edleson, *Battered Women, Their Children, and International Law: The Unintended Consequences of the Hague Child Abduction Convention* (Lebanon, NH: Northeastern University Press, 2012).

[165] Hague Convention on the Civil Aspects of International Child Abduction 1980, available at: www.hcch.net/en/instruments/conventions/status-table/?cid=24.

intention of preventing the misuse of global cross-border movement by abducting parents. Prior to the CCA, parents who worried about the outcome of a custody dispute, or were not satisfied with a custody decision, could try to remove the child to another country in the hope of receiving a more favorable decision or creating a situation in which it would be in the best interests of the child to remain in the country to which it was taken.[166] The drafters of the CCA wished to protect children *ex ante* by deterring parents from abducting their children,[167] and *ex post* by securing the quick and safe return of children who were wrongfully removed from their home country by one of their parents. The assumption guiding these goals, supported in part by empirical studies,[168] was that child abduction has a grave negative impact on the abducted child and that their prompt return home is in his/her best interests.[169] In addition, the CCA aims to prevent custody forum shopping and to secure international comity so that the "rights of custody and of access under the law of one Contracting State are effectively respected in the other Contracting States."[170] This goal can be attached to an additional possible justification for the CCA, as well as other national and regional legal tools developed to deter parental child abduction[171] – namely, that of minimizing the harms caused to the left-behind parent, including emotional damage caused by the separation

---

[166] Rhona Schuz, *The Hague Child Abduction Convention: A Critical Analysis*, Studies in Private International Law (Oxford and Portland, OR: Hart Publishing, 2013), at 7.

[167] Carolyn A. Kubitschek, "Failure of the Hague Abduction Convention to Address Domestic Violence and its Consequences" in Robert E. Rains (Ed.), *The 1980 Hague Abduction Convention, Comparative Aspects* (London: Wildy, Simmonds & Hill Publishing, 2014), pp. 132–53, at 140–1.

[168] As the literature review conducted by Rhona Schuz demonstrates, some studies found significant negative outcomes of child abduction, including adjustment and behavioral problems, while others found positive or non-significant negative effects. Schuz concludes: "whilst the research does provide some, albeit equivocal, support for the assumption that a move to another country as a result of abduction or a return may cause harm to a child, it also suggests that whether or not such harm occurs, and the extent thereof, is dependent on many other factors, including the length of the abduction, the conditions during the abduction, the degree of contact (if any) with the left-behind parent during the abduction, the information given to the child about the left-behind parent, the support available on return, the age of the child, and whether there was a separation from sibling(s)" (references omitted). See Schuz, *The Hague Child Abduction Convention*, at 65.

[169] Sudha Shetty & Jeffery L. Edleson, "Adult Domestic Violence in Cases of International Parental Child Abduction," *Violence against Women*, 11(1) (2005), 115–38, at 118.

[170] Article 1 of the CCA.

[171] Buck, *International Child Law*, Ch. 5. An extreme example of national attempts to prevent child abduction can be found in the laws of several US states that mandate supervised visitations between a parent and his/her child, if the court is convinced that there is a risk that the parent will abduct the child. These laws are suspicious of parents who have

from the child, and economic expenses caused by the search for the child and the attempts to secure the child's return.[172]

The data at the time the CCA was drafted showed that most abductors were noncustodial fathers, and the CCA was crafted as a deterrent with this factor in mind.[173] One possible explanation for the past predominance of fathers as abductors is the prevalence of legal presumptions that favored granting sole legal and physical custody to mothers. These presumptions were gradually abolished in many jurisdictions after the CCA was concluded.[174] Indeed, according to the legal scholar Merle Weiner, in the United States (the country with the consistently highest reported number of parental abduction cases),[175] until the early 1990s "the stereotypical image of an international child abduction was the following: the abductor was a male noncustodial parent, usually a foreign national, who removed the child from the child's mother and primary caretaker, typically an American national."[176]

The latest survey of the characteristics of international child abductions was conducted by the Hague Conference on Private International Law (HCCH) in 2008, and was based on the responses received from 60 contracting countries.[177] Although this survey is already nine years old at the time of writing and is partial (because not all countries are party to the CCA, not all parties cooperated with the survey and have full information, and not all parental abductions are reported to the Central Authorities (CAs)),[178] it nevertheless provides the best available

"strong familial, emotional, or cultural ties to another country, particularly a country that is not a signatory to or compliant with the Hague Convention on the Civil Aspects of International Child Abduction." See *In Re Sigmar*, 270 SW 3d 289 (Tex App 2008).

[172] Benjamin Shmueli & Rhona Schuz, "Between Tort Law, Contract Law, and Child Law: How to Compensate the Left-Behind Parent in International Child Abduction Cases," *Columbia Journal of Gender and Law*, 23(1) (2012), 65–131.

[173] Kubitschek, "Failure of the Hague Abduction Convention to Address Domestic Violence and Its Consequences," at 140–1.

[174] See Chapter 5, fn. 125.

[175] Hague Conference on Private International Law, *A Statistical Analysis of Applications Made in 2008 under the Hague Convention of 25 October 1980 on the Civil Aspects of International Child Abduction* (2011), at 9, available at: https://assets.hcch.net/upload/wop/abduct2011pd08ae.pdf.

[176] Weiner, "International Child Abduction and the Escape from Domestic Violence," at 602.

[177] Hague Conference on Private International Law, *A Statistical Analysis of Applications Made in 2008 under the Hague Convention of 25 October 1980 on the Civil Aspects of International Child Abduction*.

[178] Julia Alanen estimates, based on her work at the Legal Aid Foundation of Los Angeles, that "parental kidnapping may be grossly underreported," due to lack of awareness of the available legal remedies on behalf of the left-behind parent, or his/her illegal status in

evidence on the current characteristics of international child abduction. According to this survey, about 2,000 requests for child return were handled by the CAs in the reporting countries in 2008, involving approximately 2,700 children. This is a 45 percent increase on the number of cases found in a similar survey conducted in 2003. The HCCH does not offer an explanation for this increase, but one can surmise that it reflects a sharp increase in the number of child abductions, or a better enforcement of the CCA by the CAs, or a combination of the two. The average age of a child involved in a return application was 6.4 years, with 77 percent of the children aged 9 or younger. Of the applications that were decided in court (44 percent), 61 percent ended in a return, 34 percent in a refusal, and 5 percent in orders for access. Some 60 percent of parents who crossed the border with the child without permission did so to a country of which they were a national. In 90 percent of these cases, the abducting parent had only one nationality, that of the country to which the child was taken. Hence, this survey supports the past assumption that international abduction increases in line with the rate of breakdown in international marriages,[179] and that, for the abducting parent, the abduction is often a journey home. However, this survey, as well as the 2003 edition, also reflects the dramatic shift taking place in recent years in the identity of the abducting parent, compared to the 1980s when the CCA was drafted: 68 percent of the abducting parents in 2003 (rising to 69 percent in 2008) were the mothers. In only 17 percent of the cases reported in 2008 did the CAs manage to collect information regarding whether the abducting parent was the primary caregiver of the child or not. Within these 17 percent, most of the abducting mothers (88 percent) were sole or joint carers, whereas the abducting fathers were in most cases noncaregivers (64 percent). Hence, the gendered past assumption collapses in the face of the fact that (mostly primary carer) mothers are now twice as likely than (mostly non-primary caregiver) fathers to remove their (relatively young) child to another country without the permission of the other parent or the local court.

Several possible explanations to this gender flip can be offered. First, fathers' motivation to abduct the child diminished as national laws changed to grant fathers joint legal custody, and joint or sole physical custody, or constant and frequent access rights to their children.[180] Likewise,

the country from which the child was abducted. See Julia Alanen, "When Human Rights Conflict: Mediating International Parental Kidnapping Disputes Involving the Domestic Violence Defense," *Inter-American Law Review*, 40(1) (2008), 49–108, at 56.

[179] Schuz, *The Hague Child Abduction Convention*, at 55.

[180] See Chapter 5, fn. 125.

the statistics may reflect a growing motivation among fathers to report abduction and not simply accept the mother's international removal of the child, due to the growing social and legal importance ascribed to fatherhood. On the mothers' side, their motivation to abduct the child increased, because in many jurisdictions the law has changed so as to grant a parent the right to object to the possibility of the other parent's international relocation with the child, even if the former is a noncaregiver and the latter is the primary caregiver for the child.[181] This motivation is especially acute in the case of migrant mothers, who might desperately want to return home in the hope of finding economic and emotional support from their family of origin, as detailed in Chapter 3. Finally, as women become increasingly aware of their right to bodily integrity and safety within their home, thanks to the global anti-spousal-violence movement described earlier, they may more frequently find the courage to escape spousal violence by fleeing the border with their children. In response, their violent spouse or ex-spouse may try to stop them by approaching the CAs with a request of return.

The growing awareness of the new gendered demographics of abducting parents has led to much criticism of the CCA and its enforcement as failing to protect victims of spousal violence and their children. For example, public policy scholars Sudha Shetty and Jeffrey Edleson, who specialize in domestic violence, argue: "Mothers who abduct their children and flee to find a safe haven are not perpetuators, as the Hague Convection implies, but are victims of their partner's violence. They are also victims of an international treaty, written with good intentions, but, when implemented, had unintended negative consequences for their safety and that of their children".[182] Based on a rare example of a study that listened to the experiences of battered mothers who faced a return request after fleeing to another country with their children, together with interviews with lawyers who specialize in CCA procedures and an analysis of US court decisions on return requests, social work scholar Taryn Lindhorst and Edleson concluded: that some of the fathers who file these requests are violent spouses and fathers; that the abused mothers flee to another country because they cannot get the needed protection from the country from which they are escaping; that the mothers face significant difficulties in gaining the needed resources to defend a return request; that

---

[181] Schuz, *The Hague Child Abduction Convention*, at 58.
[182] Shetty & Edleson, "Adult Domestic Violence," at 135.

judges deciding on the return requests fail to take into consideration the empirical knowledge on the harms caused to children exposed to domestic violence; and that mothers who are forced to return the child face severe danger if they accompany their child rather than send the child back on his/her own.[183]

There is evidence that such criticism trickled down and made some judges, in some jurisdictions, more sensitive to the possibility that battered mothers may abduct their child in an attempt to escape the spousal abuse, and that the return request must be refused in the name of the child's interests. The CCA does not mention spousal violence as an exception to the rule of return. Hence, abused mothers must use Article 13(b) in an attempt to prevent the return, though it was not designed with spousal violence in mind.[184] This article states that the country to which the child was abducted does not have to return it to the country from which it was abducted, if it can be established that "there is a grave risk that his or her return would expose the child to physical or psychological harm or otherwise place the child in an intolerable situation."

This article has always been the most common ground for return refusals on part of the country to which the child was abducted. In 2008, successful applications for return refusals based on this article reached 27 percent of all successful applications, compared to 22 percent in 1999 and 19 percent in 2003.[185] Although this article is used in a variety of circumstances, this increase might suggest a growing success rate on behalf of mothers who argue that the child should not be returned due the violence of the father against the mother.[186] Still, refusals to return the child are the exception to the rule, and many still argue that the ACC is "too well implemented"[187] and is harmful to mothers who suffer spousal violence. Whereas some

[183] Lindhorst & Edleson, *Battered Women*.

[184] Brian Quillen, "The New Face of International Child Abduction: Domestic-Violence Victims and Their Treatment under the Hague Convention on Civil Aspects of International Child Abduction," *Texas International Law Journal*, 49(3) (2014), 621–43, at 625.

[185] Hague Conference on Private International Law, *A Statistical Analysis of Applications Made in 2008 under the Hague Convention of 25 October 1980 on the Civil Aspects of International Child Abduction*, at 31.

[186] Nigel V. Lowe & Victoria Stephens, "Global Trends in the Operation of the 1980 Hague Abduction Convention," *Family Law Quarterly*, 46(1) (2012), 41–85, at 60.

[187] Carol S. Bruch, "The Unmet Needs of Domestic Violence Victims and Their Children in Hague Child Abduction Convention Cases," *Family Law Quarterly*, 38(3) (2014), 529–45, at 529.

judges agree that the possibility of the child being exposed to violence inflicted on the mother by the father represents a "grave risk" or "intolerable situation" for them if returned, others do not.[188] The latter are not satisfied with the rich findings on the positive correlation between spousal and parental violence, and on the emotional harm caused to children who witness their mother being abused.[189] Judges in this camp may set a high evidentiary bar for proving the potential risk, or accept the argument that the country to which the return is demanded is able to protect the child from future risk.[190] In such cases, undertakings are often mandated (even though this is not mentioned as a tool in the CCA), requiring the abuser to promise to the court that, on the mother's and child's return, he will stay away from the abducting mother and not abuse her in any way.[191] These judges fail to recognize the difficulties in enforcing undertakings and even more formal protection orders when the perpetrator and victim reside in the same country,[192] especially in countries that do not do enough to protect victims of spousal violence, as discussed in the first part of this chapter. Nor do they appreciate the impact of these difficulties on the child who might witness his/her mother yet again being abused and hurt.[193] Going back to the test set by Article 13(b) of the CCA, even the option of sending the mother to a shelter for battered women should be perceived as a "grave risk" or "intolerable situation" for the child, because it entails either that the child reside in the shelter with the mother, away from family and friends and in an institution hardly suitable for children, or that the child be separated from the mother. If the Article 13(b) defense fails and the court orders the child's return, the mother is faced with a horrible dilemma: to send the child back on his or her own to the abusive parent and try to fight for the legal option of sole physical custody and relocation from afar, which may be costly and unsuccessful, or to return with the child and risk repeated and even escalating violence or isolation and *voluntary imprisonment* in a shelter.[194] Clearly, the attempt to use

---

[188] Kubitschek, "Failure of the Hague Abduction Convention to Address Domestic Violence and its Consequences," at 147.

[189] Quillen, "The New Face," at 633; Shetty & Edleson, "Adult Domestic Violence," at 115; Noah L. Browne, "Relevance and Fairness: Protecting the Rights of Domestic Violence Victims and Left-Behind Fathers under the Hague Convention on International Child Abduction," *Duke Law Journal*, 60 (2011), 1193–238, at 1205–6.

[190] Quillen, "The New Face."

[191] Weiner, "International Child Abduction," at 676–81.

[192] Quillen, "The New Face," at 631–2.

[193] See also Weiner, "International Child Abduction," at 676–81.

[194] Quillen, "The New Face," at 627.

an article that was not meant to assist victims of spousal violence,[195] to do exactly that, creates obstacles, inconsistencies, and failures. As Lindhorst and Edleson conclude – along similar lines to the conclusion from the discussion on abortion and torture in Chapter 4 and the discussion on spousal violence and asylum at the beginning of this chapter – like other international conventions, the CCA is caught up in the private–public dichotomy, this time at the private end, blind to the (public) human rights dimension of violence toward women.[196]

Scholars have proposed several suggestions to better adapt the CCA and its enforcement to cases of spousal violence, including by: enhancing the use of "intolerable situation," and not only "grave risk," as the relevant test in cases of domestic violence;[197] by recognizing the relevance of Article 20 of the CCA, which allows a return refusal "if this would not be permitted by the fundamental principles of the requested state relating to the protection of human rights and fundamental freedoms," to cases of domestic violence;[198] by paying special attention to the child's aversion to return in cases of spousal violence, as this is also a recognized base for return refusal according to the CCA;[199] by training lawyers and judges on spousal violence and its relevance to child abduction cases;[200] by allowing the abducting abused parent a temporary stay permit in the country to which the child was abducted until the custody dispute is settled there or in the country from which it was abducted (with the mother's long-distance participation);[201] by encouraging mediation between the parents; and by amending the CCA and national laws to clarify that exposure to spousal violence poses a grave risk to the child and that a country in which the child is exposed to such violence cannot be perceived as his/her habitual residence to which he or she should be returned.[202]

Of course, the challenge is to address the needs of victims of domestic violence who have found refuge in another country, while not compromising the important goals of the CCA and not harming innocent parents who lost their child to an abducting parent.[203] Just as in the case

---

[195] Browne, "Relevance and Fairness," at 1204.
[196] Lindhorst & Edleson, *Battered Women*, at 199.
[197] Shetty & Edleson, "Adult Domestic Violence," at 133.
[198] Weiner, "International Child Abduction," at 665; Shetty & Edleson, "Adult Domestic Violence," at 129.
[199] Article 13 of the CCA; Weiner, "International Child Abduction," at 663.
[200] Shetty & Edleson, "Adult Domestic Violence," at 134.
[201] Weiner, "International Child Abduction," at 698–703.
[202] Shetty & Edleson, "Adult Domestic Violence," at 135.
[203] Browne, "Relevance and Fairness."

of other exceptions to the rule of return, the broader their interpretation, the greater the parental incentive to abduct the child. I believe that the model proposed in relation to parental violence in the previous part of this chapter (in which harms, benefits, and cultural meaning should be considered) can assist in shaping the balance between the need to prevent child abduction and the need to allow it in cases of domestic violence. Child abduction should always be perceived as a violent act – it is an illegal and unauthorized kidnapping, which physically disrupts the child's home location, routine, and relations with others. However, as the model suggests, some violent acts are justified as their benefits significantly outweigh their harms. The CCA, and procedures conducted in light of it, must incorporate the understanding that exposure to spousal violence severely harms the child. The CCA must also be enforced with the guidance of the CEDAW 1992 General Recommendation, mentioned in the first part of the chapter, and integrate the right of the battered mother to be safe from spousal violence. Finally, return requests must take into account the understanding that a parent exposed to spousal violence cannot fairly and effectively conduct a custody dispute and might be forced to compromise or neglect the child's best interests. For all these reasons, if the court in the country to which the child was abducted is convinced that, according to the balance of probabilities, it is more likely that the mother is (or will be) exposed to violence at the hands of the father, then the immediate return request should be denied. The child will be returned only if, based on a custody hearing, the court in the country to which the child was abducted is convinced that it is in the child's best interests to be in the sole custody of the father.

Finally, the understanding that international abduction is a way for battered women, and especially migrant battered women, to escape spousal abuse, brings us back to the discussion in Chapter 3 on prenups. Any professional and responsible lawyer should advise a client who wishes to marry – especially if she or he wishes to marry a partner from another country – to sign a prenup that minimizes the chances of future child abduction *ex ante*. Minimizing measures could include, for instance, depositing the children's passports with a third party to prevent their use without both parents' consent; or an agreement to submit permanent notification to the border control authorities to ensure the children would not be able to leave the country without a notarized permission from the absent parent. Unfortunately, current data suggest that such calculated legal measures would disproportionally harm women. However, even under my antiprenups thesis presented in Chapter 3, it is hard to argue that measures such as mandatory mutual parental consent for child departure abroad should not be allowed. Hence, in cases in which the parents were to agree on such measures, a mother who would later suffer domestic violence and wish to escape it by moving to another country would be forced to approach the court with a relocation request, risking an unsympathetic judge and increased violence at the hands of the father. This is yet another reason not to encourage prenups.

Conclusion

This chapter brought together different phenomena under the umbrella of *familial violence*. Although some would argue that spousal physical violence, for example, cannot be compared to male circumcision or to child beauty pageants, and that the first is family-related violence, whereas the other two are not, I insist that they, as well as other nonphysical forms of spousal abuse, FGM, and child abduction, are all manifestations of familial violence, and that placing them side by side forces us to contemplate the circumstances in which the law should, or should not, penetrate the privacy of family life and protect one family member from another.

The chapter centers on the evolution of the global norm that prohibits spousal and parental violence and that is intolerant of any possible justifications, including cultural ones. However, the different examples show that this global norm is challenged by the ongoing prevalence of familial violence – hence, demonstrating once more the power of national and cultural norms to resist global law, and the importance of integrating top-down and bottom-up measures to change cultural perceptions that sustain familial violence. Moreover, the chapter demonstrates that globalization enhances the protection for victims of spousal violence, not only by offering them the anti-domestic-violence norm, but also, in some cases, by providing them with shelter and asylum. However, simultaneously, globalization, with its interrelations with borders, intensifies spousal violence because it creates special vulnerabilities due to unstable immigration status, and because it labels women who flee violence as child abductors who must return the child to his or her alleged home.

Perhaps even more challenging is this chapter's argument that to claim that all the acts discussed in it constitute familial violence does not mean they should all be outlawed. Rather, I suggest a three-component model that looks at harms, benefits, and cultural meaning, to judge whether a parental violent act should be tolerated by law or not. This model sets a high, but possible, bar of justification for parental violence. It supports the widespread conclusion that FGM should be globally outlawed, but also leads to the more contested conclusion that MC should be allowed, and to the even more radical conclusion, not even mentioned in the literature to date, that CBPs should be outlawed. By placing these very different violent practices side by side, I hoped to demonstrate the cultural bias and phobia that characterize current legislation, and to point to a possible way of minimizing them – urgently needed in the era of bordered globalization – while not forsaking the determinant position that most parental violence is unjustified and should be abolished.

Finally, this chapter, like those preceding and the last one following it, highlights the centrality of gender to the understanding of familiality and its regulation in this era. Girls and women are at a much higher risk of familial violence than boys and men, all over the world. Although the world made a promise, through the CRC and the CEDAW General Recommendation, to protect girls and women from domestic physical, sexual, emotional, and economic abuse, the quarter of a century that has passed since this promise was made proves that much more must be done on the familial, parochial, national, and international levels, before we can say that families are a safe place for the female section of the human race.

8

Old Age

Introduction

This final chapter of the book highlights the relevance of bordered globalization to legalized familiality in the last phase of life – old age. The interrelations between globalization and borders affect the familial lives of older persons in many different ways. Migration among this age group – increasingly prevalent – separates, unites, and alters families. On the one hand, the movement of people in the last stage of life to countries with warmer climates or more affordable health services, and the phenomenon of return migration, in which older people who emigrated when they were younger choose to retire to their birth country, separate the elderly from their children and grandchildren. This separation demands of the family members that they reconfigure their relations and identify new ways to maintain contact. On the other hand, the scenario in which adult children who immigrated to another country subsequently invite their ageing parents to live in close proximity to enable filial care unites families, at times after long periods of day-to-day separation. This reunion creates challenges of intergenerational (re)bonding.[1] Just as in other contexts of immigration, national laws play a crucial role in enabling global migration among older persons or using borders to prevent it, hence shaping familiality in old age.[2]

---

[1] For a typology of the different kinds of old-age migration, see Israel Doron and Tal Golan, "Aging, Globalization and the Legal Construction of 'Residence': The Case of Old Age Pensions in Israel," *The Elder Law Journal*, 15(1) (2007), 1–50.

[2] For a study that demonstrates the interrelations between immigration law and familial transnational movement of older persons, see Judith Treas, "Transnational Older Adults and Their Families," *Family Relations*, 57(4) (2008), 468–78; Another example, related to welfare law, is provided by Israel Doron and Tal Golan, who demonstrate that the question of whether the older person loses his/her pension rights upon emigration affects the ability of the elderly to immigrate to another country, including when the older person wishes to reunite with their children who previously immigrated. This is the case in several countries that condition governmental pension benefits on the 'residency' of the beneficiary within their territory. See Doron & Golan, "Aging, Globalization."

Notwithstanding the importance of these phenomena, which only recently started to be explored empirically and conceptualized theoretically,[3] in this chapter, I focus on a different aspect of the interrelations between globalization, borders, the law, and familiality at old age. What follows centers on older persons and their family members, who can be deeply affected by globalization even if the older person remains in her/his home country. This chapter discusses the familial causes and outcomes of in-home care provided to older persons by migrant care workers – a rapidly growing solution to the care deficit experienced by the elderly and their families in developed countries. I hope to demonstrate to both scholars and policy makers the importance and urgency of understanding the familial implications of this solution and the role of law in shaping them.

Both my research fields – family law and the sociology of the family – focus almost exclusively on family relations between parents and their minor children, as if the family story ends when the children reach the age of 18. However, most of the familial relations between parents and their children occur, in fact, after the latter have reached adulthood. People spend most of their lives being grown-up children of their parents and, later, being parents of their own grown-up children. Yet this significantly long period of familial relations is undertheorized and barely studied within the sociology of the family. Likewise, very few within academia (or indeed the public at large) perceive this significant timespan of relations between parents and grown-up children (and the grown-up children's offspring)[4] as having legal implications and as being shaped by what I term *families laws*. This unawareness exists despite the fact that,

---

[3] See, for example, Ute Karl & Sandra Torres (Eds.), *Ageing in Contexts of Migration* (Oxon: Routledge, 2016); Vincent Horn, Cornelia Schweppe, & Seong-gee Um, "Transnational Aging – A Young Field of Research," *Transnational Social Review*, 3(1) (2013), 7–10. See also all articles in this volume of *Transnational Social Review*.

[4] The relatively little discussion that exists on the legal meaning of the relations between grandparents and grandchildren, centers (as is the case with all the literature on legalized families) on grandparents and their *minor* grandchildren. See, for example, Twyla J. Hill, "Grandparents in Law: Investigating the Institutionalization of Extended Family Roles," *The International Journal of Aging and Human Development*, 54(1) (2002) 43–56; Twyla J. Hill, "Legalized Grandparenthood: A Content Analysis of State Legislation," *Journal of Intergenerational Relationships*, 5(2) (2007), 61–80; Jonathan Herring, *Older People in Law and Society* (New York: Oxford University Press, 2009), at Ch. 7. Hence, we find that the focus is on the rights and duties of grandparents toward their grandchildren rather than on, for example, the duty of grandchildren to care for their grandparents, or the right of grandchildren who perform such care to be compensated through state allowances or their grandparent's estate. The inclusion of the relations of the elderly with their grown-up grandchildren becomes more relevant as life expectancy increases and more people reach their 90s, with children in their 60s or 70s and grandchildren in their 20s and older. Although

just as in the case of parents and their minor children, these relations are configured in the shadow of the law, including family law, welfare law, inheritance law, and immigration law. Indeed, this same lack of awareness is also apparent in the sociological and legal literatures that tie together families and globalization. As mentioned in relation to the *new familial dictionary* in the Introduction to this book, although a variety of terms have emerged to capture the new impact of globalization on spousal relations and on the relations between parents and their minor children, none exists in relation to familiality in the later and final stages of life.

The sociological and legal lacunas surrounding families in the context of old age, including in globalized circumstances, have never been in such desperate need of attention as in this era. Longer life expectancy and accompanying chronic illnesses, decreasing fertility rates, higher rates and intensity of female employment, growing internal and external emigration, and the global economic recession that began in 2008, have all led to growing numbers of elderly parents in need of assistance, in conjunction with the declining will and capacity of adult children to assist.[5]

According to a recent UN survey, the demographic generational reversal already evident in many developed countries[6] is to become global. By 2030, older persons (over the age of 60) will outnumber children aged 0–9 years (1.4 billion versus 1.3 billion); by 2050, there will be more people aged 60 years or over than young people aged 10–24 years (2.1 billion versus 2.0 billion);[7] and the number of persons aged 80 or over (the "oldest old") is projected to more than triple by 2050 and to increase more than seven-fold by 2100. A staggering 83 countries already have below-replacement fertility rates. These countries differ profoundly from one another in terms of economy and culture, being as diverse as Iran, Austria, Brazil, Canada, Finland, Greece, Hungary, Italy, Japan, the Netherlands,

the discussion in this chapter does not expand to these third-generation relations, it is still very relevant to them.

[5] Martina Brandt, Klaus Haberkern, & Marc Szydlik, "Intergenerational Help and Care in Europe," *European Sociological Review*, 25(5) (2009), 585–601; Esther Iecovich & Israel Doron, "Migrant Workers in Eldercare in Israel: Social and Legal Aspects," *European Journal of Social Work*, 15(1) (2012), 29–44, at 30.

[6] In many parts of the world, the present era marks the first in history in which the average married couple has more parents than children. See Samuel Preston as mentioned in Gunhild O. Hagestad, "The Aging Society as a Context for Family Life" in Nancy S. Jecker (Ed.), *Aging and Ethics: Philosophical Problems in Gerontology* (Totowa, NJ: Humana Press, 1991), pp. 123–46, at 124.

[7] United Nations, Department of Economic and Social Affairs, *World Population Ageing* (2015), available at: www.un.org/en/development/desa/population/publications/pdf/ageing/WPA2015_Report.pdf.

Poland, Singapore, the United States, the Unites Arab Emirates, and the UK. Just nine countries (eight of them in Africa and Asia) are expected to account for more than half the world's projected population increase in the near future.[8]

For many people, old age brings with it increasing economic, physical, and mental dependency. Forced or voluntary retirement from the workforce means, in many cases, less income, often in the face of the pension crisis experienced in developed countries and the growing difficulties of individuals and governments worldwide to secure an adequate postretirement standard of living.[9] Likewise, the elderly are more at risk of physical and mental disabilities.[10] For example, according to the WHO, dementia, which correlates with old age, "is one of the major health challenges for our time." In 2015, dementia affected more than 47 million people worldwide, 60 percent of whom live in low- and middle-income countries. By 2030, it is estimated that more than 75 million people will be living with dementia, and the number is expected to triple by 2050. The different manifestations of dementia, which include Alzheimer's disease, impair the cognitive brain functions of memory, language, perception, and thought, and interfere with the ability to maintain the activities of daily living. According to the WHO: "The personal, social and economic consequences of dementia are enormous. Dementia leads to increased long-term care costs for governments, communities, families and individuals, and to losses in productivity for economies. The global cost of dementia care in 2010 was estimated to be $604 billion: 1.0 percent of global gross domestic product."[11]

The need for care in old age can be answered by public funding, as is the case, for example, in Sweden, which is considered one of the best countries for older citizens[12] and which publicly covers 96 percent of care

---

[8] United Nations, Department of Economic and Social Affairs, *World Population Prospects: Key Findings and Advance Tables* (2015), available at: https://esa.un.org/unpd/wpp/Publications/Files/Key_Findings_WPP_2015.pdf.

[9] OECD, *Pensions at a Glance* (2013), available at: www.oecd.org/pensions/public-pensions/OECDPensionsAtAGlance2013.pdf; Armando Barrientos, Mark Gorman, & Amanda Heslop, "Old Age Poverty in Developing Countries: Contributions and Dependence in Later Life," *World Development: Chronic Poverty and Development Policy*, 31(3) (2003), 555–70.

[10] World Health Organization, *World Report on Ageing and Health* (2015), at Ch. 3. Available at: http://apps.who.int/iris/bitstream/10665/186463/1/9789240694811_eng.pdf?ua=1.

[11] Ibid., at 59.

[12] Sweden is rated by Global Age Watch, as third in the social and economic wellbeing of its elderly. See "Switzerland Tops the 2015 Index," Global Age Watch Index 2015, available at: www.helpage.org/global-agewatch/population-ageing-data/global-rankings-table/.

costs, leaving only 4 percent of care expenses to be privately funded by the elderly themselves.[13] However, at the same time as the global population is ageing, welfare regimes in most countries are eroding and governments are increasingly reluctant or unable to take over responsibility for such care.[14] This global neoliberal shift exposes older persons and their families to a growing pressure to find private solutions to the needs that accompany old age.[15]

One particular solution is closely allied to globalization. Increasingly, countries are becoming dependent on migrant workers to provide round-the-clock in-home care for their older population.[16] This arrangement, which blurs the border between home and workplace and between family and stranger, is shaped by an amalgam of laws, and may have significant familial implications that have yet to receive the scholastic attention they warrant. Hence, this chapter does not, and cannot, draw on a rich seam of scholarly investigation, but rather is an invitation for future research, based on my argument that the study of the interrelations between families, the laws that govern them, globalization, and borders, must expand to the reciprocal intergenerational relations between parents and their grown-up children.

Importing Care

Aging in one's home and community is currently perceived as a better alternative than aging within an institution, even in cases in which the individual needs intense assistance day and night. In some countries, institutionalizing older persons has never been a common practice, be it for a lack of adequate government-funded homes for the elderly or a social perception that institutionalizing an ageing parent is a familial disgrace and a mark of failure in terms of filial piety.[17] In other countries, the

---

[13] "Elderly Care in Sweden," Sweden Sverige, available at: https://Sweden.Se/Society/Elderly-Care-In-Sweden/.

[14] Karin Schwiter, Christian Berndt, & Jasmine Truong, "Neoliberal Austerity and the Marketization of Elderly Care," *Social & Cultural Geography* (2015), 1–21, available at: www.tandfonline.com/doi/full/10.1080/14649365.2015.1059473.

[15] Ruth Katz, Ariela Lowenstein, & Yitzhak Brick, "Intergenerational Relations and Old Age in the Modern Era: Cross-Country Comparisons" in Yitzhak Brick & Ariela Lowenstein (Eds.), *The Elderly and the Family: Multi-Generational Aspects of Aging* (Jerusalem: Eshel, 2010), pp. 53–71 (Hebrew).

[16] Esther Iecovich, "Client Satisfaction with Live-in and Live-out Home Care Workers in Israel," *Journal of Aging & Social Policy*, 19(4) (2007), 105–22, at 107.

[17] Sjaak van Der Geest, Anke Mul, & Hans Vermeulen, "Linkages between Migration and the Care of Frail Older People: Observations from Greece, Ghana and the Netherlands," *Ageing & Society*, 24(3) (2004), 431–50.

recent move toward favoring long-term home-care is driven by a combination of a heightened desire to fulfill older persons' preference to stay at home and not to be institutionalized, and an attempt to reduce public funding.[18]

Keeping frail older persons at home raises the question of which regime will secure (or at least attempt to secure) the care they need. Each country forms this regime via its own combination of state, family, market, and NGO involvement.[19] These care regimes are constructed by a mixture of laws and regulations, including in relation to welfare, labor, immigration, and families. Indeed, it is hard to think of a better example of my argument that we need to move away from the concept of family law, to that of *families laws*, than the complex legal universe that answers the question of who should care for dependent older people.[20]

Take, for example, the story of Rachel, whom I interviewed in Israel for my current study on the question: should filial piety be legalized?[21] Rachel, an only child and a spouse and mother of two teenagers, realized that her elderly widowed mother was becoming more forgetful and less organized within her home. Having looked at several institutions for the elderly and considered the pros and cons of the institutional route, Rachel and her mother opted to sell their two apartments and buy one big apartment so the mother could live with her daughter's nuclear family. However, soon after the intergenerational reorganization, which allowed Rachel to see more closely the nature of her mother's condition, it became clear that she was, in fact, suffering from Alzheimer's. The mother's condition quickly deteriorated, and for the past two years she has been unable to recognize anyone, cannot get out of bed at all, has lost sphincter control, constantly suffers from a false sense of hunger, and is totally dependent on others for feeding, toileting, and washing. Although the mother is cared for by a migrant worker from the Philippines, Rachel felt she had to leave her job

---

[18] Esther Iecovich, "Migrant Homecare Workers in Elder Care: The State of the Art" in Karl Ute & Torres Sandra (Eds.), *Ageing in Contexts of Migration* (Oxon: Routledge, 2016), pp. 147–58.

[19] Annamaria Simonazzi, "Care Regimes and National Employment Models," *Cambridge Journal of Economics*, 33(2) (2009), 211–3; Viola Burau, Hildegard Theobald, & Robert H. Blank, *Governing Home Care: A Cross-National Comparison* (Cheltenham: Edward Elgar, 2007); Andreas Hoff, Susan Feldman, & Lucie Vidovicova, "Migrant Home Care Workers Caring for Older People: Fictive Kin, Substitute, and Complementary Family Caregivers in an Ethnically Diverse Environment," *International Journal of Ageing and Later Life*, 5(2) (2010), 7–16.

[20] Iecovich, "Migrant Homecare Workers."

[21] This reseach is supported by The Israel Science Foundation (Grant No. 138/14).

as a lawyer to better cope with and manage her mother's condition. As a result, she had been out of the paid labor marker for about two years at the time of the interview.

Rachel shared with me the difficulties she, her spouse, and her children were facing. Among them was the fact that the migrant caregiver lives with the family, and so all family members experience the loss of home privacy. Even more challenging is the fact that the paid caregiver takes the weekends off – time to which she is partially entitled by law.[22] Therefore, for the past two years Rachel has not been able to leave the house on weekends and must meet her mother's demanding physical needs. This has created familial tensions, with Rachel's spouse and children intentionally ignoring the mother-in-law/grandmother and not sharing the burden of her care in any way.

During the interview, Rachel contemplated the option of sending her mother to an institution, revealing the complex legal web that marks the path of her options and decisions, and on which she is very well informed after making many inquiries. I provide here one relevant quote, with numbers inserted that refer to the legal context that I detail immediately after:

> I always say, should we take into consideration the economic aspect or should we not? Because, in fact, there is a big incentive *not* to send [the mother] to an institution because it is cheaper to live as we live. You know there is a [migrant care] worker [*1], it does not matter that you pay [for her work] a few thousand shekels [*2], there is a care benefit so the state pays through the agency a certain percentage of the worker's salary, so it does not go through you, it does not come out of your pocket [*3]; my mother gets my father's pension [*4] and an old age allowance [*5], [...] we come out all right, we do not suffer lack of funding because we employ a foreign worker. It is manageable. But an institution costs about 15,000 shekels a month [$4,000][*6]. There is an option of receiving state support or subsidy of this cost, in what is called "Care Code," and it depends on the person's income and his family's income. And the truth is that we did save money ... I mean she [the mother] does have a certain amount of money that allows us to be certain that if she needed to live in an institution she could, but I said: I will check. If the state tells me it will fund half because it is the same amount it spends [on the migrant care worker], then I will have an incentive. But the state says: No, she [the mother] has savings. First liquidate all her savings, and only then I [the state] might subsidize something. So, in fact, I have to

---

22 Whereas, in Rachel's case, the care worker leaves the house each weekend for about 36 hours, a recent decision by the Israeli National Labor Court ruled that care workers who live with their care recipient are entitled to only 25 consecutive hours of weekly rest. See NLC 47546-10-12 *Zatelman v. Petrov* (2012) (Israel).

fund it privately [*7]. So I say, it is clear that the economic test should not be the only test, and maybe it is worthwhile for me, you know, for my peace of mind, for the family, to scrape together the 15,000 shekels a month and she will live there ... but not at the moment. It is true that transferring [mother] to an institution is to transfer a lot of the responsibility ... but still, I think the responsibility remains on us, on me. I am not sure that I would feel very good [about the idea] that she is in a place I am not entirely happy with. I have decided to wait for a crisis, I mean, if I were to have a crisis with the care worker, if she said "I've had enough," or if something about my mother's condition were to worsen [...]. If something happened to her, I could call the institution and say "here, you have a patient," but until then ...

Legal context: [*1] Israeli immigration regulation grants visas for migrant in-home care workers for dependent older persons, but not for care work at institutions for the elderly. There is no numerical cap for this kind of visa, so every eligible elderly applicant is granted the permission to import a care worker.[23] There are no demands for the worker to hold professional qualifications.[24] [*2] Labor migrants are protected by the Minimum Wage Law (the current Israeli minimum wage is about $1,250 per month), but are not compensated for overtime (except when working during their 25 hours' weekly rest), and can be paid up to 25 percent less to cover costs such as housing and health insurance.[25] [*3] Welfare law provides in-kind services to older persons who meet the eligibility criteria.[26] The eligibility test takes into consideration age (the recipient of the care must be at least of mandatory retirement age – 67 for men and 62 for women), income level, and degree of dependency.[27] If the person allowed care by a migrant worker is eligible for state support, part of the salary of the care worker (30 percent–40 percent) is state-funded,[28] and the rest is funded by the care recipient or his/her family. State-approved private

[23] Israel Population and Immigration Authority, *Criteria for Issuing a Permit to Employ a Foreign Worker in Nursing* (2014). available at: http://tinyurl.com/zwjpfl9 (Hebrew); Keren Mazuz, "The State of the Jewish Family: Eldercare as a Practice of Corporeal Symbiosis by Filipina Migrant Workers" in Fran Markowitz (Ed.), *Ethnographic Encounters in Israel: Poetics and Ethics of Fieldwork* (Bloomington: University of Indiana Press, 2013), pp. 97–111.

[24] Keren Mazuz, "The Familial Dyad between Aged Patients and Filipina Caregivers in Israel: Eldercare and Bodily-Based Practices in the Jewish Home," *Anthropology & Aging Quarterly*, 34(3) (2013), 126–34, at 128.

[25] Hila Shamir, "Migrant Care Workers in Israel: Between Family, Market, and State," *Israel Studies Review*, 28(2) (2013), 192–209; NLC 47546-10-12 *Zatelman v. Petrov.*

[26] State of Israel, Ministry of Welfare and Social Services, *Taking Care of the Elderly at Home and in the Community* (2011), available at: http://tinyurl.com/jlvklp2 (Hebrew).

[27] Shamir, "Migrant Care Workers," at 194.

[28] Iecovich, "Client Satisfaction," at 108.

agencies manage migrant labor workers' employment, including their salary. [*4] The Israeli pension legal regime requires all employers and citizen employees to deposit part of the employee's salary into a pension fund, which includes insurance for the spouse and dependent children of the worker.[29] [*5] Israel provides its citizens a modest universal state-funded old-age pension of approximately $400 per month.[30] [*6] Private residence institutions for the elderly are very costly, amounting to three times the minimum wage, 150 percent of the average salary, and up to four times the cost of a migrant in-home care worker.[31] [*7] Geriatric institutionalization is not covered by the Israeli national health insurance scheme. Assistance for geriatric institutionalization is granted by the state based on a number of factors: the allocated budget for a given year (which may not stretch to cover all those eligible); a vacancy being available in a suitable institution; and an eligibility test, based on the medical and social condition of the patient and his/her and the family's economic situation. Adult children can be forced to pay for their parents' institutionalization under the Israeli familial support law, which mandates that children must economically support their parents if the latter cannot take care of themselves and if the children have more resources than needed to support themselves, their spouse, and their minor children.[32]

As can be seen from Rachel's experience and the legal context surrounding it, the combination of laws and regulations that govern labor visas, the labor rights of migrant care workers, the public and private resources available for the elderly, and the duties of children toward their parents create a situation in which the Israeli State makes care delivered by a migrant worker a relatively affordable and preferable option for the old persons and, importantly, also for their families. These factors are summarized in Table 8.1.

Indeed, Israel is one of several countries that rely heavily on live-in migrants to care for its elderly. Currently, about 60,000 migrant workers care for about a third of Israel's frail older persons living in the

[29] In 2008, the right to pension from the employer was expanded also to migrant workers, See "Compulsory Pension Insurance for Employees," Every Right Website, http://tinyurl.com/mmwvpsm (Hebrew).

[30] "Old Age Pension Rates," National Insurance Institute of Israel, available at: www.btl.gov.il/English%20Homepage/Benefits/Old%20Age%20Insurance/Pages/Pensionrates.aspx.

[31] Iecovich, "Client Satisfaction," at 107.

[32] State of Israel, Ministry of Welfare and Social Services, Instruction No. 4.8, *Placing Feeble Elderly in Institutions* (2013), available at: http://tinyurl.com/zxs7ku4 (Hebrew); Israel Doron & Lital Bar, "Public Long-Term Care Insurance: The Need for Legislative Reform," The Association for Civil Rights in Israel (2016), available at: www.acri.org.il/he/wp-content/uploads/2016/06/reform.pdf (Hebrew).

Table 8.1. *Economic and Familial Differences between In-home Elderly Care and Institutionalized Care*

	Migrant Workers	Cost to family (before state funding)	Recipient's liquid assets	Adult children's income
In-home care by a migrant worker	Allowed into the country to work	Approx. $1,250	Taken into consideration in calculating state subsidy	Not relevant to state subsidy – adult children may voluntarily opt to assist economically
Institution-alization	Not allowed into the country to work	Approx. $4,000	Must be exhausted before eligibility for state subsidy	Adult children's income (salary and rent from real estate) is taken into consideration in calculating state subsidy. They may be forced to economically assist

community,[33] and it is estimated that these numbers will only increase.[34] In the majority of cases, and as in other countries, the care worker is a women.[35] Most of the care workers are Asian, mainly from the Philippines, and are considered most suitable due to their cultural norm of filial piety and the stereotypical perception of their feminine nature as devoted and obedient.[36] A similar scenario can be found in Italy, for example, which

[33] Iecovich & Doron, "Migrant Workers in Eldercare in Israel," at 33.

[34] Shamir, "Migrant Care Workers," at 200.

[35] Ohad Green & Liat Ayalon, "Whose Right Is It Anyway? Familiarity with Workers' Rights among Older Adults, Family Caregivers, and Migrant Live-In Home Care Workers: Implications for Policy and Practice," *Educational Gerontology*, 41(7) (2015), 471–81, at 472.

[36] Interestingly, Asian care workers who have spent many years in Israel are considered "damaged goods," because, allegedly, their filial piety norms have been eroded by the exposure

has also witnessed a shift in recent years from family-based elderly care to paid in-home care, and where 70 percent of in-home workers who care for older persons are migrants.[37] Other countries that answer the growing demand for non-family-based elderly care mainly by employing migrant in-home care workers include Spain, Portugal, Austria, and Switzerland.[38] In many other countries, migrants account for a larger proportion of the care workforce, including in-home and institutional elderly care labor, than of the workforce in the rest of the economy.[39]

Due to prolonged life expectancy, demand for migrant care workers is constantly rising, and it may increase also in countries that currently only moderately rely on migrant in-home care of the elderly, such as Britain, Canada, and the United States.[40] Demand may even grow in countries such as France, the Netherlands, and Sweden, which rely the least on migration, at present, because of their publicly funded, well-paid local care workforce.[41] In France, for example, to maintain the current ratio of care workers to older people, the care workforce would have to increase by 74 percent by 2050.[42] As the demographer Alessio Cangiano demonstrates, it is vital that these figures be part of the current debates over the immigration policies of governments in the Global North.[43] From a very preliminary and tentative examination of the online discourse on immigration policies, my impression is that the question of who would care

---

to the norms of the host society. See Liat Ayalon, "Family and Family-Like Interactions in Households with Round-the-Clock Paid Foreign Careers in Israel," *Ageing & Society*, 29(5) (2009), 671–86, at 683.

[37] Iecovich, "Migrant Homecare Workers," at 149; Francesca Bettio, Annamaria Simonazzi, & Paola Villa, "Change in Care Regimes and Female Migration: The 'Care Drain' in the Mediterranean," *Journal of European Social Policy*, 16(3) (2006), 271–85.

[38] Matteo Luppi, Rosanne Oomkens, Trudie Knijn, & Bernhard Weicht, "Citizenship in the Context of Migrant Care Work: Regimes, Rights and Recognition," Grant No. 320294, Beucitizen – Barriers Towards EU Citizenship (2015), available at: http://beucitizen .eu/wp-content/uploads/Deliverable_9.6_final1.pdf; EU Expert Group in Gender and Employment, *Long-Term Care for the Elderly: Provisions and Providers in 33 European Countries* (2010), at 94, available at: http://ec.europa.eu/justice/gender-equality/files/ elderly_care_en.pdf. Unlike the Mediterranean countries, most migrant care workers in Switzerland are from nearby countries – Poland and Hungary – and so are, in fact, "long-distance commuters." See Schwiter, Berndt, & Truong, "Neoliberal Austerity."

[39] Alessio Cangiano, "Elder Care and Migrant Labor in Europe: A Demographic Outlook, Data and Perspectives," *Population and Development Review*, 40(1) (2014), 131–54.

[40] In these countries, the rate of migrants among the homecare workers is 18 percent–27 percent. See Iecovich, "Migrant Homecare Workers," at 149.

[41] Ibid.

[42] Cangiano, "Elder Care," at 145.

[43] Ibid.

for older persons in the absence of migrants is hardly addressed.[44] Even countries that have already become transnational employers of care workers still treat the question of elderly care as if it were an entirely national concern, ignoring the major cross-border dimension.[45]

Interestingly, Rachel's account also demonstrates how being assisted by a migrant care worker does not necessarily mean that the children of the elderly are no longer present nor care about them. Indeed, the empirical evidence does not support the common argument that we live in an individualistic era of declining intergenerational family ties in which adult children's commitment to their parents is weakening.[46] Recent studies that examined both adult children's and aging parents' normative perceptions regarding filial care, as well as actual practices of such care, provide strong evidence that, in developing as well as developed countries, adult children are still highly involved in filial caregiving and form the backbone of the support system.[47] In the EU, for example, 80 percent of the total number of hours devoted to elderly care are provided by the family, mainly by female spouses and daughters.[48] Indeed, in one of the earliest attempts to explore the meaning of our "graying world," journalist Ted C. Fishman provides a beautiful account of aging within an intimate intergenerational context, which I would call *familial aging*:

> One wonderful quality of families is that their members do not readily label one another as old. Families have a better sense of the continuity of life because they see one another over very long periods, often as long as sixty or seventy years. Such spans traverse all the great life events and create deep affinities. Families see how the parents are the kids and how a kid lives on inside the adults. There are shared mythologies that provide

[44] For a rare example that targets the relevance of elderly care to the debated immigration US legal regime, see Guillermo Cantor, "Will Immigration Reform Address Our Need for Eldercare Workers?" *Aging Today* (August 22, 2013), available at: www.asaging.org/blog/will-immigration-reform-address-our-need-eldercare-workers.

[45] For example, Norway. See Umut Erel, "Introduction: Transnational Care in Europe – Changing Formations of Citizenship, Family, and Generation," *Social Politics*, 19(1) (2012), 1–14, at 7.

[46] Usha Narayanan, "The Government's Role in Fostering the Relationship between Adult Children and their Elder Parents: From Filial Responsibility Laws to ... What? A Cross-Cultural Perspective," *Elder Law Journal*, 4 (1996), 369–406; Isabella Aboderin, "Modernisation and Ageing Theory Revisited: Current Explanations of Recent Developing World and Historical Western Shifts in Material Family Support for Older People," *Ageing & Society*, 24(1) (2004), 29–50; Katz, Lowenstein, & Brick, "Intergenerational Relations and Old-Age in the Modern Era."

[47] Merril Silverstein, Daphna Gans, & Frances M. Yang, "Intergenerational Support to Aging Parents, The Role of Norms and Needs," *Journal of Family Issues,* 27(8) (2009), 1068–84.

[48] Simonazzi, "Care Regimes," at 5.

younger members with backstory on older generations. There is also the constant feed of new cultural information that bubbles up from the youngest members and keeps the older ones amused and somewhat up to date. Maybe that is why family life and long, heartfelt friendships help people stay healthy and vital throughout their lives.[49]

Yet whereas spouses and children in the Global North tend to willingly take it upon themselves to provide short-term care for aging spouses, parents, and parents-in-law, they (and the older people themselves) tend to prefer partial or total formal (external) care in the long term.[50] I would suggest that this is the case not only because children are less available due to geographic distance and paid labor demands, but also because the nature of old age itself has changed. Illnesses that once killed are now medically managed, and people can go on living for many years though heavily dependent on the care provided by others. As the condition of Rachel's mother demonstrates, this care might demand round-the-clock support for basic needs including dressing, feeding, washing, and toileting. Indeed, clinical psychologist Liat Ayalon found in her research that many of the Israeli family members of elderly relatives cared for by migrant workers related to the care recipient as a "powerless infant" and felt that they needed to "de facto parent" him or her.[51] However, I would suggest that caring for a disabled elderly spouse or parent can often be less rewarding and emotionally harder than caring for one's young child. Whereas parenting one's baby is perceived as a happy responsibility (albeit at times an extremely tough one) and as an investment in the future adult the baby will grow up to be, parenting one's parent can feel like an unnatural role-reversal. It is emotionally demanding, also for spouses, as even the very best of care might not be acknowledged and cannot prevent the awaiting death. One manifestation of the awkwardness that might result from this role-reversal is the refusal of grown-up children to bathe their parent or change his/her diapers, as reflected in Ayalon's study.[52]

---

[49] Ted C. Fishman, *Shock of Gray: The Aging of the World's Population and How It Pits Young Against Old, Child Against Parent, Worker against Boss, Company against Rival, and Nation Against Nation* (New York: Scribner, 2010), at 341.

[50] Ariela Lowenstein & Ruth Katz, "Taking Care of the Elderly – What is the Desirable Balance between the Family and the State?" in Brick & Lowenstein (Eds.), *The Elderly and the Family*, pp. 40–51 (Hebrew); Maria C. Stuifbergen & Johannes J. M. van Delden, "Filial Obligations to Elderly Parents: A Duty to Care," *Medicine, Health Care and Philosophy*, 14(1) (2011), 63–71.

[51] Ayalon, "Family and Family-Like," at 676.

[52] Ibid. Even within the paid care work market, caring for a child is more desirable than caring for an older person, as the latter work is more arduous and less well-paid. See Erel, "Introduction," at 8.

Hence, many families are happy to replace long-term or physically demanding elder care with paid care. Studies show that they seek to employ a paid worker who will care for the physical needs of the older person, leaving family members to act as *familial administrators* and as providers of social and emotional support.[53] However, local paid workers are, in many countries, in short supply and relatively expensive, and cannot meet the growing demand.[54] Particularly when around-the-clock care is needed, it is very hard to find local care workers who would readily agree to leave their family and move to live with the elderly care recipient.[55] Hence, more and more older persons and their families turn to (mainly female) migrant workers who, due to the global inequality discussed in this book, leave their families behind and fill the care deficiency in developed countries.[56] As this solution is conceptualized by geographers Karin Schwiter, Christian Berndt, and Jasmine Truong, the elderly in developing countries enjoy *privileged immobility* – that is, the ability to stay at home – and their family members enjoy *mobility* to live their own lives (that is, not tied to the dependent older person). This is thanks to the *transnational* (and I would add, *underprivileged*) *mobility* of the migrant care worker, who then experiences *forced immobility* as they are restricted to the older person's home in delivering constant day-and-night care.[57]

The solution of an in-home migrant worker blurs the borders between home and workplace, private and public, informal and formal work, emotional and physical labor, leisure time and paid time, family members and strangers, natives and immigrants.[58] The literature has paid a relatively high level of attention to the labor-related risks for the migrant care worker that are embedded in this border-blurring solution. The quasi-familial relationship, the performance of tasks previously undertaken by female family members without pay, and the high levels of familial-like intimacy, make it easier for the care recipient and his/her family to "forget" that the migrant care worker is an employee and not one of the family.

[53] Shamir, "Migrant Care Workers," at 200.

[54] Simonazzi, "Care Regimes," at 3; Lindsay B. Lowell, Susan Martin, & Robyn Stone, "Ageing and Care Giving in the United States: Policy Contexts and the Immigrant Workforce," *Population Ageing*, 3(1) (2010), 59–82.

[55] Hoff, Feldman, & Vidovicova, "Migrant Home Care Workers Caring for Older People," at 11.

[56] Simonazzi, "Care Regimes," at 3.

[57] Schwiter, Berndt, & Truong, "Neoliberal Austerity," at 4.

[58] Ibid.; Einat Albin, "From Required and Unlimited Intimacy to Troubling Unfree Labor: The Case of Domestic Workers," *Tel-Aviv University Law Review*, 39(2) (2016), 369-414 (Hebrew).

Hence the common and documented phenomena of low salaries, deprivation of free time, no compensation for overtime, demands for tasks not specified in the contract, unsuitable living conditions (for example, sharing the bedroom with the care recipient), unsatisfactory knowledge of the worker's legal rights, and sexual harassment.[59] Social work scholar Ohad Green and Ayalon add that it is the private home setting itself, characterized by its isolating effect on the employee and its lack of external supervision that locates migrant care workers as the most vulnerable within the already disempowered group of migrant workers.[60] Finally, as discussed in Chapter 5 in relation to different kinds of citizenship-related vulnerabilities, the chances that migrant care workers will complain about abuse or mistreatment – especially in countries such as the United States, in which many of the migrant care workers are undocumented and in the many countries in which they are documented but cannot become citizens or permanent residents – are extremely small.[61] These hazards have been acknowledged by the international community[62] and by scholars[63] calling

[59] Shamir, "Migrant Care Workers"; Guy Mundlak & Hila Shamir, "Between Intimacy and Alienage: The Legal Construction of Domestic and Care Work in the Welfare State" in Helma Lutz (Ed.), *Migration and Domestic Work: A European Perspective on a Global Theme* (New York: Routledge, 2008), pp. 161–76; Guy Mundlak & Hila Shamir, "Bringing Together or Drifting Apart? Targeting Care Work as 'Work Like No Other'," *Canadian Journal of Women and the Law*, 23(1) (2011), 289–308; Albin, "From Required and Unlimited Intimacy to Troubling Unfree Labor"; Schwiter, Berndt, & Truong, "Neoliberal Austerity"; Liat Ayalon, "Evaluating the Working Conditions and Exposure to Abuse of Filipino Home Care Workers in Israel: Characteristics and Clinical Correlates," *International Psychogeriatrics*, 21(1) (2009), 40–9; Asher D. Colombo, "'They Call Me a Housekeeper, but I Do Everything.' Who Are Domestic Workers Today in Italy and What Do They Do?" *Journal of Modern Italian Studies*, 12(2) (2007), 207–37.

[60] Green & Ayalon, "Whose Right Is It?"

[61] Ibid., at 473. An exception to the rule is Canada, which allows migrant domestic workers to apply for permanent residence after two years there. See Bukola Salami, Wendy Duggleby, & Fahreen Rajani, "The Perspectives of Employers/Families and Care Recipients of Migrant Live-in Caregivers: A Scoping Review," *Health and Social Care in the Community* (2016), 1–12, at 2, available at: http://onlinelibrary.wiley.com/doi/10.1111/hsc.12330/epdf. For a detailed report on the Canadian regulation of migrant care workers, see Ivy Lynn Bourgeault, Jelena Atanackovic, Jane Lebrun, Rishma Parpia, Ahmed Rashid, & Judi Winkup, "Immigrant Care Workers in Aging Societies: The Canadian Context and Experience," Ontario Health Human Resource Research Network, available at: http://rorrhs-ohhrrn.ca/images/stories/docs/immigrant-care-workers-report-.pdf.

[62] For example, United Nations, *Behind Closed Doors- Protecting and Promoting the Human Rights of Migrant Domestic Workers in an Irregular Situation* (2015), available at: www.ohchr.org/Documents/Publications/Behind_closed_doors_HR_PUB_15_4_EN.pdf.

[63] For example, Green & Ayalon, "Whose Right Is It?"; Albin, "From Required and Unlimited Intimacy to Troubling Unfree Labor"; Mundlak & Shamir, "Bringing Together."

for national and international protective legislation aimed specifically at migrant domestic workers, including those who care for the elderly.[64]

Unlike the labor-related implications, research on the *familial* implications of the border-blurring solution that places a care worker within the care recipient's home is scant. Again, we know that the spouse and children of the elderly care recipient are still involved and maintain social and emotional familial attachment although they take the opportunity to relinquish familial physical duties. But other than that, little is known about the familial impact of bringing in a stranger as an integral and indispensable part of the household and care labor.[65] In a recent systematic literature review aimed at identifying all empirical studies on the "needs and experiences" of recipients of care by a migrant live-in worker and their families, nursing specialists Bakula Salami, Wendy Duggleby, and Fahreen Rajani found only thirteen relevant articles, based on only nine studies. No less surprising is that seven of the eight articles that focused on elderly care (the remaining five dealing with childcare recipients) were based on studies conducted in Israel.[66] So most of the little we know of the perspectives of family members on the situation in which one of the family is cared for in old age by a migrant care worker is restricted to (Jewish) Israelis.

The existing research implies that not only does the home become a workplace, as emphasized within the labor law literature, but the workplace becomes a home, at least temporarily. The expectations of the family members that the migrant care worker will perform only physical care tasks, leaving to them the social and emotional sides of familial care, are based on a rigid dichotomy between physical and emotional care, which reality proves to be artificial. One paramount example of the kind of much-needed research on the familial implication of elderly care by a migrant worker exposes this artificiality. Ayalon's aforementioned study (based on twenty-two interviews with Jewish family members self-identified as

---

[64] See also "International Labour Standards on Migrant Workers," International Labour Organization, available at: www.ilo.org/global/standards/subjects-covered-by-international-labour-standards/migrant-workers/lang–en/index.htm. However, the ILO Domestic Workers Convention, 2011, was ratified only by 22 countries. See "Ratifications of C189 – Domestic Workers Convention, 2011 (No. 189)," International Labour Organization, available at: www.ilo.org/dyn/normlex/en/f?p=NORMLEXPUB:11300:0::N O::P11300_INSTRUMENT_ID:2551460.

[65] Ayalon, "Family and Family-Like," at 672.

[66] Salami, Duggleby, & Rajani, "The Perspectives of Employers." See also Kieran Walsh & Isabel Shutes, "Care Relationships, Quality of Care and Migrant Workers Caring for Older People," *Ageing & Society*, 33(3) (2013), 393–420.

the primacy caregiver of the elderly person and twenty-nine interviews and three focus groups with female Filipino care workers) found that, in many cases, the migrant care worker becomes "part of the family." She is included in family events, such as holidays and birthdays, and is given gifts and extra money above and beyond the terms of her labor contract. The family members reported feeling that they not only parent the elderly, but also the care worker. By treating the care worker as one of the family, Ayalon explains, the family members manage to maintain their normative understanding that intimate care should not be provided by a stranger but by a family member. All the family members interviewed by Ayalon appreciated the emotional support the care worker gave to the care recipient and the care recipient's spouse. Overall, they appreciated the "peace of mind" she gave them and some went as far as claiming that the care worker had given them their lives back. They also acknowledged that without the assistance of the migrant care worker they would have had to place the care recipient in an institution, as all the care they could provide as family would not be enough to sustain the older person at home.[67]

However, two quantitative studies of the care recipient/in-home migrant care worker/family member of the care recipient triad reveal that the care recipients are more likely than their family members to define the migrant care worker as a family member.[68] Interestingly, in Ayalon's qualitative study, almost all family members "described a decline in the quality of their emotional and social relationship following the illness of the care recipient and the arrival of the Filipina home-care worker." The loss of cognitive functions of the elderly, the increasing role of family members as *care managers*, and the freedom afforded by the paid worker that enables the family caregiver to move out and return to (or establish) his or her own household, were all given as explanations for this decline. These findings indicate that the family is changed by the practice of long-term care labor provided by a migrant.[69] At least for the care recipient, the migrant care worker might *do family* even more than the family itself.

The familial qualities of the attachment created within the elder care recipient–migrant care worker dyad are evident also in the accounts of the

---

[67] Ayalon, "Family and Family-Like."

[68] Liat Ayalon, "Examining Satisfaction with Live-in Foreign Home Care in Israel from the Perspectives of Care Recipients, Their Family Members, and their Foreign Care Workers," *Aging & Mental Health*, 15(3) (2011), 376–84; Esther Iecovich, "Primary Caregivers and Foreign Caregivers of the Elderly: Variables Explaining Burden and Care Satisfaction of the Primary Caregiver and the Foreign Caregiver," Research Report, Ben-Gurion University (2010) (Hebrew).

[69] See also Shamir, "Migrant Care Workers."

workers interviewed in Ayalon's study. They described their lives within the recipient's home with frequent references to love and with an emphasis on the strength of relationship they had with the care recipient, likening them to the warm relations they had, or wished to have, with their own family members. They described providing emotional care to the elderly as part of their job, and often referred to the care recipient in familial terms: *aba, ima, saba,* or *safta* (in Hebrew: father, mother, grandfather, grandmother). Notwithstanding, Ayalon detected ambivalence in the family-like relationships reflected in the accounts of the care workers, who also mentioned being treated as a slaves or machines, their regret at being away from their biological family members, and their work as caregivers being their way of supporting those left behind. Hence, I suggest that whereas the care recipient and his/her family experience familial completion thanks to the arrival of the migrant worker, in which familial order and balance are reestablished through the worker filling the care gap, the worker experiences simultaneous familial completion and loss. They may derive a sense of completion from being able to send money home to support their own family and from forming new family-like attachments in the host household. Yet, at the same time, their objectification in the household where they are employed, coupled with their emotional longing to be with their own family, can be experienced as significant losses.

Some ambivalence can also be detected among the elderly person's family members. Ayalon notes several cases in which the family members accuse the care worker of abusing the elderly by extracting financial benefits in return for emotional support.[70] One example she provides is that of an elderly man who gave his credit card to the care worker. His daughter argued that the Filipina "celebrated with this card." She tells how the family "didn't know what to do," since the Filipina "was good" to the father and "was taking good care of him."[71] Ayalon concludes her study by arguing that the migrant care worker, forced (by law) to leave her family behind, is expected by the family that employs her to become a "surrogate daughter."[72] At the same time, her findings demonstrate that this expectation usually does not translate into a family-like flow of economic giving and that, if the care recipient starts to give money to the care worker, the

---

[70] Unfortunately, there are rare cases in which the migrant care worker physically abuses the elder care recipient. See, for example, CrimC (TA) 28508-08-12 *State of Israel v. Takori* (2013) (Israel); CrimC (TA) 40020/08 *State of Israel v. Ramed* (2008) (Israel); and CrimC (RM) 30551-08-12 *State of Israel v. Lalik* (2013) (Israel).

[71] Ayalon, "Family and Family-Like," at 679.

[72] Ibid., at 681.

family members will most likely see it as a form of abuse of the older person. Another manifestation of this emotional–economic ambivalence can be found in the actions that follow the death of the care recipient. Although many families mention the migrant care worker in the obituary, together with the names of the grieving family members,[73] and might mention her in the eulogies with thanks and gratitude, the possibility that the deceased might include her as one of the estate's beneficiaries will probably be inconceivable to the deceased's relatives. Indeed, Israeli media reminds the 'true family' of the risk that the migrant care worker may take over the care recipient and his/her wealth, by marrying the elder person or persuading him/her to name the care worker as a beneficiary in the will.[74]

Returning to the legal framework that overshadows the relationship between the migrant care worker and the Israeli family, we are reminded of the profound difference between the surrogate daughter (or son, in the rare case of a male care worker) and the biological children of the elderly. Once the older person dies, the care worker can expect deportation, unless she has yet to exhaust her visa timeframe and finds another older person to care for. Although there are families that actively try to assist the care worker with finding a new family,[75] this will be in vain if the visa conditions do not allow the ongoing presence of the care worker in Israel. What prominent sociologist Arlie Russell Hochschild calls "emotional imperialism"[76] is manifested here to the full – the care worker is, in fact,

---

[73] "Avelim," Obituaries website: www.avelim.co.il/?s=%D7%9E%D7%98%D7%A4%D7%9C%D7%AA (Hebrew).

[74] For example, Elizaphan Rosenberg, "Foreign Caregiver of an Elderly Parent? Beware of a New Heir," *Ynet* (February 5, 2010), available at: www.ynet.co.il/articles/0,7340,L-3844472,00.html (Hebrew); Yanir Yagna, "The Mother's Caretaker Had an Affair with the Father – and Is Demanding Part of the Inheritance, *Walla News* (December 22, 2014), available at: http://news.walla.co.il/item/2812961 (Hebrew); Oded Bar-Meir, "'Will Hunters': Lurking after the Negev's Elderly," *Ynet* (December 20, 2012), available at: www.mynet.co.il/articles/0,7340,L-4322381,00.html (Hebrew).

[75] For example, Ma'ayan Zemach published on Facebook (July 16, 2016): "We are looking for a warm and loving home for Indika the amazing care worker of my ill father who is like a family member to us," see www.facebook.com/photo.php?fbid=1186576018047652&set=a.227263077312289.55621.100000857946256&type=3&theater (Hebrew); Sara Manor posted on Facebook (February 12, 2016): "After four years we are about to get separated from the caretaker who took care of my father ... Dad enjoyed her company, felt secured by her presence and I could have peace of mind ... If you know of a family who is looking for some peace of mind, knowing someone is taking care of their loved one, contact me," see www.facebook.com/sara.manor.5/posts/10153928016708234 (Hebrew).

[76] Arlie Russell Hochschild, "Love and Gold" in Barbara Ehrenreich & Arlie Russell Hochschild (Eds.), *Global Woman: Nannies, Maids, and Sex Workers in the New Economy* (New York: Henry Holt and Company, 2004), pp. 15–30, at 26–7.

expected to provide emotional care to, and become part of, the family, but only as long as the host family and host nation require this emotional bond. Thereafter, the care worker is treated as if the emotional care never took place and is transformed back into a nonfamilial legal alien.

The power relations in which the care recipient/in-home migrant care worker/family member of the care recipient triad is embedded are also apparent in anthropologist Keren Mazuz's rare ethnography of the encounters between the dependent elderly in Israel's geographic and social periphery and their Filipina care workers. Although, like Ayalon, Mazuz found that "profoundly familial relationships" are constituted between the care recipient and care provider,[77] she very eloquently describes the power of the older person's family members to construct a border between them and the alien care worker:

> It is the Filipina's total presence that allows the family members to choose whether, how, and when to observe and attend their aged mother's body decline. This corporeal symbiosis demands a total attendance from the Filipina until the [care recipient] dies. Thus, only a foreign female body constructed as temporary substance – uprooted and displaced in space and time, segregated into isolated Jewish households, separated from her language and culture of origin and from her family, and deprived of rights and citizenship – holds the potential to perform these tasks repeatedly. Insofar as the Filipina is grafted onto the [care recipient], her life activities and desires are suspended, thus creating an assigned category that could be considered redundant, and inferior in relation to others' lives, even that of the dying one.[78]

According to Mazuz, the cultural option to delegate the care of the older person to temporary migrants, which we saw is constructed by an apparatus of families laws, forms migrant workers as "the geared parts that lubricate the family system."[79] This option "is liberating and strengthens the young, healthy Israeli Jewish family members by simultaneously separating them from the weakened, sick and dying members through the role of the Filipina, ensuring the stability and continuity of the family without friction with the [dependent elderly] members of the family."[80]

Notwithstanding this convincing interpretation of the imbalanced power relations inherent in the care triad, I would suggest that it is somewhat affected by the unseen, yet very significant, border between Israel's geographic

---

[77] Mazuz, "The Familial Dyad," at 127.
[78] Mazuz, "The State of the Jewish Family," at 108.
[79] Ibid.
[80] Ibid., at 109–10.

and social periphery and its more affluent center. Those workers who are placed in the homes of the relatively privileged elderly might be able to express their familial subjectivity more than those placed in poorer and more remote homes. In a sense, the relative privilege of the care recipient and his/her family flows over to the migrant care worker. Some migrant care workers not only experience family-like relations while in the home of the care recipient, but also manage to create their own family while in Israel. A few marry Israelis, others marry other immigrants, and some give birth in Israel – and many manage to meet up frequently with other family members from their home country who also care for Israeli families.[81]

Take, for example, Nicole, the migrant worker who cared for my relatively wealthy grandparents, who lived in Jerusalem. Nicole came from the Philippines as a young single woman and stayed in Israel for about ten years, during which time she cared for my grandfather, and later on my grandmother. To employ Nicole for this long period, my family used the only exception available in Israeli law to the limited five-year visa for migrant workers. This exception allows workers who care for an older person (or a person with a severe disability, regardless of age) to stay for as long as the care they provide is necessary, on the condition that their deportation would cause "severe harm" to the care recipient.[82]

Two of Nicole's sisters and more distant family members also lived in Israel, and they were in regular contact. After a few years, Nicole met Joseph, who also migrated from the Philippines and cared for another older person in the same neighborhood in Jerusalem. They married, and spent their free weekends together in Tel Aviv, where a significant Filipino community had become established.[83] Away from the eyes of the immigration police (which would not have approved), and without asking any permission from their employers, Nicole and Joseph set up a small catering business that operated from my widowed grandmother's kitchen, providing Filipino dishes for several other Filipino care workers living in the area. A few months before my grandmother's death, Nicole gave birth to a baby boy and lived with him in my grandmother's

---

[81] See also discussion in Ch. 5, text accompanying fn. 154–155.

[82] Section 3a of The Entry into Israel Law 1952, available at: www.nevo.co.il/law_html/Law01/189_003.htm#Seif31(Hebrew).

[83] Tina Von Britenshtain, "The Filipino Workers in Israel" in Roby Nathanson & Lea Achdut (Eds.), *The New Workers: Wage Earners from Foreign Countries in Israel* (Tel Aviv: Hakibbutz Hameuchad, 1999), pp. 205–25 (Hebrew); "Profile of the Filipino Community in Israel," Philippine Embassy in Israel, available at: http://philippine-embassy.org.il/index.php?option=com_content&view=article&id=56:profile-of-the-filipino-community-in-israel&catid=15&Itemid=33.

home until my grandmother passed away. It was then that Nicole had to leave Israel because, according to the law detailed previously, her working visa could not be extended. I later heard that she went back to the Philippines and had two more children. These days, all three children are cared for by their grandmother in the Philippines, while Nicole looks after an older person in Canada and Joseph works as a ship's cook.

Just as in the case of the care workers in Mazuz's study, Nicole's forced departure after my grandmother passed away marked the border between her and my family and her objectification as a disposable caregiver. Still, for ten years she was part of my family's life, and, more significantly for her, established her own family in Israel. Although, as far as the Israeli policy is concerned, Nicole was supposed to be an isolated worker, totally devoted to the needs of the Jewish family and nation, she became a familial subject, and her familiality managed to find its way through the cracks in the national, gendered, and racial borders put in front of her by her employer and by the host state. Although certainly not representative, this case demonstrates that, for some migrant care workers, even in countries such as Israel, which (as detailed in Chapter 5) strive to deprive migrant workers of their familial subjectivity, the host country becomes a home and not only a workplace. This home might have abusive elements and is most often only temporary. But, there are cases in which it is a rewarding and significant home, which on rare occasions can become permanent, as the migrant care worker establishes a family in the host country, and wishes and is allowed to stay.

Toward the End

This chapter cannot be concluded because so very little is known about the impact of the interplay between globalization and borders on the legalized familiality surrounding old age. Even the most widely studied aspect of this impact – created by the presence of migrant care workers – is understood mainly in relation to Israel. Hence, many questions remain open.

Of course, attention must be devoted to the study of familial outcomes of different legal regimes governing old age and migratory care in different countries. But additional questions, not addressed even in the Israeli context, must be posed and studied. For example, who cares for the migrant care workers when they become old and dependent themselves? How does the fact that many of them were not allowed by law to have children in the host country, or were forced to be separated from their children for years and years, affect the availability of filial care when needed at old age? Do the migrant care workers manage to save money to compensate for lost filial care by paid care? And what about the parents of the migrant care workers? The *care drain* created by care immigration to developing countries was discussed in Chapter 6, in relation to left-behind children. Here, it is important to add the care drain created in relation to the left-behind elderly, less discussed in the literature. Contrary to popular belief, the majority of older people live in the less-developed parts of the world.[84] These elderly are at risk of being given the task of caring for their grandchildren while their adult children migrate to care for others, and to be lacking the physical and emotional care they need from their children as they become older and more dependent.

The lack of research on these questions echoes the lack of an international convention on the rights of older people. Overall, elder law is still in its infancy. It therefore contributes little to important discussions over elderly care and the dilemma caused by the fact that promoting migrant care workers' labor and familial legal rights will likely diminish the ability of elderly people to be assisted by them as their services will be more costly.[85]

The need to care for the world's aging population is, in my opinion, a problem of catastrophic magnitude. It is unclear how the ever-diminishing younger generations in countries with below-replacement fertility rates will manage to carry the burden of caring for the growing population of old and very old citizens. Different solutions, including some very problematic and unsatisfying alternatives, are already on the table. For instance, in Japan, one of the world's most rapidly aging countries, where people cannot afford to retire and the market is in urgent need of the elderly's participation in the workforce, there have been efforts to encourage older workers to continue in employment and thus postpone the point at which they are officially allowed to enjoy the right to be cared for.[86] Likewise, in other countries, policy makers are aiming to postpone the retirement age,[87] and cuts in pension allowances

---

[84] Hoff, Feldman, & Vidovicova, "Migrant Home Care Workers Caring for Older People," at 7.

[85] Mundlak & Shamir, "Bringing Together"; Iecovich & Doron, "Migrant Workers in Eldercare in Israel."

[86] John H. Tucker, "60 Seen as Too Young to Retire in Aging, Worker-Short Japan," *The Japan Times News* (July 15, 2016), available at: www.japantimes.co.jp/news/2016/07/15/national/60-seen-young-retire-aging-worker-short-japan/#.V4yupPl96Uk.

[87] See, for example, Chun Han Wong, "China Sets Timeline for First Change to Retirement Age Since 1950s," *The Wall Street Journal* (March 10, 2015), available at: http://blogs.wsj.com/chinarealtime/2015/03/10/china-sets-timeline-for-first-change-to-retirement-age-since-1950s/; Ed Monk, "So Exactly When Will You be Able to Retire?

are being introduced.[88] In Germany, some people are sent abroad to be cared for in more affordable homes for the elderly, including in Hungary and Thailand.[89] This legitimized "deportation" of the elderly is just one of several initiatives by individuals, families, and the state to find solutions in cases in which the resources available to the care recipients do not cover the cost of care where they currently live.[90] In China, adult children are forced by new legislative amendments to take full economic, social, and emotional responsibility for their parents.[91] Other countries are also introducing or contemplating the possibility of introducing laws that mandate parental support – in a sense, a reversal of child support.[92] Some legislators have introduced incentives for filial support, such as housing regulations that assist children who care for their elderly parent at home[93] and compensations from the deceased's estate for a caregiving child.[94] The option of legalizing euthanasia and people's right to choose the timing of their death, in cases of agonizing old age, could also be promoted, in principal, also in the name of relieving the difficulties of supporting

Government Wants to Raise Average Retirement Age by Six Months Every Year" This is Money website (October 7, 2014), available at: www.thisismoney.co.uk/money/ pensions/article-2783514/Government-hoping-delay-retirement-ages-exactly-able-retire.html; Zvi Zrahiya, "Decision to Raise Women's Retirement Age Postponed by Two Months," Haaretz (July 10, 2011), available at: www.haaretz.com/israel-news/ decision-to-raise-women-s-retirement-age-postponed-by-two-months-1.372498.

[88] For example, Mary Sanchez, "How the Feds Handle the Teamsters Pension Crisis Will Determine the Future of Union Retirees," The Kansas City Star (February 18, 2016), available at: www.kansascity.com/opinion/opn-columns-blogs/mary-sanchez/article61178627 .html; Helene Perkins, "Pension Crisis to Last for 20 Years: 11 Million Britons Face Reduced Payouts," Express (January 4, 2016), available at: www.express.co.uk/news/uk/ 631192/pension-crisis-last-20-years-11-million-Britons-face-reduced-payouts.

[89] Kate Connolly, "Germany 'Exporting' Old and Sick to Foreign Care Homes," The Guardian (December 26, 2012), available at: www.theguardian.com/world/2012/dec/26/ german-elderly-foreign-care-homes.

[90] Kathleen Peddicord, "Cheapest Places to Retire Overseas," The Huffington Post (August 6, 2015), available at: www.huffingtonpost.com/news/cheapest-places-to-retire-overseas/.

[91] Law of the People's Republic of China on Protection of the Rights and Interests of the Elderly (1996, amended 2013), available at: www.china.org.cn/english/government/ 207404.htm.

[92] Allison E. Ross, "Taking Care of Our Caretakers: Using Filial Responsibility Laws to Support the Elderly beyond the Government's Assistance," Elder Law Journal, 16 (2008), 167–209; Katherine C. Pearson, "Filial Support Laws in the Modern Era: Domestic and International Comparison of Enforcement Practices for Laws Requiring Adult Children to Support Indigent Parents," Elder Law Journal, 20 (2013), 269–314.

[93] Seymour Moskowitz, "Adult Children and Indigent Parents: Intergenerational Responsibilities in International Perspective," Marquette Law Review, 86(3) (2002) 401–55, at 441.

[94] Shelly Kreiczer Levy "The Intergenerational Bond – Rethinking Inheritance," PhD Dissertation, Faculty of Law, Tel Aviv University (2008), at 337.

the elderly.[95] Notwithstanding all these measures, real and potential, it is clear that, for many countries facing the generational inverted pyramid, nothing will suffice in the long run if they wish to survive as healthy societies, let alone care for their elderly, other than a dramatic increase in child birth rates or a massive influx of immigrants.

The scale of the challenge of caring for the old and very old is almost overwhelming and calls for drastic measures. These measures will affect our personal and cultural perceptions of life and death; our perceptions of the need for families and their desired size; and our notions of intergenerational rights and obligations. They will also force us to face the current elasticity of familial and national borders, and the possibility that these borders are in need of further reconstruction and flexibility.

[95] Charlie Sprague, "The Economic Argument for Euthanasia," The Forum (June 8, 2009), http://cmcforum.com/opinion/06082009-the-economic-argument-for-euthanasia.

Conclusion

In a recent video, watched more than 40 million times on YouTube and Facebook within a ten-week period,[1] people are briefly interviewed about themselves, their origins, and their national heritage. They provide answers such as "I'm proud to be English," "I'm really patriotic about Bangladesh," and "I am 100 percent Icelandic." Some of the interviewees also voice resentment toward other nations. For example, the Englishman is "not a fan of the Germans" and the man from Bangladesh has issues with neighboring India and Pakistan because of "the conflict." After each short interview, the participants are asked to take a DNA test that will map their ancestors' origins. Two weeks later, each is given an envelope with results that leave them surprised and even astonished. For example, the allegedly Englishman finds out he is 5 percent German; the woman who is seemingly French learns she is 32 percent British and 31 percent Italian-Greek, and not even one percent French; and the perceived Cuban learns he is a rare global combination of Native Americans and ancestors from different parts of Africa, the Middle East, and even Eastern Europe.[2] The woman who believes she is Kurd, and expresses political resentment toward the Turkish, learns she has Turkish ancestors, as well as a cousin among the 67 people who participated in this experiment. Her cousin, in turn, seems confused at discovering from his ancestors' DNA map that he is a "Muslim-Jew." A few of the interviewees (and perhaps some of the viewers, if my reaction is anything to go by) are moved to tears. The video ends with a message against extremism and the notion of pure race, and tells us that "you have more in common with the world than you know."

---

[1] *Momondo – The DNA Journey*, available at: www.youtube.com/watch?v=tyaEQEmt5ls& feature=youtu.be; "Momondo – The DNA Journey," Facebook, available at: https://www .facebook.com/momondo/videos/1741100669466167/. There are additional clips on specific interviewees.

[2] See also *Momondo – The DNA Journey Feat. Carlos*, available at: www.youtube.com/ watch?v=EYnutf0rqeY.

It is easy not to notice that this video is, in fact, a commercial adver-
tisement – part of a hypercapitalist campaign launched by a metasearch-
engine travel company, designed to encourage viewers to travel the world
and thus contribute to the tourism industry. Nevertheless, it provides a
moving reminder that many of us are the result of a very long history
of globordered families. People, since the dawn of humanity, have traveled; procreated while crossing racial, religious, and cultural borders;
and resettled. Only through socialization did the subsequent generations
learn to believe they were a part of a coherent group with a long history of
overlapping geographic, national, racial, and cultural essence.

Indeed, although globordered families are not new, the intensity of the
current movement of people makes more apparent the artificial and futile
attempts to portray human societies, in general, and familial relations, in
particular, as established and maintained within closed and coherent borders. As this book demonstrates, families in our era cannot, and should
not, be understood only within national borders. International families
(in which each spouse was born and raised in a different nation), cross-
border families (that move, in part or as a whole, to another nation),
transnational reproduction-assisted families (created by gametes or pregnancy services from abroad), and emigration-assisted families (in which
one or more family members are cared for by a paid migrant worker)
are all deeply affected by globalization. Even those families not in any of
these categories cannot truly escape globalization since almost all of us
are exposed to foreign people and messages that practice and represent
different understandings of familiality.

Moreover, familiality is a major force compelling people to cross
national borders. Short cross-border travels and long-term emigration
today cannot be understood separately from individuals' wish to create
a family (for example, by importing a spouse or adopting a child from
another country) and their incentive to support their family (by, for
instance, moving it to a more developed country or leaving it behind and
sending remittances). Hence, although most of the literature on globalization centers on political and economic macroforces, and most immigration and related human rights law centers on the microlevel of the
individual, I believe this book proves that globalization cannot be fully
understood, and international law properly shaped, without relating to
the mezzolevel of families.

This book also provides ample evidence of the ongoing significance of
borders for families. The need and ability to maneuver and take advantage
of the possibilities offered to families by globalization depend, first and

foremost, on the position of the country of origin within the global hierarchal web of economic inequalities. Those who are born and live in the
privileged parts of the world have more resources, and are usually embedded within a less dogmatic familial culture, which enables them to shop
for familial options wherever they are. However, even in the relatively rich
and pluralist parts of the world, many face difficulties in combining family life with a global market that is increasingly demanding and family-
unfriendly, reflected in, for example, the below-replacement European
birth rates. Those less fortunate, born and raised in the poorer parts of
the world, have to try to overcome hostile external national borders and,
at times, internal dogmatic religious and parochial borders, which prevent them from shaping their familial biography with relative freedom
and choice.

In particular, gender emerges from this book as a central social bordering category, which shapes the ability to enjoy the options opened to families by bordered globalization, as well to overcome the challenges created
by it. We have seen how a range of factors – including patriarchal religious
law and its increasing presence in the West, as well as the heteronormativ-
ity of much of secular law, presented in Chapter 3; surrogate motherhood,
discussed in Chapter 4, as enabling new opportunities and creating new
vulnerabilities; immigration and citizenship laws that view male spouses
as more suspicious and female spouses as more vulnerable, as discussed
in Chapter 5; children affected differently depending on whether it is the
mother or the father who immigrates, as presented in Chapter 6; gendered spousal violence and the simultaneous positive and negative impact
of globalization on the possibility of escaping it, and gendered manifestations of parental violence and the global differentiating responses to it,
presented in Chapter 7; and the feminization of immigration created by
the gendered care deficit in the Global North, discussed in Chapter 8 –
all assemble to highlight the ongoing centrality of rigid borders between
male and female within families and the role of law in maintaining or
challenging them.

Notwithstanding, again and again, this book demonstrates the elasticity of borders, its impact on families, and the role of law in trying to
prevent this elasticity and in enabling it. For example, national laws
attempt to create a border between "genuine" marriages and "sham" marriages, between citizens with full family rights and noncitizens with no
family rights, and between religious law and civil law. These attempts
fail, as families are constituted by a mixture of feelings and interests, as
citizens' familial rights are harmed by immigration laws and noncitizens

manage to establish families in the host country despite them, and as civil legislators and courts find themselves addressing religious law present in their clients' socio-legal lives. Moreover, international, regional, and transnational laws force nations to bend their borders and so alter their understanding of families, by, for example, forcing them to allow an undocumented migrant drug dealer to remain in the state in the name of his daughters' right to family life (Chapter 5).

The elasticity of borders is both one of the causes and one of the outcomes of the antagonistic, cooperative, hybrid, dilemmatic, paradoxical, and hypocritical relations between globalization and borders, explored in this book in relation to legalized families in our era. Indeed, the different issues we have explored reveal that the much-discussed antagonist relations between globalization and borders are, in fact, but one of many kinds of relations that exist (albeit one of the most important ones). Cooperative relations, for example, allow the import of cheap care labor without granting the migrant care workers family rights (Chapters 5 and 8), whereas hybridity is manifested in globordered families themselves. Most of the families discussed in this book, including the families of Bara, Nick, and baby Christopher (presented in the Introduction) and Dafna, Itamar, Kai, and Tal (presented in Chapter 3) are created by bordered globalization and integrate globalization and borders in their familial *doing* and *displaying*. Dilemmatic relations are present, when, for example, national law needs to determine whether to recognize or ignore Muslim or Jewish family arbitration, with the realization that both routes might harm women (Chapter 3); and paradoxes are created within bordered globalization, when, for example, family relations – which are supposed to be valued and promoted for their intimacy and care – become highly regulated and scrutinized because they are also one of the only remaining legitimate routes for citizenship in a developed country (Chapter 5). Hypocritical relations are created whenever national law uses globalization to export what it considers immoral familial behaviors, such as surrogacy and abortion (Chapter 4). In all these relations, the amalgam of diverse, and at times conflicting, *families laws* play a crucial role.

The diverse legal universe affecting families in the era of bordered globalization, and the inability of the international community to agree on conventions with universal regulation of issues such as same-sex marriage, cross-border surrogacy, and domestic violence as torture or a basis for asylum, demonstrate the centrality of culture to nations, societies, and communities, and the centrality of the family institution to cultures. The collectivist–individualist axis, for example, has been very much evident in the book's discussions of forced marriage (Chapter 3), child labor (Chapter 6), and care in old age (Chapter 8). This is the main reason this book does not offer overarching familial regulation to suit families' needs in the current era. Because I take cultures extremely seriously – accepting their social centrality and legal legitimacy – I understand the dangers of legal generalizations and attempts at harmonization. Families laws are faced with the very difficult challenge of protecting universal human rights while taking national interests into account and expressing cultural sensitivity and social contextualization.

Nevertheless, the discussions in the book do point to several basic normative principles that I believe should guide legislators and judges who are faced with families affected by bordered globalization, if we aim at a humane and just society and world:

1. Families are important to people, and thus individuals should enjoy the right to establish or not to establish a family, and to have significant existence as a family member.
2. The era of bordered globalization is characterized by diverse and dynamic meanings of *family*. It enables and forces individuals to create new family structures and practice complex and unorthodox family relations. The law should acknowledge familiality when it exists rather than enforce rigid notions that do not correspond with *families in action*.
3. Family-law principles should be recognized by other legal branches and their carriers. In particular, children's interests and rights should be part of immigration law and tribunals.
4. International, regional, national, and parochial laws phallocentrism should be acknowledged and corrected.
5. Families laws should be crafted with empirical (quantitative and qualitative) knowledge on the relevant stakeholders. Too little is known about the impact of bordered globalization on family members, including their needs and wishes. Uninformed policy making might lead to immoral as well as ineffective outcomes.
6. Finally, although, and because, legal risks, inconsistencies, and misunderstandings in relation to families are here to stay (because of the complex interrelations between globalization and borders), policy makers and enforcers, as well as legal professionals, must better explain to lay people the relevance of families laws to their lives. The biggest fallacy is the imagined border between the public sphere and the family, and individuals must be informed of the families laws relevant to their lives, and, with this awareness, discuss with their family

members the opportunities they have and the challenges they must face, in the era of bordered globalization.

It is my hope that those of you who have read the whole book have been left somewhat overwhelmed. This is deliberate, because one of my goals is to highlight the challenges of empirically and theoretically understanding bordered globalization and professionally assisting families affected by it. Indeed, one of the greatest challenges created by bordered globalization in relation to families is for the legal professionals who need to guide and assist them and to researchers who wish to study them. I believe that, these days, good family lawyers must acquire some understanding in comparative law, international law, and immigration and citizenship laws if they are to properly advise their clients at critical moments – such as before they marry, when they contemplate acquiring a family asset in another country, on drafting a will, or when they divorce. Because one lawyer in not likely to be able to hold all relevant knowledge, sophisticated lawyers must establish professional connections with, among others, immigration lawyers, international taxation lawyers, and family lawyers in other countries. The same goes for family judges, who must perceive themselves not only as national judges, but also as bridges to subnational and international laws, and acquire much broader legal knowledge than their niche title might suggest is necessary.

Likewise, scholars interested in families and family law must establish new alliances and develop new research methods, which I call *global methodologies*. For example, international multidisciplinary groups must become the norm, with all the funding and coordination challenges embedded in them. Moreover, multinational research assistant networks in the relevant disciplines should be established, so a researcher in one country will be able to be assisted by local assistants who have the knowledge, language, and other skills needed for contextualized and deep research. Even in relation to the seemingly easy task of exploring comparative law, I can testify from the work on this book and other projects that the challenge of truly undressing another country's law *on the books* is extremely hard, let alone that country's *law in action*. As most of us do not master more than one or two languages, and cannot afford intense fieldtrips around the world, we must cooperate with local forces in creative ways. This is so not only, as was always the case, to learn about other legal systems and societies, but also to understand our own legal system and society. As this book aims to demonstrate, Ireland's abortion law and social practices cannot be understood detached from UK, CoE, and UN laws (Chapter 4); Israeli surrogacy law and social practices cannot be understood detached from Indian law (Chapter 5); and adoption in the United States cannot be fully understood without insight into Chinese, Russian, and Guatemalan adoption law and practices (Chapter 6). Exploring families laws and legalized families in other countries becomes a must if we are to deeply understand and properly address them at home.

The overwhelming scale of the issues raised in this book also embraces the moral plane – the global economic inequalities and their detrimental impact on families, as documented here, may leave us with a sense of powerlessness and despair. Clearly, it no longer takes a family, a village, or even a nation, to secure nurturing familial ties – it takes a globe. However, this book also reveals the power of individuals, civil society, and the media to create a significant change. A specific politician who opens a (temporary) door for undocumented migrants and their families (Chapter 5), journalists who publish articles on a woman who was abortionally murdered (Chapter 4), NGOs that assist victims of forced marriage (Chapter 3), FGM, and domestic violence (Chapter 7) – they all make a difference for individuals and for families, and contribute to a humane socio-legal order. Each one of us – in our capacity as scholars, professionals, policy makers, and voters, and as family members, can make a difference. First, we have to shape an informed familial vision, and then we must act upon it.

BIBLIOGRAPHY

This bibliographic list includes academic books and articles. PhD dissertations, MA theses, reports, newspapers articles, legislation and case law are referred to only in the footnotes accompanying each chapter.

Aboderin Isabella, 2004. "Modernisation and Ageing Theory Revisited: Current Explanations of Recent Developing World and Historical Western Shifts in Material Family Support for Older People," *Ageing & Society*, 24(1): 29–50.

Abrams Kerry, 2013. "What Makes the Family Special?" *The University of Chicago Law Review*, 80(1): 7–27. Philadelphia.

Abrams Kerry and Piacenti R. Kent, 2014. "Immigration's Family Values," *Virginia Law Review*, 100(4): 629–709.

Abrego Leisy J., 2014. *Sacrificing Families: Navigating Laws, Labor, and Love across Borders* (Redwood City, CA: Stanford University Press).

Adar Bunis Mattat, 2007. *Families in Sociological and Anthropological Perspective* (Raanana: The Open University of Israel). [Hebrew]

Adelman Carol C., 2003. "The Privatization of Foreign Aid: Reassessing National Largesse," *Foreign Affairs*, 82(6): 9–14.

Ahmad Nehaluddin, 2011. "Child Labour: Ground Realities of Indian Labor Laws," *Commonwealth Law Bulletin*, 37(1): 61–74.

Akhtar Rajnaara, 2010. "British Muslims and the Revolution of the Practice of Islamic Law with Particular Reference to Dispute Resolution," *Journal of Islamic State Practices in International Law*, 6(1): 27–39.

Alanen Julia, 2008. "When Human Rights Conflict: Mediating International Parental Kidnapping Disputes Involving the Domestic Violence Defense," *Inter-American Law Review*, 40(1): 49–108.

Albin Einat, 2016. "From Required and Unlimited Intimacy to Troubling Unfree Labor: The Case of Domestic Workers," *Tel-Aviv University Law Review*, 39(2): 369–414. [Hebrew]

Aldeeb Abu-Sahlieh Sami A., 2006. "Male and Female Circumcision: The Myth of the Difference" in Rogaia Mustafa Abusharaf (Ed.), *Female Circumcision: Multicultural Perspectives* (Philadelphia: University of Pennsylvania Press), pp. 47–74.

Aldeeb Abu-Sahlieh Sami A., 1994. "To Mutilate in the Name of Jehovah or Allah: Legitimization of Male and Female Circumcision," *Medicine and Law,* 13(7–8): 575–622.

Ali Shaheen Sardar, 2013. "Authority and Authenticity: Sharia Councils, Muslim Women's Rights, and the English Courts," *Child and Family Law Quarterly,* 25: 113–37.

Almog Shulamit, 2000. *Law and Literature* (Jerusalem: Nevo). [Hebrew]

Altink Henrice and Weedon Chris, 2010. "Introduction" in Aaron Jane, Altink Henrice and Weedon Chris (Eds.), *Gendering Border Studies* (Cardiff: University of Wales Press), pp. 1–15.

Amato Paul R., 1998. "More Than Money? Men's Contributions to Their Children's Lives" in Booth Alan and Crouter Ann C. (Eds.), *Men in Families: When Do They Get Involved? What Difference Does It Make?* (New York: Psychology Press), pp. 241–78.

André Géraldine and Godin Marie, 2014. "Child Labour, Agency and Family Dynamics," *Childhood,* 21(2): 161–74.

Andreß Hans-Jürgen, Borgloh Barbara, Bröckel Miriam, Giesselmann Marco, and Hummelsheim Dina, 2006. "The Economic Consequences of Partnership Dissolution: A Comparative Analysis of Panel Studies from Belgium, Germany, Great Britain, Italy and Sweden," *European Sociological Review,* 22(5): 533–60.

Andro Armelle, Cambois Emmanuelle, and Lesclingand Marie, 2014. "Long-Term Consequences of Female Genital Mutilation in a European Context: Self Perceived Health of FGM Women Compared to Non FGM Women," *Social Science & Medicine,* 106: 177–84.

Anu, Kumar Pawan, Inder Deep, and Sharma Nandini, 2013. "Surrogacy and Women's Right to Health in India: Issues and Perspective," *Indian Journal of Public Health,* 57(2): 65–70.

Appadurai Arjun (Ed.), 2003. *Globalization* (Durham, NC: Duke University Press).

Appadurai Arjun, 1996. *Modernity at Large: Cultural Dimensions of Globalization* (Minneapolis: University of Minnesota Press).

Arbel Efrat, 2013. "The Culture of Rights Protection in Canadian Refugee Law: Examining the Domestic Violence Cases," *McGill Law Journal,* 58(3): 729–71.

Ashe Marie and Hélie Anissa, 2013. "Realities of Religio-Legalism: Religious Courts and Women's Rights in Canada, the United Kingdom, and the United States," *UC Davis Journal of International Law and Policy,* 20(2): 139–209.

Aviram Hadar, 2010. "Does the Law Achieve Its Goals? Answers from the Empirical Research World" in Hacker Daphna and Ziv Neta (Eds.), *Does the Law Matter?* (Tel Aviv University), pp. 27–62. [Hebrew]

Ayalon Liat, 2011. "Examining Satisfaction with Live-in Foreign Home Care in Israel from the Perspectives of Care Recipients, Their Family Members, and Their Foreign Care Workers," *Aging & Mental Health,* 15(3): 376–84.

Ayalon Liat, 2009. "Evaluating the Working Conditions and Exposure to Abuse of Filipino Home Care Workers in Israel: Characteristics and Clinical Correlates," *International Psychogeriatrics*, 21(1): 40–9.

Ayalon Liat, 2009. "Family and Family-Like Interactions in Households with Round-the-Clock Paid Foreign Carers in Israel," *Ageing & Society*, 29(5): 671–86.

Baal Shem Yaacov and Shinar Duv, 1998. "The Telepresence Era: Global Village or 'Media Slums,'" *IEEE Technology and Society Magazine*, 17(1): 28–35.

Bacik Ivana, 2013. "The Irish Constitution and Gender Politics: Development in the Law on Abortion," *Irish Political Studies*, 28(3): 380–98.

Bailey Alison, 2011. "Reconceiving Surrogacy: Toward a Reproductive Justice Account of Indian Surrogacy," *Hypatia*, 26(4): 715–41.

Baines Beverley, 2006. "Equality's Nemesis?" *Journal of Law and Equality*, 5(1): 57–80.

Baker Hannah, 2013. "A Possible Future Instrument on International Surrogacy Arrangements: Are There 'Lessons' to be Learned from the 1993 Hague Intercountry Adoption Convention?" in Trimmings Katarina and Beaumont Paul (Eds.), *International Surrogacy Arrangements* (Oxford, UK: Hart), pp. 411–26.

Bakht Natasha, 2004. "Family Arbitration Using Sharia Law: Examining Ontario's Arbitration Act and its Impact on Women," *Muslim World Journal of Human Rights*, 1(1): 1–24.

Balagopalan Sarada, 2008. "Memories of Tomorrow: Children, Labor, and the Panacea of Formal Schooling," *Journal of the History of Childhood and Youth*, 1(2): 267–85.

Balibar Étienne, 2004. *We, the People of Europe? Reflections on Transnational Citizenship* (Princeton, NJ: Princeton University Press).

Ballard Robert L., 2015. "Introduction" in Ballard Robert L., Goodno Naomi H., Cochran Robert F., and Milbrandt Jay A. (Eds.), *The Intercountry Adoption Debate* (Newcastle upon Tyne, UK: Cambridge Scholars Publishing), pp. 1–4.

Bano Samia, 2007. "Islamic Family Arbitration, Justice and Human Rights in Britain," *Law, Social Justice & Global Development Journal*, 1: 1–26, available at www2.warwick.ac.uk/fac/soc/law/elj/lgd/2007_1/bano/.

Barber Benjamin, 1995. *Jihad versus McWorld* (New York: Times Books).

Barnett Ola W., Miller-Perrin Cindy L., and Perrin Robin D., 2011. *Family Violence across the Lifespan: An Introduction*, 3rd ed. (Thousand Oaks, CA: Sage).

Barrientos Armando, Gorman Mark, and Heslop Amanda, 2003. "Old Age Poverty in Developing Countries: Contributions and Dependence in Later Life," *World Development- Chronic Poverty and Development Policy*, 31(3): 555–70.

Bartholet Elizabeth, 2015. "The Hague Convention: Pros, Cons and Potential" in Ballard Robert L., Goodno Naomi H., Cochran Robert F., and Milbrandt

Jay A. (Eds.), *The Intercountry Adoption Debate: Dialogues across Disciplines* (Newcastle upon Tyne, UK: Cambridge Scholars Publishing), pp. 239–44.

Bartholet Elizabeth, 2015. "The International Adoption Cliff: Do Child Human Rights Matter?" in Ballard Robert L., Goodno Naomi H., Cochran Robert F., and Milbrandt Jay A. (Eds.), *The Intercountry Adoption Debate: Dialogues across Disciplines* (Newcastle upon Tyne, UK: Cambridge Scholars Publishing), pp. 193–202.

Bartholet Elizabeth, 2010/2011. "International Adoption: A Way Forward," *New York Law School Law Review,* 55: 687–99.

Bartholet Elizabeth, 2007. "International Adoption: The Child's Story," *Georgia State University Law Review,* 24(2): 333–379.

Bartholet Elizabeth, 2006. "International Adoption" in Askeland Lori (Ed.), *Children and Youth in Adoption, Orphanages, and Foster Care* (London: Greenwood Press), pp. 63–78.

Basu Kaushik,1999. "Child Labor: Cause, Consequence, and Cure, with Remarks on International Labor Standards," *Journal of Economic Literature,* 37(3): 1083–119.

Bauman Zygmunt, 1998. *Globalization: The Human Consequences* (Cambridge, UK: Polity Press).

Bauserman Robert, 2002. "Child Adjustment in Joint-Custody Versus Sole-Custody Arrangements: A Meta-Analytic Review," *Journal of Family Psychology,* 16(1): 91–102.

Beck Ulrich, 2006. "Unpacking Cosmopolitanism for the Social Sciences: A Research Agenda," *The British Journal of Sociology,* 57(1): 1–23.

Beck Ulrich, 1992. *Risk Society: Towards a New Modernity* (London: Sage).

Beck Ulrich and Beck-Gernsheim Elisabeth, 2014. *Distant Love* (Cambridge, UK: Polity Press).

Beck Ulrich and Beck-Gernsheim Elisabeth, 2007. "Families in a Runaway World" in Scott Jacqueline, Treas Judith and Richards Martin (Eds.), *The Blackwell Companion to the Sociology of Families* (Malden, MA: Blackwell Publishing), pp. 499–514.

Beck Ulrich and Beck-Gernsheim Elisabeth, 1995. *The Normal Chaos of Love* (Cambridge, UK: Polity Press).

Bélanger Danièle and Tran Giang Linh, 2011. "The Impact of Transnational Migration on Gender and Marriage in Sending Communities of Vietnam," *Current Sociology,* 59(1): 59–77.

Ben-Naftali Orna and Shany Yuval, 2006. *International Law between War and Peace* (Tel Aviv: Ramot). [Hebrew]

Benedict Anderson, 1991. *Imagined Communities: Reflections on the Origin and Spread of Nationalism,* rev. edn. (London: Verso).

Benvenisti Eyal, 2013. "Sovereigns as Trustees of Humanity: On the Accountability of States to Foreign Stakeholders," *American Journal of International Law,* 107(2): 295–333.

Berg Rigmor C. and Denison Eva, 2012. "Interventions to Reduce the Prevalence of Female Genital Mutilation/ Cutting in African Countries," *Campbell Systematic Reviews*, 8(9): 1–155.

Berkovitch Nitza, 1999. *From Motherhood to Citizenship: Women's Rights and International Organizations* (Baltimore: Johns Hopkins University Press).

Berman Paul Schiff, 2005. *The Globalization of International Law* (Aldershot: Ashgate).

Bernstein Gaia and Triger Zvi, 2011. "Over-Parenting," *UC Davis Law Review*, 44(4): 1221–79.

Bessell Sharon, 2011. "Influencing International Child Labour Policy: The Potential and Limits of Children-Centred Research," *Children and Youth Services Review*, 33(4): 564–68.

Bettio Francesca, Simonazzi Annamaria, and Villa Paola, 2006. "Change in Care Regimes and Female Migration: The 'Care Drain' in the Mediterranean," *Journal of European Social Policy*, 16(3): 271–85.

Bhabha Jacqueline, 2003. "The Citizenship Deficit: On Being a Citizen Child," *Development*, 46(3): 53–9.

Birenbaum-Carmeli Daphna, 2016. "Thirty-five Years of Assisted Reproductive Technologies in Israel," *Reproductive Biomedicine & Society Online*, 2: 16–23, available at www.sciencedirect.com/science/article/pii/S2405661816300090.

Blair Marianne D., Weiner Merle H., Stark Barbara, and Maldonado Solangel (Eds.), 2009. *Family Law in the World Community: Cases, Materials, and Problems in Comparative and International Family Law*, 2nd edn. (Durham, NC: Carolina Academic Press).

Blecher-Prigat Ayelet, 2012. "The Costs of Raising Children: Towards a Theory of Financial Obligations between Co-Parents," *Theoretical Inquiries in Law*, 13(1): 154–207.

Blecher-Prigat Ayelet, 2010. "The Family and the Law?" in Hacker Daphna and Ziv Neta (Eds.), *Does the Law Matter?* (Tel Aviv University), pp. 275–304. [Hebrew]

Bloomer Fiona and O'Dowd Kellie, 2014, "Restricted Access to Abortion in the Republic of Ireland and Northern Ireland: Exploring Abortion Tourism and Barriers to Legal Reform," *Culture, Health & Sexuality*, 16(4): 366–80.

Blyth Eric, 2010. "Fertility Patients' Experiences of Cross-Border Reproductive Care," *Fertility & Sterility*, 94(1): e11–e15, available at www.fertstert.org/article/S0015-0282(10)00106-8/fulltext.

Boccagni Paolo, 2013. "Migration and the Family Transformations It 'Leaves Behind': A Critical View from Ecuador," *The Latin Americanist*, 57(4): 3–24.

Boellstorff Tom, 2008. *Coming of Age in Second Life: An Anthropologist Explores the Virtually Human* (Princeton, NJ: Princeton University Press).

Bonjour Saskia and de Hart Betty, 2013. "A Proper Wife, a Proper Marriage: Constructions of 'Us' and 'Them' in Dutch Family Migration Policy," *European Journal of Women's Studies*, 20(1): 61–76.

Bookey Blaine, 2016. "Gender- Based Asylum Post- Matter of A-R-C-G: Evolving Standards and Fair Application of the Law," *Southwestern Journal of International Law*, 22: 1–19.

Bosniak Linda, 2006. *The Citizen and the Alien: Dilemmas of Contemporary Membership* (Princeton, NJ: Princeton University Press).

Bourdieu Pierre, 1996. "On the Family as a Realized Category," *Theory, Culture & Society*, 13(3): 19–26.

Bourdieu Pierre, 1987. "The Force of Law: Towards a Sociology of the Juridical Field," *Hastings Law Journal*, 38: 814–53.

Bourdieu Pierre, 1984. *Distinction: A Social Critique of the Judgment of Taste*, Richard Nice (Trans.) (Cambridge, MA: Harvard University Press).

Bourdillon Michael, 2006. "Children and Work: A Review of Current Literature and Debates," *Development & Change*, 37(6): 1201–27.

Boyd Susan S., 2010. "Autonomy for Mothers? Relational Theory and Parenting Apart," *Feminist Legal Studies*, 18(2): 137–58.

Brandt Martina, Haberkern Klaus, and Szydlik Marc, 2009. "Intergenerational Help and Care in Europe," *European Sociological Review*, 25(5): 585–601.

Breuning Marijka, 2013. "Samaritans, Family Builders, and the Politics of Intercountry Adoption," *International Studies Perspectives*, 14(4): 417–35.

Brining Margaret F., Schneider Carl E., and Teitelbaum Lee E. (Eds.), 1999. *Family Law in Action: A Reader* (Cincinnati, OH: Anderson Publishing).

Brod Frommer Gail, 1994. "Premarital Agreement and Gender Justice," *Yale Journal of Law and Feminism*, 6: 229–95.

Browne Collette V. and Braun Kathryn L., 2008. "Globalization, Women's Migration, and the Long-Term-Care Workforce," *The Gerontologist*, 48(1): 16–24.

Browne Noah L., 2011. "Relevance and Fairness: Protecting the Rights of Domestic Violence Victims and Left-Behind Fathers under the Hague Convention on International Child Abduction," *Duke Law Journal*, 60:1193–238.

Broyde Michael J., 2011. "New York's Regulation of Jewish Marriage: Covenant, Contract, or Statute?" in Nichols Joel A. (Ed.), *Marriage and Divorce in a Multicultural Context: Multi-Tiered Marriage and the Boundaries of Civil Law and Religion* (New York: Cambridge University Press), pp. 138–63.

Bruch Carol S., 2014. "The Unmet Needs of Domestic Violence Victims and Their Children in Hague Child Abduction Convention Cases," *Family Law Quarterly*, 38(3): 529–45.

Bryceson Deborah and Ulla Vuorela (Eds.), 2002. *The Transnational Family: New Frontiers and Global Networks* (Oxford, UK: Berg).

Büchler Andrea, 2011. *Islamic Law in Europe?: Legal Pluralism and Its Limits in European Family Laws* (Surrey: Ashgate).

Buck Trevor, 2014. *International Child Law*, 3rd edn. (London: Routledge).

Budlender Debbie and Lund Francie, 2011. "South Africa: A Legacy of Family Disruption," *Development and Change*, 42(4): 925–46.

Burau Viola, Theobald Hildegard, and Blank Robert H., 2007. *Governing Home Care: A Cross-National Comparison* (Cheltenham: Edward Elgar).

Cameron David R., Ranis Gustav, and Zinn Anaalisa (Eds.), 2006. *Globalization and Self-Determination: Is the Nation-State under Siege?* (London: Routledge).

Cangiano Alessio, 2014. "Elder Care and Migrant Labor in Europe: A Demographic Outlook, Data and Perspectives," *Population and Development Review*, 40(1): 131–54.

Carbone June, 2014. "Legal Applications of the 'Best Interest of the Child' Standard: Judicial Rationalization or a Measure of Institutional Competence?" *Pediatrics*, 134: S111–20.

Carlson Richard, 2011. "Seeking the Better Interests of Children with a New International Law of Adoption," *New York Law School Law Review*, 55(3): 733–79.

Carsten Janet, 2004. *After Kinship* (UK: Cambridge University Press).

Castañeda Ernesto, 2012. "Living in Limbo: Transnational Households, Remittances and Development," *International Migration*, 51(s1), e13–e35, at e27, available at: http://onlinelibrary.wiley.com/wol1/doi/10.1111/j.1468-2435.2012.00745.x/full.

Castañeda Ernesto and Buck Lesley, 2014. "A Family of Strangers: Transnational Parenting and the Consequences of Family Separation due to Undocumented Migration" in Lorentzen Lois Ann (Ed.), *Hidden Lives and Human Rights in America: Understanding the Controversies and Tragedies of Undocumented Immigration* (Santa Barbara, CA: Praeger), pp. 175–202.

Castañeda Ernesto and Buck Lesley, 2011. "Remittances, Transnational Parenting, and the Children Left Behind: Economic and Psychological Implications," *The Latin Americanist*, 55(4): 85–110.

Castels Stephen and Miller Mark J., 1998. *The Age of Migration: International Population Movements in the Modern World*, 2nd edn. (Hampshire: Macmillan Press).

Chalfin Brenda, 2012. "Border Security as Late-Capitalist "Fix"" in Wilson Thomas M. and Donnan Hastings (Eds.), *A Companion to Border Studies* (Malden, MA: Wiley Blackwell), pp. 283–300.

Champenois Christina, 2015. "Does the Russian Adoption Ban Violate International Law?" *Brigham Young University International Law & Management Review*, 11(2): 29–54.

Chantler Khatidja, Gangoli Geetanjali, and Hester Marianne, 2009. "Forced Marriage in the UK: Religious, Cultural, Economic or State Violence?" *Critical Social Policy*, 29(4): 587–612.

Charsley Katharine, Storer-Church Brooke, Benson Michaela, and Van Hear Nicholas, 2012. "Marriage-Related Migration to the UK," *International Migration Review*, 46(4): 861–90.

Cheney Kristen, 2014. "'Giving Children a Better Life?' Reconsidering Social Reproduction, Humanitarianism and Development in Intercountry Adoption," *European Journal of Development Research*, 26(2): 247–63.

Christian Sandvig, 2013. "The Internet as Infrastructure" in Dutton William H. (Ed.), *The Oxford Handbook of Internet Studies* (Oxford University Press), pp. 86–106.

Coe Cati, 2011. "What is Love? The Materiality of Care in Ghanaian Transnational Families," *International Migration*, 49(6): 7–24.

Cohen Daniel, 2007. *Globalization and Its Enemies* (Cambridge, MA: MIT Press).

Cohen Jeffrey H., 2005. "Remittance Outcomes and Migration: Theoretical Contests, Real Opportunities," *Studies in Comparative International Development*, 40(1): 88–112.

Cohen Joshua, Howard Matthew, and Nussbaum Martha C., 1999. (Eds.), *Is Multiculturalism Bad for Women?* (Princeton, NJ: Princeton University Press).

Cole Jennifer and Durham Deborah (Eds.), 2007. *Generations and Globalization* (Bloomington: Indiana University Press).

Collins Kristin A., 2014. "Illegitimate Borders: *Jus Sanguinis*, Citizenship and the Legal Construction of Family, Race, and Nation," *Yale Law Journal*, 123(7): 2167–206.

Colombo Asher D., 2007. "'They Call Me a Housekeeper, but I Do Everything.' Who Are Domestic Workers Today in Italy and What Do They Do?" *Journal of Modern Italian Studies,* 12(2): 207–37.

Conroy Amanda, 2012. "Book Review: Jane Aaron, Henrice Altink and Chris Weedon (Eds.), Gendering Border Studies, Cardiff: University of Wales Press," *European Journal of Women's Studies*, 19: 399–402.

Constable Nicole, 2013. "Migrant Workers, Legal Tactics, and Fragile Family Formation in Hong Kong," *Oñati Socio-Legal Series*, 3(6): 1004–22.

Cooper Anthony, Perkins Chris, and Rumford Chris, 2014. "The Vernacularization of Borders" in Reece Jones and Corey Johnson (Eds.), *Placing the Border in Everyday Life* (Surrey: Ashgate).

Crowther Ann Luerssen, 2000. "Empty Gestures: The (In)Significance of Recent Attempts to Liberalize Algerian Family Law," *William & Mary Journal of Women and the Law*, 6(3): 611–43.

Cruz Evelyn Haydee, 2010. "Because You're Mine, I Walk the Line: The Trials and Tribulations of the Family Visa Program," *Fordham URB Law Journal*, 38(1): 155–81.

Curry Amberlynn, 2010. "The Uniform Premarital Agreement Act and Its Variations throughout the States," *Journal of American Academy of Matrimonial Lawyers*, 23: 284–355.

Dancig-Rosenberg Hadar and Levenkron Naomi, 2015. "Migratory Violence," *Tel Aviv University Law Review*, 37(2): 341–88. [Hebrew]

Dauvergne Catherine, 2009. "Globalization Fragmentation: New Pressures on Women Caught in the Immigration Law-Citizenship Law Dichotomy" in Benhabib Seyla and Resnik Judith (Eds.), *Migration and Mobilities: Citizenship, Borders and Gender* (New York University Press), pp. 333–54.

Dauvergne Catherine, 2007. "Citizenship with a Vengeance," *Theoretical Inquiries in Law*, 8(2): 489–507.

Davidov Guy, Yovel Jonathan, Saban Ilan, and Reichman Amnon, 2005. "State or Family? The 2003 Amendment to the Citizenship and Entrance to Israel Law," *Mishpat Umimshal*, 8: 643–99. [Hebrew]

de Blois Matthijs, 2010. "Religious Law versus Secular Law: The Example of the *Get* Refusal in Dutch, English and Israeli Law," *Utrecht Law Review*, 6(2): 93–114.

de Boer Ted M., 2008. "The Second Revision of the Brussels II Regulation: Jurisdiction and Applicable Law" in Boele-Woelki Katharina and Sverdrup Tone (Eds.), *European Challenges in Contemporary Family Law* (Antwerp: Intersentia), pp. 321–41.

DeBose Hawkins Cynthia and DeAngelo Ekaterina, 2015. "The New Cold War: Russia's Ban on Adoptions by U.S. Citizens," *Journal of the American Academy of Matrimonial Lawyers*, 28(1): 51–77.

de Hart Betty, 2009. "Love Thy Neighbour: Family Reunification and the Right of Insiders," *European Journal of Migration and the Law*, 11(3): 235–52.

de Hart Betty, 2006. "Introduction: The Marriage of Convenience in European Immigration Law," *European Journal of Migration and Law*, 8(3–4): 251–62.

Dejmanee Tisha, 2015. "Nursing at the Screen: Post Post-Feminist Daughters and Demonized Mothers on Toddlers and Tiaras," *Feminist Media Studies*, 15(3): 460–73.

Delanty Gerald, 2007. "European Citizenship: A Critical Assessment," *Citizenship Studies*, 11(1): 63–72.

Demleitner Nora V., 2003. "How Much Do Western Democracies Value Family and Marriage?: Immigration Law's Conflicted Answers," *Hofstra Law Review*, 32(1): 273–311.

Deomampo Daisy, 2013. "Transnational Surrogacy in India: Interrogating Power and Women's Agency," *Frontier: A Journal of Women's Studies*, 34(3): 167–88.

Dewer John and Parker Stephen, 2000. "English Family Law Since World War II: From Status to Chaos" in Katz Stanford N., Eekelaar John and Maclean Mavis (Eds.), *Cross Currents: Family Law and Policy in the US and England* (Oxford University Press), pp. 123–40.

Dezalay Yves and Bryant Garth G. (Eds.), 2002. *Global Prescriptions: The Production, Exportation, and Importation of a New Legal Orthodoxy* (Ann Arbor: University of Michigan Press).

Diduck Alison and Kaganas Felicity, 2006. *Family Law, Gender, and the State: Text, Cases and Materials* (Oxford, UK: Hart Publishing).

DiFonzo J. Herbie, 2015. "Dilemmas of Shared Parenting in the 21st Century: How Law and Culture Shape Child Custody," *Hofstra Law Review*, 43(4): 1003–24.

Dobrowolsky Alexandra, 2007. "(In)Security and Citizenship: Security, Im/migration and Shrinking Citizenship Regimes," *Theoretical Inquiries in Law*, 8(2): 629–61.

Donati Pierpaolo, 1998. "The New Citizenship of the Family" in Matthijs Koen (Ed.), *The Family: Contemporary Perspectives and Challenges* (Leuven University Press), pp. 243–61.

Doron Israel and Golan Tal, 2007. "Aging, Globalization and the Legal Construction of "Residence": The Case of Old Age Pensions in Israel," *The Elder Law Journal*, 15(1): 1–50.

Douglas Lawrence, Sarat Austin, and Umphery Martha Merrill, 2006. "Theoretical Perspectives on Lives in the Law: An Introduction" in Sarat Austin, Douglas Lawrence and Umphery Martha Merrill (Eds.), *Lives in the Law* (Ann Arbor: University of Michigan Press), pp. 1–20.

Dragiewicz Molly, 2011. *Equality with a Vengeance: Men's Rights Groups, Battered Women, and Antifeminist Backlash* (Lebanon, NH: Northeastern University Press).

Dreby Joanna, 2015. "U.S. Immigration Policy and Family Separation: The Consequences for Children's Well-being," *Social Science & Medicine*, 132: 245–51.

duRivage Nathalie, Keyes Katherine, Leray Emmanuelle, Pez Ondine, Bitfoi Adina, Koç Ceren, Goelitz Dietmar, Kuijpers Rowella, Lesinskiene Sigita, Mihova Zlatka, Otten Roy, Fermanian Christophe, and Kovess-Masfety Viviane, 2015. "Parental Use of Corporal Punishment in Europe: Intersection Between Public Health and Policy," *PloS ONE*, 10(2), available at: www.ncbi.nlm.nih.gov/pmc/articles/PMC4326463/.

Dustin Moira, 2010. "Female Genital Mutilation/Cutting in the UK," *European Journal of Women's Studies*, 17(1): 7–23.

Dwyer James G., 2016. "Diagnosing and Dispelling Denialism Regarding Children" in Moerland Ronald, Nelen Hans, and Willems Jan C. M. (Eds.), *Denialism and Human Rights* (Cambridge: Intersentia), pp. 49–68.

Earp Brian D., 2016. "Between Moral Relativism and Moral Hypocrisy: Reframing the Debate on FGM," *Kennedy Institute of Ethics Journal*, 26(2): 105–44.

Earp Brian D., 2015. "Female Genital Mutilation and Male Circumcision: Toward an Autonomy- Based Ethical Framework," *Medicolegal and Bioethics*, 5: 89–104.

Ebaugh Helen Rose and Curry Mary, 2000. "Fictive Kin as Social Capital in New Immigrant Communities," *Sociological Perspectives*, 43(2): 189–209.

Edwards Benjamin P., 2013. "Welcoming A Post-Doma World: Same-Sex Spousal Petitions and Other Post-Windsor Immigration Implications," *Family Law Quarterly*, 47(2): 173–89.

Edwards Rosalind and Gillies Val, 2012. "Farewell to Family? Notes on an Argument for Retaining the Concept," *Families, Relationships and Societies*, 1(1): 63–9.

Eekelaar John and George Rob (Eds.), 2014. *Routledge Handbook of Family Law and Policy* (Abingdon: Routledge Handbooks).

Eisenberg Theodor, 2000. "Empirical Methods and the Law," *Journal of the American Statistical Association*, 95: 665–9.

Elizabeth Vivienne, 2016. "Child Custody" in Shehan Constance L. (Ed.), *The Wiley Blackwell Encyclopedia of Family Studies*, available at: http://onlinelibrary .wiley.com/doi/10.1002/9781119085621.wbefs107/abstract?userIsAuthentic ated=false&deniedAccessCustomisedMessage=.

Elkins Jeremy, 2011. "Beyond 'Beyond the State': Rethinking Law and Globalization" in Sarat Austin, Lawrence Douglas, and Umphrey Martha Merrill (Eds.), *Law without Nations* (CA: Stanford University Press), pp. 22–65.

Enchautegui María E. and Menjívar Cecilia, 2015. "Paradoxes of Family Immigration Policy: Separation, Reorganization, and Reunification of Families under Current Immigration Laws," *Law & Policy*, 37(1–2): 32–60.

Engels Friedrich, 1985. *The Origin of the Family, Private Property and the State* (Harmondsworth: Penguin).

Erel Umut, 2012. "Introduction: Transnational Care in Europe – Changing Formations of Citizenship, Family, and Generation," *Social Politics*, 19(1): 1–14.

Erez Edna, Adelman Madelaine, and Gregory Carol, 2009. "Intersections of Immigration and Domestic Violence: Voices of Battered Immigrant Women," *Feminist Criminology*, 4(1): 32–56.

Ergas Yasmine, 2013. "Thinking 'through' Human Rights: The Need for a Human Rights Perspective with Respect to the Regulation of Cross-Border Reproduction Surrogacy" in Trimmings Katarina and Beaumont Paul (Eds.), *International Surrogacy Arrangements* (Oxford, UK: Hart Publishing), pp. 427–34.

Erikson Thomas Hylland, 2007. *Globalization: The Key Concepts* (Oxford, UK: Berg).

Estin Ann Laquer, 2014. "Foreign and Religious Law: Comity, Contract, and Constitution," *Pepperdine Law Review*, 41(5): 1029–47.

Estin Ann Laquer, 2012. "Unofficial Family Law" in Nichols Joel A. (Ed.), *Marriage and Divorce in a Multicultural Context: Multi-Tiered Marriage and the Boundaries of Civil Law and Religion* (New York: Cambridge University Press), pp. 92–119.

Estin Ann Laquar and Barbara Stark, 2007. *Global Issues in Family Law* (Eagan, MN: Thomson/West).

Ewick Patricia, 2004. "Consciousness and Ideology" in Sarat Austin (Ed.), *The Blackwell Companion to Law and Society* (Malden, MA: Blackwell Publishing), pp. 80–94.

Ewick Patricia and Silbey Susan S., 1998. *The Common Place of Law* (University of Chicago).

Ezer Nicole Lawrence, 2006. "The Intersection of Immigration Law and Family Law," *Family Law Quarterly*, 40(3): 339–66.

Farid Mahsa, 2012. "International Adoption: The Economics of the Baby Industry," *Whittier Journal of Child and Family Advocacy*, 12(1): 81–103.

Finch Janet, 2007. "Displaying Families," *Sociology*, 41(1): 65–81.

Fineman Albertson Martha, 2001. "Why Marriage?" *Virginia Journal of Social Policy & Law*, 9: 239–71.

Fishman Ted C., 2010. *Shock of Gray: The Aging of the World's Population and How It Pits Young Against Old, Child Against Parent, Worker Against Boss, Company against Rival, and Nation Against Nation* (New York: Scribner).

Fletcher Ruth, 2000. National Crisis, Supranational Opportunity: The Irish Constitution of Abortion as a European Service," *Reproductive Health Matters*, 8(6): 35–44.

Foblets Marie-Claire and Vanheule Dirk, 2006, "Marriage of Convenience in Belgium: the Punitive Approach Gains Ground in Migration Law," *European Journal of Migration and Law*, 8(3–4): 263–80.

Fogiel-Bijaoui Sylvie, 2002. "Familism, Postmodernity and the State: The Case of Israel," *Journal of Israeli History: Politics, Society, Culture*, 21(1–2): 38–62.

Fogiel-Bijaoui Sylvie, 1999. "Families in Israel: Between Familism and Post-Modernism" in Izraeli Dafna, Friedman Ariella, Dahan-Kalev Henriette, Fogiel-Bijaoui Sylvie, Hassan Manar, Herzog Hannah, and Naveh Hannah (Eds.), *Sex, Gender and Politics* (Tel Aviv: Hakibbutz Hameuchad), pp. 107–66. [Hebrew]

Folberg Jay and Milne Ann (Eds.), 1988. *Divorce Mediation: Theory and Practice* (New York: Guilford Press).

Fonseca Claudia, 2006. "Transnational Influences in the Social Production of Adoptable Children: The Case of Brazil," *The International Journal of Sociology and Social Policy*, 26(3/4): 154–71.

Fontana Lorenza B. and Grugel Jean, 2015. "To Eradicate or to Legalize? Child Labor Debates and ILO Convention 182 in Bolivia," *Global Governance*, 21(1): 61–78.

Fournier Pascale, 2010. *Muslim Marriages in Western Courts: Lost in Transplantation* (Surrey: Ashgate).

Freeman Michael, 2007. "Article 3: The Best Interests of the Child" in Alen André, Vande Lanotte Johan, Verhallen Eugeen, Ang Fiona, Berghmans Eva, and Verheyde Mieke (Eds.), *A Commentary on the United Nations Convention on the Rights of the Child* (Leiden: Brill), pp. 1–74.

Freeman Michael, 1995. "The Morality of Cultural Pluralism," *The International Journal of Children's Rights*, 3: 1–17.

Freeman Michael D. A., 1999. "A Child's Right to Circumcision," *BJU International*, 83(1): 74–8.

Friedman May and Schultermandl Silvia (Eds.), 2011. *Growing Up Transnational: Identity and Kinship in a Global Era* (University of Toronto Press).

Friedman Sara L., 2012. "Adjudicating the Intersection of Marital Immigration, Domestic Violence, and Spousal Murder: China Taiwan Marriages and Competing Legal Domains," *Indiana Journal of Global Legal Studies*, 19(1): 221–55.

Friedman Sara L., 2010. "Determining the 'Truth' at the Border: Immigration Interviews, Chinese Marital Migrants, and Taiwan's Sovereignty Dilemmas," *Citizenship Studies*, 14(2): 167–83.

Friedman Thomas L., 2007. *The World Is Flat: A Brief History of the Twenty-First Century* (New York.: Picador).

Fuchs Christian, 2008. *Internet and Society: Social Theory in the Information Age* (New York: Routledge).

Fun Cindy C. and San Mingjie, 2011. "Migration and Split Households: A Comparison of Sole, Couple, and Family Migrants in Beijing, China," *Environment and Planning*, 43: 2164–85.

Gangoli Geetanjali and Chantler Khatidja, 2009. "Protecting Victims of Forced Marriage: Is Age a Protective Factor?" *Feminist Legal Studies*, 17(3): 267–88.

Ganster Paul and Lorey David E. (Eds.), 2005. *Borders and Border Politics in a Globalizing World* (Lanham, MD: SR Books).

Gardner Andrew M., 2011. "Gulf Migration and the Family," *Journal of Arabian Studies*, 1(1): 3–25.

Garrison Marsha and Scott Elizabeth S., 2012. "Legal Regulation of Twenty-First Century Families" in Garrison Marsha and Scott Elizabeth S. (Eds.), *Marriage at the Crossroads* (New York: Cambridge University Press), pp. 303–25.

Gesneer Volkmar and Budak Ali Cem (Eds.), 1998. *Emerging Legal Certainty: Empirical Studies on the Globalization of Law* (Aldershot: Dartmouth).

Giddens Anthony, 2000. *Runaway World: How Globalization Is Reshaping our Lives* (New York: Routledge).

Glendon Mary Ann, 1989. *The Transformation of Family Law* (University of Chicago Press).

Glennon Theresa, 2009. "Divided Parents, Shared Children: Conflicting Approaches to Relocation Disputes in the USA" in Boele-Woelki Katharina (Ed.), *Debates in Family Law around the Globe at the Dawn of the 21st Century* (Antwerp: Intersentia), pp. 83–106.

Goldring Luin, 2003. "Re-Thinking Remittances: Social and Political Dimensions of Individual and Collective Remittances," *CERLAC Working Paper Series, York University*.

Gollaher David L., 2000. *Circumcision: A History of the World's Most Controversial Surgery* (New York: Basic Books).

Gornick Janet C. and Meyers Marcia K. (Eds.), 2009. *Gender Equality: Transforming Family Divisions of Labor* (New York: Verso Press).

Goulbourne Harry, Reynolds Tracy, Solomon John, and Zontint Elisabetta, 2010. *Transnational Families: Ethnicities, Identities and Social Capital* (London: Routledge).

Graham Elspeth and Jordan Lucy P., 2011. "Migrant Parents and the Psychological Well-Being of Left-Behind Children in Southeast Asia," *Journal of Marriage and Family*, 73(4): 763–87.

Graycar Reg, 2012. "Family Law Reform in Australia, or Frozen Chooks Revisited Again?" *Theoretical Inquiries in Law*, 13(1): 241–69.

Green Ohad and Ayalon Liat, 2015. "Whose Right is it Anyway? Familiarity with Workers' Rights among Older Adults, Family Caregivers, and Migrant Live-In Home Care Workers: Implications for Policy and Practice," *Educational Gerontology*, 41(7): 471–81.

Green Sarah, 2012. "A Sense of Border" in Wilson Thomas M. and Donnan Hastings (Eds.), *A Companion to Border Studies* (Malden, MA: Wiley Blackwell), pp. 573–92.

Greenberg-Kobrin Michelle, 2014. "Religious Tribunals and Secular Courts: Navigating Power and Powerlessness," *Pepperdine Law Review*, 41(5):997–1012.

Grey Colin, 2015. *Justice and Authority in Immigration Law* (Oxford: Hart Publishing).

Gross Aeyal M., 2007. "In Love with the Enemy: Justice, Truth, Integrity and Common Sense between Israel and Utopia in the Citizenship Law Case," *Hamishpat*, 23: 79–85. [Hebrew]

Grossberg Michael, 2000. "How to Give the Present a Past? Family Law in the United States 1950–2000" in Katz Stanford N., Eekelaar John, and Maclean Mavis (Eds.), *Cross Currents: Family Law and Policy in the US and England* (Oxford University Press), pp. 3–29.

Gruenbaum Ellen, 2001. *The Female Circumcision Controversy: An Anthropological Perspective* (Philadelphia: University of Pennsylvania Press).

Gunputh Rajendra Parsad and Choong Kartina Aisha, 2015. "Surrogacy Tourism: The Ethical and Legal Challenges," *International Journal of Tourism Sciences*, 15(1–2): 16–21.

Hacker Daphna, 2015. "Strategic Compliance in the Shadow of Transnational Anti-Trafficking Law," *Harvard Human Rights Journal*, 28(1): 11–64.

Hacker Daphna, 2015. "The Rights of the Dead through the Prism of Israeli Succession Disputes," *International Journal of Law in Context*, 11(1): 40–58.

Hacker Daphna, 2014. "Disappointed 'Heirs' as a Socio-Legal Phenomenon," *Oñati Socio-Legal Series*, 4(2): 243–63.

Hacker Daphna, 2012. "Religious Tribunals in Democratic States: Lesson from the Israeli Rabbinical Courts," *Journal of Law and Religion*, 27(1): 59–82.

Hacker Daphna, 2011. "Law and Society Jurisprudence," *Cornell Law Review*, 96: 727–48.

Hacker Daphna, 2009. "From the Moabite Ruth to Norly the Filipino: Intermarriage and Conversion in the Jewish Nation State" in Herzog Hanna and Braude Ann (Eds.), *Gendering Religion and Politics: Untangling Modernities* (New York: Palgrave Macmillan), pp. 101–24.

Hacker Daphna, 2008. "A Legal Field in Action: The Case of Divorce Arrangements in Israel," *International Journal of Law in Context*, 4(1): 1–33.

Hacker Daphna, 2001. "Single and Married Women in the Law of Israel – A Feminist Perspective," *Feminist Legal Studies*, 9(1): 29–56.

Hacker Daphna and Halperin Kaddari Ruth, 2013. "The Ruling Rules in Custody Disputers – On the Dangers of the Parental Sameness Illusion in a Gendered Reality," *Mishpat and Mimshal*, 15: 91–170. [Hebrew]

Hacker Daphna and Liberson Roni, 2010. "Cross Boarders Families in Israel: Between Individualism, Globalization and the Ethnos," *College of Management Law Review*, 15(2): 509–29. [Hebrew]

Hagestad Gunhild O., 1991. "The Aging Society as a Context for Family Life" in Nancy S. Jecker (Ed.), *Aging and Ethics: Philosophical Problems in Gerontology* (Totowa, NJ: Humana Press), pp. 123–46.

Hall Elizabeth C., 2011. "Where Are My Children ... and My Rights? Parental Rights Termination as a Consequence of Deportation," *Duke Law Journal*, 60(6): 1459–504.

Hallaq Wael B., 2014. *An Introduction to Islamic Law* (New York: Cambridge University Press).

Halley Janet, 2011. "What Is Family Law?: A Genealogy Part I," *Yale Journal of Law & the Humanities*, 23(1): 1–109.

Halley Janet, 2011. "What Is Family Law?: A Genealogy Part II," *Yale Journal of Law & the Humanities*, 23(2): 189–293.

Handell Günther, Zekoll Joachim, and Zumbansen Peer, 2012. *Beyond Territoriality: Transnational Legal Authority in an Age of Globalization* (Leiden: Martinus Nijhoff Publishers).

Hanson Karl, Volonakis Diana, and Al-Rozzi Mohammed, 2015. "Child Labour, Working Children and Children's Rights" in Vandenhole Wouter, Desmet Ellen, Reynaert Didier and Lembrechts Sara (Eds.), *Routledge International Handbook of Children's Rights Studies* (London: Routledge), pp. 316–30.

Hanson Karl and Vandaele Arne, 2003. "Working Children and International Labour Law: A Critical Analysis," *The International Journal of Children's Rights*, 11(1): 73–146.

Harari Yuval Noah, 2012. *Sapiens: A Brief History of Mankind* (London: Harvill Secker).

Hargittai Eszter and Hsieh Yuli Patick, 2013. "Digital Inequality" in Dutton William H. (Ed.), *The Oxford Handbook of Internet Studies* (Oxford University Press), pp. 129–150.

Hashiloni-Dolev Yael, 2015. "Posthumous Reproduction (PHR) in Israel: Policy Rationales versus Lay People's Concerns, a Preliminary Study," *Culture Medicine and Psychiatry*, 39 (4): 634–50.

Hashiloni-Dolev Yael, 2013. *The Fertility Revolution* (Moshav Ben-Shemen: Modan). [Hebrew]

Herring Jonathan, 2009. *Older People in Law and Society* (New York: Oxford University Press).

High Anna Jane, 2014. "Pondering the Politicization of Intercountry Adoption: Russia's Ban on American 'Forever Families'," *Cardozo Journal of International & Comparative Law*, 22(3): 497–560.

Hill Twyla J., 2007. "Legalized Grandparenthood: A Content Analysis of State Legislation," *Journal of Intergenerational Relationships*, 5(2): 61–80.

Hill Twyla J., 2002. "Grandparents in Law: Investigating the Institutionalization of Extended Family Roles," *The International Journal of Aging and Human Development*, 54(1): 43–56.

Hing Bill Ong, 2006. *Deporting Our Souls: Values, Morality, and Immigration Policy* (New York: Cambridge University Press).

Hochschild Arlie Russell, 2004. "Love and Gold" in Ehrenreich Barbara and Hochschild Arlie Russell (Eds.), *Global Woman: Nannies, Maids, and Sex Workers in the New Economy* (New York: Henry Holt and Company), pp. 15–30.

Hodson David, 2012. *The International Family Law Practice*, 2nd edn. (Bristol: Family Law).

Hoff Andreas, Feldman Susan, and Vidovicova Lucie, 2010. "Migrant Home Care Workers Caring for Older People: Fictive Kin, Substitute, and Complementary Family Caregivers in an Ethnically Diverse Environment," *International Journal of Ageing and Later Life*, 5(2): 7–16.

Holden Karen C. and Smoke Pamela J., 1991. "The Economic Costs of Marital Dissolution: Why Do Women Bear a Disproportionate Cost?" *Annual Review of Sociology*, 17: 51–78.

Holland Audrey, 2008. "The Modern Family Unit: Towards a More Inclusive Vision of the Family in Immigration Law," *California Law Review*, 96(4): 1049–91.

Hong Kari E., 2014. "Famigration (Fam Imm): The Next Frontier in Immigration Law," *Virginia Law Review Online*, 100: 63–81.

Honohan Iseult, 2009. "Reconsidering the Claim to Family Reunification in Migration," *Political Studies*, 57(4): 768–87.

Horn Vincent, Schweppe Cornelia, and Um Seong-gee, 2013. "Transnational Aging – A Young Field of Research," *Transnational Social Review*, 3(1): 7–10.

Htun Mala and Weldon Laurel S., 2011. "State Power, Religion, and Women's Rights: A Comparative Analysis of Family Law," *Indiana Journal of Global Legal Studies*, 18(1): 145–65.

Hunt Alan, 1993. *Explorations in Law and Society* (New York: Routledge).

Hunt Alan and Wickham Gary, 1994. *Foucault and Law: Towards a Sociology of Law as Governance* (London: Pluto Press).

Iecovich Esther, 2016. "Migrant Homecare Workers in Elder Care: The State of the Art" in Karl Ute and Torres Sandra (Eds.), *Ageing in Contexts of Migration* (Oxon: Routledge), pp. 147–58.

Iecovich Esther, 2010. "Primary Caregivers and Foreign Caregivers of the Elderly: Variables Explaining Burden and Care Satisfaction of the Primary Caregiver and the Foreign Caregiver," *Research Report*, Ben-Gurion University .[Hebrew]

Iecovich Esther, 2007. "Client Satisfaction with Live-in and Live-out Home Care Workers in Israel," *Journal of Aging & Social Policy*, 19(4): 105–22.

Iecovich Esther and Doron Israel, 2012. "Migrant Workers in Eldercare in Israel: Social and Legal Aspects," *European Journal of Social Work*, 15(1): 29–44.

Ikuomola Adediran Daniel, 2015. "Unintended Consequences of Remittance: Nigerian Migrants and Intra-Household Conflicts," *SAGE Open*, 5(3): 1–8, available at: http://sgo.sagepub.com/content/spsgo/5/3/2158244015605353.full.pdf.

Inhorn Marcia C., 2009. "Rethinking Reproductive 'Tourism' as Reproductive 'Exile,'" *Fertility & Sterility*, 94 (3): 904–6.

Inlender Talia, 2009. "Status Quo or Sixth Ground? Adjudicating Gender Asylum Claims" in Benhabib Seyla and Resnik Judith (Eds.), *Migrations and Mobilities: Citizenship, Borders and Gender* (New York University Press), pp. 356–79.

Ippolito Francesca, 2015. "(De)Constructing Children's Vulnerability under European Law" in Francesca Ippolito and Sara Iglesias Sánchez (Eds.), *Protecting Vulnerable Groups: The European Human Rights Framework* (Oxford, UK: Hart Publishing), pp. 23–47.

Isin Engin F. and Turner Bryan S., 2007. "Investigating Citizenship: An Agenda for Citizenship Studies," *Citizenship Studies*, 11(1): 5–17.

Islam Samir, 2014. "The Negative Effects of Ill-Advised Legislation: The Curious Case of the Evolution of Anti-Sharia Law Legislation into Anti-Foreign Law Legislation and the Impact on the CISG," *Howard Law Journal*, 57: 979–1031.

Jabareen Hassan, 2008. "The Rise of Transnational Lawyering for Human Rights," *Maʿasei Mishpat*, 1: 137–51. [Hebrew]

Jamieson Lynn, 2011. "Intimacy as a Concept: Explaining Social Change in the Context of Globalisation or Another Form of Ethnocentricism?" *Sociological Research Online*, 16(4), available at: https://core.ac.uk/display/6496696.

Jang Juyoung, Deenanath Veronica, and Solheim Catherine A., 2015. "Family Members' Transnational Migration, Community Contexts, and Psychological Distress in Mexican Families," *Family Science Review*, 20(2): 94–112.

Jeppesen de Boer Christina G., 2009. "Parental Relocation, Free Movement Rights and Joint Parenting" in Boele-Woelki Katharina (Ed.), *Debates in Family Law around the Globe at the Dawn of the 21st Century* (Antwerp: Intersentia), pp. 107–20.

Johnson Kay, 2002. "Politics of International and Domestic Adoption in China," *Law & Society Review,* 36(2): 379–96.

Joppke Christian, 2007. "Transformation of Citizenship: Status, Rights, Identity," *Citizenship Studies,* 11(1): 37–48.

Kaplan Yehiel, 2005. "Solving the Distress of Women who are Refused a *Get* through Punitive Alimony," *Hamishpat,* 10: 381–448. [Hebrew]

Karandikar Sharvari, Gezinski Lindsay B., Carter James R., and Kaloga Marissa, 2014. "Economic Necessity or Noble Cause? A Qualitative Study Exploring Motivations for Gestational Surrogacy in Gujarat, India," *Journal of Women and Social Work,* 29(2): 224–36.

Karl Ute and Torres Sandra (Eds.), 2016. *Ageing in Contexts of Migration* (Oxon: Routledge).

Karner Tracy X., 1998. "Professional Caring: Homecare Workers as Fictive Kin," *Journal of Aging Studies,* 12(1): 69–82.

Katz Ruth, Lowenstein Ariela, and Brick Yitzhak, 2010. "Intergenerational Relations and Old-Age in the Modern Era: Cross-Country Comparisons" in Brick Yitzhak and Lowenstein Ariela (Eds.), *The Elderly and the Family: Multi-Generational Aspects of Aging* (Jerusalem: Eshel). pp. 53–71. [Hebrew]

Katz Stanford N., Eekelaar John, and Maclean Mavis (Eds.), 2000. *Cross Currents: Family Law and Policy in the United States and England* (Oxford University Press).

Kearney M., 1995. "The Local and the Global: The Anthropology of Globalization and Transnationalism," *Annual Review of Anthropology,* 24: 547–65.

Kelly Joan B. and Emery Robert E., 2003. "Children's Adjustment Following Divorce: Risk and Resilience Perspectives," *Family Relations,* 52(4): 352–62.

Kemp Adriana, 2007. "Managing Migration, Reprioritizing National Citizenship: Undocumented Migrant Workers' Children and Policy Reforms in Israel," *Theoretical Inquiries in Law,* 8(2): 663–91.

Kenichi Ohmae, 1990. *The Borderless World* (New York: Harper Business).

Kesby Alison, 2012. *The Right to Have Rights: Citizenship, Humanity, and International Law* (Oxford University Press).

Khamasi Jennifer Wanjiku, 2015. "Transcending Female Circumcision: A Call for Collective Unmasking" in Longman Chia and Bradley Tamsin (Eds.), *Interrogating Harmful Cultural Practices: Gender, Culture and Coercion* (London: Routledge), pp. 99–110.

Khan Almas, 2006. "The Interaction between Shariah and International Law in Arbitration," *Chicago Journal of International Law,* 6(2): 791–802.

Kim Jaeeun, 2011. "Establishing Identity: Documents, Performance, and Biometric Information in Immigration Proceedings," *Law & Social Inquiry,* 36(3): 760–86.

Kojima Yu, 2001. "In the Business of Cultural Reproduction: Theoretical Implications of the Mail-Order Bride Phenomenon," *Women's Studies International Forum*, 24(2): 199–210.

Kourlis Rebecca Love, Taylor Melinda, Schepard Andrew, and Pruett Marsha Kline, 2013. "Iaals' Honoring Families Initiative: Courts and Communities Helping Families in Transition Arising from Separation or Divorce," *Family Court Review*, 51(3): 351–76.

Kricheli-Katz Tamar, 2012. "Choice, Discrimination and the Motherhood Penalty," *Law & Society Review*, 46(3): 557–87.

Kritzman-Amir Tali, 2015. "Iterations of the Family: Parents, Children and Mixed-Status Families," *Minnesota Journal of International Law*, 24(2): 245–311.

Kroløkke Charlotte, 2009. "Click a Donor," *Journal of Consumer Culture*, 9(1): 7–30.

Kron Stefanie, 2011. "The Border as Method: Towards an Analysis of Political Subjectivities in Transmigrant Spaces" in Wastl-Walter Dorit (Ed.), *The Ashgate Research Companion to Border Studies* (Surrey: Ashgate), pp. 103–20.

Kubitschek Carolyn A., 2014. "Failure of the Hague Abduction Convention to Address Domestic Violence and Its Consequences" in Robert E. Rains (Ed.), *The 1980 Hague Abduction Convention, Comparative Aspects* (London: Wildy, Simmonds & Hill Publishing), pp. 132–53.

Kunz Rahel, 2016. "'Moneymaker and Mother from Afar': The Power of Gender Myths" in van Naerssen Ton, Smith Lothar, Davids Tine and Marchand Marianne H. (Eds.), *Women, Gender, Remittances and Development in the Global South* (London: Routledge), pp. 207–28.

Kutty Faisal, 2010. "The Myth and Reality of Shari'a Courts in Canada: A Delayed Opportunity for the Indigenization of Islamic Legal Rulings," *University of St. Thomas Law Journal*, 7(3): 559–602.

Lam Theodora, Yeoh Brenda S. A., and Hoang Lan Anh, 2013. "Transnational Migration and Changing Care Arrangements for Left-Behind Children in Southeast Asia: A Selective Literature Review in Relation to the CHAMPSEA Study," *Working Paper Series No. 207*, Asia Research Institute, National University of Singapore.

Lamont Michèle and Virág Molnár, 2002. "The Study of Boundaries in the Social Sciences," *Annual Review of Sociology*, 28: 167–95.

Landes Elisabeth M. and Posner Richard A., 1978. "The Economics of the Baby Shortage," *Journal of Legal Studies*, 7(2): 323–48.

Lansdown Gerison, 2010. "The Realisation of Children's Participation Rights: Critical Reflections" in Percy-Smith Bary and Thomas Nigel (Eds.), *A Handbook of Children and Young People's Participation: Perspectives from Theory and Practice* (London: Routledge), pp. 11–23.

Lapidoth Ruth and Friesel Ofra, 2010. "Some Reflections on Israel's Temporary Legislation on Unification of Families," *Israel Law Review*, 43(2): 457–567.

Lechner Frank J. and Boli John (Eds.), 2012. *The Globalization Reader*, 4th edn. (Oxford, UK: Wiley-Blackwell).

Leckey Robert, 2008. *Contextual Subjects: Family, State, and Relational Theory* (University of Toronto Press).

Lee Catherine, 2015. "Family Reunification and the Limits of Immigration Reform: Impact and Legacy of the 1965 Immigration Act," *Sociological Forum*, 30(S1): 528–48.

Lee Donna R., 1998. "Mail Fantasy: Global Sexual Exploitation in the Mail-Order Bride Industry and Proposed Legal Solutions," *Asian American Law Journal*, 5: 139–79.

Lee Hye-Kyung, 2013. "Marriage Migration" in Immanuel Ness (Ed.), *The Encyclopedia of Global Human Migration* (Oxford: Wiley-Blackwell), available at: http://onlinelibrary.wiley.com/doi/10.1002/9781444351071.wbeghm353/abstract.

Leinonen Johanna and Pellander Saara, 2014. "Court Decisions over Marriage Migration in Finland: A Problem with Transnational Family Ties," *Journal of Ethics and Migration Studies*, 40(9): 1488–506.

Leiter Brian, 1999. "Positivism, Formalism, Realism," *Columbia Law Review*, 99: 1138–64.

Lévi-Strauss Claude, 1955. "The Structural Study of Myth," *The Journal of American Folklore*, 68(270): 428–44.

Levin Irene, 2004. "Living Apart Together: A New Family Form," *Current Sociology*, 52(2): 223–40.

Levine James A., 2011. "Poverty and Obesity in the U.S.," *Diabetes*, 60: 2667–8.

Liebel Manfred, 2015. "Protecting the Rights of Working Children Instead of Banning Child Labour: Bolivia Tries a New Legislative Approach," *The International Journal of Children's Rights*, 23(3): 529–47.

Lieberman Lindsay, 2010. "Protecting Pageant Princesses: A Call for Statutory Regulation of Child Beauty Pageants," *Journal of Law and Policy*, 18(2): 739–74.

Lifshitz Shahar, 2012. "The Liberal Transformation of Spousal Law: Past, Present, and Future," *Theoretical Inquiries in Law*, 13(1): 15–75.

Lifshitz Shahar, 2005. *Cohabitation Law in Israel: In Light of a Civil Law Theory of the Family* (Haifa University Press). [Hebrew]

Lillie Nathan, 2016. "The Right Not to Have Rights: Posted Worker Acquiescence and the European Union Labor Rights Framework," *Theoretical Inquiries in Law*, 17(1): 39–62.

Lindhorst Taryn and Edleson Jeffrey L., 2012. *Battered Women, Their Children, And International Law: The Unintended Consequences of the Hague Child Abduction Convention* (Lebanon, NH: Northeastern University Press).

Lister Ruth, 2007. "Inclusive Citizenship: Realizing the Potential," *Citizenship Studies*, 11(1): 49–61.

Lloyd Kathryn A., 2000. "Wives for Sale: The Modern International Mail Order Bride Industry," *Northwestern Journal of International Law & Business*, 20(2): 341–67.

Longman Chia and Bradley Tamsin (Eds.), 2015. *Interrogating Harmful Cultural Practices: Gender, Culture and Coercion* (London: Routledge).

López Jane Lilly, 2015. ""Impossible Families": Mixed-Citizenship Status Couples and the Law," *Law & Policy*, 37(1–2): 93–118.

Lowe Nigel V. and Stephens Victoria, 2012. "Global Trends in the Operation of the 1980 Hague Abduction Convention," *Family Law Quarterly*, 46(1): 41–85.

Lowell Lindsay B., Martin Susan, and Stone Robyn, 2010. "Ageing and Care Giving in the United States: Policy Contexts and the Immigrant Workforce," *Population Ageing*, 3(1): 59–82.

Lowenstein Ariela and Katz Ruth. 2010. "Taking Care of the Elderly – What is the Desirable Balance between the Family and the State?" in Brick Yitzhak and Lowenstein Ariela (Eds.), *The Elderly and the Family: Multi-Generational Aspects of Aging* (Jerusalem: Eshel), pp. 40–51. [Hebrew]

Maccoby Eleanor E. and Mnookin Robert H., 1992. *Dividing the Child: Social and Legal Dilemmas of Custody* (Cambridge, MA: Harvard University Press).

Macfarlane Julia, 2012. *Islamic Divorce in North America: A Sharia Path in a Secular Society* (New York: Oxford University Press).

MacIntosh Constance, 2010. "Domestic Violence and Gender Based Persecution: How Refugee Adjudicators Judge Women Seeking Refuge from Spousal Violence-and Why Reform is Needed," *Refuge*, 26(2): 147–64.

McIntosh Jennifer, Bruce Smyth, Margaret Kelaher, Yvonne Wells, and Caroline Long, 2010. "Post-Separation Parenting Arrangements: Patterns and Developmental Outcomes for Infants and Children," *collected reports prepared for the Australian Government Attorney General's Department* available at: www.ag.gov.au/FamiliesAndMarriage/Families/FamilyViolence/Documents/Post%20separation%20parenting%20arrangements%20and%20developmental%20outcomes%20for%20infants%20and%20children.pdf.

Macklin Audrey, 2007. "Who is the Citizen's Other? Considering the Heft of citizenship," *Theoretical Inquiries in Law*, 8(2): 333–66.

Maclean Mavis and Eekelaar John, 2014. "Institutional Mechanisms: Courts, Lawyers and Others" in Eekelaar John and George Rob (Eds.), *Routledge Handbook of Family Law and Policy* (Abingdon: Routledge Handbooks), pp. 372–80.

MacMaster Neil, 2007. "The Colonial "Emancipation" of Algerian Women: the Marriage Law of 1959 and the Failure of Legislation on Women's Rights in the Post-Independence Era," *Vienna Journal of African Studies*, 12: 91–116.

Mahar Heather, 2003. "Why Are There so Few Prenuptial Agreements?," *Harvard Law School John M. Olin Center for Law, Economics and Business Discussion Paper Series, Paper 436*, available at: www.law.harvard.edu/programs/olin_center/papers/pdf/436.pdf.

Mahler Sarah J., 2001. "Transnational Relationships: The Struggle to Communicate across Borders," *Identities*, 7(4) 583–619.

Mahr Jessie M., 2008. "Protecting Our Vulnerable Citizens: Birthright Citizenship and the Call for Recognition of Constructed Deportation," *Southern Illinois University Law Journal*, 32(3): 723–47.

Malhotra Anil and Malhotra Ranjit, 2012. "All Aboard for the Fertility Express," *Commonwealth Law Bulletin*, 38(1): 31–41.

Malinowski Bronislaw, 1939. "The Group and the Individual in Functional Analysis," *American Journal of Sociology*, 44(6): 938–64.

Merin Yuval, 2005. "The Right to Family Life and Civil Marriage under International Law and its Implementation in the State of Israel," *Boston College International and Comparative Law Review*, 28(1): 79–147.

Marsden Jessica, 2014. "Domestic Violence Asylum After Matter of L-R," *The Yale Law Journal*, 123(7): 2512–57.

Marson Alison A., 1997. "Planning for Love: The Politics of Prenuptial Agreements," *Stanford Law Review*, 49: 887–916.

Martin Susan Ehrlich and Jurik Nancy C., 2007. *Doing Justice, Doing Gender: Women in Legal and Criminal Justice Occupations*, 2nd edn. (Thousand Oaks, CA: Sage Publications).

Mascarenhas Maya N., Flaxman Seth R., Boerma Ties, Vanderpoel Sheryl, and Stevens Gretchen A., 2012. "National, Regional, and Global Trends in Infertility Prevalence Since 1990: A Systematic Analysis of 277 Health Surveys", *Plos Medicine*, 9(12): e1001356, available at: www.plosmedicine .org/article/info%3Adoi%2F10.1371%2Fjournal.pmed.1001356#s3.

Mauro Guillén F., 2001. "Is Globalization Civilizing, Destructive or Feeble? A Critique of Five Key Debates in the Social Science Literature," *Annual Review of Sociology*, 27: 235–60.

Mautner Menachem, 2011. "Three Approaches to Law and Culture," *Cornell Law Review*, 96(4): 839–68.

Mavunga R.A., 2013. "A Critical Assessment of the Minimum Age Convention 138 of 1973 and The Worst Forms of Child Labour Convention 182 of 1999," *Potchefstroom Electronic Law Journal*, 16(5): 121–68, available at: http:// papers.ssrn.com/sol3/papers.cfm?abstract_id=2427729.

Mayers William E., 2001. "The Right Rights? Child Labor in a Globalizing World," *Annals of the American Academy of Political and Social Science*, 575: 38–55.

Mazuz Keren, 2013. "The Familial Dyad between Aged Patients and Filipina Caregivers in Israel: Eldercare and Bodily-Based Practices in the Jewish Home," *Anthropology & Aging Quarterly*, 34(3): 126–34.

Mazuz Keren, 2013. "The State of the Jewish Family: Eldercare as a Practice of Corporeal Symbiosis by Filipina Migrant Workers" in Markowitz Fran (Ed.), *Ethnographic Encounters in Israel: Poetics and Ethics of Fieldwork* (Bloomington: University of Indiana Press), pp. 97–111.

Mazzucato Valentina, 2013. "Transnational Families, Research and Scholarship" in Immanuel Ness (Ed.), *The Encyclopedia of Global Human Migration*, availableat:http://onlinelibrary.wiley.com/doi/10.1002/9781444351071.wbeg hm541/pdf.

Mazzucato Valentina, Schans Djamila, Caarls Kim and Beauchemin Cris, 2015. "Transnational Families between Africa and Europe," *International Migration Review*, 49(1): 142–72.

Mazzucato Valentina and Djamila Schans, 2011. "Transnational Families and the Well-Being of Children: Conceptual and Methodological Challenges," *Journal of Marriage and Family*, 73(4): 704–12.

McClain Linda C., 2012. "Marriage Pluralism in the United States: On Civil and Religious Jurisdiction and the Demands of Equal Citizenship" in Nichols Joel A. (Ed.), *Marriage and Divorce in a Multicultural Context: Multi-Tiered Marriage and the Boundaries of Civil Law and Religion* (New York: Cambridge University Press), pp. 309–40.

McLaughlin Julia Halloran, 2007. "Premarital Agreements and Choice of Law: 'One, Two, Three, Baby, You and Me," *Missouri Law Review*, 72(3): 793–854.

McLaughlin Julia Halloran, 2003. "Should Marital Property Rights Be Inalienable? Preserving the Marriage Ante," *Nebraska Law Review*, 82(3): 460–98.

McWilliams Monica, Priyamvada Yarnell N. R., and Churchill Molly, 2015. "Forced Dependency and Legal Barriers: Implications of the UK's Immigration and Social Security Policies for Minoritized Women Living in Abusive Intimate Relationships in Northern Ireland," *Oñati Socio-Legal Series*, 5(6): 1536–56.

Meier Patricia J. and Zhang Xiaole, 2008. "Sold into Adoption: The Hunan Baby Trafficking Scandal Exposes Vulnerabilities in Chinese Adoptions to the United States," *Cumberland Law Review*, 39(1), 87–130.

Meisels Judith, 2014. "Reflections on the Centrality of Genetics in Parenting Following HCJ 566/11 Mamet v. Ministry of Interior Affairs," *Mivzakey Hearot Psika*, 28: 46–56, available at: https://www.colman.ac.il/sites/default/files/28_june_2014_5_meisels.pdf. [Hebrew]

Menjívar Cecilia and Salcido Olivia, 2002. "Immigrant Women and Domestic Violence, Common Experiences in Different Countries," *Gender & Society*, 16(6): 898–920.

Menzel Peter and D'Aluisi Faith, 2005. *Hungry World: What the World Eats* (Napa, CA: Material World Books).

Mercurio Bryan, 2003. "Abortion in Ireland: An Analysis of the Legal Transformation Resulting from Membership in the European Union," *Tulane Journal of International and Comparative Law*, 11:141–80.

Meria Laura (Ed.), 2014. *Transnational Families, Migration and the Circulation of Care: Understanding Mobility and Absence in Family Life* (New York: Routledge).

Merkel Reinhard and Putzke Holm, 2013. "After Cologne: Male Circumcision and The Law. Parental Right, Religious Liberty or Criminal Assault?" *Journal of Medical Ethics*, 39: 444–9.

Merry Sally Engle, 2003. "Constructing a Global Law- Violence against Women and the Human Rights System," *Law & Social Inquiry,* 28(4): 941–77.

Mezmur Benyan Dawit, 2012. "Acting Like a Rich Bully: Madonna, Mercy, Malawi, and International Children's Rights Law in Adoption," *International Journal of Children's Rights,* 20(1): 24–56.

Michie Jonathan (Ed.), 2011. *The Handbook of Globalization,* 2nd edn. (Cheltenham, UK: Edward Elgar).

Milanovic Branko, 2013. "Global Income Inequality in Numbers: In History and Now," *Global Policy,* 4(2): 198–208.

Milanovic Branko, 2012. "Evolution of Global Inequality: From Class to Location, from Proletarians to Migrants," *Global Policy,* 3(2): 125–34.

Milanovic Branko, 2007. "Globalization and Inequity" in Held David and Kaya Ayse (Eds.), *Global Inequality* (Cambridge: Polity Press), pp. 26–49.

Minow Martha and Shanley Mary Lyndon, 1996. "Relational Rights and Responsibilities: Revisioning the Family in Liberal Political Theory and Law," *Hypatia,* 11(1): 4–29.

Mnookin Robert H. and Kornhauser Lewis, 1979. "Bargaining in the Shadow of the Law: The Case of Divorce," *Yale Law Journal,* 88: 950–96.

Modelski George, Devezas Tessaleno and William Thompson R. (Eds.), 2008. *Globalization as Evolutionary Process* (London: Routledge).

Morag Tamar, Rivkin Dori, and Sorek Yoa, 2012. "Child Participation in the Family Courts – Lessons from the Israeli Pilot Project," *International Journal of Law, Policy and the Family,* 26(1):1–30.

Morgan David H. J., 2011. *Rethinking Family Practices* (Basingstoke: Palgrave).

Morgan David H. J., 1996. *Family Connections: An Introduction to Family Studies* (Cambridge, UK: Polity Press).

Morris Brian J. and Krieger John N., 2013. "Does Male Circumcision Affect Sexual Function, Sensitivity, or Satisfaction?- A Systematic Review," *Journal of Sexual Medicine,* 10(11): 2644–57.

Moskowitz Seymour, 2002. "Adult Children and Indigent Parents: Intergenerational Responsibilities in International Perspective," *Marquette Law Review,* 86(3): 401–55.

Mullally Siobhan, 2011. "Domestic Violence Asylum Claims and Recent Developments in International Human Rights Law: A Progress Narrative?" *International and Comparative Law Quarterly,* 60(2): 459–84.

Mulongo Peggy, McAndrew Sue, and Martin Caroline H., 2014. "Crossing Borders: Discussing the Evidence Relating to the Mental Health Needs of Women Exposed to Female Genital Mutilation," *International Journal of Mental Health Nursing,* 23(4): 296–305.

Mundlak Guy, 2007. "Industrial Citizenship, Social Citizenship, Corporate Citizenship: I Just Want My Wages," *Theoretical Inquiries in Law,* 8(2): 719–48.

Mundlak Guy and Shamir Hila, 2011. "Bringing Together or Drifting Apart? Targeting Care Work as "Work Like no Other," *Canadian Journal of Women and the Law*, 23(1): 289–308.

Mundlak Guy and Shamir Hila, 2008. "Between Intimacy and Alienage: The Legal Construction of Domestic and Care Work in the Welfare State" in Lutz Helma (Ed.), *Migration and Domestic Work: A European Perspective on a Global Theme* (New York: Routledge), pp. 161–76.

Munjal Diksha and Munjal Yahita, 2014. "The "Wanted" Child: Identifying the Gaps and Challenges in Commercial Surrogacy in India," *Asian Bioethics Review*, 6(1): 66–82.

Musalo Karen, 2007. "Protecting Victims of Gendered Persecution: Fear of Floodgates or Call to (Principled) Action?" *Virginia Journal of Social Policy & the Law*, 14(2): 119–43.

Mutcherson Kimberly M., 2013. "Open Fertility Borders: Defending Access to Cross-Border Fertility Care in the United States" in Glenn Cohen (Ed.), *The Globalization of Health Care: Legal and Ethical Issues* (New York: Oxford University Press), pp. 148–63.

Muthumbi Jane, Svanemyr Joar, Scolaro Elisa, Temmerman Marleen, and Say Lale, 2015. "Female Genital Mutilation: A Literature Review of the Current Status of Legislation and Policies in 27 African Countries and Yemen," *African Journal of Reproductive Health*, 19(3): 32–40.

Myrdahl Eileen Muller, 2010. "Legislating Love: Norwegian Family Reunification Law as a Racial Project," *Social & Cultural Geography*, 11(2): 103–16.

Narayanan Usha, 1996. "The Government's Role in Fostering the Relationship between Adult Children and their Elder Parents: From Filial Responsibility Laws to ... What? A Cross-Cultural Perspective," *Elder Law Journal*, 4: 369–406.

Neagu Mariela, 2015. "Children by Request: Romania's Children between Rights and International Politics," *International Journal of Law, Policy and the Family*, 29(2): 215–36.

Nelson Julie A., 2012. "Are Women Really More Risk-Averse than Men?" *Global Development and Environment Institute, Working Paper No. 12-05, Tufts University.*

Newman David, 2011. "Contemporary Research Agendas in Border Studies: An Overview" in Wastl-Walter Dorit (Ed.), *The Ashgate Research Companion to Border Studies* (Surrey: Ashgate), pp. 33–47.

Newman David, 2006. "The Lines that Continue to Separate Us: Borders in our 'Borderless' World," *Progress in Human Geography*, 30(2): 143–61.

Newman Jonah, 2012. "Whose Home? The Role of Jewish Identity in Israel's Policy towards the Children of Foreign Workers," *Washington University International Review*, 1: 42–54.

Nhenga-Chakarisa Tendai Charity, 2010. "Who Does the Law Seek to Protect and from What? The Application of International Law on Child Labour in an African Context," *African Human Rights Law Journal*, 10(1): 161–96.

Nichols Joel A., 2012. "Multi-Tiered Marriage" in Nichols Joel A. (Ed.), *Marriage and Divorce in a Multicultural Context: Multi-Tiered Marriage and the Boundaries of Civil Law and Religion* (New York: Cambridge University Press), pp. 11–50.

Nieuwenhuys Olga, 1996. "The Paradox of Child Labor and Anthropology," *Annual Review of Anthropology*, 25 (1): 237–51.

Noguchi Yoshie, 2010. "20 Years of the Convention on the Rights of the Child and International Action against Child Labour," *The International Journal of Children's Rights*, 18(4): 515–34.

Nyers Peter, 2007. "Introduction: Why Citizenship Studies," *Citizenship Studies*, 11(1): 1–4.

Nygren Karl, Adamson David, Zegers-Hochschild Fernando, and de Mouzon Jacques, 2010. "Cross-Border Fertility Care – International Committee Monitoring Assisted Reproductive Technologies Global Survey: 2006 Data and Estimates," *Fertility and Sterility*, 94(1): e4–e10, available at: www.fertstert.org/article/S0015-0282(09)04298-8/pdf.

Nwaogu Uwaoma G. and Ryan Michael J., 2015. "FDI, Foreign Aid, Remittance and Economic Growth in Developing Countries," *Review of Development Economics*, 19(1): 100–15.

Obrien John, 1999. *Conflict of Laws*, 2nd edn. (London: Cavendish).

O'Halloran Kerry, 2015. *The Politics of Adoption: International Perspectives on Law, Policy and Practice*, 3rd edn. (Dordrecht: Springer).

Okin Moller Susan, 1999. "Is Multiculturalism Bad for Women?" in Joshua Howard Matthew and Nussbaum Martha C. (Eds.), *Is Multiculturalism Bad for Women?* (Princeton, NJ: Princeton University Press, 1999), pp.7–26.

Okin Moller Suzan, 1989. *Justice, Gender, and the Family* (New York: Basic Books).

Okyere Samuel, 2013. "Are Working Children's Rights and Child Labour Abolition Complementary or Opposing Realms?" *International Social Work*, 56(1): 80–91.

Olsen Frances E., 1985. "The Myth of State Intervention in the Family," *University of Michigan Journal of Law Reform*, 18: 835–64.

O'Neill Mary, Bagheri Parisa, and Sarnicola Alexis, 2015. "Forgotten Children of Immigration and Family Law: How The Absence of Legal Aid Affects Children in the United States," *Family Court Review*, 53(4): 676–97.

Ong Debbie, 2012. "Prenuptial Agreements Affirming TQ v. TR in Singapore," *Singapore Academy of Law Journal*, 24: 402–32.

Orgad Liav, 2008. "Love and War: Family Migration in Time of National Emergency," *Georgetown Immigration Law Journal*, 23(1): 85–127.

Paasi Anssi, 2011. "A Border Theory: An Unattainable Dream or a Realistic Aim for Border Scholars?" in Wastl-Walter Dorit (Ed.), *The Ashgate Research Companion to Border Studies* (Surrey: Ashgate), pp. 11–31.

Palacios Jesús, 2015. "Crisis in Intercountry Adoption, Crisis in Adoptive Families," *Family Science*, 6(1): 43–9.

Pande Amrita, 2010. ""At Least I Am Not Sleeping with Anyone": Resisting the Stigma of Commercial Surrogacy in India," *Feminist Studies*, 36(2): 292–312.

Pande Amrita, 2010. "Commercial Surrogacy in India: Manufacturing a Perfect 'Mother-Worker'," *Signs: Journal of Women in Culture and Society*, 35(4): 969–92.

Pande Amrita, 2009. "'It May Be Her Eggs but It's My Blood': Surrogates and Everyday Forms of Kinship in India," *Qualitative Sociology*, 32(4), 379–405.

Pande Amrita, 2009. "Not an 'Angel'," Not a 'Whore': Surrogates as 'Dirty' Workers in India," *Indian Journal of Gender Studies*, 16(2): 141–73.

Panitch Vida, 2013. "Global Surrogacy: Exploitation to Empowerment," *Journal of Global Ethics*, 9(3): 329–43.

Panitch Vida, 2013. "Surrogate Tourism and Reproductive Rights," *Hypatia*, 28(2): 274–89.

Parness Jeffrey A., 2014. "Parentage Prenups and Midnups," *Georgia State University Law Review*, 31(2): 343–76.

Parreñas Salazar Rhacel, 2005. *Children of Global Migration: Transnational Families and Gendered Woes* (CA: Stanford University Press).

Parreñas Salazar Rhacel, 2004. "The Care Crisis in the Philippines: Children and Transnational Families in the New Global Economy" in Ehrenreich Barbara and Hochschild Arlie Russell (Eds.), *Global Woman: Nannies, Maids, and Sex Workers in the New Economy* (New York: Henry Holt and Company), pp. 39–54.

Parsons Talcott, 1964. *Social Structure and Personality* (New York: Free Press).

Pearson Jessica, 2000. "A Forum for Every Fuss: The Growth of Court Services and ADR Treatment for Family Law Cases in the United States" in Katz Stanford N., Eekelaar John and Maclean Mavis (Eds.), *Cross Currents: Family Law and Policy in the US and England* (Oxford University Press), pp. 513–31.

Pearson Katherine C., 2013. "Filial Support Laws in the Modern Era: Domestic and International Comparison of Enforcement Practices for Laws Requiring Adult Children to Support Indigent Parents," *Elder Law Journal*, 20: 269–314.

Peled Yoav, 2007. "Citizenship Betrayed: Israel's Emerging Immigration and Citizenship Regime," *Theoretical Inquiries in Law*, 8(2): 603–28.

Peterson Richard R., 1996. "A Re-Evaluation of the Economic Consequences of Divorce," *American Sociological Review*, 61(3): 528–36.

Phillips Anne and Dustin Moira, 2004. "UK Initiatives on Forced Marriage: Regulation, Dialogue and Exit," *Political Studies*, 52: 531–51.

Plummer Ken, 2003. *Intimate Citizenship, Private Decision and Public Dialogue* (Seattle: University of Washington Press).

Polikoff Nancy, 2008. *Beyond (Straight and Gay) Marriage, Valuing All Families under the Law* (Boston: Beacon Press).

Quillen Brian, 2014. "The New Face of International Child Abduction: Domestic-Violence Victims and Their Treatment Under the Hague Convention on Civil

Aspects of International Child Abduction," *Texas International Law Journal,* 49(3): 621–43.

Rabin Nina, 2013. "At the Border between Public and Private: U.S. Immigration Policy for Victims of Domestic Violence," *Law & Ethics of Human Rights,* 7(1): 109–53.

Rafiq Aayesha, 2014. "Child Custody in Classical Islamic Law and Laws of Contemporary Muslim World (An Analysis)," *International Journal of Humanities and Social Science,* 4(5): 267–77.

Rains Robert E., 2011. "A Prenup for Prince William and Kate? England Inches Toward Twentieth Century Law of Antenuptial Agreements: How Shall It Enter the Twenty-First?" *Florida Journal of International Law,* 23: 447–80.

Raiti Gerard C., 2007. "Mobile Intimacy: Theories on the Economics of Emotion with Examples from Asia," *Journal of Media and Culture,* 10(1), available at: http://journal.media-culture.org.au/0703/02-raiti.php.

Ram Uri, 2012. "McDonaldization" in Ritzer George (Ed.), *The Wiley-Blackwell Encyclopedia of Globalization* (Malden, MA: Blackwell Publishing), pp. 342–7.

Randall Melanie, 2015. "Particularized Social Groups and Categorical Imperatives in Refugee Law: State Failures to Recognize Gender and the Legal Reception of Gender Persecution Claims in Canada, the United Kingdom, and the United States," *Journal of Gender, Social Policy & the Law,* 23(4): 529–71.

Ray Larry, 2007. *Globalization and Everyday Life* (London: Routledge).

Roach Anleu Sharyn, 1992. "Women in The Legal Profession: Theory and Research," *Law Institutional Journal,* 66: 193–208.

Roberts Albert R. (Ed.), 2007. *Battered Women and Their Families: Intervention Strategies and Treatment Programs,* 3rd edn. (New York: Springer).

Robertson Roland, 2012. "Globalisation or Glocalisation?" *Journal of International Communication,* 18(2): 191–208.

Rogerson Sarah, 2013. "Lack of Detained Parents' Access to the Family Justice System and the Unjust Severance of the Parent-Child Relationship," *Family Law Quarterly,* 47(2): 141–72.

Rome Sunny Harris, 2010. "Promoting Family Integrity: The Child Citizen Protection Act and Its Implications for Public Child Welfare," *Journal of Public Child Welfare,* 4(3): 245–62.

Root Veronica S., 2007. "Angelina and Madonna: Why all the Fuss? An Exploration of the Rights of the Child and Intercountry Adoption within African Nations," *Chicago Journal of International Law,* 8(1): 323–54.

Ross Allison E., 2008. "Taking Care of Our Caretakers: Using Filial Responsibility Laws to Support the Elderly beyond the Government's Assistance," *Elder Law Journal,* 16: 167–209.

Rossiter Ann, 2009. *Ireland Hidden Diaspora: The 'Abortion Trial' and the Making of a London-Irish Underground, 1980-2000* (London: IASC Publishing).

Rudrappa Sharmila, 2012. "Working India's Reproduction Assembly Line: Surrogacy and Reproduction Rights?" *Western Humanities Review,* 66(3): 77–101.

Ruggie John Gerard, 2014. "Global Governance and ""New Governance Theory"": Lessons from Business and Human Rights," *Global Governance,* 20: 5–17.

Sabar Galia, 2012. "African Migrant Workers in Israel: Between Extended Family, Money and a Sense of Evil" in Ehud R. Toledano (Ed.), *African Communities in Asia and the Mediterranean: Between Integration and Conflict* (London: Africa World Press), pp. 255–84.

Salami Bukola, Duggleby Wendy, and Rajani Fahreen, 2016. "The Perspectives of Employers/ Families and Care Recipients of Migrant Live – In Caregivers: A Scoping Review," *Health and Social Care in the Community,* 1–12, available at: http://onlinelibrary.wiley.com/doi/10.1111/hsc.12330/epdf.

Samonova Elena, 2014. "Socioeconomic Impacts of Child Labour," *Journal of Education, Psychology and Social Sciences,* 2(1): 50–4.

Sănduleasa Bertha and Matei Aniela, 2015. "Effects of Parental Migration on Families and Children in Post-Communist Romania," *Revista de Stiinte Politice,* 46: 196–207.

Sanger Carol, 2006. "A Case for Civil Marriage," *Cardozo Law Review,* 27: 1311–23.

Sarat Austin and Silbey Susan S., 1998. "The Pull of the Audience," *Law & Policy,* 10(2–3): 97–166.

Saravanan Sheela, 2013. "An Ethnomethodological Approach to Examine Exploitation in the Context of Capacity, Trust and Experience of Commercial Surrogacy in India," *Philosophy, Ethics, and Humanities in Medicine,* 8(10), available at: http://peh-med.biomedcentral.com/articles/10.1186/1747-5341-8-10.

Sassen Saskia, 2007. *A Sociology of Globalization* (New York: W. W. Norton).

Sassen Saskia, 2003. "Globalization or Denationalization?" *Review of International Political Economy,* 10(1): 1–22.

Sassen Saskia, 1991. *The Global City: New York, London, Tokyo* (Princeton, NJ: Princeton University Press).

Schiff Berman Paul, 2012. *Global Legal Pluralism: A Jurisprudence of Law Beyond Borders* (New York: Cambridge University Press).

Schiratzki Johanna, 2011. "Banning God's Law in the Name of the Holy Body – The Nordic Position on Ritual Male Circumcision," *The Family in Law,* 5: 35–53.

Schmidt Garbi, 2014. "Troubled by Law: The Subjectivizing Effects of Danish Marriage Reunification Laws," *International Migration,* 52(3): 129–43.

Scholte Jan Aart, 2005. *Globalization: A Critical Introduction,* 2nd edn. (New York: Palgrave Macmillan).

Schuerkens Ulrike, 2010. "Theoretical and Empirical Introduction: Globalization and Transformation of Social Inequality" in Schuerkens Ulrike (Ed.), *Globalization and Transformation of Social Inequality* (New York: Routledge), pp. 3–28.

Schueths April M., 2012. "'Where are My Rights?' Compromised Citizenship in Mixed-Status Marriage: A Research Note," *Journal of Sociology & Social Welfare*, 39(4): 97–109.

Schueths April and Lawston Jodie (Eds.), 2015. *Living Together Living Apart: Mixed Status Families and US Immigration Policy* (Seattle: University of Washington Press).

Schuz Rhona, 2015. "The Dangers of Children's Rights' Discourse in the Political Arena: The Issue of Religious Male Circumcision as a Test Case," *Cardozo Journal of Law & Gender*, 21: 347–91.

Schuz Rhona, 2013. *The Hague Child Abduction Convention: A Critical Analysis, Studies in Private International Law* (Portland, OR: Hart Publishing).

Schuz Rhona, 1997. *A Modern Approach to the Incidental Question* (Netherlands: Springer).

Schuz Rhona, 1996. "Divorce and Ethnic Minorities" in Michael Freeman (Ed.), *Divorce: Where Next?* (Aldershot: Dartmouth), pp. 131–57.

Schwiter Karin, Berndt Christian, and Truong Jasmine, 2015. "Neoliberal Austerity and the Marketization of Elderly Care," *Social & Cultural Geography*, 1–21, available at: www.tandfonline.com/doi/full/10.1080/14649365.2015.1059473.

Sear Rebecca, Lawson David W., Kaplan Hillard, and Shenk Mary K., 2016. "Understanding Variation in Human Fertility: What Can We Learn from Evolutionary Demography?" *Philosophical Transactions of the Royal Society B*, 371: 20150144, available at: http://rstb.royalsocietypublishing.org/content/royptb/371/1692/20150144.full.pdf.

Selby Jessica, 2008. "Ending Abusive and Exploitative Child Labour Through International Law and Practical Action," *Australian International Law Journal*, 15: 165–80.

Selman Peter, 2015. "Intercountry Adoption of Children from Asia in the Twenty-First Century," *Children's Geographies*, 13(3): 312–27.

Selman Peter, 2012. "The Global Decline of Intercountry Adoption: What Lies Ahead?" *Social Policy & Society*, 11(3): 381–97.

Seron Carroll and Silbey Susan S., 2004. "Profession, Science, and Culture: An Emergent Canon of Law and Society Research" in Sarat Austin (Ed.), *The Blackwell Companion to Law and Society* (Victoria, Australia: Blackwell Publishing), pp. 30–59.

Serour G. I., 2013. "Medicalization of Female Genital Mutilation/Cutting," *African Journal of Urology*, 19: 145–49.

Sethna Christabelle and Doull Marion, 2012. "Accidental Tourism: Canadian Women, Abortion Tourism, and Travel," *Women's Studies*, 41: 457–75.

Shachar Ayelet, 2013. "Privatizing Diversity: A Cautionary Tale from Religious Arbitration in Family Law" in Fishbayn Joffe Lisa and Neil Sylvia (Eds.), *Gender, Religion & Family Law: Theorizing Conflicts between Women's Rights and Cultural Traditions* (Waltham, MA: Brandeis University Press), pp. 38–75.

Shachar Ayelet, 2009. *The Birthright Lottery: Citizenship and Global Inequality* (Cambridge, MA: Harvard University Press).

Shachar Ayelet, 2007. "The Worth of Citizenship in an Unequal World," *Theoretical Inquiries in Law*, 8(2): 367–88.

Shachar Ayelet, 2001. *Multicultural Jurisdictions: Cultural Differences and Women's Rights* (UK: Cambridge University Press).

Shahar Ido, 2015. *Legal Pluralism in the Holy City: Competing Courts, Forum Shopping, and Institutional Dynamics in Jerusalem* (Surrey: Ashgate).

Shakargy Sharon, 2013. "Israel" in Trimmings Katarina and Beaumont Paul (Eds.), *International Surrogacy Arrangements* (Oxford, UK: Hart Publishing), pp. 231–46.

Shakargy Sharon, 2013. "Marriage by the State or Married to the State: Choice of Law in Marriage and Divorce," *Journal of Private International Law*, 9(3): 499–533.

Shamir Hila, 2013. "Migrant Care Workers in Israel: Between Family, Market, and State," *Israel Studies Review*, 28(2): 192–209.

Shamir Hila and Mundlak Guy, 2013. "Spheres of Migration: Political, Economic and Universal Imperatives in Israel's Migration Regime," *Middle East Law and Governance*, 5(1–2): 112–72.

Shanley Mary Lyndon, 2004. *Just Marriage* (New York: Oxford University Press).

Shaw Katerina, 2009. "Barriers to Freedom: Continued Failure of U.S. Immigration Laws to Offer Equal Protection to Immigrant Battered Women," *Cardozo Journal of Law & Gender*, 15: 663–89.

Sheleff Leon, 1981. *Generations Apart: Adult Hostility to Youth* (New York: McGraw-Hill).

Shenfield Françoise, De Mouzon Jacques, Pennings Guido, Ferraretti Anna Pia, Anders Nyboe Andersen, De Wert Guido, Veerle Goossens, and the ESHRE Taskforce on Cross Border Reproductive Care, 2010 "Cross-Border Reproductive Care in Six European Countries," *Human Reproduction*, 25(6): 1361–68.

Shetty Sudha and Edleson Jeffery L., 2005. "Adult Domestic Violence in Cases of International Parental Child Abduction," *Violence Against Women*, 11(1): 115–38.

Shifman Pinhas, 2005. "On the New Family: Introductory Notes," *Tel Aviv Law Review*, 28(3): 643–70. [Hebrew]

Shirpak Khosro Refaie, Maticka-Tyndale Eleanor, and Chinichian Maryam, 2007. "Iranian Immigrants' Perceptions of Sexuality in Canada: A Symbolic Interactionist Approach," *The Canadian Journal of Human Sexuality*, 16(3–4): 113–28.

Shmueli Benjamin and Schuz Rhona, 2012. "Between Tort Law, Contract Law, and Child Law: How to Compensate the Left-Behind Parent in International Child Abduction Cases," *Columbia Journal of Gender and Law*, 23(1): 65–131.

Shultz Marjorie Maguire, 1982. "Contractual Ordering of Marriage: A New Model for State Policy," *California Law Review*, 70(2): 204–334.

Siddiqi Faraaz and Harry Anthony Patrinos, 1995. "Child Labor: Issues, Causes and Interventions," *Human Capital Development and Operations Policy, Working Paper No. 56.*Sifris Ronli, 2014. *Reproductive Freedom, Torture and International Human Rights* (London: Routledge).

Silverstein Merril, Gans Daphna and Yang Frances M., 2009. "Intergenerational Support to Aging Parents: The Role of Norms and Needs," *Journal of Family Issues,* 27(8): 1068–84.

Simonazzi Annamaria, 2009. "Care Regimes and National Employment Models," *Cambridge Journal of Economics,* 33(2): 211–3.

Sims Roxanne, 2009. "A Comparison of Law in the Philippines, the U.S.A., Taiwan, and Belarus to Regulate the Mail Bride Industry," *Akron Law Review,* 42(2): 607–37.

Simms Shelley, 1993. "What's Culture Got to do with It? Excising the Harmful Tradition of Female Circumcision," *Harvard Law Review,* 106(8): 1944–61.

Singer Anna, 2009. "'Active Parenting or Solomon's Justice?' Alternative Residence in Sweden for Children with Separated Parents" in Katharina Boele-Woelki (Ed.), *Debates in Family Law around the Globe at the Dawn of the 21st Century* (Antwerp: Intersentia), pp. 55–81.

Sirman Nükhet, 2005. "The Making of Familial Citizenship in Turkey" in Keyman Emin Fuat and İçduygu Ahmet (Eds.), *Citizenship in a Global World: European Questions and Turkish Experiences* (London: Routledge), pp. 147–72.

Smart Carol and Sevenhuijsen Selma (Eds.), 1989. *Child Custody and the Politics of Gender* (London: Routledge).

Smearman Claire A., 2009. "Second Wives' Club: Mapping the Impact of Polygamy in U.S. Immigration Law," *Berkeley Journal of International Law,* 27(2): 382–447.

Smerdon Usha Rengachary, 2013. "India" in Trimmings Katarina and Beaumont Paul (Eds.), *International Surrogacy Arrangements* (Oxford, UK: Hart Publishing), pp. 187–217.

Smolin David M., 2010. "Child Laundering and the Hague Convention on Intercountry Adoption: The Future and Past of Intercountry Adoption," *University of Louisville Law Review,* 48(3): 441–98.

Smolin David M., 2007. "Child Laundering as Exploitation: Applying Anti-Trafficking Norms to Intercountry Adoption under the Coming Hague Regime," *Vermont Law Review,* 32: 1–55.

Smolin David M., 2006. "Child Laundering: How the Intercountry Adoption System Legitimizes and Incentivizes the Practices of Buying, Trafficking, Kidnapping, and Stealing Children," *Wayne Law Review,* 52(1): 113–200.

Smolin David M., 2005. "The Two Faces of Intercountry Adoption: The Significance of the Indian Adoption Scandals," *Seton Hall Law Review,* 35(2): 403–93.

Smolin David M., 2000. "Strategic Choices in the International Campaign against Child Labor," *Human Rights Quarterly,* 22(4): 942–88.

Snow Robert L., 2008. *Child Abduction: Prevention, Investigating and Recovery* (Westport, CT: Praeger).

Sooryamoorthy Radhamany, 2015. "Introduction to the Special Issue," *Journal of Comparative Family Studies,* 46(1): 1–8.

Sorokan Todd S., Finlay Jane C. and Jefferies Ann L., 2015. "Newborn Male Circumcision," *Paediatrics & Child Health,* 20(6): 311–5.

Spatz Melissa, 1991. "A "Lesser" Crime: A Comparative Study of Legal Defenses for Men Who Kill Their Wives," *Columbia Journal of Law and Social Problems,* 24(4): 597–639.

Sperling Daniel, forthcoming. *Suicide Tourism: Understanding the Legal, Philosophical and Socio-Political Dimensions* (Oxford University Press).

Stark Barbara, 2006. "When Globalization Hits Home: International Family Law Comes of Age," *Vanderbilt Journal of Transnational Law,* 39(5): 1551–604.

Stark Barbara, 2005. *International Family Law: An Introduction* (Aldershot, UK: Ashgate).

Staver Anne, 2013. "Free Movement and the Fragmentation of Family Reunification Rights," *European Journal of Migration and the Law,* 15(1): 69–89.

Storrow Richard F., 2013. "The Proportionality Problem in Cross-Border Reproduction Care" in Glenn Cohen (Ed.), *The Globalization of Health Care: Legal and Ethical Issues* (New York: Oxford University Press), pp. 125–47.

Storrow Richard F., 2011. "Assisted Reproduction on Treacherous Terrain: The Legal Hazard of Cross-Border Reproductive Travel," *Reproductive BioMedicine Online,* 23(5): 538–45, available at: http://www.rbmojournal.com/article/ S1472-6483(11)00412-3/fulltext.

Storrow Richard F., 2010. "The Pluralism Problem in Cross-Border Reproductive Care," *Human Reproduction,* 25(12): 2939–43.

Storrow Richard F., 2005-2006. "Quest for Conception: Fertility Tourism, Globalization and Feminist Legal Theory," *Hastings Law Journal,* 57: 295–330.

Strasser Mark, 2014. "Family, Same-Sex Unions and the Law" in Eekelaar John and George Rob (Eds.), *Routledge Handbook of Family Law and Policy* (Abingdon: Routledge Handbooks), pp. 45–60.

Strathern Marilyn, 2005. *Kinship, Law and the Unexpected: Relatives are Always a Surprise* (New York: Cambridge University Press).

Stuifbergen Maria C. and van Delden Johannes J. M., 2011. "Filial Obligations to Elderly Parents: A Duty to Care," *Medicine, Health Care Philosophy,* 14(1): 63–71.

Swatek-Evenstein Mark, 2013. "Limits of Enlightenment and the Law – On the Legality of Ritual Male Circumcision in Europe Today," *Merkourios,* 29(77): 42–50.

Swyngedouw Erik, 2004. "Globalisation of 'Glocalisation'? Networks, Territories, and Rescaling," *Cambridge Review of International Affairs,* 17(1): 25–48.

Tagari Hadas, 2012. "Personal Family Law Systems – A Comparative and International Human Rights Analysis," *International Journal of Law in Context*, 8(2): 231–52.

Thai Hung Cam, 2014. *Insufficient Funds: The Culture of Money in Low-Wage Transnational Families* (Redwood City, CA: Stanford University Press).

Thomas Philip A., 1997. "Socio-Legal Studies: The Case of Disappearing Fleas and Bustards" in Thomas Philip A. (Ed.), *Socio-Legal Studies* (Aldershot: Dartmouth), pp 1–22.

Thym Daniel, 2008. "Respect for Private and Family Life Under Article 8 ECHR in Immigration Cases: A Human Right to Regularize Illegal Stay?" *International and Comparative Law Quarterly*, 57(1): 87–112.

Trask Bahira Sherif, 2010. *Globalization and Families: Accelerated Systemic Social Change* (New York: Springer).

Treas Judith, 2008. "Transnational Older Adults and Their Families," *Family Relations*, 57(4): 468–78.

Treviño Javier, 2001. "The Sociology of Law in Global Perspective," *The American Sociologist*, 32(5): 5–9.

Triger Zvi, 2016. "On the Regulation of Fertility Services in Israel" in Blank Yishai, Levi-Faur David, and Kreitner Roy (Eds.), *Regulation: Law and Policy* (Tel Aviv University), pp. 269–309. [Hebrew]

Triger Zvi, 2015. "A Different Journey: Experiences of Israeli Surrogacy Parents in India," *Theory and Criticism*, 44: 177–202. [Hebrew]

Triger Zvi, 2012. "Introducing the Political Family: A New Road Map for Critical Family Law," *Theoretical Inquiries in Law*, 13(1): 361–84.

Trimmings Katarina and Beaumont Paul, "General Report on Surrogacy" in Katarina Trimmings and Paul Beaumont (Eds.), *International Surrogacy Arrangements* (Oxford, UK: Hart Publishing, 2013), pp. 439–549.

Trubek David M., 1990. "Back to the Future: The Short, Happy Life of the Law and Society Movement," *Florida State University Law Review*, 18: 1–55.

Tsong Yuying and Yuli Liu, 2008. "Parachute Kids and Astronaut Families" in Tewari Nita and Alvarez Alvin N. (Eds.), *Asian American Psychology: Current Perspectives* (Mahwah, NJ: Erlbaum), pp. 365–79.

Unnithan Maya, 2013. "Thinking through Surrogacy Legislation in India: Reflections on Relational Consent and the Rights of Infertile Women," *Journal of Legal Anthropology*, 1(3): 287–313.

Urbanek Doris, 2012. "Forced Marriage vs. Family Reunification: Nationality, Gender and Ethnicity in German Migration Policy," *Journal of Intercultural Studies*, 33(3): 333–45.

Urry John and Larsen Jonas, 2011. *The Tourist Gaze 3.0* (Los Angeles: Sage).

van Der Geest Sjaak, Mul Anke, and Vermeulen Hans, 2004. "Linkages between Migration and the Care of Frail Older People: Observations from Greece, Ghana and the Netherlands," *Ageing & Society*, 24(3): 431–50.

van Houtum, Henk, 2012. "Remapping Borders" in Wilson Thomas M. and Donnan Hastings (Eds.), *A Companion to Border Studies* (Malden, MA: Wiley Blackwell), pp. 405–18.

Van Rossem Ronan, Meekers Dominique, and Gage Anastasia J., 2015. "Women's Position and Attitudes towards Female Genital Mutilation in Egypt: A Secondary Analysis of the Egypt Demographic and Health Surveys, 1995–2014," *BMC Public Health* 15: 874–87.

van Walsum Sarah K., 2009. "Transnational Mothering, National Immigration Policy, and European Law: The Experience of the Netherlands" in Benhabib Seyla and Resnik Judith (Eds.), *Migration and Mobilities: Citizenship, Borders and Gender* (New York University Press), pp. 228–51.

Vanderplatt Madine, Ramos Howard, and Yoshida Yoko, 2012. "What Do Sponsored Parents and Grandparents Contribute?" *Canadian Ethnic Studies*, 44(3): 79–96.

Vink Maarten Peter, Prokic-Breuer Tijana, and Dronkers Jaap, 2013. "Immigrant Naturalization in the Context of Institutional Diversity: Policy Matters, but to Whom?" *International Migration*, 51(5): 1–20.

Vitikainen Annamari, 2013. *Limits of Liberal Multiculturalism* (Helsinki: Theoretical Philosophy).

von Britenshtain Tina, 1999. "The Filipino Workers in Israel" in Nathanson Roby and Achdut Lea (Eds.), *The New Workers: Wage Earners from Foreign Countries in Israel* (Tel Aviv: Hakibbutz Hameuchad), pp. 205–25. [Hebrew]

Wade Lisa, 2011. "Learning from "Female Genital Mutilation": Lessons from 30 Years of Academic Discourse," *Ethnicities*, 12(1): 26–49.

Wallace Harvey and Roberson Cliff, 2016. *Family Violence: Legal, Medical and Social Perspectives*, 7th edn. (London: Routledge).

Walsh Kieran and Shutes Isabel, 2013. "Care Relationships, Quality of Care and Migrant Workers Caring for Older People," *Ageing & Society*, 33(3): 393–420.

Wang H. and Zhai F., 2013. "Programme and Policy Options for Preventing Obesity in China," *Obesity Reviews*, 14:134–40.

Wang Lee Ann, 2013. "'Of the Law, but Not Its Spirit': Immigration Marriage Fraud as Legal Fiction and Violence against Asian Immigrant Women," *UC Irvine Law Review*, 3(4): 1221–50.

Wasserstein Fassberg Celia, 2013. *Private International Law* (Jerusalem: Nevo), vol. I. [Hebrew]

Wastl-Walter Dorit (Ed.), 2011. *The Ashgate Research Companion to Border Studies* (Surrey: Ashgate).

Watson James L, 2006. *Golden Arches East: McDonald's in East Asia*, 2nd edn. (CA: Stanford University Press).

Weiner Merle H., 2000. "International Child Abduction and the Escape from Domestic Violence," *Fordham Law Review*, 69(2): 593–706.

Weinrib Loraine E., 2008. "Ontario's Sharia Law Debate: Law and Politics under the Charter" in Moon Richard (Ed.), *Law and Religious Pluralism in Canada* (Vancouver: UBS Press), pp. 239–63.

Weinstein Brynn, 2012. "Reproductive Choice in the Hands of the State: The Rights to Abortion under the European Convention on Human Rights in Light of A, B, & C v. Ireland," *American University International Law Review*, 27: 391–437.

Weinstein Jeffrey A., 1993. ""An Irish Solution to an Irish Problem": Ireland's Struggle with Abortion Law," *Arizona Journal International and Comparative Law*, 10: 165–200.

Weitzman Lenore J., 1985. *The Divorce Revolution: The Unexpected Social and Economic Consequences for Women and Children in America* (New York: The Free Press).

West Robin, 2009. "A Reply to Pierre," *Georgetown Law Journal*, 97: 865–75.

Wheeler Patricia, 2004. "Eliminating FGM: The Role of the Law," *The International Journal of Children's Rights*, 11: 257–71.

White Ben, 1996. "Globalization and the Child Labor Problem," *Journal of International Development*, 8(6): 829–39.

Wilkinson Eleanor and Bell David, 2012. "Ties that Blind: On Not Seeing (or Looking) beyond 'The Family," *Families, Relationships and Societies*, 1(3): 423–9.

Williams Joan, 2000. *Unbending Gender: Why Family and Work Conflict and What to Do About It* (New York: Oxford University Press).

Williams Joan C., 2010. *Reshaping the Work-Family Debate: Why Men and Class Matter* (Cambridge, MA: Harvard University Press).

Willing Indigo, Fronek Patricia, and Cuthbert Denise, 2012. "Review of Sociological Literature on Intercountry Adoption," *Social Policy and Society*, 11(3): 465–79.

Wilson Fretwell Robin, 2012. "The Perils of Privatized Marriage" in Nichols Joel A. (Ed.), *Marriage and Divorce in a Multicultural Context: Multi-Tiered Marriage and the Boundaries of Civil Law and Religion* (New York: Cambridge University Press), pp. 253–83.

Wilson Fretwell Robin, 2007. "The Overlooked Costs of Religious Difference," *Washington and Lee Law Review*, 64(4), 1363–83.

Wilson Thomas M. and Donnan Hastings, 2012. "Borders and Border Studies" in Wilson Thomas M. and Donnan Hastings (Eds.), *A Companion to Border Studies* (Malden, MA: Wiley Blackwell), pp.1–25.

Wilson Thomas M. and Donnan Hastings (Eds.), 1998. *Border Identities Nation and State at International Frontiers* (UK: Cambridge University Press).

Wimmer Andreas, 2007. "Boundaries (Racial/Ethnic)" in George Ritzer (Ed.), *Blackwell Encyclopedia of Sociology Online*, available at: http://www.sociologyencyclopedia .com/subscriber/uid=960/tocnode?query=Boundaries+(Racial%2FEthnic) &widen=1&result_number=1&from=search&id=g9781405124331_yr2015_ chunk_g97814051243318_ss1-42&type=std&fuzzy=0&slop=1.&authstatusc ode=202.

Wolfe Lucy, 2012. "Darling Divas or Damaged Daughters? The Dark Side of Child Beauty Pageants and an Administrative Law Solution," *Tulane Law Review*, 87: 427–55.

Wonderlich Anna L., Ackard Diann M., and Henderson Judith B., 2005. "Childhood Beauty Pageant Contestants: Associations with Adult Disordered Eating and Mental Health," *Eating Disorders* 13(3): 291–301.

Woodhouse Barbara Bennett, 2009. "A World Fit for Children Is a World Fit for Everyone: Ecogenerism, Feminism, and Vulnerability," *Houston Law Review*, 46: 818–65.

Worthington Rebecca, 2009. "The Road to Parentless Children is Paved with Good Intentions: How the Hague Convention and Recent Intercountry Adoption Rules are Affecting Potential Parents and the Best Interests of Children," *Duke Journal of Comparative & International Law*, 19(3): 559–86.

Wray Helena, 2006. "An Ideal Husband? Marriages of Convenience, Moral Gate-Keeping and Immigration to the UK," *European Journal of Migration and Law*, 8(3–4): 303–20.

Wray Helena, Agoston Agnes, and Hutton Jocelyn, 2014. "A Family Resemblance? The Regulation of Marriage Migration in Europe," *European Journal of Migration and Law*, 16(2): 209–47.

Yilmaz Ihsan, 2002. "The Challenge of Post-Modern Legality and Muslim Legal Pluralism in England," *Journal of Ethnic and Migration Studies*, 28(2): 343–54.

Yntema Hessel E., 1953. "The Historic Bases of Private International Law," *The American Journal of Comparative Law*, 2(3): 297–317.

Young Alexandra, 2012. "Developments in Intercountry Adoption: From Humanitarian Aid to Market-Driven Policy and beyond," *Adoption & Fostering*, 36(2): 67–78.

Zafran Ruth, 2005. "The Relational Discourse as a Theoretical Basis for Resolving Family Disputes: Some Thought about Care and Justice" in Ben-Naftali Orna & Naveh Hannah (Eds.), *Trials of Love* (Tel Aviv: Ramot), pp. 605–55. [Hebrew]

Zayas Luis, 2015. *Forgotten Citizens: Deportation, Children, and the Making of American Exiles and Orphan* (New York: Oxford University Press).

Zayas Luis H. and Bradlee Mollie H., 2014. "Exiling Children, Creating Orphans: When Immigration Policies Hurt Citizens," *Social Work*, 59(2): 167–75.

Zee Machteld, 2014. "Five Options for the Relationship between the State and Sharia Councils: Untangling the Debate on Sharia Councils and Women's Rights in the United Kingdom," *Journal of Religion and Society*, 16: 1–18.

Zelig Campos Kaylah, 1993. "Putting Responsibility Back into Marriage: Making a Case for Mandatory Prenuptials," *University of Colorado Law Review*, 64: 1223–45.

Zelizer Viviana A., 2005. *The Purchase of Intimacy* (Princeton, NJ: Princeton University Press).

Zelizer Viviana A., 1994. *Pricing the Priceless Child: The Changing Social Value of Children* (Princeton, NJ: Princeton University Press).

Zetter Roger, 1991. "Labelling Refugees: Forming and Transforming a Bureaucratic Identity," *Journal of Refugee Studies*, 4(1): 39–62.

NAME INDEX

Aaron, Jane, 32–33
Abrams, Kerry, 194
Abrego, Leisy, 203–04, 208
Abu-Sahlieh, Sami Aldeeb, 269–70
Adelman, Carol, 200
Alanen, Julia, 282–83n178
Ali, Syed Muntz, 95n90
Alstein, Howard, 227n119
Altink, Henric, 32–33
Appadurai, Arjun, 26–27
Arbel, Erfat, 258, 258n56, 258n57, 259
Arendt, Hannah, 150n9
Ashe, Marie, 98n111
Astakhov, Pavel, 232–33
Ayalon, Liat, 303, 305, 306–09, 310

Bacik, Ivana, 123
Baines, Beverly, 96
Balibar, Étienne, 34–35, 41
Barber, Benjamin, 42–43
Bassan, Sharon, 137, 139–40
Bauman, Zygmunt, 24
Beck, Ulrich, 3, 6, 59, 67, 73–74n3, 76
Beck-Gernsheim, Elisabeth, 3, 6, 59, 73–74n3, 76
Benvenisti, Eyal, 254–55, 255n42
Berndt, Christian, 304
Bernstein, Gaia, 173
Bhabha, Jacqueline, 184
Blecher-Prigat, Ayelet, 62, 110
Blood, Diane, 49
Boccagni, Paolo, 209
Bonjour, Saskia, 166
Bookey, Blaine, 258n58

Bourdieu, Pierre, 36, 51–52, 63
Bradlee, Mollie, 184
Büchler, Andrea, 75n9
Buck, Lesley, 206

Cangiano, Alessio, 301
Castañeda, Ernesto, 200–01n15, 206
Champeonis, Christina, 232
Churchill, Molly, 253
Curry, Mary, 12n43

D'Alusio, Faith, 197
Dancig-Rosenberg, Hadar, 251–52
Dauvergne, Catherine, 154, 155
de Blois, Matthijs, 93, 93n81
de Boer, Ted M., 104
de Hart, Betty, 159, 166
Demleitner, Nora, 194–95
Dobrowsky, Alexandra, 149–50
Donati, Pierpaolo, 150n6
Doron, Israel, 291n2
Dreby, Joanna, 208
Duggleby, Wendy, 306
Durkheim, Emil, 54
Dwyer, James G., 241n184

Earp, Brian, 270–71
Ebaugh, Helen Rose, 12n43
Edleson, Jeffrey, 284–85, 287
Elkabetz, Roni, 84n38
Elkabetz, Shlomi, 84n38
Elkins, Jeremy, 69
Engels, Friedrich, 56
Erez, Edna, 254
Erikson, Thomas Hylland, 19